Rotten States?

LESLIE HOLMES

Rotten States?

CORRUPTION, POST-COMMUNISM,

AND NEOLIBERALISM

Duke University Press   Durham & London

2006

© 2006 Duke University Press

All rights reserved

Printed in the United States of America

on acid-free paper ∞

Designed by C. H. Westmoreland

Typeset in Galliard by Keystone Typesetting, Inc.

Library of Congress Cataloging-in-Publication Data

appear on the last printed page of this book.

FOR BECKY AND SANNA

Contents

Tables

Abbreviations

BPCWR	*Bulgarian Press on Corruption Weekly Review*
CBOS	[Centre for Social Opinion Research]
CCP	Chinese Communist Party
CD	*China Daily*
CDPSP	*Current Digest of the Post-Soviet Press*
CEE	Central and Eastern Europe
CIS	Commonwealth of Independent States
CPI	Corruption Perceptions Index
CSD	Center for the Study of Democracy
EECR	*East European Constitutional Review*
EiSP	*Ekonomicheskie i Sotsial'nye Peremeny: monitoring obshchestvennogo mneniya*
EU	European Union
FOZZ	[Foreign Debt Servicing Fund]
FSB	[Federal Security Service]
GDP	Gross Domestic Product
GDR	German Democratic Republic
IMF	International Monetary Fund
INDEM	[Centre for Applied Political Research]
NGO	nongovernmental organization
OECD	Organization for Economic Cooperation and Development
OMRI DD	*Open Media Research Institute Daily Digest*
PRC	People's Republic of China
RFE/RL	*Radio Free Europe/Radio Liberty*
RFE/RL OCTW	*Radio Free Europe/Radio Liberty Organized Crime and Terrorism Watch*
SLD	[Democratic Left Alliance]

SWB/EE	BBC Summary of World Broadcasts, Eastern Europe
TI	Transparency International
UNODCCP	United Nations Office for Drug Control and Crime Prevention
UNICRI	United Nations Interregional Crime and Justice Research Institute
VTSIOM	[All-Russian Centre for the Study of Public Opinion]

Preface

In 1993 I published a book — *The End of Communist Power: Anti-corruption Campaigns and Legitimation Crisis* — that focused on the relationship between corruption and legitimation crises in the communist world, and on the role of both in the collapse of communist power. At the time of completing that book (late 1991), I had intended to move away from the study of corruption and legitimation crises. But I soon changed my mind, for two reasons. First, various people who knew the book invited me to present seminars that would update my research, and analyze corruption and legitimation in the early phases of post-communism. Second, the issue of corruption appeared to be becoming far more salient not only in that part of the world which I had spent most of my life studying, but also in the part in which I lived, the West. It would have been perverse to abandon the study of corruption just at the moment when it was becoming one of the hottest topics in social science. Moreover, so many regimes in so many types of system were being brought down during the 1990s at least partly because of corruption-related scandals that I began to wonder whether the legitimation crisis that some believed had emerged in the West during the 1970s, and then in the communist world in the late 1980s, might be an early symptom of a general crisis of *any* type of state. Hence I decided to continue my research into corruption, and to relate it once again to notions of political legitimacy and crisis. This book is the largest fruit of that research and deliberation.

The focus here is on what can still be called, for want of a better term, the post-communist world[1] — primarily Central and Eastern Europe (CEE) and the Commonwealth of Independent States (CIS), although for reasons elaborated below there is also more on the People's Republic of China (PRC) than on many other countries.[2] But a number of comparisons with countries in other parts of the world and with different systems are also drawn at appropriate junctures. The arguments about the legitimacy problems of the state, and about the connections between corruption and neoliberalism, are offered as *general* ones, for others to test with reference to countries and regions about which they know far more than I.

Since theorizing is usually of limited value unless based on and applicable to empirical findings, I have focused in particular on four countries in which I have conducted original research for this study — Bulgaria, Hungary, Poland, and Russia. Because there is also more material on the PRC than on most CEE and CIS states, it is appropriate to argue that there are in effect four and a half case studies. Between 1996 and 2004 I visited all five states — the choice of which is justified in chapter 1 — to conduct interviews and gather crime statistics. In the three CEE states and Russia, I also organized surveys and gathered data from others' surveys; unfortunately the Chinese authorities would not permit me to perform the same exercise in the PRC.

At this point it is important — for the sake of something frequently mentioned in this book, transparency — to acknowledge my own limitations. While my knowledge of both spoken and written Russian is reasonable, my command of Polish and Bulgarian is weaker. My knowledge of Mandarin is slight, and is only of the spoken language. I have no knowledge of Hungarian, and usually use German or English when I visit Hungary and conduct interviews. Despite these weaknesses, I have during the course of this research visited all of these countries several times, for reasonably lengthy periods (several weeks) in Russia, China, and Poland; my trips to Bulgaria and Hungary have been shorter, though I do maintain regular contact with both (mainly through e-mail and through meeting Bulgarian and Hungarian colleagues in third countries). I have visited most but not all of the countries referred to in this book. While I would have preferred to visit them all, the book is ultimately comparative, and I make no claims to being a specialist on any particular country.

Another limitation arises from the time it has taken me to complete this work. As mentioned above, I have received a large number of invitations in recent years to present seminar and conference papers based on my research, and to produce articles, book chapters, and reports. I have usually accepted these invitations, since they often result in more responses to my research and arguments, and an opportunity to increase my knowledge of others' work in the field. But they have had the disadvantage of delaying completion of this book, with the result that some of the ideas and research findings included here have already appeared elsewhere. Parts of this book overlap heavily in particular with L. Holmes 1997a, L. Holmes 1997c, L. Holmes 1999, and a report on corruption in CEE and the CIS that I produced in early 2000 for the World Bank. However, the second of these items is not widely accessible outside Poland, the third is no longer available on line, while the last is not publicly available at all. I wish to thank the World Bank for permission to use parts of my report here.

My thanks also go to a large number of other people and organizations which helped me in a range of ways. Much of the basic research for the project was conducted by my principal research assistant, Dr. Yuri Tsyganov, who was a model of efficient, trouble-free collaboration; his knowledge of Slavic languages and Mandarin was invaluable. Dr. Tsyganov's salary was paid for out of a research grant generously awarded to me by the Australian Research Council (Grant No. A79930728); I wish publicly to express my gratitude to the Australian Research Council for this funding. For critiques of my arguments, I am grateful to the many academics, students, and practitioners — too numerous to name individually — who made comments at seminars and conferences in Berlin, Brisbane, Budapest, Canberra, Dublin, Florence, Grenoble, Hobart, Oxford, Salford, Seoul, Singapore, Sofia, Swansea, Tampere, Uppsala, Warsaw, and Wellington between 1996 and 2004. I also thank my numerous postgraduate students in Bologna, Melbourne, and Warsaw, whose questions forced me to refine and occasionally even change my arguments, and who provided me with additional material and insights.

One person I wish to single out for particularly detailed, insightful, and constructive criticism, who helped me far more than she realizes, is Helen Sutch of the World Bank. For assistance in arranging interviews and obtaining data I wish to thank Antoaneta Dimitrova, Ivan Krastev, and Alexander Stoyanov in Sofia; Zolna Berki, Gábor Tóka, and András Sajó in Budapest; Jiang Tingyao and Michael Dutton in Beijing; Ewa Balcerek, John Fells, and Ryszard Zelichowski in Warsaw; and Slava Amirov, Donald Bowser, Boris Demidov, Bobo Lo, and Elena Panfilova in Moscow. Some of these people also helped me with more mundane but crucial administrative assistance during my travels, like obtaining access to e-mail, fax machines, and photocopiers; for this kind of help I wish also to thank Marianne Möller and Natalja Eisenblätter in Berlin; Zsolt Enyedi in Budapest; Monique Cavallari in Florence; and Jackie Wilcox in Oxford.

At various points the book refers to the results of four opinion surveys that I commissioned during 2000. For their helpfulness and efficiency in organizing these I am grateful to Alexander Stoyanov of Vitosha Research (Bulgaria), Kata Csizér of TÁRKI Social Research Centre (Hungary), Krzysztof Zagórski of CBOS (Poland), and Yuri Levada and Alexander Grazhdankin of VTSIOM (Russia). I am indebted to Ewa Karafilowska for technical assistance in reprocessing some of the survey data to make them directly comparable.

I also wish to thank the numerous interviewees in several countries (not just the five on which I concentrated), without whose time and helpfulness this book would have been much poorer. There are so many that it would be impracticable to list them all (though several are referred to in the text, when I thank them for particular contributions), and several asked not to be identified. Even some interviewees who did not seek anonymity have had to be granted it because of much stricter ethics regulations in my university since the early days of the research for this project; I have been unable to track down some of these people in their new positions. My thanks also to the anonymous reviewers of the manuscript, whose suggestions helped me tighten the argument at various points, alerted me to additional sources, and updated my information. Of course I am solely responsible for remaining ambiguities in the argument, omissions, outdated information, and errors.

Finally, at Duke University Press I would like to thank two people in particular. The first is Fred Kameny, whose thorough and thoughtful copy editing substantially reduced the number of ambiguities in my text, and rendered it more user-friendly. The second is Valerie Millholland — for her encouragement of this project, for appreciating the reasons why I did not want to sign a contract before I had a full-length draft manuscript completed, and for being so tolerant and polite when I delivered the final manuscript late; if only all publishers were as understanding.

Rotten States?

CHAPTER 1

Introduction

This book is about a phenomenon that has become a salient aspect of politics in most parts of the world: official corruption.[1] There is a particular focus on the post-communist world, here meaning those countries that were ruled by communist parties until the revolutions of 1989–91.[2] This focus has been adopted partly because of my own expertise and research, but also because one part of this area, the CIS, was by the late 1990s considered by some analysts the most corrupt region in the world;[3] another major part, Central and Eastern Europe (CEE), was perceived as less corrupt than the CIS, but still as having a major problem.[4] Given that as influential and powerful an agency as the World Bank has identified corruption as the single greatest source of poverty in today's world, it becomes clear why the topic is important, and why it is relevant to concentrate on the post-communist regions. Meanwhile in China, Jiang Zemin during his tenure as president and as general secretary of the Communist Party identified corruption as the problem that could bring about the collapse of the communist system (*Renmin Ribao*, 22 August 1993, 1; *BR* 36, no. 36:5–6).[5] By studying an area in which the problem is particularly acute, it is hoped to shed light on the problem, and perhaps even contribute to overcoming it elsewhere.

Despite its principal focus, the study raises issues that are relevant to every type of state and large-scale society, since there is none in which corruption does not exist. Moreover, examples of corruption can be found in all the political institutions of the contemporary state, including ministries, local councils, the police, the judiciary, customs and immigration offices, the military, and political parties. An analysis of corruption helps to illuminate both the particular difficulty of building political systems in the post-communist world and the more general reality that states everywhere are beset with problems, including actual or potential crises of identity and legitimacy.

The focus is on post-communist states *generally*, particularly the European ones, since it is a basic premiss here that all of them shared the legacy of communism and the international context of the 1990s; at least in theory, most also shared a commitment to the same basic goals of democracy and a market economy. This said, the precommunist history and traditions, the political culture more broadly, and the methods chosen for reaching the basic goals are unique to each country; it would be impossible in a single book to examine them all, or even several, properly. Hence, although a comparative approach is employed here and aspects of corruption from most post-communist states are examined, the emphasis is on four CEE and CIS countries — Bulgaria, Hungary, Poland, and Russia; there is also more on China than on most other countries. Because a detailed analysis of five case studies is provided, the comparative and theoretical arguments become more persuasive.

Despite the putative focus on five countries, it would be more accurate to claim four and a half, with the half being China. This does not reflect an indifferent attitude toward China, which is of indisputable size and significance. Rather, it reflects the status of China as a post-communist state; as is argued below, the PRC is post-communist only in some ways. In others China still is clearly communist. For example, most post-communist states had high levels of censorship until their communist regimes collapsed or were on the verge of collapse (depending on the country). China still does, and it does not permit foreigners to conduct surveys of politically sensitive issues, of which corruption is an example.[6] At various points in this book, reference is made to four surveys conducted in mid-2000 in Bulgaria, Hungary, Poland, and Russia; since we were unable to conduct a similar exercise in China, and since even the findings of surveys on corruption by the Chinese themselves are not generally available to outsiders, our database on China is considerably poorer than for the other countries.

For the sake of simplicity, however, a focus on five countries is claimed. The reasons for focusing on these five are several, and relate to some of the major factors most frequently adduced for explaining differences in levels and types of corruption. First, this choice means that both large and small countries (in terms of population and area) have been included. Moreover, in terms of political and administrative structures, one of the two large countries (Russia) is federalized, while the other (China) is essentially unitary.[7] Second, the choice provides a wide range of cultural backgrounds. Poland and to a lesser extent Hungary are both Catholic countries that nowadays consider themselves increasingly part of "the West," and certainly European; this image will only strengthen now that they are members of the European Union (May 2004). Russia is predominantly Orthodox, and cannot decide whether it is European or sui generis, leading Samuel Huntington (1996, 139–54) to describe it as one of the world's four major "torn" countries.[8] Indeed, it has been experiencing profound problems with its own identity since 1991, in the wake of one of the fastest and most extensive imperial collapses ever (on Russia's identity problems see Dunlop 1997; Tolz 1998). Bulgaria is also predominantly Orthodox, but it clearly considers itself European, and does not suffer from the "loss of empire" identity problems that Russia is experiencing.[9] China has a mainly Confucian tradition and is much more confident about its own identity than Russia is; it is Asian, and has no desire to become western in any significant way.

Third, the countries chosen include both ethnically homogeneous countries (Poland, Hungary, and to a lesser extent China); a country with just one numerically significant ethnic minority (Bulgaria, with a large Turkish minority); and a country that ethnically is highly diverse (Russia has in excess of one hundred recognized ethnic groups, even though Russians account for some 87 percent of the population). Fourth, the five countries have adopted diverse approaches and sequencing to their economic transitions, and have experienced very different success rates. Both Poland and Hungary are among the most successful post-communist states. Yet they are often seen as having adopted radically different approaches to their economic transitions, with Poland considered by many to have adopted "shock therapy" and Hungary a "gradualist" policy. Although this contrast is usually overdone (L. Holmes 1996; see too Murrell 1993, on how the concept of Polish shock therapy has been exaggerated), there have been important differences in the way the Poles and the Hungarians have approached economic restructuring. One of our interests was to see if this difference was reflected in different rates or types of corruption. In contrast, Bulgaria is often seen as a "late starter" in terms of both economic and political transition, and in this limited sense it constitutes a different kind of post-communist state. Russia has been among the most troubled post-communist states, inconsistent in its attitudes toward major reform. Having begun to adopt radical economic policies in the early

1990s under the influence of Gaidar, it then lost its way and in some ways virtually stagnated in the late Yeltsin era. Vladimir Putin's ambiguous approach to ownership—state versus private—has only compounded and prolonged the problem of inconsistency. Moreover, Russia's problems tend to affect other countries more than the problems of smaller states do; it would be eccentric not to include such an influential state.

China might appear to be an anomaly, since many would question the application of the concept of "post-communism" to a country in which, at the time of writing, the communists still appeared to be well ensconced (the country is still communist politically). But China is already post-communist in the economic sphere, and increasingly so in terms of social (class) structure. Indeed, if the "radical critics" referred to by Gordon White (1996, 157–58, 167) are correct in referring to a "value vacuum," a "crisis in values," and a collapse in faith, China is already much more post-communist than is generally appreciated. It therefore constitutes yet another kind of state emerging from the communist past, despite its significant differences from the other four. And since many believe—in my view erroneously—that the USSR could have survived both as a country and as a communist state had its leaders introduced the kinds of policies that Deng Xiaoping and others introduced into China from the late 1970s, a comparison of the situation in the PRC with countries that have had political as well as economic revolutions is warranted.

Despite the emphasis here on post-communist countries, corruption is ubiquitous in the contemporary world, and reaches the highest levels.[10] For instance, investigations of Willy Claes, secretary general of the North Atlantic Treaty Organization (NATO), began in February 1995 after allegations that he had been involved in the acceptance by his party (the Flemish Socialist Party) of a $1.7 million kickback in 1988, when he was the Belgian economics minister. The kickback was linked to the purchase of forty-six helicopters from the Italian company Agusta, which secured the order despite fierce competition from French and German companies. There was allegedly a further kickback to his party of $3 million (approximately) from the French arms company Dassault. As a result of the allegations and investigations, Claes resigned his NATO post in October 1995, when the Belgian parliament lifted his parliamentary immunity so that he could stand trial. He was found guilty of corruption in December 1998 and sentenced to a three-year suspended prison sentence and a small fine; he was also barred from holding public office for five years.

In considering corruption relating to Italy since the start of the Tangentopoli ("bribe city") scandal and the *mani pulite* ("clean hands") campaign in 1992, the western mass media have had a field day listing alleged misconduct by literally thousands of Italian businesspeople and politicians, including the former and current prime ministers Giulio Andreotti, Silvio Berlusconi, and Bettino Craxi (on Italian corruption see Magatti 1996; Scamuzzi ed. 1996; Barbacetto, Gomez, and Travaglio 2002; Newell and Bull 2003). In Spain, many see corruption as the main reason for the failure of Felipe Gonzalez's socialist government to continue its thirteen-year rule beyond the elections of March 1996, after a major scandal that broke in late 1994 (see *Time*, 25 September 1995, 38–39; on Spanish corruption more generally see Heywood 1995; Jiménez and Caínzos 2003). In France, Prime Minister Pierre Bérégovoy committed suicide in May 1993, after allegations that he had been involved in corruption. Between 1990 and 2000, mayors in Cannes, Grenoble, Lyon, Nice, and Paris were forced to resign, and in some cases prosecuted, because of alleged corruption, as were at least five French cabinet ministers (see for example *International Herald Tribune*, 7 February 1997, 5; *Wall Street Journal Europe*, 3 November 1999, 1, 12, 14; *Age* [Melbourne], 3 March 2000, 12), while the reputation of the Socialist Party (PS) has been severely tarnished by corruption (for the effects on the reputation of the French PS see Mény 1997). After allegations of corruption in the Paris branch of his party (the Rally for the Republic), President Jacques Chirac was accused in October 1999 of being involved in fraudulent activities, relating specifically to his unsuccessful presidential candidacy in 1988 and more generally to his tenure as mayor of Paris from 1977 to 1995, when he was elected president in his second attempt. Chirac's reelection as president in May 2002 meant among other things that he could stave off possible legal action for another seven years (on corruption in France see Evans 2003).

Even West European countries with a reputation for being relatively clean appear to have experienced an increase in corruption in recent years. This is true of both Germany and the Netherlands, for instance (on Germany see for example Claussen 1995; J. Roth 1997; McKay 2003; Ramge 2003; on the Netherlands see Kroes and de Boer 1996; van

Duyne, Huberts, and van den Heuvel 2003). In Germany a major corruption scandal erupted in late 1999 around the man who had headed the political system for some sixteen years, Chancellor Helmut Kohl. Kohl eventually paid a substantial fine in early 2001 to bring legal closure to this sorry episode; political closure had to await the tabling of a parliamentary commission's report in July 2002 that found the Christian Democratic Union, or CDU (Kohl's party), guilty of illegally raising millions of Marks, although the commission was unable to determine the source of the funds.

Ireland's prime minister, Charles Haughey, had to resign in 1992 *partly* because of allegations of corruption; in May 2000 he was accused by the Moriarty Tribunal of having improperly received more than six million Irish pounds between 1979 and 1996.[11] And many commentators saw the "sleaze factor" as one of the two or three principal causes underlying the end of eighteen years of Conservative rule in the UK in May 1997 — although the "New Labour" government of Tony Blair that succeeded it has not been without corruption scandals either, despite Blair's promise in 1997 and on various occasions since to clean up public life.[12]

The problem is by no means confined to Europe. While this did not bring him down, President Bill Clinton's reputation was dented by the so-called Whitewater scandal that emerged in 1993. Corruption has played a significant role in toppling long-standing governments in Japan and India, as seen in the poor electoral performances of the Liberal Democratic Party in 1993 in Japan and of the Congress Party in 1996 in India (on Japanese corruption see Woodall 1996; Bouissou 1997; Rothacher 2003; on India see Singh 1997). The Thai military used the corruption of the government of Chatichai Choonhawan as an excuse for staging a coup against an elected civilian government in February 1991 (on this and other aspects of Thai corruption see Pasuk Phongpaichit and Sungsidh Piriyarangsan 1996). It has been alleged that the election victory in 1994 of the Colombian president, Ernesto Samper, was secured partly because of substantial campaign funding from the Cali drug cartel (though a congressional committee cleared Samper of these charges in late 1995 — according to some reports because too thorough an investigation of the matter would have had embarrassing consequences for many members of Congress), while the former Ecuadorean vice president Alberto Dahik fled the country in late 1995 shortly before being found guilty of embezzlement and illicit enrichment. Two former South Korean presidents, Chun Doo Hwan and Roh Tae Woo, were found guilty in August 1996 of having accepted large-scale bribes when in office from household company names such as Daewoo and Samsung (on Korean corruption see Kim 2002).

Nor are Islamic countries immune to corruption. High-level corruption is said to have been the major reason for the dismissal of Benazir Bhutto and her government in Pakistan in November 1996. Few would dispute that corruption was a major factor in the collapse of the Soeharto regime in Indonesia in 1998. Indonesia, Nigeria, and Bangladesh often figure prominently in comparative tables (considered in chapter 4) of the world's most corrupt states. Of all the post-communist states that have been assessed by Transparency International (TI) for its annual Corruption Perceptions Index (CPI), Azerbaijan and Tajikistan (both Muslim) were perceived to be two of the three most corrupt in 2003.[13] The CPI for 2003 assessed a total of eighteen Arab states (including Palestine), of which Oman was perceived to be the least corrupt (twenty-sixth out of 133 states altogether, scoring 6.3), and Libya the most (118th, scoring 2.1).[14] But even the lowest-ranked Arab state was perceived to be less corrupt than either Azerbaijan or Tajikistan. One concrete example of a corruption scandal in an Islamic state of the Middle East is that which surrounded the mayor of Teheran, who was formally charged with corruption in April 1998. He was found guilty in July and sentenced to two years' imprisonment, a fine equivalent to more than half a million dollars, and a ten-year ban on seeking public office.

It is not only Islamic states in the Middle East that have had major corruption scandals. In Israel Benyamin Netanyahu was accused in October 1999 both of illegally keeping gifts made to him and his wife in their official capacities while he was premier (1996–99) and of involvement in a building scam; although the legal charges were dropped in September 2000 because of insufficient evidence, Netanyahu's behavior was described by the Israeli attorney general as "improper." And a new corruption scandal, in which allegations were made publicly about both Prime Minister Ariel Sharon and his Likud Party, erupted in early 2003 (*Economist*, 11–17 January 2003, 40). Although the Israeli authorities dropped the case in 2004 for lack of sufficient evidence, they did not fully clear Sharon. In sum, while the perceived scale and role of corruption varies from country to country, there are clearly no neat Huntingtonian dividing lines on this issue.[15] Many more examples from many more countries could be cited.

So far, reference has been made only to examples of corruption at the higher levels of the political system. But there also appears to have been a substantial increase in corruption at the lower levels. One of the most disturbing trends is corruption among police forces: there have been several cases, both alleged and proven, in Australia, many involving drugs, wildlife smuggling, and pedophilia (see for example New South Wales Royal Commission 1997; Queensland Criminal Justice Commission 1997; Hoser 1999). Following earlier spates of corruption (see for example Maas 1973), the New York Police Department was again rocked by a number of scandals in 1994 and 1995, particularly in the 30th precinct in Harlem and parts of the Bronx; many officers were dealing drugs and guns (*Age*, 10 June 1995, 20). In Thailand, surveys conducted in the early 1990s revealed that the police were considered the most corrupt branch of the state apparatus (Pasuk Phongpaichit and Sungsidh Piriyarangsan 1996, esp.156). Even New Zealand, which enjoys a reputation as one of the least corrupt countries in the world, has experienced corruption scandals involving both the police (see T. Lewis 1998) and judges.

The listing of countries and state agencies tainted by corruption allegations in recent years could continue for hundreds of pages. Interesting — even titillating — as such an exercise might be, it is unnecessary, since it is already possible on the basis of the examples cited above to make a persuasive argument that corruption has become a salient feature of contemporary politics almost everywhere. Indeed, in a thought-provoking article in the British newspaper the *Independent* (13 March 1993), Terry McCarthy asked whether a new era was dawning around the world with the end of the cold war, in which corruption was becoming a key feature of the political scene. Certainly many professional political scientists have argued that corruption became the salient political issue of the 1990s, as revealed in the following extract from the publicity blurb for a conference on corruption organized by the European Studies Research Institute at the University of Salford in November 1996: "Each decade sees the emergence of at least one major new area of political science enquiry. In the 1970s it was terrorism. In the 1980s it was ecol-

ogy. In the 1990s the new area is corruption: the first half of the decade
has witnessed the exposure of corruption on an unprecedented scale."

The references by McCarthy to a new era, and by the organizers of the
Salford conference to the unprecedented exposure of corruption, jointly
serve as an introduction to this book. In particular, they help to explain
its three principal and related theoretical foci — timing, including the
role of neoliberalism; the relationship between corruption and the specific features of post-communism; and the interplay between corruption
and the delegitimation and weakening of the state. Although these issues are explored further in later chapters (especially chapters 6 and 8),
each requires an initial consideration.

As for timing, we cannot be certain, for reasons elaborated in chapter
4, that the explosive increase in reports of corruption reflects a commensurate increase in corruption itself, either in the post-communist world
or more generally. Mény (1996, 313–15) argues that it does, and that
the marked increase in corruption began as far back as the late 1970s, for
various reasons. In the western democracies, corruption increased
largely because of the growing needs of political parties and the "Ameri-
canization" of electoral campaigns, whereas in communist states, the
need to circumvent "excessive regimentation and bureaucracy" was the
driving force. Most commentators agree with McCarthy and the organizers of the Salford conference that the 1990s witnessed a major increase in corruption — or at least our awareness of it. Blankenburg
(2002) has suggested four reasons for enhanced awareness in Western
Europe during the 1990s: the financial implications of the breakdown of
traditional ideological party loyalties, including the rise of "business
politicians"; the enhanced anticorruption role of judges and prosecutors
in Latin countries; the growth of investigative journalism; and the ramifications of globalization, specifically the needs of international businesses to defeat the protectionism that often stemmed from corruption.
He goes on to argue that this growing awareness of corruption, plus a
reformulated social construction of it, may simply have made it appear
that there was more corruption. He may be correct. But the various
imperfect methods used to measure corruption collectively provide
strong circumstantial evidence that it really did increase. There is certainly abundant empirical evidence that the public in many countries
perceived a growing problem, and believed that its scale had increased

(see my tables 2 and 3). In the particular case of the post-communist states, it can be argued that the apparent increases in corruption owe something to the rise of investigative journalism, though this change is for reasons different from those pertaining in the West. They are in no small measure a function of the much lower levels of censorship in most countries compared with their communist eras. But both East and West were affected in the 1990s by yet another factor.

That factor — which is not mutually exclusive of the arguments cited above — involves extending McCarthy's argument about the impact of the end of the cold war. As has been suggested by Mosés Naím (*New York Times*, 28 November 1996), the increase of corruption reporting may be due to a much greater willingness by the West to criticize corrupt regimes elsewhere, since the end of the cold war diminished the need to keep such states within the western camp.[16] Naím's argument too can be further developed. Many countries, particularly in the West, may have become more introspective with the decline of the principal external threat. This is not to suggest a lack of interest post-1990 in events in other parts of the world. The collapse of the former Yugoslavia and the feuding that accompanied it constituted one major focus of the western media for much of the 1990s. But such external events were not seen as threatening the West in the same way or at the same level as tensions with the USSR once did; in many ways, it was not until 11 September 2001 that the major new threat finally became obvious and was agreed upon.

The 1990s were also marked by the emergence of post-communism, as both a cause and an outcome of the end of the cold war. It would take an extraordinary leap of logic and a romantic imagination to suggest that the worldwide explosion in the reporting of corruption is in some direct sense connected with the emergence of post-communism. That is not being suggested here. Rather, it is posited that in light of the above examples from different kinds of system in different parts of the world, it is not surprising that there is evidence of increased corruption and its reporting in post-communist states: it would be more surprising if there were not. While this point may seem obvious and even trivial, it needs to be remembered that according to the predictions of analysts such as George Schöpflin (1984, esp. 400), if communist states were ever to move toward the western model, corruption would decline or even disappear.[17]

The reference to "the Western model" brings us to the final dimension of the timing question, and relates to corruption — as distinct from merely the reporting of corruption — in both the post-communist states and the world more generally. It is hypothesized in this book that the spread of neoliberalism since the 1970s, which accelerated in the late 1980s, has significantly contributed to the apparent rise in corruption.[18] Neoliberalism's focus on ends over means, flexibility, competition, *homo economicus*, consumption, free trade, and reducing the role of the state (state "downsizing"; monetarism rather than Keynesianism) helps to explain the connection. This said, it will be further argued that the relationship between neoliberalism and corruption is a complex one, and that the effects differ depending on a given country's starting point.

Our second hypothesis is that the very nature of post-communism encourages the spread of corruption, or is at least highly conducive to it. One major reason is that the communist legacy is characterized by a fuzziness of boundaries between state institutions, and between the state and society; an ideology in which ends are often more important than means; and a near-absence conceptually and in practice of the rule of law. But the influence of contemporary factors, notably various dimensions of the multiple and simultaneous transition, is also important. All this is elaborated in chapter 6 (though see too L. Holmes 1997b, esp. 15–21).

A third hypothesis is that the many revelations of corruption are altering public perceptions of the state. Expressing this view at its most extreme, the substantially increased coverage of corruption everywhere is leading to yet another version of the crisis of the state. This is a question that I have already addressed elsewhere (L. Holmes 1997a), and it would be inappropriate to repeat the argument in full here. Because there are practical limits to the measurement of legitimacy, strong circumstantial evidence is the most that can realistically be expected. Thus, as with the first two hypotheses, this one can ultimately only be argued on the basis of strong indications and inductive reasoning. But this book does provide limited survey evidence on the connection between corruption and system legitimacy, and in a general way can contribute to the debate on the putative crisis of the state. At the specific level of the post-communist countries, the major theoretical concern relating to the impact of so much reporting of corruption is the extent to which it is potentially more dangerous — more destructive and delegitimizing — in these states than in systems that are more consolidated. The post-communist states are in aggregate still more fragile than western states, even though this statement is by now, some fifteen years after the revolutions of 1989–91, becoming ever less true of the transition trail-blazers such as Hungary, Poland, and Slovenia.

The term delegitimation might appear to be an inappropriate one, since it implies there was legitimacy to start with. This can be questioned in the case of the post-communist states. However, it is assumed that there was initially strong normative support from a majority of the population for the new approaches and macropolicies of post-commu-nist governments, even if this was short-lived. Readers who reject this assumption should still be able to accept the more basic premiss, namely that corruption is rendering the task of increasing popular legitimacy for regimes, and systems more generally, even more difficult than it would already be.

Because of the scope and particular problems of post-communism, it is further argued that there is a need for a strong state in the early stages of the transition from communist power. But the concept of a strong state needs to be interrogated. It is certainly not argued here that post-communist societies need authoritarian or quasi-authoritarian political systems. The sorry situation of post-communist countries ruled by dictators — such as Belarus and Turkmenistan — should make it abun-dantly clear why such an option should be discarded not merely from a principled, pro-democratic perspective (though I do hold that view), but even from a pragmatic, cost-benefit perspective. In general, authori-tarian and quasi-authoritarian systems simply do not perform as well as other types of system. In particular, in view of the focus here, the evi-dence not only from the more authoritarian post-communist states, but also from other types of authoritarian and dictatorial system, soon re-veals that corruption can be at least as pervasive in such systems as in more open ones; while the problem may be largely concealed for years, the Soehartoes and Marcoses of this world usually discover that sooner or later, the past catches up with them.

Thus the argument for strong states is for effective, competent states that can establish democratic institutions, pass and implement laws, promote the rule of law, raise taxes to pay for what society needs and demands, encourage and support civil society, and fight organized crime and corruption. The need for such states is even greater where civil society is weak, as is still true in most post-communist states. But such states must be subject to democratic control. As a minimum, the élites that direct such states must be subject to regular, competitive, and fair elections, and must accept the results of those elections. There must be free mass media, though it is also important in the transition phase that such media be reasonably responsible. In sum, the argument is for a strong *democratizing* state, and does not necessarily pertain to consolidated democracies. How the democracy is structured will vary from one country to the next (for four types of post-communist democratization see Dryzek and Holmes 2002, 268–73); but it must be effective. Radical or fundamentalist neoliberalism, with a heavy emphasis on deregulation, does not provide a suitable model for a strong democratizing and legitimizing transition state.[19]

In the next chapter the term "corruption" is closely interrogated. If the phenomenon is to be studied comparatively — even "just" within the post-communist world, let alone globally — then a working definition or approach must be found that can largely transcend genuine and supposed cultural differences. Otherwise, if notions of corruption are really as culturally specific as is often maintained, the task of demonstrating a general delegitimizing effect would be much more difficult, if not impossible. Another objective of the first part of the chapter is to examine the conceptual connections between corruption and other phenomena with which it is related, including organized crime or "mafia" activity. That part of the chapter concludes by suggesting a set of criteria for determining whether an action or nonaction constitutes corruption: for the purposes of empirical research, such a list is more useful than a simple definition. The second part of the chapter considers the numerous methodological and empirical problems associated with attempting to create either a typology or a taxonomy of corruption.

Chapter 3 provides examples of both alleged and proven corruption from throughout the post-communist world, albeit with a focus on our five countries. It is also explained why it is neither possible nor desirable to provide a highly systematic overview of "post-communist corruption." Nevertheless, the chapter is structured in terms of categories of corruption and types of official. In chapter 4 some of the methodological problems that arise in attempting to measure the scale of corruption are elaborated, and some of the sketchy data available are presented. Four basic methods — some with subdivisions — for assessing the amount of corruption in a country are analyzed. While none is satisfactory in its own right, it is maintained that if virtually all methods yield substantially similar overall results (at its most general, that the amount of corruption is increasing or decreasing), then these findings must be accepted in the absence of more accurate methods. The onus is on skeptics to provide alternative — better — methods, or simply to convince others that there is no significant problem of corruption.

One of the methods analyzed in chapter 4 is based on survey research, and this is an appropriate point at which to provide details of the four surveys specially commissioned for this book. All four were conducted in mid-2000 as omnibus surveys and used the same basic questionnaire; this was translated into the languages spoken in the countries being analyzed by the various survey organizations involved: Vitosha Research in Bulgaria, TÁRKI Social Research Centre in Hungary, CBOS (Centrum Badania Opinii Społecznej or Centre for Social Opinion Research) in Poland, and VTSIOM (Vserossiiskii Tsentr Izucheniya Obshchestvennogo Mneniya or All-Russian Centre for the Study of Public Opinion) in Russia. To minimize the risk of influencing respondents, lists of variables (such as the factors that respondents considered most responsible for the apparent rise in corruption levels) within questions were arranged alphabetically in each of the four languages, so that the sequence varied across the surveys. The number of valid responses[20] in the Bulgarian survey (conducted in September–October) was 1,870; in the Hungarian (conducted in July), 1,526; in the Polish (conducted in June), 1,066; and in the Russian (conducted in July), 1,000. Sampling was nationally representative, random within clusters; responses were elicited by face-to-face interviews.[21] Results of the four surveys appear in various parts of the book, so that it is more appropriate to elaborate the details once here than to keep repeating them.

The surveys were scheduled with three criteria in mind. First, for the sake of comparability, they were to be as temporally close to each other as their omnibus ("piggy-back") nature would permit. Second, they had to be conducted within the time frame of the research grant for this project. Third, a period was chosen which minimized the background "noise" of elections, since election periods are typically associated in post-communist states — as often elsewhere — with abnormally intensive media coverage of alleged corruption. With the partial exception of

Hungary, none of the four surveys was within three months of a national parliamentary or presidential election.[22]

The impact of corruption is the focus of chapter 5. Its importance is considered from various perspectives, including that of the individuals affected by it; environmental, economic, and social impacts; effects on other countries; and political and more general effects on legitimacy. Chapter 6 provides an analysis of the factors causing corruption. Since I have elsewhere provided a detailed analysis of the reasons for corruption in late communist states (L. Holmes 1993, 157–201), this chapter concentrates on the effect of changes since about 1990. It provides most of the evidence and the detailed reasoning necessary for assessing the three hypotheses outlined in this chapter.

Chapter 7 considers what can be and is being done to bring corruption under control. It begins by describing and critiquing the various methods available to individual states, then analyzes the role of external agencies (including foreign governments, international organizations, transnational corporations, and international banks), and the role to be played by civil society. The chapter concludes with an assessment of the likely impact of the various measures.

Chapter 8, the last, returns to the major theoretical questions outlined here. It considers the general lessons and conclusions to be drawn from the five countries; the extent to which the problem is more serious than in other types of system; the possible functionalities of corruption if one moves beyond purely ethical considerations; and once more how both neoliberalism and the very nature of post-communism contribute to corruption. It also addresses likely scenarios in the post-communist world — the dynamism of corruption — in terms both of corruption and more generally of the putative crisis of what can be called the irresponsible state. In a nutshell, the irresponsible state is one that does not perform the tasks that it should, does not do what citizens legitimately expect of it: performing tasks and providing services that it is unrealistic to expect from underdeveloped civil societies or from the subjective and fickle abstraction called the market. All too often, neoliberals can sound remarkably like Marxists in de facto advocating the "withering away of the state." The chapter also considers briefly the thesis that there is a crisis, particularly of legitimacy, in post-communist countries and elsewhere — a thesis that is supported by a substantial literature, but a literature that does not in general focus on either corruption or post-communist states. At the very end of chapter 8, the validity of the term "rotten" is assessed. The possible interactivity between "rotten" states and "rotten" societies is considered, since an exclusive focus on corruption among state officials would not only be inappropriately state-centered, but would also represent a serious blind spot in our attempts to understand corruption in post-communist states.

CHAPTER 2

Definitional and Taxonomical

Aspects of Corruption

There are several reasons why it is impossible to produce a universally acceptable definition of corruption. One is cultural: something considered a bribe in one society might be seen as not merely acceptable but even appropriate business etiquette in another. For example, anyone familiar with Chinese customs will know that gift giving is expected — virtually required — in a number of contexts in which doing so would not be normal in most western cultures.[1] Even within "a" given culture, subcultures can and do have different views, as can different groups, such as socioeconomic classes, within subcultures. For instance, what a wealthy businessperson in one society would regard as a small gift to an official might appear to someone on a low income as a significant bribe. Views within a society can also change over time, often even more so during times of transition (Yan Sun 2001; Humphrey 2002, 127–46). Hence, claims that Russians or Poles or the Chinese would not see a particular act as corruption should be treated with extreme caution; the observation by Pasuk Phongpaichit and Sungsidh Piriyarangsan (1996, 188) about Thailand that "public opinion remains far from clear or coherent on the issue of what is corruption" — a conclusion based on interviews, focus group research, and survey research — applies more or less to all societies.[2] A second reason why definitions of corruption are elusive is that many actions or nonactions are not clearly forbidden by law, which in any case varies from country to country and over time, and might therefore be more appropriately judged using more subjective concepts like "popularly legitimate" or "proper."[3]

Third, there is currently a heated debate among specialists on corruption as to whether improper "B2B" — business to business — activity should be considered corruption. The numerous scandals in the early years of the new millennium concerning major corporations such as Enron and WorldCom have certainly been described in many of the media as corruption, and an argument can be made that since so many people now apply the term to a wider range of activities than they used to, it is time to reassess its meaning. This issue is addressed below; suffice it to note here that this is another reason why there can be no universally accepted definition of corruption.

These problems notwithstanding, there is a common, solid core of actions and nonactions that are generally considered corrupt in virtually any society. For instance, public officials who demand a bribe before they will perform a duty they should normally be expected to perform anyway are perceived to be corrupt, and are condemned, almost every-where—even where such demands have become common, and in this specific sense normal. Similarly, officials who surreptitiously divert pub-lic funds to build themselves private weekend retreats are almost univer-sally considered corrupt and to be doing something unacceptable. Such forms of corruption, directly relating to financial resources, are some-times labelled "economic" or "western" corruption (Satarov 2001, 9); they often involve rent-seeking activities by officials.[4]

Around this core is a large number of questionable activities — there is a grayness at the margins, or penumbra. An obvious example is what is sometimes called "social" or even "Asiatic" corruption (Satarov 2001, 9–10), such as patronage and clientelism. Attitudes toward this, and inter-pretations of what constitutes it, do vary from culture to culture, over time, and even from individual to individual.[5] Yet there are often more similarities between what are held to be culturally specific concepts than is often acknowledged. Is the British concept of the "old school tie" network so different from the Chinese concept of *guanxi* (connec-tions)?[6] And is the American concept of networking (or developing connections) so qualitatively different from either of them, or from the Russian concept of *blat*?[7] Which, if any, of these four concepts constitutes corruption? Or does the answer depend in each country on the circum-stances? As demonstrated in chapter 6, some have explained the Poles' apparently greater tolerance of clientelism and nepotism than of bribery partly in terms of Catholic values (or culture), according to which loyalty to the family is considered more important than loyalty to the state or society generally. According to these interpretations, the communist era, during which most Poles were believed to have been alienated from—

even hostile to — the communist state, only reinforced such attitudes. If this interpretation is correct, it is possible that attitudes will be modified if, over time, the legacy of communism in terms of perceptions of the state is replaced by greater respect for and legitimacy of the post-communist state. But can we be certain that attitudes in countries with neither a Catholic tradition nor experience of communist power would be radically different, especially if the question (relative attitudes toward bribery and clientelism) were framed in "local" terminology?

Another gray area is what constitutes a bribe.[8] Earlier it was argued that most people consider it wrong, even if it is common, when officials demand a bribe before they will perform a function that they should perform anyway. There is even less ambiguity in most publics' perceptions that the demand for a bribe in return for breaking state rules is unacceptable. But what of the situation in which an official is offered a "gift," or is presented with one as a token of gratitude? In a pure, Weberian bureaucracy, there would be no such exchanges between members of the public and state officials. Tidy and appealing as such a situation might be, it bears little resemblance to reality in many parts of the globe, including the post-communist world. To highlight this problem with a simple example — is an apple for the teacher a form of bribery?

Ultimately, there can be no universally accepted answer to this question, since a person's perspective on a number of factors determines that person's assessment. The most important variables to consider are:

1. The intention of the person giving the apple (the donor);
2. The expectation of the person receiving the apple (the recipient);
3. The timing of the giving;
4. The value of what is offered;
5. The perceived social acceptability of the transaction.

Each of these requires some discussion. If the donor does not expect anything in return for the apple, such as a better grade in a test, there is less reason for describing the apple as a bribe than if there is such an expectation. Similarly, if the recipient does not expect the apple, there is less likelihood that what is given would be widely perceived as a bribe. Leading on from the latter point, offering something before someone has performed a certain task is more likely to look like bribery than giving something after the task has been performed, particularly if the recipient was genuinely not expecting any form of reward. The value of what is offered is in practice often taken into consideration in determining what does and does not constitute a bribe. In principle, the value should not matter; a gift is a gift (or a bribe is a bribe), whatever its pecuniary worth. But in practice, survey and focus group research in various parts of the world reveals that many people do distinguish between giving the teacher an apple and giving the teacher a new motor car. Finally, the observation by Humphrey (2002, 128–29) that the bribe is generally seen as negative whereas the gift has a positive connotation in virtually all cultures is useful in attempting to understand the difference between these two concepts.

It is argued here that an apple for the teacher does not constitute bribery as long as there is no expectation on the part of the donor of a payback or benefit in any meaningful sense; there is no expectation of or demand for the apple from the recipient; and the apple is not offered before any event in which the donor has a personal interest — or, ideally, in connection with *any* personal interest of the donor. In the case of an apple, the value is also clearly very small, which supports the argument that the gift does not constitute a bribe. If it did, the study of bribery would become redundant or tautologous, since it would cover so many aspects of human existence — who among us has never either offered or been offered gifts of this sort? — that it would become essentially meaningless. The dangers of conceptual stretching are well known in the social sciences (Sartori 1970, esp. 1034–36). The study of corruption specifically would remain a somewhat more manageable task, since most people are not state officials.[9] Nevertheless, limiting the notion of what does and does not constitute a bribe renders the study of the bribery of officials, as one form of corruption, a less amorphous and unbounded topic.[10]

The above notwithstanding, it is worth noting that ambiguity in public and even judicial attitudes pertains to many crimes, not merely corruption. Just because it is impossible neatly to categorize every act as either criminal or not criminal does not mean that all attempts either to define a phenomenon or to deal with it should be abandoned. The world is a messy and complex place.

With these caveats in mind, it is possible to move closer to a definition of corruption. Leslie Palmier (1983, 207) is one of many who have cited the most widely used definition, "the use of public office for private advantage."[11] This definition is not without problems. In the real world, the distinction between public and private is often blurred. Private advantage can take a wide range of forms, including status and influence, and this point is not explicitly acknowledged in the definition. Moreover, the definition is so general that it does not reflect an important point: "corruption" may sometimes involve the use of public office for what appears to be both private *and* public advantage.

For example, let us suppose that a high-ranking state official in the mythical land of Nortistan has awarded a contract to a foreign supplier of military equipment, in return for a substantial bribe. Assuming that this equipment is demonstrably as good as what is offered by other suppliers and cheaper, it could be argued that both the official and the Nortistani population have benefited from the corruption (in other words, the transaction is a positive-sum game). The population apparently gains because it is being defended as adequately as it would have been otherwise, but more cheaply. This is not to deny that the actions of the Nortistani official constitute corruption. The official engaged in these actions clandestinely, and almost certainly against the law. Moreover, he or she is putting personal interests before those of the state and society, in that the contract could have been awarded to whichever supplier offered the lowest price for a comparable (adequate) product without any demand for or expectation of a kickback. It is reasonable to assume that the final price was not actually the lowest possible, since the official's bribe had to be factored in by the supplier. These points notwithstanding, this hypothetical case does underscore that different acts or forms of corruption can be perceived in very different ways by citizens, who can sometimes appreciate a degree of corruption if it is perceived to be to their benefit as well as the official's. Thus there are times when an official is perceived by others to be reaping a just reward, even though he or she may not have abided by the formal rules.

Most definitions of corruption are essentially similar to that just cited, although some are more specific because they include examples. Thus until 2000 the international NGO Transparency International defined corruption as "the misuse of public power for private benefits, e.g. the bribing of public officials, taking kickbacks in public procurement or embezzling public funds" ("1996 Transparency International Corruption Perceptions Index" (press release), 2 June 1996, 6), while the Russian Criminal Code in effect until the end of 1996 defined it as "the misuse of power or of an official position, exceeding one's powers or official positions, the acceptance of bribes, involvement [lit. mediation —*posrednichestvo*] in bribery, official forgery" (in Marsov and Poleshchuk 1993).[12]

These two definitions help to refine the first definition cited, although the terms "misuse of power" and "exceeding one's powers" are ultimately vague. Moreover, both treat bribery as one form of corruption. But in Chinese and Thai law, to take just two examples, corruption (*tanwu, fuhua*, or *fubai* in Chinese; *khorrapchan* or *chor rat bang luang* in Thai) and bribery (*huilu* in Chinese; *sinbon* or *dtai dto* in Thai) are seen as related but distinct.[13] Some Russian analysts have also treated corruption and bribery as separate in some circumstances.[14] One fully justified —and universally applicable—reason is that bribery might occur between two private individuals (such as the manager of a private company wanting to build a new plant and a building contractor), which means that it would not constitute corruption as most widely interpreted.[15] Another reason is that in such approaches, corruption often involves embezzlement. Since officials can engage in embezzlement as individuals, not through any direct interaction with other people, it follows that corruption does not necessarily involve two or more persons, whereas bribery does.[16] Despite this, in both China and Thailand the two concepts are nearly always treated as a pair—exactly as in the English expression "bribery and corruption." Hence it is justifiable to include as a form of corruption any sort of bribery that involves officials, despite the cultural variations in usage.

Even this brief discussion of the concept of corruption highlights its vagueness and ambiguities, and one can to some extent sympathize with analysts such as Werlin (1972, esp. 249–50; 1994, 547) who have consciously opted in some of their work on corruption to avoid defining it at all. People often disagree on what constitutes corruption, even in a particular society and at a particular point in time. Moreover, some people tolerate and even more or less accept some forms of corruption, so that we can talk of "good," "bad," and disputed cases of corruption. For instance, most people would condemn all forms of "meat-eating" corruption (officials demand a bribe before they will perform a task on a supplicant's behalf), but in some circumstances might accept "grass-eating" corruption (officials will accept a bribe, but do not expect it). As with the teacher's apple, the timing of a "gift" will often affect perceptions of its social acceptability. In addition, levels of condemnation sometimes vary considerably between cases in which officials are corrupt primarily for personal (individual) gain,which are often seen as purely selfish, and those in which they have engaged in corrupt actions mainly for the benefit of an allegedly underfunded organization such as a political party, which are sometimes seen as more justifiable.[17]

To address some of the issues of subjectivity and ambiguity, the "grandfather" of the academic comparative study of corruption in the English-speaking world, Arnold Heidenheimer (Heidenheimer ed. 1970b, 24, 26–27), devised a schema more than three decades ago in which he distinguished between black, white, and gray corruption. In drawing these distinctions, he focused separately on the perceptions of élites and ordinary citizens: black acts of corruption were perceived by both groups as fundamentally detrimental to society, white acts were seen by both to have some justification and to be of some benefit to society, while gray acts were those about which the two groups had different views.[18]

It will by now be clear that conceptions of corruption depend largely on perception, rather than clearcut definitions. But the question then arises of how to study corruption. If it is so amorphous, *can* it be studied? The answer is that it can and should be, in light of its significance in most parts of the world. Indeed, the very fact that examples have been cited from several continents and different types of political and economic system suggests that the common core referred to above is more substantial than is usually acknowledged by those epistemologically and ideologically concerned about the potential dangers of cultural imperialism or transference. This common core means that the concept of corruption is less amorphous than is sometimes maintained. It is only perceptions of ambiguous cases, and of the significance of corruption in a society, that are so variable and that can be culturally specific. But how can we determine what does and does not constitute corruption in particular instances? Expressed differently, how can we know what constitutes the core — unambiguous corruption — and what constitutes the penumbra?

One minimalist approach is the legalistic one, which maintains that only laws and formal rules should be considered when attempting to determine whether an act constitutes corruption. Scott (1972, 3–5) and LaPalombara (1994, esp. 328–34) are two who favor this approach. This is certainly one way of determining what constitutes "core" corruption. Not only does it provide an unambiguous conception of corruption in any one country, but a comparison of laws in several countries can produce a minimal definition of the core that is universally, or near universally, applicable. A major drawback, however, is that this approach excludes the gray areas that are often so important in terms of public perception. Another is that purely law-based definitions can lack dynamism, and treat the law as if it were above, outside, or independent of the real world in which it exists, from which it emanates, and which it reflects. Yet many laws are made or amended primarily in response to public demand or new developments. Since laws can change or be amended in this way, they themselves are reflective of changing attitudes, perceptions, and realities, with which they are in a dynamic and interactive relationship. Approaches that focus overwhelmingly on specific laws at specific times are thus unduly self-limiting and narrow; they are also inadequate for the purposes of the present analysis, in light of its theoretical concern with the relationship between legitimation problems and corruption.

Another minimalist approach advocates the exclusion of all acts other than those that involve direct material benefit, bilateral exchange, or both. In the first category can be included Kaufmann and Siegelbaum (1997, esp. 422), who prefer to exclude any form of patronage, and focus simply on two forms of corruption — "misappropriation of wealth for the benefit of a government official" and "the extraction of rents" (such as bribes and kickbacks) from private entities. Kim (2002, 169) can be located in both the direct material benefit and bilateral exchange camps, since he would limit the notion of corruption just to cases of bribery (mainly to bureaucrats) and illegitimate contributions to politicians. In a similar but slightly broader vein, Offe (2004, esp. 77–81) advocates a definition of corruption that focuses on the "selling and buying of public decisions," though he points out that purchase is not restricted to cash transactions, and can include "in-kind" exchanges. Approaches like those of Offe and Kim have their advantages, especially to analysts wanting to engage in empirical research on corruption, who therefore prefer a relatively narrow, bounded concept. But the linguistic problems of identifying bribery with corruption have already been outlined, while Kim's specification of "bureaucrats" as the main recipients of bribes might suggest excluding agents of the law; as will be seen in subsequent chapters, many citizens become particularly incensed by demands or requests for bribes made by police or customs officers. Both Kim and Offe (though not Kaufmann and Siegelbaum) also exclude official embezzlement, largely because it is a unilateral activity; this too is overly restrictive, since — as indicated above and demonstrated empirically in chapters 4 and 5 — legal systems and citizens' values frequently treat embezzlement by officials as a concrete form of corruption.

At the other end of the spectrum is what can be called the radically subjective approach. Thus Moran (2001, 380) advocates a flexible "moving target" approach in defining corruption. Simcha Werner (1983, 147) goes even further when he argues that corruption, like beauty, is in the eyes of the beholder. These approaches also have their attractions, not least of which are their inherent dynamism and their capacity to be all-inclusive. All-inclusiveness in particular is also a weakness; since the radically subjective approach cannot be adequately operationalized for comparative analysis (or even for serious studies of individual cases over time), it is not adopted here.

It is contended in this book that the optimal approach to identifying what constitutes corruption — there can be no ideal approach — falls somewhere between minimalist and radically subjective approaches, and combines both hard and soft components. The hard component focuses on legality: if authorities treat as illegal an act that is considered by many observers to be a form of corruption, then it is corrupt. The second component is a soft one, and is reflected primarily in moral condemnation. This second component is useful for identifying the gray (penumbra) areas of corruption, although time-series analysis reveals that moral condemnation has often resulted in legislation that has closed loopholes and, in the process, redefined previously ambiguous activities as unambiguously corrupt. Evidence of moral condemnation includes speeches by politicians, and articles in and letters to the press. In theory, such condemnation could also be tested through opinion surveys, but this is often impractical regarding particular acts (as distinct from general attitudes toward corruption).[19]

One difference between the communist and post-communist eras concerning definitions is that some of the former problems of distinguishing private from public have now either disappeared or else been reduced.[20] The situation of managers is a good example. In economies that are overwhelmingly state-owned and -run, most employees could be described as public officials. There was thus always a potential danger that attempts to compare the scale of corruption across systems — notably capitalist and communist—would indicate higher rates in communist states, primarily because of the expansive definition of "public office"; this is not to deny that many communist systems were very corrupt by most standards anyway (on the USSR see Clark 1993). The privatization moves undertaken since the 1990s mean that this problem has been substantially reduced in many countries. To the extent that there is confusion over what constitutes public and private in particular post-communist states, it is a problem that often exists in established mixed economies too.[21]

Before concluding this brief semantic section, it is worth noting the issue of delimitation and overlap. In addressing this issue, it is appropriate to start by considering specifically matters relating to the communist and post-communist eras, and then much broader questions. During the communist era, there was often confusion between corruption and a number of related concerns, such as the roles of the second economy, the black economy, the gray economy, and the unplanned economy.[22] This conceptual problem has not disappeared; but it has decreased as the planned economy has been phased out and the private sector officially approved.[23] But there is often confusion in the post-communist news media between corruption on the one hand and organized crime, "mafia" activity, and economic crime on the other.

In this book, corruption is clearly distinguished from both organized crime and mafia activity, in that it consists exclusively of malfeasance by state officials and does not necessarily involve several individuals working together in a gang. Conversely, organized crime can operate independently of the state and its officials, and is necessarily a group activity. Many writers use the terms organized crime and mafia essentially interchangeably. This is not the usual practice in Poland, however. Many specialists argue there that organized crime has minimal ties with and influence on the state and its officers, whereas mafia activity does interact with the state and influences it. A typical example of this kind of usage was provided by Marek Ochocki, then director of the Office for Combatting Organized Crime in the Polish police headquarters, who drew the following distinction in April 1994: "Mafia-style crime has a decisive influence on state structures, that is political and economic structures; organized crime does not have such a decisive influence" (SWB/EE, 3 May 1994). Such a distinction makes sense at an abstract and definitional level. But in the real world, organized crime often develops into mafia crime, and the two types of crime become increasingly intertwined. Moreover, and as mentioned above, many analysts outside Poland examine connections between organized crime and state officials in a manner that would be inappropriate according to this Polish perspective.[24] Hence, while this Polish usage has its advantages, the terms "organized crime" and "mafia activity" are treated here as interchangeable.

As demonstrated below, corruption is not defined *ex ante* for the purposes of this book. Rather, a set of criteria is provided for determining whether a given action or nonaction is corrupt. Our approach to organized crime is essentially similar. Thus, for actions to constitute examples of organized crime, they should in principle meet the following five criteria:

1. necessarily carried out by a group, but not of officials;[25]
2. necessarily coordinated;
3. probably targeted (concentrating on a particular type or types of criminal activity, such as drug dealing, prostitution, gambling, or arms smuggling);
4. necessarily illegal at least in part;
5. usually involving violence, actual or threatened.

The criteria used for identifying corruption are different. It therefore follows that while corruption and organized crime (or mafia activity) are often connected, they are conceptually distinct.[26]

Officials can engage in economic crime; if they do so in the context of their official position, this constitutes one form of corruption. But ordinary citizens can also engage in economic crime (such as smuggling or tax evasion), which does not constitute corruption. Conversely, corruption can involve improper acts by officials that are not directly of an economic nature. A prime example is nepotism, which is formally condemned in many societies. Hence corruption overlaps with economic crime, but they too are conceptually distinct.

The reference to nepotism raises a much broader issue of delimitation and overlap. In studying corruption, one of the most difficult problems is deciding the point at which "normal" practice ends and corruption begins. While doing so is difficult enough in terms of exchanges that are primarily material—determining the difference between a bribe and a gift, notably—it is even more problematic with advantages based on personal contacts, as already noted. If junior people cultivate more senior people through networking and vice versa, for instance, does this overlap with clientelism?

There are no easy or agreed answers to this question. Della Porta and Mény (Della Porta and Mény eds. 1995c, esp. 171–72) have argued quite persuasively — citing analysts such as Weingrod (1968), Graziano (1980), and Vannucci (1993) — that corruption and clientelism should be treated as analytically distinct, and provide several reasons. First, there is an important difference in the resource of exchange: whereas corruption involves an exchange of public decisions for money, clientelism involves an exchange of protection for consensus. Second, there is generally a vertical distinction in clientelism (patron, client), whereas such a distinction does not necessarily exist in cases of corruption. Third, the currencies and mechanisms of exchange are different: in clientelism, the payback is associated with general obligations of a personal nature and recognition, whereas in corruption, it rests more on an instrumental rationality connected with financial reward and often the expectation of an iteration of "the game." Finally, Della Porta and Mény argue that those involved in corruption know they are doing wrong and seek to hide their actions, whereas clientelism has long been considered normal, and is conducted openly.[27]

Some of these points, especially the last, are persuasive. In an ironic twist, a former Australian state premier (Nick Greiner of New South Wales) established the by now well-regarded Independent Commission against Corruption to fight corruption — and was then himself accused by the commission of a form of clientelistic corruption. Greiner apparently could not see that he had done anything wrong, and argued that what the commission considered corruption was both open and "normal" politics (Philp 1997, esp. 436–40). Moreover, the need for definitional consistency means that since clientelism can exist purely in the private sector, we cannot argue that all clientelism is a form of corruption; rather, some examples of clientelism can constitute one form of corruption.

Even if one acknowledges these points, however, there are problems with the sharp distinctions drawn by Della Porta and Mény. One is the suggestion that corruption involves the exchange of public decisions for money; according to the Chinese and Thai definitions cited earlier, as well as the English-language pairing rather than merging of "bribery and corruption," such an approach is overly exclusive. For instance, corruption does not necessarily involve any exchange; an example is embezzlement by officials.[28] Another problem is the suggestion that clientelism does not involve instrumental rationality; in many cases it does, with expectations of future payoffs (sexual, status-related, or even pecuniary).[29] Moreover, corruption does not necessarily involve an expectation of an iteration of "the game," though it can and often does.

Partly for these sorts of reason, other analysts have been less willing to draw a neat distinction between clientelism and corruption. Thus the late Jacek Tarkowski (1995, 34), building on Clapham (1982, 5), has written: "Clientelism . . . contradicts two key principles of rational bureaucracy: the separation of the 'private' and the 'official' spheres and the principle of impartiality. The logic of clientelism stands in sharp contrast . . . to more general values of egalitarianism and impartiality which should bind the holders of public offices. It is for these reasons that in many societies, including the ones in which clientelism is widely accepted as a mechanism of allocating goods, it is surrounded with an aura of ambiguity, immorality and corruption." More recently, the Hungarian legal scholar András Sajó (2002, 3) has argued that "one can imagine clientelism without corruption, although the two often go hand in hand. In the post-communist context, the two phenomena seem fused at the hip," and Sajó proceeds to analyze what he calls "clientelist corruption."

In light of all the above, which is a highly truncated overview of just some of the numerous definitional issues involved, we can, for want of a better working definition, return to the traditional one cited by Palmier. By now, however, the reader new to corruption studies is better aware of the many possible ramifications and interpretations of the component parts. Borrowing heavily from the definition of a nation by Hugh Seton-Watson (1965, 5), we can say that corruption exists if the authorities or a large section of the population believes that it exists; ultimately, not objective characteristics but perception is the all-important defining factor. This said, and in line with the earlier argument about a core and a penumbra, it is accepted here that the existence of legal definitions of corruption helps to translate perceptions into more concrete and observable social norms.

Although it is acceptable to use a working definition of corruption for everyday purposes, it is preferable when conducting empirical research to employ a checklist of criteria for determining whether something constitutes an example of corruption. The following is designed to allow for "penumbra" cases of corruption, while at the same time limiting the concept, so that it does not become so broad as to be meaningless. For the purposes of this book, an action or nonaction (such as deliberately "turning a blind eye" in return for some benefit) should in principle meet five criteria in order to qualify as an example of corruption:

1. It must be engaged in by an individual or group of individuals occupying or intending to occupy a public office, typically a state position; in short, it must be carried out by actual or aspiring *officials*, whether elected or appointed.[30]

2. The public office must involve a degree of decision-making or law-enforcing or state-defensive *authority*. Hence, while military officers could be corrupt, ordinary soldiers would be excluded under this definition. Similarly, even though they might be state employees, postal delivery workers or train drivers could not be corrupt under this approach.

3. The officials must commit the act at least in part because of either *personal interest* or the *interests of an organization* to which they belong (such as a political party), if these interests run counter to those of the state and society.[31] Expressing this another way, the officials commit the act for *particular* (micro- or meso-)interests, and at least partly against the *general* (macro-)interest.[32]

4. The officials act (or do not act) partly or wholly in a *clandestine* manner, and are aware that their actions (or nonactions) either are or might be considered illegal or improper. In cases of uncertainty, the officials opt not to find out whether their actions or nonactions are legal and proper — not to subject their actions to the so-called sunlight test (in other words, they are not prepared to allow open and thorough scrutiny of their actions) — ultimately because their intention is to maximize their interests.[33]

5. It must be *perceived* by significant sections of the population as corrupt.

This set of criteria for assessing whether an action or nonaction constitutes corruption is less problematic than a definition, but it is not watertight; no definition or set of criteria could be. Notably, it does not adequately address the case in which a patron openly makes a questionable appointment or promotion and simply rejects the criticisms of others (assuming that there are no clear laws or even guidelines on such matters), which does not fulfil our fourth criterion.[34] But the primary focus in this book is on corruption that involves clear and immediate or imminent material advantage, even though there are references at appropriate points to more ambiguous forms of corruption, such as nepotism. This narrower focus is adopted partly because it is less problematic than one that places considerable emphasis on highly contested (subjective) phenomena such as clientelism, and partly because the theoretical arguments can be made adequately without recourse to ambiguous cases that some readers can then dismiss as "not corruption." The approach to corruption adopted here, and to its possibly delegitimizing role for the state, is based primarily on perception, but it seeks to avoid a dependence on highly disputed types of corruption. It is thus close to the second group of minimalist conceptions identified above, but — in keeping with our broader objective — does allow for social forms of corruption such as patronage. It suffices for our purposes, despite its acknowledged deficiencies.

However, it is accepted here that many actions and nonactions that do not directly involve material advantage can legitimately be described as corruption. That so little emphasis is placed on various forms of clientelism, for the purposes of a more effective and persuasive methodology, should not be mistaken by the reader for neglect: there is an acknowledgment here that clientelism is often widely perceived as — and hence is — a form of corruption.

PROBLEMS IN PRODUCING A TYPOLOGY AND TAXONOMY OF CORRUPTION

Corruption assumes many forms. In her study of corruption in rural China, Jean Oi (1989) identified seventeen types, while Ting Gong (1994, 9), classifying Chinese corruption more generally, identified eighteen. My own study of corruption in late communism employed a twenty-type classification (L. Holmes 1993, esp. 78–88); but since several of these categories, such as false reporting for personal advantage, were more relevant to a planned economy than to the kind of increasingly marketized system typical of post-communist states, that taxonomy is inappropriate for this book. Any attempt at a comprehensive taxonomy should incorporate both unambiguous and contested forms of corruption, including various forms of patronage; the forging of documents for personal advantage; bribe taking and bribe giving; extortion; embezzlement; smuggling that involves abuse of office — and a host of other forms. One form of corruption of particular relevance to a study of the post-communist countries is that practice of former communists, while still in positions of authority, of using their offices and insider knowledge to take advantage of the privatization process. This form of corruption — nomenklatura privatization — will be explored in later chapters, since it is a particular form of more generic types considered here (notably corrupt insider trading and the acceptance of kickbacks). At this point, the differences between a taxonomy and a typology need to be addressed, as do the problems in creating a typology.

As with many other terms considered in this chapter, there is disagreement over the appropriate usage of the terms "taxonomy" and "typology," with some using them interchangeably. For those who draw a distinction, it lies in the nature of the relationship between categories. Whereas some dictionaries and social scientists see a taxonomy as basically a list of categories (groupings or aggregates of similar individual constituents), others insist that it connotes some form of ordered relationship between the categories. The same point applies to typology. Because the few attempts at classification in corruption studies tend to use the term "typology" to refer to rank-ordered classifications, that practice has been adopted here. Thus a taxonomy in this book refers simply to a list of identified types, with no necessary implication of structured relationship between or rank ordering of those types, whereas a typology is a more advanced and ambitious classification that does imply rank ordering.

In principle, producing a typology of corruption is a highly desirable project, since doing so would make it possible to target the most disruptive (system-delegitimizing) forms; assuming limited resources in the fight against corruption, it makes sense to concentrate efforts on the most damaging manifestations. Constructing such a typology is fraught with difficulties, as will become obvious. Yet citizens do tend to perceive some officials and actions as deserving of greater criticism than others are. In terms of popular legitimacy, it is thus important to note these differences, even if it proves ultimately impossible to measure and classify them in a satisfactory way. What are the variables to be included in such a typology?

Rank-Ordering Types of Officials

Within any state, there is a hierarchy of responsibility, even at the higher levels. In general, democracies — and democratizing countries — privilege elected officials over appointed (or career) officials, who are answerable to the elected officials. This is because the elected officials are themselves more directly answerable to the electorate than appointed officials are; this superiority of the elected officials is a key element of a democracy. Hence in a democracy, since senior police or military officers are not usually elected, they are formally subordinate to politicians. Given this hierarchy, it initially appears that the public should be more incensed by corruption among politicians than among senior police or military officials. Certainly TI's first ever Global Corruption Barometer (2003) appears to support this: in three quarters of the forty-four countries for which there are survey data, the group or institution whose corruption incensed the highest proportion of citizens was political parties (Galtung 2003).

However, the next-most criticized group of institutions in the barometer was law-enforcing agencies, which suggests that the clear logic and divide inferred a priori in the previous paragraph might have to be interrogated, for two reasons. First, many citizens believe that the law-enforcing agencies of the state (primarily the police and the judiciary) are those that should be the most trustworthy. These are the bodies responsible for investigating and dealing with the malfeasance of others, including politicians. If even the police and the judiciary cannot be trusted, it may appear to citizens that there is no other agency to which they can turn for justice. In such a situation, the state experiences a serious legitimacy deficit.[35]

Second, the law-enforcing agencies can be seen as enjoying a monopoly position that politicians do not. If citizens are disappointed with particular politicians or parties — perhaps because of their corruption — they can replace them with other politicians and parties, at the ballot box. This release valve implies that while the public may be highly incensed by the corrupt practices of a party or prime minister, it knows that it will sooner or later have an opportunity to demonstrate its disapproval. In this sense, it is not clear that corruption among high-ranking elected officials is more delegitimizing to the system (as distinct from the regime) in a democracy than the corruption of high-ranking appointed officials, notwithstanding the formal subordination of the appointed officials to the elected ones and the results of the TI Corruption Barometer.

A final problematic rank ordering is that between a president and a prime minister. Predicting how the public would react to an identical act of corruption by each of these two most senior officials is difficult. One problem arises from the distinction drawn by Walter Bagehot (1928) in the nineteenth century between the "dignified" and "efficient" elements of a constitutional arrangement. In many countries the head of state is supposed to be above politics; in practice this means above *party* politics. In a real sense, the implication is that the president in a republic (and all post-communist states are republics) is expected to be particularly honest and trustworthy, an ultimate arbiter and authority. From this perspective, it could reasonably be assumed that corruption engaged in by the supreme symbol of the "dignified" element of the constitution would be even more of a disappointment to the public than the corruption of what could be seen as the top official in the "efficient" part of the system, the premier. On the other hand, precisely if the president is seen primarily as a figurehead, many citizens may feel that his or her corruption is more disappointing but less significant than the corruption of the most powerful politician. To place this in a familiar CEE context — would the Czech public have been even more incensed had Václav Havel been accused of corruption than they were about the allegations concerning Václav Klaus when he was still prime minister?

There is a further complication to this issue, especially if a typology that applies across polities is to be constructed. Until this point, the argument has implicitly been premised on an assumption that the system is parliamentary; this was certainly the kind of arrangement that Bagehot was examining, and it applies to Czechia. But many post-communist countries are either presidential or mixed.[36] In his classification of twenty-five early post-communist states, Thomas Remington (1994, 13–15) identified seven as presidential systems (Azerbaijan, Georgia, Kazakhstan, Kyrgyzstan, Russia, Turkmenistan, and Uzbekistan), nine as semipresidential (Armenia, Croatia, Estonia, Lithuania, Moldova,

Poland, Romania, Ukraine, rump Yugoslavia), and only nine as parliamentary (Albania, Belarus, Bulgaria, Czecho-Slovakia, the GDR, Hungary, Latvia, Slovenia, and Tajikistan). Parts of this classification are now outdated, and even at the time could be challenged on the grounds that there were often significant differences between formal constitutional descriptions and actual practices. Nevertheless, citing Remington's classification is a reminder that assumptions about parliamentarism, at least in the post-communist context, can be misplaced. In presidential systems, the problem of determining which senior politician's corruption will be more destabilizing is simplified. If the president is the supreme symbol of both the dignified and the efficient elements, then his or her corruption will be even more unacceptable to the masses than corruption engaged in by a prime minister. Conversely, the task of rank ordering is further complicated in mixed systems (Remington's semipresidential systems).

Corrupt Official's Level

It would seem a priori that citizens will be more incensed by a high-ranking official's corruption than by that of a low-ranking one. This is because, ceteris paribus, the higher-ranking official enjoys greater authority and carries more responsibility, so that the abuse of office appears more serious. But such an assumption about public attitudes is not always correct. Not only may the nature and scale of the officials' corrupt acts matter more than the rank of the officials, but some citizens simply do not relate in any meaningful sense to distant officials, whereas they become incensed by corrupt behavior among local officials with whom they interact day to day.

Types of Corruption

Rasma Karklins (2002) is one of the few scholars to have produced a typology of post-communist corruption. She lists sixteen types, which are then grouped and rank-ordered according to their level of seriousness; seriousness is defined primarily in terms of political costs ("squandering of political capital") or damage. The first group, "low level administrative corruption," is seen as the least politically costly of the three groups, and subsumes three subtypes of corruption (such as bribery of public officials to bend rules). The intermediate category, "self-serving asset-stripping by officials," includes five subtypes; examples are profiteering from privatization; nepotism, clientelism, and selling of positions; and malpractice in public procurement. The most serious category is "state capture by corrupt networks," which in Karklins's schema embraces eight types of corruption. These include the undermining of free elections (such as through slush funds and hidden advertising); misuse of legislative power; corruption of the judicial process; and securing and using *kompromat* (compromising materials for political blackmail).[37] Karklins's is a bold and intuitively sensible approach. But the hierarchy is not always as clearcut as it might initially appear. It is often difficult to determine in practice, when comparing actual cases, which types of corruption the public considers the most serious, and which less. One major reason is that the judgment typically depends on the precise circumstances. Thus, a case of embezzlement involving millions of dollars will probably appear worse than accepting a bribe of $10,000, whereas the bribery case may seem worse if the sums involved are reversed.

In the following taxonomy, the only attempt at macro-classification of types of corruption is indicated by subheadings; but there is no rank order implied, and it is far from clear that such an ordering could be justified. In all cases, the assumption is that the official's action or inaction is at least partly the result of partiality — a personal interest or an interest of the official's political party; this is self-evident in some cases but not others. The interest may apply immediately (as when a bribe is accepted), or there may be an assumption of a future payback (as when a crony is promoted in the expectation of future favors from that person). The other important caveat is that the types of corruption have been separated purely for the sake of clarity; in reality, many cases involve two or more of the types listed below.

A. Deliberate Dereliction of Duties, Inaction, and Obstruction
 1. Willful ignorance
 2. Refusal to investigate or charge, obstructing an investigation
 3. Avoidance of specified procedures
B. Improper Filling of Office and Clientelism
 4. Nepotism (relatives)
 5. Cronyism (friends and close associates)

6. Actions on the basis of shared interests (cases not covered by 4 or 5; an example is where a patron fills a post primarily because someone originates from the patron's home town, is of the same ethnicity, or worked in the same branch as the patron, even though the patron and the client may never have met)

C. Party-Related Corruption
   7. Vote rigging
   8. Improper financing

D. Other Overtly Materialistic Forms
   9. Accepting bribes and kickbacks
   10. Extortion (demanding bribes or kickbacks)
   11. Embezzlement
   12. Insider trading (broadly understood, to include taking advantage of public office to benefit from the privatization process)
   13. Money laundering
   14. Smuggling[38]

Some of the variables below overlap with some of the types identified above (for example, level of predacity overlaps with types 9 and 10). But it is important to distinguish between, on the one hand, types of corruption and, on the other, the factors that can help us to understand why citizens are likely to rank-order pairs or small numbers of cases of corruption in a particular way.

Scale of Corruption: Pecuniary Value

While there is no qualitative difference between the two acts, it seems reasonable to infer that citizens will be more incensed by a prime minister who has embezzled $10 million than one who has embezzled $10,000. Hence one variable in any taxonomy should take into account the value of the corrupt gain. The problem is the usual difficulty of knowing in practice where to insert cutoff points on a continuous monetary scale between, say, "not very serious," "moderately serious," and "very serious"; only empirical opinion research — for instance, focus groups followed by surveys — could be expected to produce any guidelines on this. Even then, such guidelines would vary from country to country, and probably also over time and by income group.

Scale of Corruption: Number of Agencies

It is also reasonable to assume that ten major scandals of corruption among officials within country X in one year are more delegitimizing than just one or two such cases. This is because a relatively small number of cases of high-level corruption will typically be perceived as examples of corrupt *individuals*, whereas a large number of cases makes the corruption appear *systemic*.

This said, it is also a priori important to distinguish a situation in which ten officials within one state agency, such as the police or judiciary, are found to be guilty in the same year from one in which the same number of officials, but from several agencies, are found guilty. Again, the latter case might suggest widespread systemic corruption. In contrast, where cases appear to be concentrated or localized, there can be a general perception that other state bodies will be able to deal with the problem from outside the particularly corrupt agency.

Scope of Corruption

There are several ways in which the scope of corruption can be interpreted. In this analysis, this factor refers to whether an official engages in a *one-off* corrupt activity or *iterated* activities. Ceteris paribus, the latter would be seen by most people as worse than the former.

Nature of Activity

Another variable measures the extent to which an incident of corruption is seen as overt action or rather inaction (as in cases of willful ignorance, or "turning a blind eye"); other things being equal, the former type would be expected to attract more public criticism.[39]

Nature of Lawbreaking

An eighth factor is the extent to which an action or nonaction is considered (1) at least partly the result of unclear or nonexistent legislation; (2) a more questionable bending of the rules (the rules are reasonably clear, but officials consciously interpret any gray areas so as to maximize their personal advantage); or (3) explicit and conscious breaking of the rules. Ceteris paribus, the last category is perceived as worse than the second, which in turn would usually be seen as worse than the first.

Once again, the situation is less clearcut than it initially appears. Occasionally laws lack legitimacy. A simple everyday example — common enough to most automobile drivers in Australia, and probably in many other countries — will highlight this point. All too often, contractors undertaking roadworks commissioned by state authorities take days or even weeks after completion to remove temporary speed limits they had imposed while making repairs, so that drivers, seeing that the repairs have been made, will often speed (thus breaking the law) by traveling at the normal limit on that stretch of road. These drivers do not observe the law, since they consider it illegitimate; the state, which is ultimately responsible for the roadworks, has been irresponsible in not fulfilling its duty to ensure prompt removal of the signs. In situations in which some laws are illegitimate, what initially appears in the previous paragraph to be an obvious rank-ordering of malfeasance begins to blur.

Level of Predacity

The distinction mentioned above — and drawn some three decades ago during investigations into police corruption in New York by the Knapp Commission (Knapp et al. 1973, 4) — between "grass eating" and "meat eating" should be incorporated into our list of variables. Meat eating, which is in essence extortion, normally raises public ire more than grass eating.

Perceived Level of Greed

A distinction should be drawn between officials who engage in corruption for personal gain and others who engage in corruption on behalf of their political party or some other organization to the detriment of the state or society. The latter type of activity is still corruption, since officials are improperly using their position to place the interests of a group before those of the larger collective, and do so wittingly and secretly. Perhaps counterintuitively, the TI Barometer referred to above suggests that publics are often less tolerant of this type of corruption.[40] A priori, cases in which officials benefit both themselves and their party or organization should be ranked as worse than either of the first two types.

Potential Impact

An important factor is the perceived potential impact of corruption. If an official engages in corruption that could endanger citizens' lives, that conduct would almost certainly be more strongly condemned than if the same official committed essentially the same act for the same motive and for the same level of personal gain, but in a manner that did not endanger people. The range of potentially life-threatening instances of corruption is broader than it might initially appear. It includes selling military secrets or weapons to actual or potential enemies (including materials that could be used for nuclear, biological, or chemical warfare), or merely to groups that might endanger third parties; approving substandard building practices for housing blocks, bridges, or other structures that subsequently lead to collapse; and diverting funds intended for disaster relief, such as after a famine, flood, or forest fire.

Social Tolerance of Different Types of Corruption

As indicated above, Heidenheimer has advocated distinguishing between "black," "white," and "gray" corruption. Assessing this trichotomy entails examining the perceptions of both the public and the state's own officials (élites, in Heidenheimer's terminology). White corruption is seen as relatively benign, and potentially even beneficial in its effects (corruption in a highly bureaucratized system is often likened to "lubrication"), by both citizens and officials; it is relatively tolerable, in marked contrast to black corruption. As pointed out earlier, gray corruption is the most ambiguous, in that different sections of the community evaluate its impact differently, and hence have different levels of tolerance toward it.

Involvement with Organized Crime

Citizens can be expected to be more incensed by corrupt officials who collaborate with organized crime than by those who do not. Concrete allegations along these lines are not difficult to find in CEE. For example, the Polish newspaper *Gazeta Wyborcza* alleged in March 1994 that the police chief in Poznan had links with organized crime (SWB/EE, 20 June 1994; the police chief appears to have been subsequently cleared of these allegations—*SWB/EE*, 5 January 1995), while the head of the Crime Department of the Hungarian National Police headquarters, Antal Kacziba, claimed in January 1995 that organized crime was attempting to infiltrate the police and the judiciary, and to influence political decision making (*SWB/EE*, 12 January 1995). In October 1995 Yurii Baturin, assistant to the Russian president on national security, stated that state officials were colluding with a quarter of all organized-crime gangs (*Izvestiya*, 14 October 1995, 1). More recently, the Polish police claimed in 2003 to have discovered close cooperation between the SLD authorities in Starachowice and organized crime groups; possibly exaggerating the significance of this alleged cooperation, the *Warsaw Voice* (3 April 2003—*http://www.warsawvoice.pl/view/1879*, visited April 2003) asserted that it had a "disastrous effect on the image of the Left."

The reasons why the public can be assumed to be concerned about such connections are largely self-evident. For one thing, citizens expect the state's officers to protect them against criminal gangs, not to collude with them. Another reason that needs highlighting is that organized crime typically involves violence, whether actual or threatened; if violence is threatened, the threat may be overt or implicit. If numerous officials are involved or believed to be involved in such violence, the state can begin to look as if it is tolerant of, or even encourages, arbitrary coercion against the citizenry. Given so many post-communist countries' experiences of terror during the communist era (see Dallin and Breslauer 1970), this would be a most unwelcome development.

Close Relatives of High-Level Officials

Although in principle only an official can be guilty of corruption, in practice many citizens will see corruption-emulating behavior by close members of a senior official's family as "corruption," reflecting rottenness in the state. Hence while the behavior of family members should in formal terms be excluded from our consideration, given that it is often associated by the public with the state and can play a delegitimizing role, a comprehensive approach should include such activities in a taxonomy of high-level corruption.

Fourteen variables have been identified—and there are doubtless more—each of which has at least two dimensions. Because of the large number of possible permutations, it becomes obvious why it would be highly problematic to produce a comprehensive and hierarchical (rank-ordered) typology of corrupt acts and their perpetrators. With some of our variables, notably the first and second, it is not even clear how the dimensions should be rank-ordered. Rather, having identified the variables and rank-ordered the dimensions within most of them, it should be possible — given sufficient information — to classify, compare, and rank three or four actual cases of corruption in terms of each of these variables and dimensions, produce an aggregate number corresponding to the "level of seriousness," and suggest which case has been the least delegitimizing and which the most. In all such analyses, only cases from within one country should be compared, since cultural and structural "noises" must be heeded. Moreover, the rank-ordering so produced would still ultimately be speculative; only appropriate, targeted opinion surveys could confirm whether the speculations appeared to be accurate.

In view of all the difficulties of producing a typology of corruption, it might appear pointless to attempt any rank ordering or even classification of it. But to refrain from doing so would be unnecessarily self-limiting. It has been argued that intuition, logic, and empirical research can provide a guide to how at least some of the variables listed above interrelate. As will be demonstrated in chapters 4 and 5, data are available on popular attitudes toward different types of corruption; these findings can be added to intuitive and logical assumptions to produce a limited typology of corruption. In addition, it has been demonstrated in this chapter that it is possible to produce a taxonomy of corruption.

Having identified the problems involved in creating a sophisticated typology of corruption, it should be noted that in addition to the typology of Karklins (2002) discussed above, the World Bank has produced its own typology of CEE and CIS states based on its rankings of just two variables — the level of state capture and the level of administrative corruption (Pradhan, Anderson, Hellman, Jones, Moore, Muller, Ryterman, and Sutch 2000, esp. 14–16; Gray, Hellman, and Ryterman 2004, 31–32). Both these variables are problematic, for reasons that will not be examined in detail here.[41] Nevertheless, the exercise is an interesting one, and suggests that it is possible to produce simple, if limited and imperfect, typologies of corruption in and of post-communist states.[42]

This chapter has sought to highlight the many serious problems involved in defining corruption, and in both classifying and rank-ordering examples of it (in terms of significance and potentially delegitimizing effects). For some, the problems are sufficiently severe to suggest that all attempts to analyze corruption in a systematic and scholarly manner should be abandoned. But this conclusion would be unjustified, and in a real sense would play into the hands of corrupt officials. Just because a watertight definition or typology of corruption cannot be produced does not mean that corruption does not really exist, just as the difficulties in defining a nation do not mean that attempts to improve our understanding of nationalism should be abandoned.

CHAPTER 3

Actual, Alleged, and

Arguable Corruption

There is so much corruption throughout the post-communist world that it would be impossible for anyone to provide a comprehensive picture. Moreover, much still goes unreported or uninvestigated. During a visit to Melbourne in 1993, Emil Constantinescu, then leader of the principal opposition alliance (the Democratic Convention) and later president of Romania, alleged that corruption had become a salient feature of post-communist Romania, adding that no significant cases had yet been tried. But Romania was at the time something of an exception.[1] While widespread corruption is a feature of all post-communist states, so too are well-publicized allegations and trials in most. Rather than attempt systematically and pedantically to cite evidence from every country, it is more appropriate to classify different types of charges and officials, and to provide just a few examples, with a primary focus on our five case studies.

The following analysis is structured to conform where appropriate with the list of officials included in the four surveys we have conducted (see chapter 4 for this list). In a few cases, categories have been either collapsed or disaggregated. The main reason for disaggregation (primarily in the last category, "Other Officials") is to acknowledge the results of others' surveys as well as our own. Conversely, some categories have been merged, particularly where one group's corruption was so common and low-level that the news media generally did not find it interesting enough to report. Thus corruption among traffic police is not accorded its own separate category, even though surveys reveal that it is perceived as very common. The overall structure also draws some distinction between different types of corruption, not merely types of official.

Two further introductory caveats are necessary. The first is that actual

cases are often untidy, involving several officials from different categories. To have reported such cases in disaggregated form would have been
more precise, but would also have gutted them of any "feel." Therefore,
cases are on occasion reported here under one type of official that actually include details on other types, on the grounds that the case as a
whole will make more sense presented this way. Since there are several
examples of each type of official in almost every category, the general
argument is not weakened by this practice.

The second caveat is very important, and relates to the veracity of
cases. Included in this chapter are cases of both proven and alleged
corruption that have been reported in publicly available sources. I have
endeavored to ascertain (and report) the outcomes of allegations. But
this has frequently proved impossible; all too often, as noted by Levin
(2001, 2) with reference to contemporary Russian corruption scandals,
cases simply peter out in terms of media coverage. Often investigations
are terminated, for reasons not publicly reported. Since, as emphasized
at various points in this book, the true scale of corruption cannot be
gauged, and because of the interest here in perceptions and their impact
on legitimacy and the post-communist transition generally, it is ultimately not of major significance whether a case is subsequently proven if
the reporting of allegations has meant that Desdemona's handkerchief
has already been dropped (that is, once an impression of wrongdoing
has been created, whether justified or not). Indeed, that positive outcomes for the accused — notably, court findings of innocence — are so
rarely published only strengthens the argument that perceptions, as in
so many other areas of politics, are often more important than the so-
called facts. The intention here is neither to trivialize nor personalize;
the less serious media can be left to do that. But if we are to understand
better why so many citizens in so many post-communist countries have
so little trust in their authorities, it is important to provide concrete
examples of the type of material that is likely to be affecting those perceptions. This all said, sincere apologies and sympathies are extended to
those whose names have been unfairly sullied in the news media, and
whose alleged improprieties are mentioned again here. Unfortunately,
any damage to their reputation was already done in their own countries
and in their own languages, with a constituency that is broader and
politically more significant than the readership of this book, by the time
their alleged wrongdoings reached these pages.

CHARGES AGAINST LEADING OFFICIALS
OF THE COMMUNIST ERA OR THEIR RELATIVES

There are numerous reasons why charges of corruption have been brought against senior officials of the communist era. One is revenge or retribution; new officials of the post-communist era whose careers suffered at the hands of the old élites are sometimes unable to resist the temptation to retaliate. Linked to this motive is a more general public catharsis — a mass purging of the soul after decades of repression. While this might on one level be seen as another dimension of revenge, it can also represent a mass psychological need to believe in the reality of a fresh start. Third, new governments often wish to demonstrate their commitment in the post-communist era to the rule of law, and trying corrupt leaders from the previous system can be a symbolically significant way of doing so. Expressing this differently, new authorities may be anxious to appear neither soft on their predecessors nor too similar to them in their selective application of the law. Finally, and developing out of the previous point, élites managing new systems can expect to enhance their regime's and the system's legitimacy through appropriate application of the law. But quite what is considered appropriate is rarely straightforward, as the heated debates, confused practices, and differing opinions relating to lustration in so many post-communist states in recent years have highlighted (see for example S. Holmes 1994; T. Rosenberg 1995; Šiklová 1996; Brown 1997; Cybulska, Sęk, Wenzel, and Wójcik 2000, 84–87; Letki 2002; Horne and Levi 2004). Nevertheless, the general principle holds that appropriate (universal) application of the law ultimately has legitimating effects. Before beginning our survey of actual cases, it is worth noting that the four explanations identified here are not peculiar to post-communist states. Rather, they are particularly common in states and societies that have been experiencing radical systemic change. Examples from other types of system include the charges against Presidents Soeharto in Indonesia and Marcos in the Philippines.

It might be considered inappropriate to include cases involving close relatives of senior officials. But as explained in chapter 2, they are included on the grounds that malfeasance by those close to the most senior public figures is often linked in the citizenry's mind to those top officials; the officials may then, whether fairly or otherwise, be suspected of being either corrupt themselves or at least aware and tolerant of corruption in those close to them.[2] The inclusion of cases involving family members thus reflects the focus here on public perceptions of corruption and its possibly delegitimizing effects.

Leading Bulgarian communist officials who have been charged with corruption or the vaguer but closely related "abuse of office" include the former Politburo member and economics minister Stoyan Ovcharov (tried twice, in 1991 and 1992 — for sending the grandson of the former Bulgarian supreme leader Todor Zhivkov to Switzerland for education at the state's expense and for abuse of office; he was sentenced to a nine-year prison term); the former prime minister Georgi Atanasov (found guilty in November 1992 of abuse of office, sentenced to ten years' imprisonment — RFE/RL, 4 November 1992); the former prime minister Andrey Lukanov, who was charged with abuse of office in August 1993;[3] the former deputy leader of the Bulgarian Communist Party, Milko Balev (sentenced in September 1992 to two years' imprisonment for illegal currency transactions); and Zhivkov himself (convicted in September 1992 of the illegal transfer of party funds, and sentenced to seven years' imprisonment; charged with embezzlement, again in connection with his party, in August 1993 — RFE/RL, 10 August 1993 and 26 October 1993).[4]

In December 1991 the widow of the former Albanian leader Enver Hoxha, Nexhmije, was arrested and charged with misuse of government funds between 1985 (the year of her husband's death) and 1990. She was tried in January 1993, found guilty, and sentenced to nine years' imprisonment. She appealed, and for her efforts had her term of imprisonment extended by two years in May; the Court of Appeal resolved that the scale of misappropriation of funds was much greater than had been revealed at trial. In September 1992 the former president Ramiz Alia (Hoxha's successor) was placed under house arrest, after charges arose of misusing state funds and abuse of power. He was eventually convicted in July 1994 of abuse of power and conspiring to violate civil rights, and sentenced to nine years' imprisonment.

The former Estonian prime minister Indrek Toome (1988–90) was arrested in Tallinn in November 1994 for allegedly attempting to purchase three forged passports; apparently the supposed seller was an undercover police officer taking part in a sting operation. Toome was charged with attempting to bribe a police officer, and faced up to two years' imprisonment if found guilty. But he was acquitted in March 1995, largely on the grounds that the sting (entrapment) method had not yet been legalized in post-communist Estonia (*RFE/RL*, 30 November 1994; *OMRI DD*, 17 March 1995).

CHARGES AGAINST POST-COMMUNIST OFFICIALS OR THEIR RELATIVES

Corruption Less for Personal Gain Than for Political Interests

We turn now to corruption among politicians who have been accused of corruption not to line their own pockets (at least not primarily), but in an improper attempt to gain advantage over political rivals.

Attempting to Secure the Presidency Allegations in Russia that Boris Yeltsin's presidential campaigns benefited from questionable financing and improper use of funds — mainly by spending far more than was legally permitted — were frequent (see for example *Segodnya*, 21 June 1996; *Kommersant*, 2 July 1996; Korzhakov 1997, 10–20; White, Rose, and McAllister 1997, esp. 250–51; Sakwa 2000, 131), but until 1999 there had been remarkably few suggestions that the president had engaged in corruption for his own private ends.[5]

In late 1995 in Poland it was alleged that President Lech Wałęsa's electoral campaign had been improperly assisted by the head of the Warsaw police force, Arnold Superczynski, who was rumored to have lent a police car and communications equipment to a man claiming to be in charge of the president's electoral committee, Andrzej Pastwa (*SWB/EE*, 10 November 1995). Superczynski resigned amid the allegations. However, Wałęsa himself denied any knowledge not only of the improprieties, but even of Pastwa.

In Belarus the victor in the presidential election of June–July 1994, Aleksandr Lukashenka, had headed the parliament's Interim Anti-Corruption Commission until its dissolution by the prime minister in April, after allegations in January that the premier himself was corrupt. Lukashenka's presidential campaign focused on his reputation as a fighter against corruption — yet he himself was accused in December by both a former deputy prime minister and a parliamentarian of accepting illegal funding for his election campaign (*Keesings Record of World Events* 40, no. 12:40326).

There are too few cases of this sort of real and alleged corruption from which to be able to draw valid conclusions. However, the very limited numbers, plus logical inference, would suggest that the likelihood of this type of corruption is greater where a system is presidential or semi-presidential than in parliamentary arrangements, where the stakes are lower.[6]

Corruption for the Advantage of a Political Party This type of corruption benefits mostly groups, particularly political parties. This said, individual leaders from those parties are often implicated. For analytical purposes, two main forms of this sort of corruption can be distinguished: corrupt acquisition of funds to fight elections and administer parties; and electoral fraud, notably vote rigging.

As indicated in chapter 1, many of the biggest corruption scandals in Western Europe over recent years have surrounded the illicit acquisition of funds for a political party rather than personal gain as such.[7] Even where there has been personal gain it has typically been secondary, at least in terms of the sums of money involved, to the securing of finances for party coffers.

In the infamous corruption scandal that engulfed the privatization board in Hungary in 1996 (see below), opposition parties and elements of the news media alleged that some of the very large fee paid to consultant Marta Tocsik was ultimately intended for the coffers of the ruling Socialist Party (the former communists—see Z. Szilagyi 1996b). Ultimately this had to remain speculation, since the scandal broke before the alleged intended transfer could occur. Nevertheless, it was claimed that large sums had already been deposited in the accounts of companies close to both the Socialist Party and its junior coalition partner (*OMRI*, 22 January 1997). Certainly one of the members of the privatization board, Laszlo Boldvai, was found guilty in February 1999 of abuse of power; Boldvai, who had been the treasurer of the Hungarian Socialist Party, was found to have pressured Tocsik into transferring millions of forints into various companies. The implication was that these companies would in time have transferred much of this money to the coffers of the Hungarian Socialist Party.

While Poland had not until late 2002 had such a high-profile case of this type, it too has experienced corruption relating to the financing of political parties. For example, the director of the parliamentary office of the Centre Alliance was arrested in February 1993 for allegedly accepting a bribe of 1.5 billion złoty ($94,000) from a company based in Sopot eager to secure a fuel import license; it was assumed by some at the time that the director had done this for the sake of his party (*SWB/EE*, 10 March 1993). In 1998 the magazine *Wprost* alleged that President Aleksander Kwaśniewski, together with Leszek Miller, had illegally used funds of the PZPR (the Polish United Workers' Party, the communist party) to pay workers of the communist party's successor, Social Democracy of the Republic of Poland (SdRP). This would have contravened a ruling of the Supreme Court in 1996 that the SdRP would have to pay its workers from its own funds, even if it did see itself as the successor to the PZPR. The allegation by *Wprost* led the general public prosecutor, Hanna Suchocka, to order an investigation. After an investigation lasting almost two years, it was announced in early 2000 that there was insufficient evidence of any crime having been committed, and the investigation was suspended pending the emergence of any more concrete evidence (all from *DONOSY Liberal Digest*, 27 February 1998, 4 March 1998, 15 January 2000).

The so-called Rywingate scandal of 2002–4 was a more significant Polish case; once again allegations were made about Leszek Miller. In late December 2002 the newspaper *Gazeta Wyborcza* claimed that the film producer Lew Rywin had in July 2002 offered the newspaper's editor (Adam Michnik) advantageous changes to the law governing the news media in return for a bribe of $17.5 million. During a meeting in July with Michnik, Rywin is alleged to have mentioned the Polish prime minister, Leszek Miller, and to have claimed that the bribe would be channeled to the ruling party, the SLD. In February 2003 Rywin was required to testify before a Sejm (lower house of parliament) commission. At this he categorically denied ever having referred to the prime minister at the meeting with Michnik, or having ties with either Miller or the SLD (*Warsaw Voice* on line — *http://www.warsawvoice.pl/view/24*, visited March 2003). Michnik also testified to this commission and declared his belief in Miller's innocence (*EECR* 12, nos. 2–3 (2003): 36–37). In April 2003 Miller himself testified before the parliamentary commission and denied any wrongdoing. He also argued that he had not taken the Rywin case seriously or reported it, as some had claimed he should have done, since the whole matter was so absurd. In July prosecutors in Warsaw dropped charges against Miller for not reporting the case to them, apparently accepting his argument that he did not take it seriously enough to seek a formal investigation. Nevertheless, some observers believed that the impact of the allegations was significant enough to have prompted Prime Minister Miller's call for early elections in April 2003 (*Age* [Melbourne], 4 April 2003, 13; in the event, the call for early elections was abandoned). By late 2003 it was clear that Lew Rywin would be tried for corruption, and that Prime Minister Miller would probably be testifying at the trial (*Warsaw Voice*, 17 October 2003 — *http://www.warsawvoice.pl/view/3783*, visited October 2003).

The allegations continued to haunt the prime minister, who resigned his position as president of his party (the SLD) under pressure in February 2004.[8] Rywin was sentenced to thirty months' imprisonment and a fine for attempted fraud in April 2004; the court determined that Rywin had acted alone, thus exonerating Miller and other politicians whose names had been mentioned in connection with the case (*Warsaw Business Journal*, 27 April 2004). However, in late May the Polish Sejm unexpectedly voted in favor of a report — the so-called Ziobro report — asserting that Miller had been one of those who had sent Rywin to Michnik to offer the bribe, and urged the State Tribunal to try both Miller and President Kwaśniewski for not having reported Rywin's attempted bribe to the authorities. In September the Sejm formally adopted this report. While all this can on one level be seen as political point scoring, it contributed to the deteriorating image of high-level politics in Poland. In all events, Miller had resigned as prime minister at the beginning of May, having seen Poland formally admitted to the European Union; while the "Rywingate" scandal was not the only possible reason for this resignation, many Poles considered it a major contributory factor. Rywin appealed his sentence, which was reduced in December 2004 to two years' imprisonment (plus the original fine of 100,000 złoty); the classification of his crime was changed from attempted fraud to aiding and abetting paid protection (*Warsaw Voice* on line, 15 December 2004, visited December 2004).

The downfall of the Klaus government in Czechia in late 1997 certainly related to party-financing corruption. Allegations were made that the Civic Democratic Party had not only improperly accepted about 7.5

million crowns (over $220,000), but had also made inappropriate privatization decisions that favored the donors, including a former tennis star. President Václav Havel made clear his strong disapproval of Klaus's alleged behavior, accusing his prime minister of mendacity — although it should be noted that the two men had a long history of strained relations anyway (on recent Czech corruption see Appel 2001).

There were numerous allegations of vote rigging in the Russian parliamentary elections of December 1993. Western monitors initially reported that there had been little or no such fraud. But in light of the allegations from within Russia, President Yeltsin established a special "panel of experts" headed by Aleksandr Sobyanin to investigate the claims. The panel reported in early May 1994 (*Izvestiya*, 4 May 1994, 4), and provided mathematical "proof" of malpractice. It therefore endorsed the claims that some election results had been falsified.

Since the main beneficiaries of this falsification were said to have been the communists, the pro-communist Agrarians, and Zhirinovskii's cynically named Liberal Democratic Party, which collectively represented the main opposition to Yeltsin, it might be inferred that the president would have enthusiastically endorsed these findings. However, the panel also alleged that turnout figures for the referendum held at the same time as the elections were almost 9 percent lower than had been officially reported, thus rendering the results of the referendum invalid. Since the referendum had essentially "legitimized" the so-called Yeltsin constitution, it becomes clearer why the president was less pleased with the report than might have been expected. Indeed, the presidential chief of staff soon described it as a provocation. The panel was dissolved, and when the Central Electoral Commission reported in July it endorsed the results of the December election and referendum. It also claimed that the membership of the panel either had been incompetent or else had deliberately attempted to destabilize Russia. Although an authoritative western analysis of post-communist Russian elections concluded that there was probably little electoral fraud (see White, Rose, and McAllister 1997, 128–29), the evidence is ultimately inconclusive; moreover, the various allegations in the mass media (for example *Izvestiya*, 4 May 1994, 4) suggest that many ordinary citizens will have had their doubts about the whole process. Allegations of electoral fraud and bribery of candidates were also made about the parliamentary election of December 1999 (*Izvestiya*, 4 December 1999, 3; *Nezavisimaya Gazeta*, 4 December 1999, 2) and the presidential election of March 2000 (*Moscow Times*, 9–10 September 2000).

Other allegations of bribery or fraud relating to elections include those surrounding the Albanian local elections of September 1993 (*RFE/RL* 2, no. 39, 13); the Azerbaijani elections of November 2000 (*Transitions*, 7 November 2000 and 7 January 2001); the Kyrgyz parliamentary elections of February–March 2000; the Kyrgyz presidential election of October 2000 (*Transitions*, 1 November 2000); and the Ukrainian presidential elections of November 2004.

Corruption Less for Personal Gain than for the Advantage of the Country One of the clearest examples of "white" corruption — assuming that the reports on it are more or less reliable — occurred in Albania, which experienced the so-called Arsidi scandal in late 1994 and early 1995. The former prime minister Vilson Ahmeti was tried for a second time (he had already received a two-year sentence in August 1993 for abuse of power) for involvement in the misappropriation of approximately $1.2 million to pay a French citizen, Nicola Arsidi, in 1991, to negotiate a waiver of Albania's debt (Zanga 1995, 13). This constitutes white corruption if the action was ultimately intended to help the whole Albanian population.

Corruption (Both Alleged and Proven)
Primarily for Personal Gain

All proven cases in the rest of this chapter constitute either gray or, in most cases, unambiguously black corruption, as do cases where allegations were based on fact (whether proven or not).

Presidents There have been relatively few allegations of overt corruption by presidents, other than in connection with presidential election campaigning, as outlined above. But a few have been made, including in some of our five chosen countries.

At about the time of the Polish presidential elections of 1995, an investigation into alleged tax evasion by Wałęsa focused on income earned by him. He had received payment in 1989 from Warner Brothers in California for granting permission to make a film about him. Although the tax office stated that it was illegal to publish the results of their investigations because of privacy laws, it was revealed that it had imposed a substantial tax bill on Wałęsa, categorizing the money as a fee rather than the donation that Wałęsa had claimed it was (*SWB/EE*, 14 November 1995, 21 and 22 December 1995). Wałęsa's archrival did not escape entirely unscathed either. Thus there were allegations that Aleksander Kwaśniewski's wife had not declared her shares in the Polisa insurance company, which, it was claimed, she should have done (*SWB/EE*, 10 November 1995); Jolanta Kwaśniewska was again embroiled in a scandal that some alleged involved corruption — "Orlengate" — in 2004 (*Warsaw Voice*, 19 September 2004, 6), although she appeared by mid-2005 to have cleared her name.

In Russia, after various vague allegations were made against President Yeltsin throughout the 1990s, a major investigation of his alleged Swiss accounts was launched in 1999, and formal accusations followed. The head of a Swiss building firm (Mabetex) responsible for renovating the Kremlin claimed that his company had paid off credit card bills for both Yeltsin's daughters and the president himself over a period of more than three years; the sum paid amounted to almost $90,000 (see *Literaturnaya Gazeta*, 8 December 1999). In October 1999 the head of a Swiss bank (Banca del Gottardo) confirmed publicly that his bank had been requested by Mabetex to guarantee three credit cards for Yeltsin and members of his family. This said, virtually the first action taken by the man who succeeded Yeltsin, Acting President Vladimir Putin, was to pass a decree guaranteeing to his predecessor immunity from prosecution.[9] From many perspectives, this was symbolically an unfortunate start for a new leader ostensibly committed to substantially reducing corruption in Russia. It certainly suggests that Yeltsin will never be formally charged with corruption; indeed, Russian investigations were closed at the end of 2000, officially because of insufficient evidence.[10] In addition to the accusations against Yeltsin, Pavlo Lazarenko, a former prime minister, in early 2000 raised allegations of corruption among those immediately surrounding Ukrainian president Kuchma — and there were implications that they involved Kuchma himself (*Financial Times*, 28 January 2000; *RFE/RL*, 7 July 2000).[11]

Allegations of corruption were a salient feature of politics in Belarus in 1994. In January the de facto president, Stanislau Shushkevich, had to step down after losing a vote of no confidence amid vague allegations of corruption. In April 2001 the former Yugoslav president Slobodan Milošević was formally charged by the Yugoslav authorities with corruption and abuse of office, and placed under arrest. The president of Albania, Sali Berisha, was publicly accused in December 1997 of being involved in smuggling, though it should be noted that the person making the allegations (a former finance minister) had himself been accused by Berisha of similar activities in 1995 (Schmidt 1998, 52). And in April 2004, the Lithuanian parliament voted to impeach President Paksas, *in part* because of allegations of corruption; according to the *Financial Times* (7 April 2004), this was the first time a European head of state had been impeached. A grayer area was the public airing of the warning given by the head of the Latvian taxation office to President Vaira Vike-Freiberga in 1999 that she needed to bring her income reporting into order, after it was alleged that she had failed to declare some of her income (*Baltic Times*, 5–11 August 1999).

Finally, some of the most concrete allegations have concerned the Kazakh president, Nursultan Nazarbayev, in a scandal now often called Kazakhgate. In March 2003 an American businessman, James Giffen, was arrested and charged with paying more than $20 million in bribes to Kazakh officials, in connection with the securing of contracts for American oil companies. In April it was alleged that far larger sums amounting to almost $80 million had been paid to very senior Kazakh officials, one of whom was the president (*Wall Street Journal*, 23 April 2003, § A, 2; another official accused was the former prime minister Nurlan Balgimbayev). Pretrial hearings took place in New York in June and July 2004, and the case was ongoing at the time of writing (the trial itself was expected to start in early 2005). According to the *Wall Street Journal* (23 April 2003, § A, 2), the case has been described by experts as "the largest investigation of possible bribery abroad since the US started prosecuting such cases a quarter century ago" (that is, since the introduction of the Foreign Corrupt Practices Act—see chapter 7). One of the potentially most damaging aspects of the case is Giffen's claim that he was working with the authority of the U.S. government.

Prime Ministers and their Deputies   There have been far more allegations of corruption among CEE and CIS prime ministers than among presidents. Some have been made while the person was in office, while others have surfaced subsequently, such as the Kazakh case just cited. Examples are numerous: listed here are just some of the more widely publicized cases.

Allegations have been made about post-communist prime ministers in at least four of the five countries on which we are concentrating. In Bulgaria allegations of impropriety relating to the holding of shares in a bank were made against Zhan Videnov in 1996 (*SWB/EE*, 8 March 1996). These were soon rejected and no charges were laid; but even if the charges were true, the conduct would less obviously be a case of corruption than most of the analogous cases considered here. In 2000 Prime Minister Kostov acknowledged that his wife had accepted a party "donation" of $80,000. The most serious issue was that the donor was believed by some to be an organized-crime boss. Kostov denied any impropriety, and maintained that both he and his wife were unaware of the source when accepting the donation (Allnutt, Druker, and Tracy 2001, 125). In 1999 and 2000 allegations were also made about the former deputy prime ministers Aleksandr Bozhkov and Yevgenii Bakardzhiev (*Bulgarian Media on Corruption Weekly Review*, 12–18 June 1999; *EECR* 9, no. 3:9); Bozhkov was eventually indicted for "administrative irresponsibility" (*RFE/RL*, 20 October 2000), but acquitted in 2003.

In Hungary there have been allegations about several prime ministers, although most of these have been vague, and of "gray" or ambiguous corruption (mainly nepotism, cronyism, and "turning a blind eye" to alleged corruption by others).[12] In August 2001 more concrete allegations were made about Prime Minister Viktor Orbán, when the opposition unsuccessfully sought to initiate formal investigations into his role (if any) in a corruption case centered on the Ministry for Agriculture and Rural Development. At the same time, the opposition also sought a formal investigation into the prime minister's father, whose mining company was alleged to have received preferential treatment (concerning orders for dolomite) from a state-owned enterprise (*Budapest Sun*, 16 August 2001).

One of the best-known "allegations" about a post-communist Polish prime minister was vague, and little more than innuendo. Thus it was alleged during the second term of Prime Minister Waldemar Pawlak that a company belonging to a close friend, which had been in financial difficulties, was inappropriately awarded a state contract worth several billion złoty (Fuszara 1999, 5). More recently and much more concretely, allegations were made relating to Prime Minister Leszek Miller in the Rywingate scandal already outlined above.[13]

Early in 1993 President Yeltsin charged his own deputy, Vice-President Aleksandr Rutskoi, with the task of investigating rumors of corruption at the very top of the Russian system. By April Rutskoi had made allegations of corruption against many of the most senior members of Yeltsin's team, including the former acting prime minister Yegor Gaidar, Yeltsin's aide Gennadii Burbulis, and two deputy prime ministers (Aleksandr Shokhin and Vladimir Shumeiko). All were alleged to have profited improperly from the privatization process. Rutskoi alleged in a speech to the Supreme Soviet that they were attempting to legalize the shadow economy (*Pravda*, 17 April 1993; see too *Rossiiskaya Gazeta*, 30 March 1993).

The allegations were made at a time when relations between the president and his deputy were rapidly deteriorating. But relations between the president and parliament were also at a nadir, and in July parliament voted in favor of a criminal investigation of Shumeiko for alleged embezzlement of money intended for the purchase of baby food. In the following month Rutskoi himself was charged with corruption; it was alleged that through the Vozrozhdenie foundation, of which he was chairman, he had been illegally transferring millions of dollars into a Swiss bank account. Rutskoi immediately refuted the allegations (Rubnikovich and Rodin 1993). But the president suspended both him and Shumeiko at the beginning of September, and Rutskoi's name was not finally cleared until December 1995. The charges against those accused by Rutskoi also were eventually dropped, in the absence of any firm evidence.[14]

Gaidar is not the only Russian prime minister against whom reasonably specific allegations of corruption have been made. Another is the longest-serving prime minister in post-communist Russia, Viktor Chernomyrdin. A political scandal erupted in the United States in November 1998 after it was alleged in the *New York Times* that Vice President Al Gore had been informed by the CIA of considerable evidence of Chernomyrdin's corruption, but had essentially dismissed it; this said, it appears that the evidence is ultimately circumstantial (for an overview see Kupchinsky 2002).[15] In Albania, Fatos Nano was charged in July 1993 with misuse of Italian aid in 1991 while he was premier; he was found guilty in April 1994 of misappropriation of state funds and falsification of official documents, and sentenced to twelve years' imprisonment (though he was released early in 1997). After corruption allegations were made against him in 1993, a vote of no confidence in Prime Minister Vyacheslau Kebich of Belarus was moved in January 1994. The motion was lost, and in April Kebich called for an end to unsubstantiated claims of corruption. Having lost the presidential race to Lukashenka, Kebich resigned in July and was succeeded as prime minister by Mikhas Chygir; Chygir was accused of corruption in December, in what proved to be a bumper year for allegations of high-level corruption in Belarus.

Perhaps counterintuitively in light of their relatively clean image during the communist era, and perhaps also their proximity to the Nordic states, all three Baltic states have been very prone to corruption-related scandals focusing on the prime minister. Allegations of corruption, relating among other matters to the privatization of apartments in Tallinn, were made against Prime Minister Tiit Vahi of Estonia in early February 1997. Although he narrowly survived a no-confidence motion in parliament, he resigned two weeks later to focus on the charges (*Monitor*, 11 and 14 February 1997; *Oxford Analytica East Europe Daily Brief*, 11 March 1997).

At first sight, the best-known case of a Latvian prime minister — Andris Škēle — involved in corruption scandals seems to have arisen because of the corruption of others, rather than that of the prime minister himself. Škēle felt obliged to resign in July 1997. Nearly a year before, at the beginning of August 1996, new anticorruption legislation — basically a conflict-of-interest law — had become effective, and Škēle had promised a clampdown. But the man who had been Latvian prime minister since December 1995 was initially accused by some of being soft on allegedly corrupt officials. In January 1997 Škēle had tendered his resignation for the first time that year, after criticism of his appointment of Vasilijs Melniks as finance minister; Melniks was a former businessman who had been accused of corrupt practices (*Warsaw Voice*, 26 January 1997, 8; *Business Central Europe* 5, no. 38 (1997): 15).[16] Although Škēle's resignation was not accepted, he seems to have decided to become tougher in dealing with allegations of corruption among his immediate entourage. On 17 June Škēle appeared on television to discuss a number of allegations of corruption (of various forms, including conflicting interests, tax evasion, and acceptance of bribes) among members of his cabinet and ministries. At the time of the television broadcast, the minister of culture had already resigned. By late June the prosecutor's office had charged no fewer than seven ministers with breaking the conflict-of-interest law; they included the ministers of defense, agriculture, transport, education, and science. Šķēle also dismissed the health minister for tax evasion. But many of the political parties—ironically, considering the earlier criticisms—now felt that Šķēle had been too heavy-handed in implementing the conflict-of-interest law and encouraging investigation into ministers' private affairs. It was in this conflictual situation, in which the prime minister refused to capitulate to the pressure from the parties, that Šķēle this time did step down (all information from *RFE/RL* and *Monitor*, June and July 1997). However, allegations were made a little over six months later that Šķēle himself had accepted a kickback from a German company in 1992, before he was prime minister (when he was deputy minister of agriculture—*RFE/RL*, 17 February 1998). It seems that all too often in CEE and the CIS, senior political actors have been unaware of the old adage about not throwing stones if one lives in a greenhouse. This said, the whole, complex story appears not to have done Šķēle any serious long-term political harm: he became prime minister again in July 1999.

In January 1996 President Algirdas Brazauskas of Lithuania asked his prime minister, Adolfas Šleževičius, to resign, after the suspension of operations by the Lithuanian Incorporated Innovation Bank (LAIB) in December 1995 and by the Litimpeks Bank in the following month. The request followed an investigation by the prosecutor general's office into allegations that Šleževičius had withdrawn a considerable sum (about $30,000) from his LAIB account just two days before its activities were halted by the central Bank of Lithuania; the prosecutor general's office subsequently announced its intention to initiate criminal proceedings against the premier for having received abnormally high interest rates on his account at LAIB and, more generally, abuse of office (basically, benefiting from insider information). When Šleževičius refused to resign, Brazauskas called on the Lithuanian parliament to approve a presidential request for ratification of a decree to dismiss him; the decree would also have lifted the prime minister's parliamentary immunity (*OMRI DD*, 26 January 1996). Parliament approved the decree in February, and Šleževičius lost his post. A later case in Lithuania was in many ways more akin to the Latvian case mentioned earlier, in that a prime minister's resignation was due primarily to charges of corruption around him, rather than allegations of his own corruption. After a number of allegations about several members of the government, made over the preceding weeks and relating principally to the energy sector, Gediminas Vagnorius resigned in April 1999; his resignation was eventually accepted by

President Adamkus in May (*Baltic Times*, various issues from March to May 1999).

In 1994 a former prime minister of Ukraine, Yukhim Zvyagilsky, fled to Israel, accused of embezzling approximately $25 million; he was granted immunity by the Ukrainian legislature in February 1997. A more recent case is that of Pavlo Lazarenko, Ukrainian prime minister in 1996–97. He was arrested in December 1998 as he attempted to cross into Switzerland, and charged with money laundering; although he had by then left Switzerland, he was found guilty in absentia and given an eighteen-month suspended sentence by a court in Geneva in June 2000. Lazarenko was also charged by the Ukrainian authorities with large-scale embezzlement while in office, and he returned to Ukraine shortly after the attempt to enter Switzerland. He later fled to the United States, where he was charged with laundering $114 million while he was premier in 1996–97. From there Lazarenko admitted to the Ukrainian authorities that he had laundered some $9 million through Swiss banks. But this admission was considered an attempt at securing a much lighter sentence than he might otherwise have expected; investigators claimed in court that Lazarenko had embezzled about $880 million between 1994 and 1997 (see for example RFE/RL, 7 July 2000; *Ukrayinska Pravda*, 16 June 2003, at *http://www2.pravda.com.ua/en/archive/2003/june/14/1.shtml*, visited August 2003).

Lazarenko eventually went on trial in San Francisco in March 2004, after almost five years in detention. The presiding judge dismissed many of the charges on the grounds that it was not clear whether Lazarenko had broken Ukrainian law; nevertheless, he was to be tried on almost thirty counts (RFE/RL OCTW 4, no. 12 (2004)). He was convicted on the remaining counts in June 2004; his lawyers claimed in January 2005 that the new Ukrainian government would be able to clear Lazarenko's name, but that possibility was still pending at the time of writing. Whatever the precise figures, or the deficiencies in Ukrainian law, there is no doubting that in terms of the sums involved, this former Ukrainian prime minister has been seen by some as one of the most corrupt senior officials in the post-communist world. It is therefore on one level surprising, and of particular relevance to our interest in the formation of perceptions, that the Ukrainian media should have devoted so little attention to the trial in 2004 (RFE/RL OCTW 4, no. 12 (2004)). Perhaps the authorities were concerned that Ukraine's already poor image with regard to corruption would be even further tarnished by excessive pub-licity of this case—although one Ukrainian whom I interviewed in mid-2004 believed that the real reason was Lazarenko's closeness to very senior members of the government, who wanted to minimize any likeli-hood of being besmirched by the case, and had sufficient leverage over the media to ensure that media coverage would be kept to a minimum.

Although the focus here is on prime ministers, they are such high-profile and high-ranking officials that alleged "corruption" by close rela-tives also annoys many citizens and is likely to have some impact on the legitimacy of the regime, and possibly of the system. Once again, there is no need to look beyond our five countries for examples. In April 2000 allegations were made that the son-in-law of Prime Minister Ivan Kos-tov of Bulgaria had been profiteering improperly from recent privatiza-tion processes. The allegations appear to have been largely a "beat-up," or distortion. But they were particularly embarrassing to Kostov at that time because, according to President Stoyanov, there were widespread criticisms of the prime minister for being weak in fighting corruption; some observers evidently and perhaps unfairly interpreted this weakness as evidence of complicity and conflict of interest. Poland has also experi-enced this type of allegation and scandal. In 1995 *Życie Warszawy* wrote that the wife of Prime Minister Józef Oleksy had improperly acquired shares in the Polisa insurance company; she sued the newspaper for libel (*SWB/EE*, 6 November 1995).[17]

To conclude this discussion, we can refer to some of the numerous allegations that have been made against deputy prime ministers (in addition to the cases of Shokhin and Shumeiko cited earlier): these claims are included here rather than in the discussion of ministers that follows on the assumption that many citizens treat such officials as being much more senior than mere ministers. An example is the former deputy prime minister of Albania, Rexhep Uka, who together with the former finance minister Genc Ruli was charged with abuse of office and corrup-tion relating to the export of timber (Zanga 1995, 13). The once high-flying Russian deputy prime minister Boris Nemtsov may have lost some of his luster in 1997 when it was alleged that he had accepted a substantial payment ($100,000) for a small book (*Provintsial*) that had not yet been begun, and which some believed was unlikely ever to get written.[18] A similar type of scandal affected the first deputy prime minis-ter Anatolii Chubais, the mastermind of Russian privatization, in November 1997. Together with four other officials, including Maksim Boiko, deputy prime minister and chairman of the State Property Management Committee, and Alfred Kokh, also a deputy prime minister and former head of the committee, Chubais was accused of having accepted an advance for an unpublished book on privatization; the advance amounted to $90,000 for each of the five men accused and was seen by some as a bribe (*Nezavisimaya Gazeta*, 13 November 1997, 1–2). While he lost his post as finance minister, no formal charges were laid against Chubais (Glinkina 1998, 19; for English-language details and analysis from the Russian press see CDPSP 49, no. 44:1–8), who vigorously denied any wrongdoing (*Kommersant*, 28 November 1997, 1).[19]

In November 1999 the Czech deputy prime minister Egon Lansky resigned. The official reason given for this was poor health. However, there was speculation that another reason was that he had been discovered to have an illegal bank account in Austria, in which he had been depositing questionably acquired funds and via which he had been avoiding paying taxes (*Radio Prague E News* — http://archiv.radio.cz/news/EN/1999/29.10.html, visited February 2004; *Carolina* — http://www1.cuni.cz/carolina/archive-en/Carolina-E-No-354.txt — visited July 2004).

Ministers (or Approximate Equivalents)   So many allegations of corruption have been made against ministers or their equivalents in our five countries that there is no need to range beyond them to exemplify this form of malfeasance.

Bulgarian ministers about whom allegations of corruption or abuse of office have been made and in some cases proven are numerous, and include the industry minister Rumen Bikov (October 1993); the trade minister Valentin Karabashev (October 1993); the labor minister Evgeni Matinchev (1994); the defense minister Valentin Aleksandrov (1994–5); the transport minister Stamen Stamenov (November 1996); the former interior minister Lyubomir Nachev (April 1997); and the transport minister Wilhelm Kraus (dismissed in December 1999, formally indicted in October 2000 for abuse of office — RFE/RL 20 October 2000). Many of these were not ultimately charged, but at least some damage, in terms of public image, had in most cases been done.

Several Hungarian ministers were involved in the so-called Oilgate scandal of 1996. This was a case in which ministers sought to reach an agreement with Russia over its debt to Hungary of almost $900 million.[20] Another high-profile case emerged in October 2000, when Jozsef Torgyan, minister of agriculture (and head of the Independent Small-holders' Party, or ISP), was accused of incorrectly reporting his income; there were also suggestions that he might have accepted bribes. Torgyan constantly changed his story concerning the origins of the funds that paid for an expensive new villa he had recently built, and resisted serious attempts by other parliamentarians and even Prime Minister Viktor Orbán to force him to declare openly all his sources of income. Torgyan failed to appear before a committee responsible for investigating con-flicts of interest in mid-December 2000, and briefly managed to avoid excessive scrutiny. However, his behavior had a detrimental effect on the ISP's standing, and several of his fellow party members were among those demanding and bringing about his resignation not only as head of the ISP in February but also as minister of agriculture in March 2001 (all from *EECR* 9, no. 4:18–19; *EECR* 10, no. 1:20).

In Poland formal charges of corruption were laid against the minister for foreign economic relations in August 1994 (*RFE/RL*, 8 February 1995; Roszkowski 1997, 93–94). In October 1994 the minister of foreign affairs, Andrzej Olechowski, offered his resignation, after the minister of justice, Włodzimierz Cimoszewicz, included Olechowski's name on a list of officials who had broken the conflict-of-interest ("anti-corruption") law.[21] Although an external observer might have some sympathy for Olechowski's argument that the broadcasting of the list was premature and in this sense political, it did reveal that the Polish authorities were serious about tackling the problem of double dipping by politicians (see *SWB/EE*, 28 and 29 October 1994). More recently, the Polish deputy defense minister was formally charged with corruption in June 2002, but denied any wrongdoing (*RFE/RL Newsline*, 13 June 2002).

China has also had its problems with allegedly corrupt ministers, though the authorities tend to be vague about rumored misdemeanors. For example, the minister of justice Gao Changli resigned in November 2000 — officially because of ill health, but at the same time as investiga-tions began into alleged economic irregularities committed by him and his mistress (*Financial Times*, 5 December 2000). Less ambiguous is the case of the former deputy minister of public security Li Jizhou, who in October 2001 was sentenced to death (deferred for at least two years) for his involvement in the major Fujian corruption scandal that broke in 2000 (see chapter 7).

As for Russia, it is difficult to know where to start, and just a few examples will be cited. In July 1993 President Yeltsin dismissed the minister for security, Viktor Barannikov, for alleged corruption relating to Barannikov's wife (*Izvestiya*, 29 July 1993, 1–2). However, dismissal was typically the only punishment in the early post-communist years. Thus when the head of the State Statistics Committee, Yuri Yurkov, was arrested for alleged manipulation of business data in June 1998, *Izvestiya* (10 June 1998) stated that this was the first time a minister had been arrested in contemporary Russia.[22] But the precedent had now been set, and the (former) minister of justice Valentin Kovalev was arrested and charged with misuse of public funds in February 1999; he was subsequently prosecuted for embezzlement and bribe taking, convicted, and sentenced to nine years' probation (*Segodnya*, 4 April 2000; TI *Newsletter*, September 2000).[23] More recently, the Russian procurator general, Vladimir Ustinov, announced in October 2001 that the minister for railways, Nikolai Aksenenko, was being investigated for alleged corruption (EECR 10, no. 4:34). In early January 2002 Putin announced that Aksenenko had been found to have been involved in his ministry's deliberate tax evasion, and to have benefited from improper use of funds amounting to more than $1 million. Aksenenko was pressured to resign (*Russia Reform Monitor*, 3 January 2002; RFE/RL, 4 January 2002).[24]

Parliamentarians There have been allegations of corruption among members of parliament in most post-communist countries; our five states are no exception. Thus the Bulgarian prosecutor general Ivan Tatarchev announced in November 1994 that several former parliamentarians were under investigation for corruption (SWB/EE, 4 November 1994). More recently, the parliamentarian Valentin Stoyev was reported in the press to have been improperly involved with businesspeople in connection with the running of a pyramid scheme (cited in Fuszara 1999, 6).

An unambiguous case of a Hungarian parliamentarian acting corruptly was reported in October 2000. Zoltan Szekely, chairman of the parliament's procurement committee and a member of the ISP, was caught accepting a bribe for 20 million forints (about $65,000); he was later arrested, found guilty, and in May 2002 sentenced to six years' imprisonment and a ten-year ban on holding public office (EECR 9, no. 4:18; RFE/RL, 30 May 2002).

In a report by the World Bank on Poland made public in March 2000, it was claimed that some parliamentarians had been prepared to block or amend laws in return for bribes, for which the going rate had increased from about $500,000 in 1992 to $3 million by 1999 (Sutch with Dybula and Wojciechowicz 2000, ch. 3 n. 13; *Business Central Europe* 7, no. 71:44; for verification and updating by a Polish analyst see Piotr Golik's article in *Warsaw Voice*, 2 April 2000). An entertaining recent example of conflict of interest in Poland is the story of a Polish member of parliament who advocated a ban on the use of mobile telephones by car drivers; according to Fuszara (1999, 9), he omitted to mention publicly that he owned a company that manufactured hands-free telephones for use in motor vehicles.

Once again, and only partly because of the much larger scale of the country, examples of Russian corruption in this category greatly outnumber those in our other three CEE countries. One case is that of the chairman of the Upper House (Federal Council), Yegor Stroyev, who was alleged in 1997 to have used his position to promote companies close to him in bids to acquire the most attractive assets being privatized by the state (*Izvestiya*, 15 February 1997, 1–2). As in Poland, there have been allegations in Russia that parliamentarians are sometimes prepared to agree to vote a particular way in parliament in return for a reward (see *Izvestiya*, 30 May 1997). Zhirinovskii's Liberal Democratic Party of Russia has been accused by many of being particularly prone to this practice (see for example *Los Angeles Times*, 3 October 1999).[25] In late 2002 *Komsomol'skaya Pravda* (21 November) outlined how many Russian parliamentarians supplement their rather meager official salaries. In addition to the method just mentioned, they might demand an official investigation into a company in return for a payment from one of that company's competitors.

China has also acknowledged that it has corrupt parliamentarians. Thus it was announced in late December 2000 that three deputies to the National People's Congress (NPC) had been expelled, two for suspected corruption; at least one of these was subsequently dismissed from office for large-scale bribe taking (CD, 28 December 2000, 18 May 2001). A better-known and higher-profile case is that of Cheng Kejie, former vice-chairman of the Standing Committee of the NPC. Cheng was placed under house arrest in August 1999, on suspicion of taking bribes and purchasing political office. After official investigations he was expelled from the CCP in April 2000; a few days later he was dismissed from his senior NPC position and then arrested (CD, 21 and 26 April 2000). In August he was found guilty of having corruptly acquired some 41 million yuan (about $4.9 million), and after an unsuccessful appeal he was executed in September 2000 (CD, 1 August and 15 September 2000; BR 43, no. 33:7).

Czechia provides an example of parliamentarians involved in what can best be described as smuggling. In 1993 it was revealed that sixteen deputies had taken advantage of their parliamentary immunity to import cars without paying the requisite duty; one member of parliament had in fact done this three times (Kettle 1995, 36). And Poland and Russia are certainly not the only countries in which there have been attempts — both successful and unsuccessful — to bribe parliamentarians to vote in a particular way. In June 1999 the leader of the Social Democratic Workers' Party in Latvia, Juris Bojars, claimed publicly that an unidentified Russian-speaking businessperson had offered his party a substantial financial inducement to vote for Anatolijs Gorbunovs (of the Latvia's Way party) in the Latvian presidential elections. Latvia's Way denied these allegations (RFE/RL, 21 June 1999).

Local Officials The range of public offices that are elected rather than appointed varies from country to country. This is true of the office of the mayor, for instance. Mainly for this reason, the two groups have been collapsed into one here. But for differences in perceptions of corruption levels between elected and appointed local officials in specific countries, the reader is directed to chapter 4. A second introductory caveat is that "local" is used here in a broad sense, to refer to any level below the central (federal in a federated state); this can include Russian regions (such as republics and *oblasty*) and Chinese provinces, for example.

The former mayor of Veliko Turnovo (Bulgaria) was convicted in 1994 for corruption (RFE/RL, 14 June 1994). A report to the Bulgarian government from the Central Service for Organized Crime Control in May 1997 named a number of local state officials who had corruptly assisted the recently arrested organized-crime boss nicknamed Rocco (SWB/EE, 16 May 1997). Less than two years later, the head of the National Audit Office claimed that "if all the reports produced by the National Audit Office were published, not a single minister *or mayor* would survive in his position" (*BPCWR*, 13–19 February 1999; emphasis added).

Our research uncovered little detailed evidence of corruption among local officials in Hungary. However, the head of the Hungarian State Audit Office referred in 1999 to various recent corruption scandals in local governments, and to the likelihood that there would be more in connection with municipal investments (A. Kovács 1999, 12–14).

Without doubt, the foremost corruption scandal in Poland in late 2000 related to local officials in Katowice (Silesia). A report in the newspaper *Rzeczpospolita* in late November alleged that officials close to the provincial governor had been abusing their offices for personal gain for at least three years. A commission was immediately sent to investigate, and by early December confirmed that there had been corruption. The governor himself was not accused of any wrongdoing. But he had built his reputation largely on a commitment to clean government and as a crusader against corruption, so the revelations were a serious embarrassment to him. He offered his resignation to the Polish prime minister, Jerzy Buzek. Buzek announced on 6 December in Warsaw that his government would now have a policy of zero tolerance toward corruption — and he accepted the governor's resignation (*RFE/RL*, 7 December 2000).

Corruption appears to be alive and well in Russian local and regional government. According to city police statistics, the Moscow force investigated 17 percent more bribery cases in the first six months of 1999 than in the whole of 1998 (Handelman 2000, 89). The former governor of Vologodskaya province, Nikolai Podgornov, was sentenced in October 1999 to seven years' imprisonment for bribe taking and abuse of office; he served only a few months before being amnestied in June 2000 (*Izvestiya*, 6 July 2000, 2). In the late 1990s the Russian prosecutor's office formally investigated allegations of corruption against the former mayor of St. Petersburg, the late Anatolii Sobchak.[26] And the governor of Tula was arrested in 1997 for accepting bribes (*Izvestiya*, 14 June 1997, 1).

In China one of the most sensational cases of corruption in the 1990s concerned the leadership of Beijing municipality; but since the principal figure in this was most recently a senior party official (although at one time also mayor), the case is considered later in the chapter. Early in 2000 the former deputy governor of Jiangxi province, Hu Changqing, was found guilty of accepting bribes worth some 5.4 million yuan and almost immediately executed; the Chinese news media reported that Hu was the highest-ranking official to have been executed in "new" (communist) China (BR 43, no. 39:4; CD, 10 and 12 March 2000). In August of that year the deputy chairman of the Ningxia Regional Committee of the Chinese People's Political Consultative Conference was accused of nepotism and cronyism, and expelled from the CCP (BR 43, no. 35:7). The mayors of Shenyang and Simao were both found guilty of corruption in 2001 (BR 44, no. 26:6; 44, no. 35:6; 44, no. 39:4), while Xinhua (the official Chinese news agency) announced early in 1994 that about a fifth of officials (more than 300,000 people) in Anhui province had been caught misappropriating state funds (report cited in the *Age* [Melbourne], 6 January 1994, 8).

Senior Public Servants (Ministerial Staffs) This group of officials is large, so it is not particularly surprising that allegations and proven cases of corruption have been common in many post-communist states. Just a few examples will suffice.

According to reports in various national daily newspapers, several senior Bulgarian officials from the Interior Ministry were accused in October 1993 of corruption, in the report of an enquiry by a parliamentary subcommittee that focused on the dismissal of the head of the National Security Service. The veracity of these reports is difficult to determine, and the president's office refuted them; however, it is likely that at least some citizens were prepared to believe them.

In what has been described as "the biggest scandal of the transition era" in Poland (Łoś and Zybertowicz 2000, 164), several senior officials — including the director and deputy director of FOZZ (Foreign Debt Servicing Fund) — were charged in 1993 with fraud and embezzlement in connection with a sophisticated scheme by which they bought into Poland's foreign debt when its value declined. FOZZ was formally established in 1989 (having had a predecessor since 1985), partly to enable the state to accumulate funds for repaying Poland's debt to western creditors. With the discovery of "irregularities" in FOZZ's activities already by late 1989, a full-scale investigation was launched in 1991. By September the director and a number of his assistants had been accused of misappropriating some 1.9 billion złoty (about $1.25 million) intended for debt repayment, and seeking to make private profit where the state should have been benefiting. The director spent fifteen months in prison between 1991 and 1993. But the case was complex, and investigations continued. In February 1993 formal charges were laid. The investigations suggested that embezzled funds amounted to a higher figure of 3.8 billion złoty (more than $2.2 million — all from *SWB/EE*, 5 October 1991, 23 July 1992, and 21 January 1993), while the losses to the state caused by the embezzlement were estimated at 1.6 trillion złoty. But in October 1993 a Polish court decided there was insufficient evidence in the FOZZ case, and it was formally dropped. There followed appeals by prosecutors and new investigations. Eventually, in January 1998, new figures were produced in court suggesting that the losses to the state amounted to approximately $128 million. The FOZZ affair had still not been finally resolved several years later (*Warsaw Voice*, 1 July 2001; for a detailed analysis of this case, particularly some of its more sinister aspects, see Łoś and Zybertowicz 2000, 164–73).

In 1995 a former Russian deputy minister for foreign economic relations was charged with abuse of office, forgery, and smuggling, in connection with the improper issuance of export quotas and licenses (*Izvestiya*, 27 October 1995, 3). This case followed one some two years earlier involving the head of the quotas department in the same ministry, who was prosecuted for accepting bribes in return for granting export licenses (*Izvestiya*, 22 December 1993, 4). In 1997 a number of Defense Ministry officials were reported to have been involved in large-scale embezzlement, and to have transferred most of their ill-gotten gains abroad (*Izvestiya*, 14 May 1997, 1, 3). And in April 2002 a former senior financial officer of the Defense Ministry was sentenced to three years' imprisonment for large-scale embezzlement (of some $450 million) (*RFE/RL*, 7 August 2002).

Finally, an example of a senior Chinese public servant found guilty of corruption is Kang Hui, director of the Wages and Welfare Department of the Ministry of Personnel, who was sentenced to ten years' imprisonment (*BR* 43, no. 21:17).

Police Officers   As will be seen in chapter 4, the surveys conducted for this research project distinguished between traffic police and regular police: the two groups differ markedly in their perceived level of corruption in some countries, suggesting that this was an appropriate decision. But for the purposes of this chapter, the two groups can be collapsed. As for which of the two should be setting an example, it is reasonable to infer that it is the regular police, because of their broader and higher-level responsibilities.

Starting once again with our five target countries, the police chief of Sofia was dismissed in November 1991 for "irregularities" that appear to have involved corruption (*swb/ee*, 30 November 1991). Another Bulgarian case of police corruption was reported in mid-1997, when two police officers were arrested for alleged involvement in people smuggling (*swb/ee*, 3 July 1997). And the head of Sofia's Economic Police was caught red-handed in August 1999 accepting a bribe worth some $75,000 from a local businessperson (*rfe/rl*, 5 August 1999; *Bulgarian Media on Corruption Weekly Review*, 4–7 January 2000); at the end of 2002 he was sentenced to twenty years' imprisonment, though he announced his intention to appeal (Centre for Liberal Strategies 2003, 2).

A report in July 1996 claimed that corruption in the Hungarian police force was increasing, and referred to the widespread perception that police officers often collaborated with organized crime. Following on from this, four senior police officials were dismissed in December 1996 for failing to deal adequately with the violence of organized-crime gangs (*omri*, 4 December 1996). The Hungarian Ministry of Domestic Affairs acknowledged widespread police corruption in 1999; 240 officers had been discharged "in recent years" because of it (*Central European Review*, 29 July 1999).

There were several official references to police corruption in the Polish police force in the early 1990s (see for example those by the deputy minister of the interior, *swb/ee*, 13 December 1991, and by the police chief Zenon Smolarek, *swb/ee*, 29 April 1992). But what was to become one of the most widely publicized and discussed examples of corruption in Poland — despite its eventual outcome (see below) — entered the public arena in a major way in early March 1994, although rumors had already been circulating for some weeks. In its weekend edition of 6–7 March, *Gazeta Wyborcza* alleged that there was widespread corruption in the police force in Poznan. The matter was soon addressed by the central authorities. Within days the Sejm's Commission for Administration and Internal Affairs had announced an investigation. At the same time, Smolarek — who was still Poland's police chief, and who had been implicated in the newspaper report — offered to resign; shortly afterward, his deputy made a similar offer. An initial investigation into the police force found evidence of several irregularities, but no corruption as such. By April, although a number of officers from the Poznan police force had been charged with breach of duty, the deputy minister of internal affairs declared that there was still no evidence of actual corruption.

The full report on the Poznan case was not produced until late December 1994. Although the report was classified top secret, disgruntled members of the Poznan police force leaked aspects of it to the news media. By then charges of corruption had been laid against a small number of officers; but the number of accusations was hardly compatible with any notion of a systemically corrupted police force.

One chapter of the Poznan case was in a sense closed when Smolarek was formally "recalled" in February 1995, his earlier attempts to resign having been rejected. He himself had not been found corrupt, media allegations notwithstanding; rather, his resignation offers had been made to symbolize his acceptance of ultimate responsibility for what had allegedly happened in Poznan. That Prime Minister Pawlak now publicly thanked him for his work as Poland's top police officer testified to his continued high standing.[27] The final chapter of this affair was closed in 1997, when a small number of officers in Poznan were found guilty of improper behavior, but not corruption (*Donosy Liberal Digest*, 17 June 1997). The verdict did not mark the end of allegations of police corruption, and in September 1997 the minister of internal affairs and administration, Leszek Miller, acknowledged that there was still corruption in the force and that several investigations were under way (*SWB/EE*, 12 September 1997).[28]

There have also been news reports of corruption among the Polish traffic police. Evidently one familiar practice during the 1990s was for the police to mount additional security patrols in more affluent parts of cities, especially at night during weekends, in return for private recompense (Fuszara 1999, 4); local wealthy people caught speeding or being under the influence of alcohol could pay bribes to police officers to avoid being charged, thus further supplementing these officers' incomes.[29]

Two articles published in *Izvestiya* in mid-2000 (21 June 2000, 3; 27 June 2000, 2) provided typical examples of Russian police corruption. In the first, the new head of the police department in Stavropol informed the news media of a scam by police officers who provided false registration documents for expensive foreign cars. The second article referred to reports from Tula of police officers who kidnapped civilians and demanded ransoms, and to the arrest of the local head of the traffic police for accepting bribes. By 2003 the problem of corruption among senior officers annoyed the minister of internal affairs (Boris Gryzlov) sufficiently that he referred to one gang of them, based in Moscow, as "werewolves in police epaulets," thus using a phrase that has become more popular in Russia since the launch of "Operation Werewolf" in June 2003 (*New York Times*, 26 June 2003; *Washington Post*, 2 July 2003). In addition to cases involving the regular police force, there have been reports of corruption in the security (secret) police. For example, two officers in the FSB (successor organization to the KGB) were arrested in February 1997 for alleged drug smuggling. And a group of FSB officers was arrested in November 2002 for allegedly running a scheme designed to extort money from Russian owners of foreign cars (RFE/RL, 14 November 2002).

China has also experienced serious police corruption. In November 2000 the former deputy chief of police in Fujian province was sentenced to death for his role in a major smuggling case (see chapter 7). And seven police officers were arrested in Henan province in April 2001, accused of assisting organized-crime gangs (BR 44, no. 36:6).

Customs and Border Control Officers Predictably, many corruption cases involving smuggling focus on customs and border control officers. In early 1991 the Bulgarian government announced a major crackdown on corruption among customs officers, expressing particular concern about alleged cooperation between customs officers and the burgeoning Bulgarian "mafia." One senior customs officer was arrested at Sofia airport on New Year's Eve 1991 while attempting to smuggle out $10,000 in a custom-made belt (SWB/EE, 20 January 1992). In June 1997 the new director of the Bulgarian Main Customs Administration, Elka Vladova, announced that forty customs officers had been dismissed in the ten days since she had assumed office because of corruption (SWB/EE, 9 June 1997; see too RFE/RL, 3 June 1997). Within a short period, the directors of all sixteen regional customs offices were removed, while 377 customs officers lost their posts—154 of them apparently because of various offenses, including corruption (Todorov, Shentov, and Stoyanov 2000, 16–17). In 1998 a tough new law on customs was passed. But all this still did not solve the problem. By 2000 a new project entitled

Fight Against Corruption in the Bulgarian Customs Administration had been launched, symbolic of the continuing problem in this branch of the state (Todorov, Shentov, and Stoyanov 2000, 43); and by mid-2002, according to the director of the National Border Police Service, fifteen border police officers had recently been dismissed because of corruption (RFE/RL, 30 August 2002).

There has been no shortage of reports of corruption among Hungarian customs officers and border guards. For instance, it was reported in October 1995 that there had been a tenfold increase in corruption cases involving border guards since the previous year; the number of guards charged for accepting bribes increased from five to fifty (SWB/EE, 23 October 1995). Some of these cases involved senior officers. Thus the former deputy head of the customs and tax section at the national head-quarters of the Customs and Revenue Police was arrested in December 1996 for allegedly allowing companies to defer payment of customs duties in return for bribes (SWB/EE, 24 December 1996).

In August 1995 the Main Customs Office in Poland announced the arrest of thirty-six of its officers. It added that preparatory legal proceedings were at that time being mounted against 102 officers. According to a spokesperson, further actions would follow. Of particular concern was the widespread collusion between customs officers and criminal gangs (SWB/EE, 25 August 1995). Some eighteen months later, in February 1997, the head of Poland's border guards announced an official campaign against corruption. He revealed that seven officers had already been arrested in 1997 for suspected bribe taking, compared with six for the whole of 1996, while forty-one people were under investigation. And in mid-1997, the head of the Main Customs Office resigned, partly in connection with a major corruption scandal at the border crossing at Terespol (SWB/EE, 29 February and 3 July 1997).

Neither Russia nor China is an exception with regard to corruption among border guards and customs officials. According to a report in the Estonian media, Russian border officials permitted a bus full of Kurdish refugees to cross into Estonia on Christmas Day 1992 in return for some $14,000 (Express Chronicle, 13 January 1993). Two years later, the head of customs in Bryansk was arrested, along with more than ten of his junior colleagues, for alleged smuggling (Izvestiya, 30 December 1994, 7). In 2002 the Russian minister of internal affairs was allegedly frustrated by the procurator general in his bid to prosecute several businesspeople and customs officials for corrupt collusion; the officials were said to be cutting tariffs on imported furniture in return for bribes (Shlapentokh 2003, 152). And the head of the customs house in Grodekovo, Primorskii Krai, was arrested in November 2003 for allegedly running a smuggling gang (*Zolotoi Rog*, 13 November 2003). In China the former head of customs in Shenzhen was arrested in August 2000 for allegedly accepting bribes in connection with a smuggling racket, while his functional equivalent from Xiamen was sentenced to death (later commuted) for corruption in November 2000 (*BR* 43, no. 47:7; *People's Daily*, on-line English-language edition, 8 November 2000; for an earlier example of corruption among Chinese customs officers see Ting Gong 1997, 283–84).

Judicial Officials In many instances, cases of corruption among court officials involve both judges and others. Moreover, prosecutors general are often seen as belonging to more or less the same branch of law enforcement as judges, rather than the same branch as the police. Because of this, and because there are already more categories in this chapter than is desirable, judges and prosecutors are grouped together here.

After similar claims made by President Zhelyu Zhelev in the preceding year (see *SWB/EE*, 27 February 1996), the Bulgarian minister of the interior, Bogomil Bonev, claimed in 1997 that corruption was widespread among judges and prosecutors, although this charge was strongly denied by the prosecutor general Ivan Tatarchev (*SWB/EE*, 16 and 17 May 1997; *RFE/RL*, 11 November 1997). A commission of the Supreme Judicial Council announced in May 1997 that a number of judges (mostly at the local level) had established inappropriate relations with organized-crime groups — although the prosecutor general questioned the commission's findings (*SWB/EE*, 9 May 1997).[30] The allegations that the judiciary was highly corrupt were repeated by Prime Minister Kostov in April 1998 (*RFE/RL*, 8 April 1998).

During 2000 the Polish media reported that some two hundred judges were under investigation for corruption. This figure appears to have been a serious exaggeration, with "only" sixty-five judges under investigation by the end of the year, many of whom were not suspected of anything that would normally be classified as corruption — at least according to Janusz Niemcewicz, a judge in the Constitutional Tribunal (World Bank 2001, 109). Nevertheless, there were still enough investigations to raise the possibility that corruption was systemic in the Polish judiciary.

In October 1995 the acting prosecutor general in Russia since February 1994, Aleksei Ilyushenko, was placed in detention in Lefortovo prison, charged with accepting bribes and abuse of office. He was said to have been involved in the illegal export of oil in a scheme involving the Balkar Trading company — and to have been the first Russian prosecutor general to have been arrested for corruption since the time of Catherine II (*Izvestiya*, 17 February 1996, 1; 14 March 1996, 2; 19 September 1996, 1; *OMRI DD*, 26 February 1996). However, investigations failed to prove any serious wrongdoing (*Izvestiya*, 13 January 1998), so Ilyushenko was eventually released, and the case against him closed (May 2001 — *http://www.svoboda.org/hotnews/2001/05/11/27.asp*; visited August 2004). But he had gone blind in prison, and many Russians believe that the case against him was a political fabrication. On the other hand, many regular Russian judicial officials, notably judges, have escaped prosecution in the past, even when they have been caught red-handed in corrupt acts, because of judicial immunity (*Izvestiya*, 10 March 1995, 5).

Finally, China has also reported cases of corrupt judicial officials and prosecutors in recent years, as a result of its anti-corruption campaign (see *CD*, 26 August 1998). Two deputy presidents of the Municipal Intermediate People's Court in Shenyang (capital of Liaoning Province) were dismissed in August 2001 for bribe taking (*BR* 44, no. 33:6). And 694 prosecutors were investigated in 1999 for wrongdoing, including corruption, of whom 544 were disciplined and 55 prosecuted (*CD*, 28 February 2000).

Military Officers   Several military officers have been accused of corruption in Bulgaria. In May 1993 the commander of Bulgarian Land Forces resigned after both the chief of general staff and the defense minister accused him of corruption, among other charges (*RFE/RL*, 10 May 1993). Many observers did not believe the corruption charges, and believed that they stemmed from marked political differences between accusers and accused, as in several other cases cited in this chapter. Far less ambiguous was the so-called Atia case, uncovered in 1993, which involved a cigarette- and oil-smuggling ring at the Atia military base. It was clear that senior officers were implicated, but as of 2000 the case had still not reached the Bulgarian courts (all from Todorov, Shentov, and

Stoyanov 2000, 10). In December 1997 twelve military officers, mostly colonels, were convicted of various forms of corruption (*SWB/EE*, 18 December 1997), after an admission by the minister of defense in November of large-scale corruption in the military, and the dismissal of twenty-five army officers (*RFE/RL*, 14 and 17 November 1997).

When several senior military officers were arrested in Hungary in mid-1993 for alleged fraud, it was reported by the authorities that the officers' actions — selling supplies of fuel — had endangered the country's military preparedness (*SWB/EE*, 23 June 1993). In March 1995 the principal defendant in this so-called oil colonels case was found guilty and sentenced to a fine and three and a half years' imprisonment (*SWB/EE*, 1 April 1995).

In March 1992 *Gazeta Wyborcza* reported the arrest of seven Poles in Germany accused of smuggling arms to Iraq in defiance of a UN arms embargo; those named included a former general (*RFE/RL*, 27 March 1992; see too *SWB/EE*, 7 January 1993). But there do not appear to have been many cases reported — which would help to explain why, as demonstrated in chapter 4, military officers in Poland are perceived to be much less corrupt than most other public officials.

One of the most significant corruption scandals in Russia during the second half of the 1990s erupted in July 1996, when major allegations were made of corruption in the senior ranks of the military. At the beginning of the month, the chairman of the Duma defense committee, Lev Rokhlin, accused the recently dismissed defense minister Pavel Grachev of permitting "massive criminal embezzlement in the armed forces," and five generals (including Grachev's brother-in-law) of corruption (Fel'gengauer 1996).[31] The Duma formally demanded a legal investigation; but nothing came of this (Rokhlin was murdered in July 1998; his wife was found guilty of the murder).

Among the numerous other cases reported of corruption among senior Russian military officials, several give rise to particular concern, since they involve the corrupt sale of arms and even nuclear materials. One such case, described sensationally if inaccurately in *Izvestiya* (11 February 1997) as the "theft of the century," involved the supply of explosives by a colonel to a businessman friend. A military court ruled that it did not constitute bribery — the colonel was simply being generous to a friend! — and dismissed the case; the officer retained his position. Precisely this type of judicial decision undermines citizens' trust in the state.

Other significant Russian cases include the accusations in 1995 against the Russian major general commanding the eastern sector of the UN peacekeeping forces in Croatia, for allegedly being involved in smuggling arms to Serbs living in Croatia (*Segodnya*, 13 April 1995, 1; for the general's claim that he was being accused for political reasons see *Segodnya*, 15 April 1995, 2; see too *TI Newsletter*, September 1995); and those against Rear Admiral Vladimir Morev of the Russian Pacific Fleet, who was found guilty in April 2000 of selling military equipment for personal gain and sentenced to eight years' imprisonment (*Izvestiya*, 25 March 2000, 3, and RFE/RL, 2 May 2000; for a generic analysis of Russian military corruption see *Komsomol'skaya Pravda*, 16 August 2002, 8–9).[32]

There has long been evidence of corruption in the Chinese military; such corruption apparently peaked in the late 1980s and early 1990s (Mulvenon 2003, 21). But it is only since the late 1990s that outsiders have been permitted to investigate alleged corruption and other forms of malfeasance in the People's Liberation Army, and even more recently (2000) that the Chinese media have begun to name allegedly corrupt officers. Such developments are in line with the senior Chinese leadership's vow on various occasions during the 1990s to deal with corrupt tigers (senior officials), not just flies (lower-ranking officials), as part of an attempt to increase the state's legitimacy. Thus the sentencing to fifteen years' imprisonment for corruption in October 2000 of a very senior officer, General Ji Shengde, head of the general staff's Department of Intelligence, was widely publicized.[33]

In Czechia two senior military officers were charged in January 1996 with corruption relating to the awarding of defense contracts. The two, a lieutenant colonel and a colonel, allegedly demanded not only a bribe, but also a share of the contractor's profits and shares in the company (*OMRI DD*, 23 January 1996). The order, for heating equipment, was canceled in December 1995 — the third such cancellation in recent months because of alleged corruption. Research by Fuszara (1999, 5, 7) into the Czech press reveals that there has been a large number of reports on military corruption, and that some of the cases have had almost Pythonesque overtones.[34] For example, corruption was apparently a major reason why the Czech military purchased parachutes that were unusable — reportedly at some ten times their "true" value, though one must ask if unusable parachutes would have any value at all — and computers that were mutually incompatible.

Many other post-communist states have reported cases of alleged corruption in the military. For example, the head of the Estonian general staff's financial department was accused in September 1995 of conducting illegal arms deals, including some with organized-crime gangs (*Baltic Independent*, 17 November 1995). This is but one of many cases suggesting that while military officers are generally considered less corrupt than other government officers in most post-communist states, the potential impact of those who are corrupt is often even greater.

Diplomats A priori, it seems unlikely that corruption among diplomats incenses the public as much as corruption elsewhere in the state apparatus. Moreover, there is much less reporting of corruption among this group than among other groups of state officials. Nevertheless, a comprehensive analysis of official corruption should include a reference to corruption among diplomats.

In 1997 several Russian diplomats were arrested in Finland for arms smuggling (*Izvestiya*, 16 May 1997). One particularly disturbing aspect of the case was that some of the diplomats were said to have been working for the FSB. In Bulgaria the daily newspaper *Duma* published an article in June 1999 alleging that a former Bulgarian ambassador to Colombia had been involved in large-scale embezzlement and had colluded with organized-crime gangs (BPCWR, 5–11 June 1999). And the Bosnian ambassador to the UN was granted bail by a judge in New York in July 2004 after being accused of embezzlement amounting to almost $2.5 million.

Other Officials The following groups are included as "temporary state officials." The first group includes officials engaged in the essentially transient phase of privatization, while the second includes those engaged in banking, which in many countries is gradually being privatized.

Members of Privatization Boards and Agencies — Most post-communist states have experienced at least one corruption scandal relating to the membership of the privatization boards and agencies. Significant corruption cases involving the privatization agencies have been reported or alleged in Romania (March 1994), Slovakia (April 1994), Ukraine (November 1995), the former GDR (April 1997), Georgia (March 2001), Ukraine (June 2004), and elsewhere. The five countries examined in this book provide many more examples.

Serious allegations of corruption among Bulgarian privatization officials were made in 1996, in an open letter to the prosecutor general from
Edvin Sugarev, member of parliament belonging to the Union of Democratic Forces (UDF). Sugarev focused on the privatization of the country's second-largest oil refinery, the Plama refinery in Pleven (SWB/EE,
24 October 1996). His claim was rejected, however, and a number of
senior officials called for lifting his parliamentary immunity so that he
could be sued. Quite how much substance there was to Sugarev's allegations is unclear. A parliamentary commission found them groundless,
and my own interviews in Bulgaria suggest that Sugarev's allegations
should be treated with extreme caution. But in 1997 the relatively new
prime minister, Ivan Kostov, did expel two local party chiefs from his
own party (the UDF) for their allegedly corrupt involvement in the
privatization of a Ruse yeast plant (SWB/EE, 3 October 1997). The
problem continued to plague Kostov's administration, however, and as
of late 2000 six high-ranking ministerial officials had been dismissed
and were under investigation for alleged involvement in privatization-
related corruption (Center for the Study of Democracy 2001, 27).

Of the four CEE and former Soviet Union countries examined here,
Hungary has arguably had the most high-profile scandals relating to
privatization. Serious allegations were already being investigated in
1993, and some formal charges relating to the privatization had been
laid (see SWB/EE, 3 June 1993). But this was tame compared with what
happened during the mid-1990s. In October 1994, after investigations
initiated in September by the interior ministry into alleged corruption
in the sale of formerly state-owned enterprises, eight of the ten members
of the privatization board (ÁPV) were forced to resign. But the lesson
of this experience was apparently not learned vicariously by the new
members of the board; in late 1996 all eleven members of the newly
constituted board had to resign amid revelations that they had been
complicit in a payment of over $5 million (804 million forints) to the
legal consultant Marta Tocsik, an enormous sum particularly by Hungarian standards. At the same time, the minister for trade, industry, and
privatization, Tamas Suchman, was also required to resign (for details
see Z. Szilagyi 1996b). This was all the more embarrassing since Suchman had only taken over part of his portfolio a few weeks previously,
after his predecessor had resigned—formally for reasons of ill health,
but in the view of some because of involvement in the so-called Oilgate

corruption case referred to above. In June 1997 eight officials connected to ÁPV were formally charged, variously with mismanagement, fraud, and forgery. One of these was Marta Tocsik. Tocsik was acquitted in February 1999. However, some members of the ÁPV were found to have acted improperly in the privatization process they were supposed to be overseeing. In short, the court concluded that there had been what many would see as corruption in this affair.

One of the best-known but most debatable examples from Poland is that of the former privatization minister Janusz Lewandowski. He was formally charged in January 1997 with improper behavior in connection with the privatization of a chemical plant in Krakow in 1993; although leading politicians had claimed in late 1996 that the charges were politically motivated (see *SWB/EE*, 12 October 1996), and Lewandowski himself called the charges absurd (*Warsaw Voice*, 13 October 1996), the investigating authorities in Krakow concluded that there was sufficient evidence of wrongdoing to warrant formal charges (*Warsaw Voice*, 26 January 1997). It is important to note that the charge was not of corruption as such, but of questionable management of the privatization process. But discussions conducted during research for this book in Poland in the late 1990s indicated that many people had not read the fine print, and had assumed that corruption was at issue.

A deputy chairman of the State Property Committee in Russia was dismissed in February 1992 for what *Izvestiya* (28 February 1992, 2) described as an example of improper nomenklatura privatization. Allegations were made in 1994 that the first deputy prime minister Oleg Soskovets had benefited in an inappropriate manner, through insider agreements, from the privatization of a huge tin processing plant in Novosibirsk, the largest in Europe (*Izvestiya*, 28 June 1994, 5); but nothing came of these allegations. And the reader is reminded of the allegations, referred to above, against the chairman of the Federal Council (Stroyev).

Despite its image of having been on the capitalist road for more than two decades, it is only relatively recently that China formalized the private ownership of enterprises. The CCP advocated outright privatization at its 15th Congress in September 1997. From the early 1980s until the late 1990s, private individuals or groups could only lease enterprises, on renewable five-year contracts from the state, and manage them on an essentially capitalist and entrepreneurial basis. While there is some valid-

ity to the argument that this phasing-in arrangement represents a pecu-
liarly Chinese approach to privatization (Lan Cao 2000), it was clearly
ripe for corruption, especially where two or more private agents sought
the same enterprise and state officials had wide discretionary powers.
Another variant on the theme is the practice by companies of bribing
state officials for permission to offer shares to the public. This happened
extensively in Jiangsu province from the late 1990s, according to official
Chinese reports published in June 2002 (initially by the Xinhua News
Agency, 12 June); the majority of such companies were state-owned but
sought partial privatization. Several senior officials were sentenced in
connection with this corruption scandal, for terms of up to eleven years.
In addition, the recent trend toward more conventional privatization
methods is making China susceptible to the same types of privatization-
related corruption as have occurred in so many other parts of the world
— and not only in post-communist transition states.

The worst privatization-related corruption scandal in Czechia emerged
at the end of October 1994, in what was described in the mid-1990s
(Kettle 1995, 36) as "the biggest scandal to date in the Czech Republic."
The head of the privatization agency (the Centre for Voucher Privatization), Jaroslav Lizner, was caught in a Chinese restaurant in Prague with
what prosecutors subsequently described as a bribe that he had just
accepted in connection with the sale of a dairy. He had with him a
briefcase containing more than eight million Crowns (approximately
$260,000 at that time), the value of the bribe (Kettle 1995, 38–39).[35]
Lizner claimed that he had simply accepted a deposit from the potential
purchasers as a sign of their good faith. But there was no reference to a
deposit in the sale agreement signed in the restaurant. In all events,
Lizner was found guilty of bribe taking in October 1995 and sentenced to
seven years' imprisonment and a fine of one million crowns; at the end of
January 1996 the prison sentence was reduced on appeal to six years
(OMRI DD, 31 January 1996; for an update on the Lizner case see chapter
7). Although Lizner's is the most spectacular and best-known case, it is
not the only one in Czechia. For example, in 1992 the head of the
privatization program in the city of Vsetin was arrested for having been
discovered with a large sum of money that he subsequently acknowledged was a bribe (though he claimed that it was only an *attempted* bribe,
and that he had intended to report the attempt to the police and hand

them the evidence — all from Kettle 1995, 39; on Czech corruption relating to privatization see Reed 1995, Perlez 1997, Reed 2002, and more broadly Appel 2001).

CEOs and Board Members of State-Run Banks — In July 1992 the head of the Bulgarian National Bank attempted to resign, after recent media allegations of his corruption. But the Bulgarian parliament refused to accept his resignation (RFE/RL, 8 July 1992; SWB/EE, 29 July 1992).[36]

Hungary has experienced a number of banking scandals. One concerned three fairly small banks, and broke in 1992 (Okolicsanyi 1992). This was followed by a much bigger scandal that according to Reisch (1993) and other sources (SWB/EE, 11 September 1993) dominated the Hungarian press in late 1993. It affected several banks, one of the most prominent being the YbL Bank, which had been bailed out by the state in 1992 as it was about to go bankrupt; the chairman of this bank's board of directors, the bank's director general, and the deputy director general were all accused of corruption and malpractice. Yet another scandal emerged in 1995, when the former director general of Agrobank (of which the state was the largest shareholder) and its president were both officially charged with bribery (SWB/EE, 5 June 1995).

In March 1993 the former president of the National Bank of Poland was charged in connection with the so-called Art-B banking corruption scandal, as well as the FOZZ scandal. He was accused of having caused losses to the Polish state amounting to more than $8 million — officially because of poor supervision (RFE/RL, 30 March 1993), though Łoś and Zybertowicz (2000, 166, 170) claim that the accusation was actually for corruption. In all events, the charges were dropped in October 1993 because of insufficient evidence.

Unsurprisingly, Russia has not been immune to corruption scandals in the banking sector. In February 1999 the prosecutor general's office published a report alleging numerous improprieties in the Russian Central Bank, although the allegations were soon rejected by the chairman and deputy chairman of the bank's board of directors. Some two months later, a warrant was issued for the arrest of the head of the SBS Agrobank in connection with bank loans that had allegedly been made illegally and from which, it was claimed, he had benefited (RFE/RL, 7 April 1999; Sovershenno Sekretno, June 1999).

What proved to be possibly China's most serious banking scandal was made public by the National Audit Office in January 2002. It involved fraud and embezzlement at the Bank of China amounting to some 2.7 billion yuan (more than $320 million at the time; the value of the loss was reassessed in March at some 6 billion yuan, or $725 million). The man who had headed the bank at the time of the fraud was removed from office, pending investigation of his role in the affair; he was expelled from the Communist Party in November 2002 (*People's Daily*, online English-language edition, 6 November 2002), while criminal investigations into his alleged bribe taking and embezzlement continued (*BR* 45, no. 47:7). In August 2002 the official previously in charge of China's foreign currency reserves went on trial, formally charged with corruption. He was found guilty of bribe taking and sentenced in October to fifteen years' imprisonment; some believe that he would have received a harsher punishment had it not been for his whistle blowing, and perhaps his connections at the very top of the political system (Sheng and Gao 2002).[37]

Czechia has also experienced corruption-related banking scandals. One of the best-known involved the country's third-largest bank, the partly state-owned IPB. In April 1997 the chairman and deputy chairman of the bank were arrested and charged with embezzlement (*Economist*, 3 May 1997, 99; for other examples see Kettle 1995, 39). And in January 1997 the chairwoman of the National Bank of Belarus was dismissed for "abuses of her official position" and detained by the police, pending investigation.

Officials and High-Profile Political Figures Not Covered by Previous Categories
Bulgaria experienced a major corruption scandal in April 2000, when the head of the government press service felt obliged to resign amid allegations that he had accepted bribes (*Business Central Europe*, July 1971, 17); but the case was not proven.

In July 1996 the newspaper journalist A. Minkin of *Novaya Yezhednevnaya Gazeta* leveled charges of corruption and other offenses against the former head of the presidential security service, Aleksandr Korzhakov (who had been dismissed from Yeltsin's presidential staff in June), the former head of the FSB Mikhail Barsukov, and the chairman of the State Committee on Physical Culture and Tourism, Shamil Tarpishchev. There followed reports in the Russian news media in January 1997 that Korzhakov had been granted a loan of 200 million roubles at well below the official interest rate (*Izvestiya*, 17 January 1997). But Korzhakov contested a by-election for the Duma in February and won, thus securing parliamentary immunity;[38] he has not since been formally charged, and many now believe that the allegations were politically motivated. Boris Fedorov, deputy prime minister and one-time minister of finances, was also affected by this scandal, in that he was said to have been threatened by the allegedly corrupt officials (*OMRI DD*, 9 July 1996).

Finally, it is important to remember that China is still formally communist, politically at least, and thus has a group of officials — communist party officials — that no longer have direct equivalents in most of the CEE and CIS countries. One CCP official found guilty of serious corruption was a local party head in Guangxi province, He Jianlin. He was sentenced to eight years' imprisonment in February 1999 after being found guilty of selling official positions in the local government (*Renmin Ribao*, 7 February 1999, 4; *New York Times*, 11 March 1999). But a much higher-profile corruption scandal erupted in 1995. During a visit to Beijing in May–June 1997, several academics and officials informed me that the most significant (widely discussed and potentially delegitimizing) case of corruption in China in recent years concerned Chen Xitong, the former head of the CCP in Beijing, former mayor of Beijing, and member of the Politburo. He was obliged to resign his CCP post in April 1995 after allegations that he had played a key role in corruptly allocating various redevelopment projects in Beijing. The transactions included the sale of a significant block very close to the center of the capital (near Tiananmen Square) to a Hong Kong consortium that sought to build a vast shopping and residential complex on the site (*Weekend Australian*, 29–30 April 1995). In July 1998 Chen was sentenced to sixteen years' imprisonment for various misdemeanors, including twelve for corruption.[39]

Numerous further examples of corruption in CEE, the CIS, and the PRC could be cited. But five points can be highlighted on the basis of the evidence produced in this chapter. The first point about corruption is that "there's a lot of it about" — certainly if media reporting and allegations are to be believed. The news media in most countries have not been hesitant about making accusations.

However, and following on from this, it appears that many of the allegations, particularly of very senior officials and politicians, are above all politically motivated. In the case of senior officials from the communist period, the political motivation can be interpreted as retribution and the need for a symbolic fresh start as much as the search for justice. Yet some of these cases have eventually seen the allegedly corrupt official either cleared (as with the former Estonian prime minister Indrek Toome in March 1995), permitted not to stand trial because of ill health (as with the former East German leader Erich Honecker in January 1993), or treated relatively leniently. For instance, the former prime minister of the GDR, Hans Modrow, was sentenced to only a suspended (nine-month) sentence in August 1995, after a court in Dresden found him guilty of vote rigging during local elections in May 1989.[40] Because many post-communist politicians who have been accused have subsequently been cleared—after investigations that themselves have varied considerably in terms of thoroughness—it seems indisputable that charges of corruption are often made to undermine one's opponents. This is certainly the view of Marsov and Poleshchuk (1993), who argued in a front-page article in a leading Russian newspaper that "today, the struggle against corruption is above all a struggle against a political opponent." Preliminary investigations in July 1996 into alleged corruption among Russian military officers revealed improprieties, but also activities that while questionable were not clearly improper (Veslo 1996). Perhaps there was some truth in the claim of one of the generals charged that the allegations were intended primarily to sully the reputation of prospective candidates for the position of defense minister.

Third, and again relating closely to the previous point, there is often a discrepancy between how the news media portray a case and how the judiciary eventually assesses it. In some instances, journalists have been less than thorough in investigating the reliability of their sources. But that is not invariably so, or indeed the whole story. A detailed analysis of just four Bulgarian cases was under way at the Centre for Liberal Strategies in Sofia in the early years of the century.[41] The researchers in this project sought to compare media allegations with judicial rulings. As of mid-2004 the research had not been completed in three of the four cases analyzed, so that no conclusions could be drawn. However, early findings based on this tiny sample suggested that legal agencies and the media might have had quite different perceptions of the same phenomena. Another pertinent observation is that the long time needed to resolve so many cases of alleged corruption, especially by senior officials, in the courts is symptomatic of the difficulties inherent in investigating this type of crime. In view of these complications, it is often difficult to know which media are merely being troublemakers, and which are making serious but ultimately frustrated attempts to ascertain whether a rumor is based in fact.

Fourth, while there are also continuities with the past, new forms of corruption have emerged in the post-communist world, at the same time as some old ones are disappearing. In my earlier study of corruption in the late communist era, cases were cited of corruption that related to fulfillment of the central plan (L. Holmes 1993, 101–4); with the increasing privatization, marketization, and economic decentralization typical of post-communist states, such plan-related corruption has all but disappeared. Conversely, it is clear even from the few cases cited that a common form of corruption nowadays is an outgrowth of the privatization process. The reasons for this are considered in chapter 6.

Another source of corruption under post-communism is taxation, particularly the taxation of personal and corporate income, which some taxpayers seek to evade. Income taxation was on an essentially negligible scale for most people during the communist era, whereas it has now become a salient feature of life. With maximum personal rates having been as high as 45 percent in Poland, it is not surprising that some individuals should resent the new arrangements and seek to circumvent them.[42] Many private enterprises—which apart from those on the smallest scale are a new feature of post-communism—have also illegally sought to reduce or escape their tax liabilities, sometimes by bribing tax officials to obtain lower tax bills. While the excessive discretionary powers enjoyed by many tax officials help to explain why enterprises can engage in this sort of questionable behavior, their willingness to engage in it in the first place can be largely explained by what Varese (1997, 580), referring in particular to early post-communist Russia, has called a "predatory tax system."[43]

Electoral rigging also appears to have become far more significant now that elections matter. Despite moves during the 1980s toward real competition in some communist states—notably Poland and Hungary—elections were still only for bodies that were for the most part and in practice subordinate to the communist party. But now that elections are really for power, the stakes have been raised. Closely related to the last point is the real or apparent increase in corruption because of genuine party competition in new and impoverished democratizing systems. The new political parties have in most cases very limited funds. In some countries, despite measures to make political opportunities more nearly equal, the former communists still have considerable access to large funds, which often renders the newer parties even more willing to break the rules (assuming that there are any) requiring transparent funding of political activities. Włodzimierz Cimoszewicz, former prime minister of Poland and later minister of foreign affairs, was publicly arguing in the 1990s that partly to overcome corruption, political parties in his country should be funded from only two sources, the state and membership dues (World Bank 2001, 120). Such a proposal is attractive in the abstract, since it should end the democratically questionable relationship that often exists between large-scale donors and political parties in any system (Poland did move in this direction in April 2001, when corporate sponsorship of political parties was banned).[44] However, several practical problems arise in attempting to implement such a scheme.

Our fifth and final observation is that there appears to be a pecking order in the reporting of corruption among officials, just as there is in other parts of the world. In general, the higher-ranking the official, the more attention his or her alleged corruption is likely to attract. While it cannot be conclusively proven, it is a priori highly probable that the legitimacy of a system is undermined more by widespread corruption at the top than at lower levels (see Miller, Grødeland, and Koshechkina 2001b, 61–70).

As emphasized at the beginning of this chapter, one of its main objectives has been to provide examples of both alleged and proven cases of corruption as one way of better understanding why so many citizens have little trust in their post-communist institutions, and believe that corruption is a major problem.[45] This is all part of a general interest in the delegitimizing effects of perceived corruption in transition states; chapter 4 considers the evidence of such perceptions. But to conclude this chapter, it is worth considering the general impact that the news media have on public perceptions of corruption. As with all perceptions, this impact is difficult to measure. But one of the more persuasive methods is to survey citizens about how they acquire their knowledge and views of corruption.

Our brief overview starts with some Polish data from the mid-1990s. When a survey in April 1994 (Centrum Badania Opinii Społecznej 1994b, 4) asked respondents where they obtained their information on dishonesty and bribery in the Polish legal system, "television, radio and newspapers" was cited by 76 percent, "hearing from personal acquaintances" by 15 percent, "personal experience" by 5 percent, and "other means" by 4 percent. Yet it is worth noting that the weekly newspaper *Nie* has on occasion been surprised and disappointed at the apparent lack of impact of its investigative journalism, especially vis-à-vis the former president Lech Wałęsa (Fuszara 1999, 2).[46]

Some of the recent World Bank surveys of corruption in individual post-communist states have directly addressed the impact of the news media, though none in the five countries analyzed in this book. But data on Kazakhstan, Kyrgyzstan, and Romania are instructive, and may have resonance with other post-communist states (further research on this is required). Thus a survey of Romanians in 2000 suggested that 83 percent of citizens (households), 78 percent of public officials, and 75 percent of enterprise managers identified the mass media as either the most important or second-most important source of their information about corruption; overall, this was easily the most significant source, well ahead of personal experience, which ranked second, or relatives and friends, which ranked third (Anderson, Cosmaciuc, Dininio, Spector, and Zoido-Lobaton 2001, 6–7). In a survey conducted in Kazakhstan in 2001, the results were similar — in some cases remarkably so — to the Romanian ones. Thus the mass media were overall the principal source of information, identified by 83 percent of households, 84 percent of public officials, and 75 percent of enterprise managers as their most important or second-most important source. Relatives and friends were overall the second-most important source, ahead of personal experience (Anderson and Mukherjee 2002, 17). The Kyrgyz results were slightly different, in that the principal source of information was relatives and friends, while the mass media were the second major source. However, it is not possible directly to compare the Kyrgyz results, which provide percentages only for the principal source cited, with those from Kazakhstan and Romania, which provide the combined percentage for the two most frequently cited sources (Kyrgyz results from Anderson 2002,

21).[47] But even allowing for this shortcoming, it is clear that the mass media are a major source of information on corruption in all three post-communist countries for which World Bank survey data are available.[48] It is therefore reasonable to infer that the media are heavily influencing perceptions of corruption in post-communist countries.

CHAPTER 4

On the Scale and

Main Areas of Corruption

This chapter analyzes the four main methods used to assess the extent of corruption in particular societies — legal statistics, perception-based estimates, experience-based estimates (also called the proxy method), and tracking methods — and summarizes the findings indicating which branches of the state appear to be most and least prone to corruption.[1]

MEASURING AND COMPARING
THE SCALE AND DYNAMISM OF CORRUPTION

There are many reasons why it is impossible to provide an accurate picture of the scale of corruption in any country. One is the nature of the beast: corruption is unusual among crimes in that there is often no obvious victim to report particular instances of it. In many cases, two or more agents collude for mutual benefit, while in others, individuals work alone. But in both situations, the loser or victim is the essentially amorphous and impersonal state or society. Second, the lot of those who do make allegations concerning others' corruption — whistleblowers — is often an unhappy one. This is particularly true of insiders — people working within the same organization as the allegedly corrupt official(s). This point is explored in more detail in chapter 7; here it is noted simply that the disincentives to reporting suspected or even known corruption are typically strong.

Third, the broad range of opinions in any society over the precise boundaries of the concept renders complete agreement on its magnitude an unachievable goal. In an interview in October 2000 with Nikolai Kovalev, head of the Duma's Commission for the Fight against Corruption and of the National Anti-Corruption Committee, it was pointed out that it was impossible to assess the scale of corruption in Russia because "there is no legal definition of corruption as such" (*Izvestiya*, 6 October 2000, 3).[2] Fourth, even where the compilers of legal and other statistics can agree on what constitutes corruption, official data sets on registered crimes and other forms of impropriety are in most cases insufficiently disaggregated to provide any clear picture. Finally, there is strong circumstantial evidence to suggest that *all* crime is substantially underreported in at least some post-communist states.[3]

Despite these difficulties, there is a need to form an impression of the extent of corruption, and of where it is most heavily concentrated in any society, if it is to be combated. Researchers have therefore devised numerous methods for "guesstimating" the scale and dynamism of corruption in individual countries. None of the four major methods elaborated here is satisfactory — adequate or comprehensive — in itself. But if the general pictures produced by several methods appear to be essentially similar, it is reasonable to infer that our perception is as close to reality as it can be.

Legal Statistics

It comes as a surprise to many that according to official statistics the twelve countries with the highest crime rates at the beginning of the twenty-first century were, in descending order, Suriname, Iceland, Rwanda, Finland, New Zealand, Sweden, the Virgin Islands, Guam, Norway, the United Kingdom (England and Wales), Denmark, and Greenland. It will emerge below that the Nordic countries and New Zealand are also perceived to be among the least corrupt countries in the world. Conversely, according to official statistics, several of the countries perceived as most corrupt also have the lowest overall crime rates: the twelve countries with the lowest rates, in ascending order, were Nepal, Burkina Faso, Togo, Congo, Angola, Indonesia, Ivory Coast, Albania, Cameroon, Syria, Gambia, and Bangladesh (rank ordering calculated by the author on the basis of comparative crime statistics in *Britannica Book of the Year 2002*, 874–79).[4] What is to be made of these "facts"?

It is partly because of the impossibility of compiling comprehensive and satisfactory comparative statistics on corruption that so many ana-

lysts turn to perception indices. If it can be accepted that such perceptions mostly have a positive correlation with reality, then the phenomenon described in the previous paragraph is a curious one, since there
appears to be a strong negative correlation between crime rates and
levels of corruption. This might be purely coincidental, but that seems
unlikely. A more persuasive argument is that the crime statistics are
misleading unless deconstructed. The data refer to the number of offenses reported to the police, standardized to produce a figure per
100,000 inhabitants. According to the official statistics, the crime rate in
Sweden is more than 216 times higher (12,982 per 100,000) than that in
Indonesia (60), while New Zealand's (13,854) is almost 185 times
higher than Albania's (75). Almost anyone who has visited these countries will find it difficult to reconcile these figures with his or her own
experiences and perceptions. Part of the explanation might be that there
appear to be lower crime rates in countries in which traditions encourage citizens to deal with antisocial behavior themselves, rather than turn
to the state for assistance. But an even more convincing solution to this
conundrum — though it is not incompatible with the first — is that ceteris
paribus, countries in which the police are highly trusted and respected
are likely to appear to have higher crime rates than countries in which
citizens hold the agents of the state in low regard. If citizens believe that
the police are themselves likely to be corrupt or incompetent, then they
are less likely to report crimes than if the police are seen as basically
trustworthy and effective.[5] There is also the issue of honesty among the
police as it affects accuracy in reporting. Where the police are under
pressure to demonstrate high "clear-up" rates but are not strictly monitored, there is an incentive to underreport crime. Finally, citizens are less
inclined to report crime where the process is perceived to be complicated (see Anderson, Cosmaciuc, Dininio, Spector, and Zoido-Lobaton
2001, 16). Other things being equal, this tendency suggests that education levels in individual countries are a relevant variable in reporting
rates. Hence, with knowledge of the political and social cultures of
individual countries, as well as their education levels, it is in many cases
possible a priori to explain the strong negative correlation between corruption and crime rates.

It has been demonstrated that official crime statistics must be treated
with extreme caution, and can be highly misleading.[6] Nevertheless, a
starting point is the scattered available data: these provide a sketchy

impression at least of known (registered) cases of corruption in a few countries, and indicate the minimum scale of the problem.

As with many post-communist states, the available data on Russia are incomplete and sometimes inconsistent.[7] The official annual statistical yearbooks provide details on the number of all registered crimes (these increased from 1.84 million in 1990 to almost 3 million in 2000 — Goskomstat 2001, 273), and, starting with the 1996 yearbook, the total number of economic crimes (sometimes registered, sometimes uncovered).[8] The latter are defined in broad terms, and include "abuse of power" — thus providing further evidence to support our assumption in chapter 3 that abuse of power sometimes embraces pecuniary corruption. According to the yearbooks, the numbers more or less steadily increased over the period 1996–2002, from 212,000 in 1995 to 321,900 in 2000 to 325,900 in 2001 (Goskomstat 1996, 244; Goskomstat 2001, 273; Goskomstat 2002, 273).

The most authoritative source of information — the annual report on criminality produced by the Ministry of Internal Affairs — is difficult for outsiders to obtain (though see below). But piecing together and comparing numerous reports can produce a general picture. Thus, to begin with more aggregated data before gradually focusing on the more specific, a detailed analysis of crime of all types published in 1995 stated that nearly 40 percent of the almost three million offenses dealt with in 1994 had been in the economic sphere — this figure includes burglary, theft, and related crimes. Approximately 180,000 economic crimes were registered in 1994. In the first four months of 1995, more than 80,000 economic crimes were reported, representing an increase of 33 percent over the same period a year earlier (Kirichenko, Privalov, Chetokin, and Shvyrkov 1995, 17). But the estimate that the figure would reach 240,000 for the whole of 1995 proved too conservative. Thus the editor of *Moskovskie Novosti* revealed later in the year that 110,000 economic criminal acts were committed in 1993, and that this figure grew to 183,000 in 1994 and 300,000 for most of 1995 (Zhilin 1995, 9; note that this figure is different from the official figure for 1995 cited earlier).

Research by Louise Shelley (1995, 59) suggests that bribery in Russia increased by 35 percent in 1993 over the previous year. Mikhail Glukhovsky (1992, 16) assessed the proportion of corrupt acts to all organized crime in the USSR at 2.0 percent in 1989, 3.0 percent in 1990, and 8.8 percent in 1991. According to Stephen Handelman (1994, 255), who unfortunately does not cite his source, the acting prosecutor general Aleksei Ilyushenko stated that over 46,000 state officials at all levels were brought to trial in 1993 on charges of corruption and abuse of office. These figures are much higher than others more recently published — probably in part because they include abuse of office, which is vague and sometimes includes actions or nonactions that few observers would consider corruption. At a meeting on corruption held at the Russian prosecutor general's office in July 1996, the first deputy prosecutor general, Yurii Chaika, revealed that approximately fourteen thousand corruption cases had been filed in the previous two years — one third of which involved state officials (suggesting that he was using a very broad definition of corruption). "Recently," over a thousand violations connected with privatization had been reported (*OMRI DD*, 9 July 1996). These figures are closer to those cited (again, unreferenced) by Glinkina (1998, 16); according to her, legal proceedings for corruption were initiated against 3,504 officials in 1995, of whom 66 percent were government officials and 27.4 percent law enforcement officers. But even these figures are higher than some cited in February 1996 by Yeltsin. According to the president, twelve hundred officers of the state were charged with corruption during 1995 (*OMRI DD*, 26 February 1996).[9] In September of the following year, Yeltsin revealed that more than 2,500 officials were being investigated because of suspected corruption (*Rossiiskaya Gazeta*, 27 September 1997).

During a visit to Moscow in April–May 1997, I obtained a copy of the Ministry of Internal Affairs annual report on criminality for 1996. According to this, the number of "economic crimes and crimes by officials" (*dolzhnostnye prestupleniya*) reported in 1996 was 239,453; this represented an increase of 13.0 percent over 1995. Since the number of crimes of all types declined by 4.7 percent from 1995 to 1996, economic and official crime, at least in terms of cases reported, strongly resisted the trend. The number of crimes by officials was 14,758; the growth in this sector was more modest than the overall growth in economic and official crime, at 3.9 percent from 1995 to 1996. The number of cases of official bribe taking reported in 1996 was 5,453, or 11.5 percent higher than in 1995. However, there was a substantial increase in "large-scale" and "particularly large-scale" bribery cases, at 21.7 percent.[10] But it must also be noted that the percentage of cases being tried in the courts increased at even higher rates: of the total number of cases of official crime reported, almost half (7,306) resulted in prosecution, representing an increase of 34.9 percent over the previous year's figure. Of the bribery cases, 52.7 percent (2,874) were tried in court; this was up 28.1 percent since 1995 (all figures either directly cited from, or calculated by the author on the basis of, data in Glavnyi Informatsionnyi Tsentr 1997, 6).

Figures cited by Mukhin (2000, 125) are close to those just provided — and, since they were presented at a conference in 1999, also indicate how difficult it remains to obtain comprehensive and up-to-date statistics. Piecing together various sources, Mukhin states that the number of officials convicted of bribe taking was 1,114 in 1994, 1,071 in 1995, and 1,243 in 1996. His figures appear to tally with — but update — those in Luneev. According to Luneev (1997, 277), the number of registered cases of bribe taking by Russian officials was 2,691 in 1990, 2,534 in 1991, 3,331 in 1992, 4,497 in 1993, 4,919 in 1994, 4,889 in 1995, and 5,453 in 1996; the last figure is identical to that in the official source cited in the preceding paragraph, so it is likely that the time-series data are based on official Ministry of Internal Affairs sources. It was reported in 1997 that only about one third of the five thousand or so cases investigated by the procuracy end up in court (Mukhin 2000, 125, citing *Nezavisimaya Gazeta*, 2 October 1997). These figures are slightly lower than official figures from "the law enforcement agencies" cited by Mukhin, according to which there were 2,469 prosecutions for official corruption in 1993, 2,678 in 1994, and 3,504 in 1995.[11] However, the figures are sufficiently close for us to assume that they provide a reasonably accurate picture of how many officials were actually investigated, prosecuted, and convicted in Russia during the mid-1990s.

Three final statistics are worth noting. According to one Russian source, only one eleventh of the number of cases of official corruption registered between the mid-1980s and the mid-1990s in Russia resulted in convictions (Luneev 1996, 87; also Luneev 1997, 277–78). This situation may have further deteriorated recently. Thus in a report to Parliament, Deputy Prosecutor General S. Kekhlerov revealed in late 2004 that although more than two thousand officials were convicted of corruption in 2003, and a further two thousand were "brought to account" for abuse of power, this meant that "only one or two per cent of all instances of bribery lead to criminal penalties" (*Johnson's Russia List* 8467, 23 November 2004). This estimate suggests that the number of bribery cases could have been some 400,000 or even higher in 2003.

Finally, the Russian police uncovered more than seven hundred cases linking corrupt bureaucrats with organized crime between 1995 and 1997 (Glinkina 1998, 17; for further general data on Russian corruption see Nomokonov 2000, 123).

We turn now to three CEE countries. As in most post-communist states, the authorities provide relatively little guidance on the scale of corruption in Bulgaria. However, the number of economic offenses uncovered increased in most years in the first dozen years of post-communism, at 8,170 in 1991, 8,665 in 1992, 7,835 in 1993, 9,446 in 1994, 9,956 in 1995, 10,449 in 1996, 12,498 in 1997, 14,986 in 1998, 15,470 in 1999, 12,385 in 2000, 12,446 in 2001 and 13,706 in 2002. The 2002 figure was thus some 60 percent higher than the 1991 figure, while the 1999 figure was higher still.

The number of cases of bribery discovered did not show such a clear upward trend, being 84 in 1991, 61 in 1992, 85 in 1993, 69 in 1994, 71 in 1995, 107 in 1996, 119 in 1997, 95 in 1998, 136 in 1999, 52 in 2000, 59 in 2001, and 64 in 2002.[12] The number of "crimes relating to documents" (*dokumentni prest'pleniya*)[13] does show an underlying upward trend, however, despite downturns in 1998 and 2000: 1,093 in 1991, 1,381 in 1992, 1,606 in 1993, 2,117 in 1994, 2,443 in 1995, 2,433 in 1996, 2,827 in 1997, 2,197 in 1998, 3,040 in 1999, 2,525 in 2000, 2,694 in 2001, and 3,570 in 2002. Another category of crime that almost certainly includes cases of corruption is "crimes in office" (*prest'pleniya po sluzhba*); the number of these discovered each year was 1,301 in 1991, 1,669 in 1992, 1,515 in 1993, 1,587 in 1994, 1,543 in 1995, 1,842 in 1996, and 1,922 in 1997; there was a major increase to 2,489 in 1998 and 2,846 in 1999, followed by a solid decline to 2,393 in 2000, 2,054 in 2001, and 1,891 in 2002. The category "fraud and extortion" also probably includes cases of corruption: the official number of cases discovered was 912 in 1991, 1,122 in 1992, 1,215 in 1993, 1,840 in 1994, 1,811 in 1995, 1,876 in 1996, 2,099 in 1997, 2,594 in 1998, 3,179 in 1999, 3,222 in 2000, 3,183 in 2001, and 3,601 in 2002. Thus despite occasional plateaux, a comparison of the 1991 and 2002 figures reveals an almost fourfold increase.

Finally, the number of cases of misappropriation (*prisvoyavane*) showed no consistent pattern: 1,775 in 1991, 1,790 in 1992, 1,451 in 1993, 1,626 in 1994, 1,583 in 1995, 1,480 in 1996, and 1,698 in 1997 — with a substantial decline in 1998 to 888, followed by a rise again in 1999 to 1,235, a less dramatic but still significant decline again in 2000 to 938, then 1,032 in 2001 and 938 again in 2002 (all statistics from Natsionalen Statisticheski Institut 1995, 388–89; 1999, 312–13; 2001, 405; 2003, 435).

While not unmistakably corruption-related, it is worth noting statistics cited by the national director of police in Bulgaria, Hristo Gatsov. According to Gatsov, the number of financial crimes was 20.6 percent higher in 1994 than in 1993, which is a substantial increase. However, he also claimed that the real number of such crimes was "eight to ten times" higher than reported, with money laundering, embezzlement, tax evasion, and crimes relating to the privatization process all having gone up. Gatsov blamed much of the country's corruption, which he saw as an integral part of this problem, on delays in structural reforms (all from OMRI, 23 January 1995).[14] Finally, the very limited data available on Bulgarian convictions for corruption indicate that there as in other countries, their numbers appear to be considerably lower than the reported number of instances of corruption. Thus in 1997 there were twenty-six convictions of officials for accepting bribes (and three acquittals); there was little change in 1998 (twenty-one convictions, four acquittals), 1999 (twenty-five convictions, two acquittals), and 2000 (twenty-one convictions, one acquittal) (Open Society Institute 2002, 86).

The statistics in the Hungarian statistical yearbooks are, like their Bulgarian equivalents, insufficiently disaggregated to provide a clear picture specifically on corruption, so that once again the best we can do is provide the statistics that are likely to include cases of corruption (see for example Központi Statisztikai Hivatal 1995, 381–91; Központi Statisztikai Hivatal 1996, 222–33, esp. 226). This said, the published Hungarian crime data became more detailed in the late 1990s. Thus the statistical yearbook for 1998 (Központi Statisztikai Hivatal 1998, 255–56) provides for the first time numbers for various types of crime not previously listed separately, which almost certainly include cases of corruption, for a number of years in the 1990s. In the following lists of statistics, the incomplete time series data in the 1998 yearbook have been added to appropriate earlier data to provide as complete a series as possible.

Thus the number of cases of fraud (*csalás*) discovered amounted to 7,762 in 1990, soaring to 26,296 in 1994, 112,592 in 1995,[15] 50,923 in 1996, 69,312 in 1997, and 119,646 in 1998. The number of cases of economic crime (*gazdasági*) was somewhat more stable, at 9,858 in 1990, 5,409 in 1996, 6,543 in 1997, and 13,454 in 1998. Embezzlement also increased modestly in comparison with fraud, from 3,027 in 1990 to 4,587 in 1994, 6,148 in 1995, 5,085 in 1996, 5,171 in 1997, and 5,133 in 1998. These figures suggest a stabilization from the mid-1990s. On the other hand, the number of cases of "abuse of authority" increased substantially — almost sixfold — over this eight-year period, from 50 cases in 1990 to 225 in 1996, 266 in 1997, and 291 in 1998. Finally, the number of cases of bribery discovered more than doubled over this same period, from 324 in 1990 to 724 in 1996, 650 in 1997, and 664 in 1998.[16]

In addition to providing data on the number of cases discovered, more recent Hungarian statistical yearbooks have included data on convictions. Thus the number of people sentenced in 1998 for fraud was 2,450 (of whom 523 received prison sentences), while 274 were convicted of bribery (of whom 138 were given prison sentences). These figures compare with 2,460 for fraud in 1997 (1,987 in 1996) and 227 for bribery. The number of people convicted in 1997 for abuse of authority was 70, and for embezzlement 2,283. When these various figures are compared with the number of cases of the various crimes discovered each year, it becomes clear that in Hungary as elsewhere, the number of convictions is markedly lower than the number of cases uncovered.

Although the published Hungarian statistics can only hint at minimum levels of corruption, private interviews conducted in Budapest during September 1996 revealed that the number of cases of corruption (including cases involving businesspeople) officially uncovered in Hungary in the early years of post-communism was 385 (1990), 432 (1991), 899 (1992), 582 (1993), 983 (1994), 676 (1995), and 682 (first six months of 1996). Even allowing for different cultural interpretations of corruption and different laws in different countries, these figures reveal a disturbing trend, given that they are internally consistent (that is, based in each case on a similar definition and methodology). According to the head of the Hungarian fraud squad (financial crime unit), Ernő Kiss, the number of fraud and embezzlement cases in Hungary increased sevenfold between 1990 and 1992 alone (RFE/RL, 22 March 1993). One area in which there appeared to be some improvement in early post-communist Hungary was the police force. In 1991 thirty-six officers were charged with corruption, compared with twenty-nine in 1992, seventeen in 1993, and nine in 1994. However, this positive trend had apparently reversed by the mid-1990s (OMRI, 19 July 1996 and 4 December 1996).

Finally, the Open Society Institute managed to obtain from the Hungarian Ministry of Justice aggregated data on the "number of detected crimes of bribery and trafficking in influence." These were 902 in 1998, 609 in 1999, 650 in 2000, and 836 in 2001. The ministry also provided figures on the "Number of persons convicted for bribery and trafficking in influence"; these were relatively low and consistent, at 274 in 1998, 289 in 1999, and 274 in 2000 (no figures were available for 2001; all data from Open Society Institute 2002, 239).

Detailed, sufficiently disaggregated data on Poland are also difficult to obtain — and as in other countries, they almost certainly represent only a tiny fraction of the total number of crimes. The Polish Institute of the Administration of Justice estimated in early 2000 that only about 25 percent of crimes committed in Poland are reported in the official police statistics, although that estimate pertained to *all* crime, not specifically corruption (*DONOSY Liberal Digest*, 3 March 2000, on line; the reader is reminded here of the point made in note 3, above). With this important caveat in mind, the data can be examined.

Official figures on the number of confirmed cases of corruption following initial investigation (those contravening Articles 228–31 of the Criminal Code that came into effect September 1998) were first published in the Statistical Yearbook for 2001, according to which there were 794 cases in 1990, 1,247 in 1995, 1,349 in 1999, and 1,899 in 2000; the 2003 yearbook reveals that there were 2,331 cases in 2001 and 2,408 in 2002 (Główny Urząd Statystyczny 2001, 63; 2003, 64). Thus there had been more than a threefold increase in confirmed cases in just twelve years.

Although the direct reporting of corruption in the Statistical Yearbook is a recent development, earlier yearbooks do provide details on the number of economic crimes reported.[17] There is confusion in the numbers reported for the early and mid-1990s, which were revised upward later in the decade. This much can be seen by citing both the lower and higher figures here — 3,844 or 6,042 in 1990, 2,041 in 1991, 3,037 in 1992, 2,564 in 1993, 1,716 in 1994, 1,701 or 17,529 in 1995, 2,448 or 22,253 in 1996, 26,773 in 1997; 27,000 in 1998; 7,459 in 1999; 12,220 in 2000; 10,918 in 2001 and 9,995 in 2002.[18] Again, these figures cannot be disaggregated so as to make clear the amount of officially recorded corruption (Główny Urząd Statystyczny 1994, 91; 1995, 97; 1996, 97; 1997, 68; 1998, 60; 1999, 65; 2001, 64; 2003, 65).

One category of crime that has mushroomed in Poland in recent years, and that many academics consulted in Warsaw in February 1997 and June 2001 believe involves a great deal of corruption, is "crimes against documents" or "crimes against the reliability of documents" (*przeciwko dokumentom* to 1998; thereafter *przeciwko wiarygodności dokumentów*). This category includes hiding, stealing, and — easily the largest subcategory — falsifying documents. The numbers increased from 6,357 in 1990 to 9,511 in 1991, 22,180 in 1992, 42,383 in 1993, 37,279 in 1994, 40,063 in 1995 (*Główny Urząd Statystyczny* 1996, 97; the statistical yearbooks for 1998, 60, and 1999, 65, have a slightly higher figure for 1995 of 43,554), 51,885 in 1996 (1998, 60), 56,206 in 1997, 61,746 in 1998 (1999, 65), 80,640 in 1999, 70,591 in 2000 (2001, 64), 76,183 in 2001, and 71,395 in 2002 (2003, 65). There was thus almost a thirteenfold increase during the 1990s, with only a marginal improvement after that. But it has proved impossible to have the Polish Ministry of Justice confirm the interpretation provided here.

Despite the lack of clear or full Polish data on corruption, it is possible to add further references to all the above to form general impressions. Thus in late 1993 Prime Minister Hanna Suchocka's government published a report on the first four years of democracy in Poland that included an analysis of numerous problem areas and various data. Among the contents of the report was a complaint that corruption and bribery among state officials was a cause for concern — with the 250 registered cases of bribery in 1992 representing an increase of some 80 percent over the previous year (Sabbat-Swidlicka 1993, 21).

One very questionable statistic provided by the Polish Ministry of Justice in 1997 is the number of public officials ostensibly convicted of corruption; between 1990 and the end of 1996, this figure amounted to four.[19] More recently, the Open Society Institute has been able to obtain what appear to be more convincing data from the same ministry. According to these, the number of convictions for "passive bribery" was 96 in 1993, 71 in 1994, 68 in 1995, 72 in 1996, 106 in 1997, 116 in 1999, 104 in 2000, and 99 in 2001 (Open Society Institute 2002, 400).[20] Full data on convictions for both active bribery and traffic in influence are available only since 1999; they are 305 and 16 for 1999, 395 and 22 for 2000, and 415 and 20 for 2001 (Open Society Institute 2002, 400).[21] Even taking into consideration only the data on convictions for "harm to public or private interest by a public functionary," the numbers, while low, are still higher than the figure provided to me in 1997: 34 (1993), 30 (1994), 30 (1995), 46 (1996), 62 (1997), 57 (1999), 59 (2000), and 100 (2001).[22] Clearly the fight against corruption in Poland still had a long way to go.

But the Polish case, in which there appears to be a substantial discrepancy between the number of cases of corruption reported and those actually resulting in prosecution and conviction, might not be atypical. Certainly the Hungarian data provided above would bear out this possibility, which is also compatible with the secrecy surrounding investigation and prosecution figures in many countries. For instance, the confidential Russian data cited above do not indicate how many cases of bribery registered were solved or resulted in prosecution, whereas full details were provided on many other types of crime (Glavnyi Informatsionnyi Tsentr 1997, 8). According to Kettle (1995, 39), only twelve officials, of whom ten were police officers, were charged with bribe taking in Czechia in 1994; there also appear to have been fewer cases in Hungary than in some other early post-communist states (Kránitz 1994, 107–8).

Because of its communist political system, it is perhaps surprising that quite detailed official data on corruption in China should have become available in recent years. The procuracy collects data and produces aggregate surveys. During a visit to Beijing in May–June 1997, I was able to obtain some of these data.[23] Although this book is primarily concerned with the 1990s and the early years of the new century, data from the 1980s provide a basis against which to make comparisons. Between 1982 and 1988 a total of 218,238 cases of economic crime were filed with and investigated by the procuracy; of these 73.4 percent, or some 160,000 cases, were instances of corruption (about 127,000) or bribery (about 31,000). These figures yield an annual average of nearly 23,000 cases, although it seems that the figure was higher than this in 1986, which was apparently a bumper year for economic crime. But the number of corruption and bribery cases filed and investigated then increased substantially, to 58,926 in 1989 (all data either directly cited or calculated from He Bingsong 1992, 246–48). The number of cases of bribery and corruption reported to the procuracy in the early 1990s was 94,686 in 1990 and 81,110 for 1991 (my Chinese source was unable to provide subsequent figures). As for cases leading to full investigations and charges (that is, those directly comparable with the data for the 1980s just cited), these numbered 51,373 in 1990, 46,219 in 1991, 50,088 in 1994,[24] 63,953 in 1995, and 61,099 in 1996 (data for 1992 and 1993 are not available). Hence the turning point appears to have been 1989, although there was also a noticeable increase in 1995 over 1994.[25]

In many ways more important than these aggregate figures are the numbers of "big cases" involving 10,000 yuan or more; these amounted to 11,295 in 1990, 11,894 in 1991, 19,055 in 1994, 29,419 in 1995, and 34,879 in 1996, so that there had been more than a threefold increase in just six years. The Chinese procuracy usually distinguishes between corruption, which involves mainly embezzlement, and bribery; using this distinction, the aggregate figures on "big cases" can be further broken down for 1990 and 1991. In 1990 there were 7,435 cases of large-scale corruption and 3,860 cases of large-scale bribery; in the following year there were 8,050 cases of large-scale corruption and 3,844 cases of large-scale bribery. In completing this analysis of Chinese statistics to the mid-1990s, it should be noted that according to my Chinese source they represent only a small portion of the crimes that were committed.

While the Chinese statistical yearbook provides little guidance on the scale of corruption, the *Law Yearbook of China* has for several years provided data on the number of trials relating to abuse of office and, since 1998, corruption and bribery. The number of trials opened on abuse of office was 7,119 in 1992, 4,105 in 1993, 10,160 in 1994, 12,281 in 1995, 15,357 in 1996, 8,338 in 1997, 1,340 in 1998, 1,250 in 1999, 1,473 in 2000, and 1,839 in 2001. Thus there was a fairly marked increase in the number of trials relating to abuse of office in most years of the early and mid-1990s, a substantial decline in 1997, and then a very marked drop in the late 1990s. Even though the numbers began to creep up again at the turn of the millennium, they are currently still much lower than they were for most of the 1990s. They are also much lower than the number of trials opened on corruption and bribery; these amounted to 18,604 in 1998, 18,946 in 1999, 21,431 in 2000, and 21,800 in 2001 (all data from *Zhongguo Falu Nianjian 1993*: 935; *1994*: 1,025; *1995*: 1,063; *1996*: 1,029; *1997*: 1,055; *1998*: 1,238; *1999*: 1,029; *2000*: 1,209; *2001*: 1,256; *2002*: 1,239). In comparison with other post-communist states — and reflecting the ongoing influence of the communist approach to law in China (people sent to trial are presumed guilty, and unlikely to be cleared) — the proportion of convictions to prosecutions is usually high. In 1999, for example, more than 15,700 people were convicted on corruption-related charges (CD, 11 March 2000).

Once again, the data on the number of trials can only be seen as a minimum indicator of the scale of corruption. Indeed, it is possible (though in the Chinese case improbable) that a reduction in the number of trials reflects less concern on the part of the authorities, rather than a decline in the amount of corruption. Expressed differently, there could be a negative correlation between the number of trials and the number of cases of corruption. Certainly the Communist Party tends to punish many of its officials through internal disciplinary measures, rather than processing misdemeanors through the legal system. Some indication of the imbalance between the number of defendants facing the courts and the number punished by the CCP is provided by comparing the number of trials cited in the preceding paragraph with the number of party officials subject to CCP sanctions. The number of officials subject to various kinds of punishment for corruption by the CCP's disciplinary and supervisory departments was "approximately 158,000" in 1998 and 132,447 in 1999 (CD, 14 March 2000), while almost one million (983,000) CCP members were disciplined in various ways because of corruption between 1998 and 2002; the latter figure represented a substantial increase on earlier years (People's Daily, on-line English-language edition, 15 September 2004).

Yet another problem in using official statistics is that the way data are sometimes presented in sources available to foreign observers makes for uncertainty that like is being compared with like. It is worth noting that some statistics on corruption were published in Beijing Review in September 2000 (BR 43, no. 39: 4), although these data may not be directly comparable to the very detailed ones cited above. Between 1994 and 2000 the Chinese authorities recorded more than 270,000 cases of corruption and bribery (an annual average of approximately 37,500 to 45,000 cases;[26] since the exact starting and finishing dates are not given, it is not possible to be more precise); there were more than 60,000 major cases of "corruption, bribery and embezzlement of public funds" in this period, costing the state almost 23 billion yuan in losses. More than 10,000 officials at county level and above were investigated. Another source (People's Daily, on-line English-language edition, 13 April 2002) suggests that 36,447 cases of bribery and corruption were recorded in 2001 — although the Politburo member Wei Jianxing was re-ported in the same source (*People's Daily*, on-line English-language edi-tion, 24 January 2002) as saying that 174,633 corruption cases were uncovered; once again, the data can be very confusing. Perhaps a more authoritative figure was that provided by the procurator general to the 10th National People's Congress (NPC) in March 2003; in the roughly five years that had elapsed since the 9th full session of the NPC (1998), 20,7103 cases of corruption had been investigated (Saich 2004, 331). Finally, the number of Communist Party officials expelled between 1992 and 1998 because of various offenses, including bribery and embezzle-ment, exceeded 100,000 (BBC News on line, 31 July 1998).[27]

Despite the increased availability of crime statistics in most of the countries that were once under communist rule,[28] it is clear from the discussion above that the pictures we can produce of their corruption, based on official data, are at best patchy. It is therefore necessary to consider other approaches.

Perception-Based Approaches

Domestic Élite and Staff Perceptions   One method used to gauge the scale of corruption is to survey members of the political élite — people who might be expected to have a more direct interest than the general public in such matters, and to have access to more accurate information. Relatively little research of this nature has been conducted in or on the post-communist world. But a survey of 101 randomly selected members of the Polish parliament (Sejm) was conducted in the autumn of 1998 on behalf of the Institute of Public Affairs, and produced interesting results.

When asked whether they believed that corruption was "very frequent or frequent" among Polish politicians, only about 18 percent (18 mem-bers) answered affirmatively, whereas about 32 percent believed it "rare or very rare." However, some 41 percent believed that the amount of corruption among politicians was about average; since corruption is generally seen as a serious problem within Poland, "about average" is of concern. Surprisingly, ten of the respondents replied that they did not know the answer; for parliamentarians to be either so noncommittal or so ignorant is also of concern (all data, and many more, in Kurczewski 1999a, those cited here at 263 — though readers must also see the errata slip inserted into the book to appreciate that the data have not been incorrectly cited here; English-language summaries can be found in Kurczewski 1999b and Kurczewski 2004, 175–78).[29]

A more recent study, based on research conducted in 2000 that includes the responses of parliamentarians in Russia and the three Baltic states, is that conducted by the University of Oslo's Department of Political Science (Steen 2004). Unfortunately for our purposes, the data published so far do not distinguish between the responses of parliamentarians, directors of state-run enterprises, heads of local cultural institutes, and members of other "élite" groups, and in this sense are not directly comparable with Kurczewski's findings.[30] But one interesting point to emerge from the Steen team's research is that Estonian élites perceive corruption as less of a problem than their Latvian, Lithuanian, and Russian counterparts do. Another is that whereas over 60 percent of Russian élite respondents believed that public officials pursued their own interests to a greater extent than the public good, less than 40 percent of Estonian élite members did. A final revealing finding was that Russian élites trusted their own ministries even less than they believed the public did; this was a reversal of the balance identified in the three Baltic states.

While the number of relevant élite surveys is tiny, there have been several surveys of the perceptions of public officials — "staffs," in Weberian terms. The most readily accessible are those organised by the World Bank since 1998. So far, such surveys have been conducted in Albania (1998), Georgia (1998), Latvia (1998), Slovakia (1999), Bosnia and Hercegovina (2000), Romania (2000), Kazakhstan (2001), Kyrgyzstan (2001), and Russia (2001). Space limitations preclude any detailed comparative analysis of these here. But some of the results, relating to perceived levels of corruption in different state agencies, are summarized later in the chapter.[31]

Business and Public Perceptions   There has been a large number of surveys of businesspeople's and citizens' attitudes toward corruption in both individual post-communist states and groups of states; some of these are considered in further detail below and in chapter 5. At this point, the focus is on comparative cross-polity and general surveys, in which the scale of corruption in a particular country is suggested largely in relation to other countries, and in which there is little if any disaggregation by type of official or type of corruption.[32]

Easily the best-known and most frequently cited of these surveys is the
TI CPI, which has appeared annually since 1995.[33] Before analyzing the
position of post-communist states in the CPIs, a few words of warning
are necessary, since it is easy to misinterpret the data if insufficient heed
is paid to the small print that accompanies their publication. First, both
the methodology and the selection of countries vary somewhat from
year to year, so that strictly speaking, it is not appropriate to perform
direct comparisons over time. Obviously if only thirty countries are
compared in one year, while eighty countries are compared the next, a
country that retains its place in the middle of the grouping will be
ranked fifteenth in the first year, and fortieth in the second. It can thus
appear as if it has deteriorated markedly, whereas in fact there may have
been no perceptible change.

It is also important to note who has been polled for the surveys used
by TI to produce its composite scores. The earliest index was based on
surveys of foreign businesspeople and financial journalists involved with
the country being assessed, whereas some later ones include a limited
amount of local (indigenous) survey data, mainly based on responses
from local businesspeople and foreign specialists (including embassy
staff) resident in the country; they also include the views of expert
assessors (country analysts), primarily in the United States. But whereas some of the earlier CPIs included surveys of the general public (two in
1999, one in 2000), the views of the public have been neither sought nor
reflected by TI in more recent surveys.

Even if the questionability of omitting the general public's perceptions is overlooked, the mixing of somewhat different kinds of sources
over the years limits the value of the CPIs for diachronic analysis. This
said, the distinction is not necessarily as neat as it might appear. Informal, random, and small-scale interviews conducted with western businesspeople when I have been traveling in CEE and the CIS have made
me aware that the impressions they form of the level of corruption in a
given country are sometimes based on their own experiences, and sometimes on what their native hosts tell them. In short, the views of people
living in a country can seep into surveys of foreign businesspeople; at
the same time, the very existence of the CPI, and its reporting in much of
the post-communist media, mean that the opposite also pertains. The
potential dangers of mutual endorsement of misguided views — myths
even — based on originally fallacious perceptions are obvious.

A third potential problem is that the tables have since 1998 been based on three-year averages. TI now emphasizes this, and defends its policy on the grounds, to quote its former executive director Jeremy Pope, that a "multi-year approach is more accurate and realistic. The rankings fail to fully take into account the impact of recent scandals that have damaged perceptions of the integrity environment of a country, nor do the rankings tend to reflect recent efforts by governments to introduce anti-corruption reforms in their countries" (Transparency International 2000a, 3). The main reason for TI's approach is thus to produce country images that are less susceptible to, and influenced by, short-term (transient) factors. If the impact of those factors is more long term, that will eventually manifest itself in averages over time. But one of the most strident critics of all attempts to measure corruption, in particular the TI methodology, has argued that such an approach can be inflexible and misleading, since it provides inadequate recognition of major new initiatives by a government, for example, to deal with corruption (Sík 1999; see too Sík 2002, esp.107–13). While Sík has a point, TI's approach is methodologically defensible, since even energetic and well-intentioned new campaigns can soon fizzle out, and be of little if any long-term significance.[34]

Bearing these important caveats in mind, two ways of presenting the TI CPI data are used here. The first is designed to ascertain whether individual post-communist states are perceived as having become more or less corrupt, or else little changed, since the mid-1990s. Despite the potential hazards involved (because of the different numbers and types of surveys used each year), there is no alternative at present to comparing the actual scores of individual countries over time (as distinct from their rankings).[35] As long as there is full awareness of the dangers of fetishizing the images so produced, the exercise is of value. We start by considering the four CEE countries singled out for particular consideration. The reader is reminded that CPI scores are on a scale of ten; the higher the score, the less perceived corruption.

Bulgaria first appeared in a TI CPI in 1998, and since then its scores have slowly but steadily improved, from 2.9 to 4.1 in 2004, though it still has a long way to go to reach the generally much lower levels of corruption in Western Europe.[36] Unlike the three other CEE countries on which we are concentrating, there are no TI aggregated scores over time for Bulgaria before 1998. Hungary has appeared in all TI CPIs since

1995. In that year it scored 4.12; the number climbed to 5.0 or higher until 2001, then fell to 4.9 in 2002 and 4.8 in both 2003 and 2004. Thus according to this comparison—which TI itself emphasizes is hazardous—the corruption situation in Hungary improved somewhat from the mid-1990s to the early years of the new century, but then marginally deteriorated again. Since there were at the time of writing only three recent figures below 5.0, it is too soon to assume any general trend.

As with Poland and Russia, aggregated longitudinal data on Hungary's perceived levels of corruption during the communist and early transition eras were published by TI in 1996. Aggregate figures were published for two periods, 1980–85, and 1988–92. Hungary's score in the earlier of these was 1.63, and 5.22 in the later. Thus Hungary was seen as very corrupt in the early 1980s (a purely communist period), to have improved dramatically in the early transition period, then to have hovered around the 5.0 mark, and finally to have started declining again —albeit marginally—after the turn of the century. At the time of writing, it was somewhat below the average for the late communist and early transition periods.

Poland has been included in all TI CPIs since 1996, and has since steadily deteriorated; it scored 5.57 in 1996, 4.2 in 1999, and 3.5 in 2004. Despite the various methodological limitations, a decline of this magnitude strongly suggests that Poland has become more corrupt since the mid-1990s. Comment on this is made below. At this juncture, it is worth comparing Poland's more recent performance with the TI averaged scores for 1980–85 (an interesting period in modern Polish history, coinciding with the heady days of the Solidarity challenge and the subsequent declaration of martial law and political clampdown) and 1988–92 (early transition). Poland scored 3.64 for the earlier period and 5.20 for the later. Thus like Hungary, early post-communist Poland was seen as having improved in comparison with the communist period, then as having improved further, but then as having deteriorated again by the late 1990s. By 2003 it was perceived as being back at the levels of the early 1980s, and to be more corrupt than Bulgaria; that gap widened in 2004.

Like Poland, Russia has been included in all TI CPIs since 1996, and it has since fluctuated within a relatively narrow band; its lowest score was 2.1 in 2000, its highest 2.8 in 2004. To be charitable, one can say that Russia was fairly consistent over this period, albeit consistently rather bad. There has been an improvement in the first four years of Vladimir Putin's presidency; but as in Hungary, it is too early to be sure that recent changes represent a long-term trend. Certainly the scores for 2002–4 could be interpreted as indicating stagnation in Russia in terms of an effective fight against corruption. Unlike Hungary and Poland, Russia may have become significantly worse in the post-communist period than it was in the Soviet period. The reason for being even more cautious in interpreting (and using) the earlier data is that they are for the USSR as a whole, not merely Russia. However, doing so does not seem unreasonable when it is borne in mind just how centralized in Moscow the former Soviet state was. Thus according to the averaged figures published by TI in 1996, the Soviet Union's score for 1980–85 was 5.13; this figure declined to 3.27 for the period 1988–92 (end of the communist era, and the very start of the post-communist era; the reader is reminded that Russia made the transition a little later than Hungary and Poland). But the latter figure is still higher than the recent scores, even those for 2002–4. In sum, Russia's corruption image has deteriorated markedly in recent times in comparison with the communist era; only time will tell whether it really has turned the corner under Putin, or essentially stagnated after a very modest improvement.

Since China has been included as an "add-on" in this study, it is worth noting that its perceived corruption pattern is different again from that of our other countries. Its performance improved quite markedly between 1995 (2.16) and the end of the 1990s, but then stabilized at around 3.5 (2000 appears to have been an aberrant year). Like Russia's, China's image in terms of corruption has declined over the past two decades. According to TI, the average annual score for 1980–85 was 5.13, and for 1988–92 was 4.73; this is in line with most external analysts' intuition and evaluations, while the improvement since the mid-1990s suggests that the major campaign against corruption that began in 1993 has had an effect (all data from TI website, on which the slightly changing methodologies from one TI CPI to the next are also elaborated).

The results of the various TI CPIs are summarized in table 4.1.

As emphasized throughout this book, our focus on four or five post-communist countries does not reflect a lack of interest in the others. It is appropriate to make a few observations on the fate in the TI CPI of CEE and CIS states other than the four selected for this book. In the earliest CPIs the only post-communist state to be included beyond our four was

TABLE 4.1.   TI Corruption Scores of Five States, 1995–2004

	1995	1996	1997	1998	1999	2000	2001	2002	2003	2004
Bulgaria	n.a.	n.a.	n.a.	2.9	3.3	3.5	3.9	4.0	3.9	4.1
China	2.16	2.43	2.88	3.5	3.4	3.1	3.5	3.5	3.4	3.4
Hungary	4.12	4.86	5.18	5.0	5.2	5.2	5.3	4.9	4.8	4.8
Poland	n.a.	5.57	5.08	4.6	4.2	4.1	4.1	4.0	3.6	3.5
Russia	n.a.	2.58	2.27	2.4	2.4	2.1	2.3	2.7	2.7	2.8

Note: Higher scores indicate less perceived corruption.

Czechia. It was ranked slightly lower than Poland in 1996, with a score of 5.37; its score had declined by 2000 to 4.3, and further still to 3.7 by 2002. It then improved marginally to 3.9 in 2003 and 4.2 in 2004. In short, not only was it considered more corrupt than Hungary and sometimes Poland, but often also Bulgaria (though they ranked more or less equally in 2003 and 2004); its image has deteriorated markedly since 1996, despite a small improvement recently. According to the TI averaged figures published in 1996, corruption levels were not perceived to have changed significantly from the communist years of the early 1980s (average score of 5.13 for 1980–85) through the early transition phase (5.20 for 1988–92) to the mid-1990s, though a slight improvement is suggested by the data before the decline in the late 1990s.[37]

At the end of the 1990s the TI CPI began to include many more post-communist countries. While it would be inappropriate to elaborate all the findings, it is worth noting that the countries that emerged as the least corrupt of the CEE and CIS states were Estonia and Slovenia, a position they maintained in 2004. By then the most corrupt post-communist state was perceived to be Azerbaijan (scoring 1.9), closely followed by Georgia, Tajikistan, and Turkmenistan (all 2.0), with Kyrgyzstan, Kazakhstan, and Ukraine forming another equally rated group with a score of 2.2. Indeed, in the 2004 CPI these seven were among the most corrupt countries of the 146 assessed; only Chad, Myanmar, Nigeria, Bangladesh, and Haiti emerged as even more corrupt than Azerbaijan.

A second way in which the TI CPI assessments can be used is to compare them with those of Freedom House, which uses a different methodology. Although this methodology has changed over the years, comparing the assessments of Freedom House with those of TI produces interesting results. In the late 1990s the Freedom House survey team produced assessments on the basis of news reports, publications by NGOs, analyses by think tanks and academic specialists, and individual professional contacts. In its 1998 report on the post-communist transition countries, Freedom House provided a four-tier classification of perceived corruption levels, from group A (least corrupt) to group D (most corrupt). The groupings were as follows:

GROUP A (least corrupt): three East Central European states (Hungary, Poland, and Slovenia)

GROUP B: three Baltic post-communist states (Estonia, Latvia, and Lithuania), plus Czechia

GROUP C: several South East European states (Bulgaria, Croatia, Republic of Macedonia, Romania) plus Slovakia, as well as three CIS states (Belarus, Georgia, and Moldova) and Mongolia

GROUP D (most corrupt): Albania, Armenia, Azerbaijan, Kazakhstan, Kyrgyzstan, Russia, Tajikistan, Turkmenistan, Ukraine, and Uzbekistan. With the exception of Albania (South Eastern Europe), all the countries in this group are CIS states (Karatnycky 1998, 13).

There is clearly a relatively high degree of congruence between the TI and Freedom House assessments for 1998. TI ranked our four CEE states in the order Hungary (5.0), Poland (4.6), Bulgaria (2.9), and Russia (2.4). But it is also worth comparing the Freedom House list with that provided in the TI CPI for 1999, which includes many more CEE and CIS states than the 1998 version. TI does not cluster countries in the way Freedom House did. However, if the countries in the CPI are grouped according to their rank orderings, which is appropriate for the synchronic exercise being performed here, the results look remarkably similar to those produced by Freedom House. The most significant difference is that the TI rankings suggest much greater variation between the Baltic states than the Freedom House list does.[38] The TI listing of CEE and CIS countries plus China can be clustered as follows, with the countries in each cluster ranked in ascending order of perceived corruption (countries with equivalent scores are arranged alphabetically in subgroups, separated by commas):

GROUP A (least corrupt—CPI score 5.0): Slovenia; Estonia; Hungary

GROUP B (4.9–4.0): Czechia; Poland

GROUP C (3.9–3.0): Lithuania; Slovakia; Belarus, China, Latvia; Bulgaria, Republic of Macedonia, Romania

GROUP D (most corrupt—CPI score < 3.0): Croatia; Moldova, Ukraine; Armenia; Russia; Albania, Georgia, Kazakhstan; Kyrgyzstan; Yugoslavia; Uzbekistan; Azerbaijan

As in the Freedom House listing, the Central Asian and Transcaucasian countries emerge as the most corrupt post-communist countries, along with Albania and Russia (Yugoslavia also performs poorly in the TI list, but it is not included in the Freedom House list). Thus the suggestion that geographic proximity to the West is a good indicator of likely levels of corruption is supported by these clusterings, although statistical correlations do not prove causal relationships.

Freedom House has not produced a similar clustering in recent years —and it now uses a different method for assessing countries[39]—but one can be created by grouping countries according to their individual corruption ratings. (Of course the breakpoints between categories are determined by the person performing this exercise, not Freedom House.) To compare assessments made in 2004 with those of the late 1990s that sort of grouping is done below, using the Freedom House scale of 0 to 7.00, with higher scores indicating *more* corruption:

GROUP A (least corrupt—Freedom House score < 3.00): Slovenia; Estonia, Poland; Hungary

GROUP B (3.00–3.99): Slovakia; Czechia, Latvia, Lithuania

GROUP C (4.00–4.99): Bulgaria; Romania; Bosnia, Croatia

GROUP D (5.00–5.99): Republic of Macedonia, Serbia; Albania, Montenegro; Armenia, Belarus, Russia, Ukraine

GROUP E (most corrupt—Freedom House score > 6.00): Georgia, Kosovo, Kyrgyzstan, Uzbekistan; Azerbaijan, Moldova, Tajikistan, Turkmenistan; Kazakhstan

These results can now be compared with the TI CPI for 2004 (scale of 0 to 10.00, with 10.00 indicating the *least* corruption):

GROUP A (least corrupt—CPI score > 6.0): Estonia, Slovenia [no scores between 5.9 and 5.0]

GROUP B (4.9–4.0): Hungary; Lithuania; Czechia; Bulgaria; Latvia, Slovakia

GROUP C (3.9–3.0): Croatia, Poland; China; Belarus; Armenia, Bosnia and Hercegovina; Mongolia

GROUP D (2.9–2.5): Romania; Russia; Republic of Macedonia, Serbia and Montenegro; Albania

GROUP E (most corrupt—CPI Score < 2.5): Moldova, Uzbekistan; Kazakhstan, Kyrgyzstan, Ukraine; Georgia, Tajikistan, Turkmenistan; Azerbaijan

Both the Freedom House ratings and the CPI for 2004 include slightly more countries (an increase of three in each case) than in the earlier period just analyzed; the list of countries is very similar, though not identical (for example, the CPI does not rate Kosovo; but it does rate Mongolia and China, which Freedom House does not). Otherwise, what is striking is the similarity between the assessments, in terms of both rankings and continuities. Thus Estonia and Slovenia continue to be seen as the least corrupt post-communist states, while the most corrupt are still perceived to be Central Asian and Transcaucasian states, plus Ukraine. Despite a few interesting differences between the Freedom House rankings for 2004 and the TI rankings — notably, in terms of this book, the rankings of Poland and Hungary — the scale of difference is in most cases fairly marginal.[40]

The findings of our own survey in 2000 of four post-communist states relevant to this part of the analysis are summarized in table 4.2. Over all, the table reveals a remarkable similarity of perception across the four countries. But there are some interesting (if mostly marginal) differences. Perhaps counterintuitively, Hungarians were more likely than any of the other three nationalities to assume that the number of people engaging in corruption had increased since the collapse of communist power. Moreover, Hungarians had clearer views than any other respondents on what had been happening, with only 6.3 percent answering "don't know." That more Bulgarians answered "don't know" than anyone else was also an unexpected result. One possible explanation is that many respondents were unclear whether the government's major campaign against corruption was working.[41] One unambiguous result is that very few people in any of the four countries believed that the level of corruption had decreased in the first decade of post-communism.

Table 4.3 also reveals a remarkably high level of similarity of response across the four countries. Again, however, there are some interesting

TABLE 4.2.   Popular Perceptions of the Number of People Involved in Corruption since the Collapse of Communist Power, 2000 (in Percent)

	Increased	Decreased	Stayed about the same	Don't know
Bulgaria	69.6	1.8	12.6	16.0
Hungary	76.6	2.0	15.0	6.3
Poland	66.9	2.8	16.0	14.3
Russia	68.5	2.4	19.0	10.0

Note: The question read: "Is it your impression that the scale of corruption (here referring to the number of people engaged in it) has increased, decreased, or stayed about the same since 1989 [1991 for Russia]?"

TABLE 4.3.   Popular Perceptions of the Current Scale of Corruption, 2000 (in Percent)

	Increasing	Decreasing	Stabilizing	Don't know
Bulgaria	56.7	2.5	23.7	17.1
Hungary	68.0	4.1	21.2	6.7
Poland	62.7	2.7	16.6	18.0
Russia	65.9	3.1	19.7	11.4

Note: The question read: "Is it your impression that the scale of corruption (here referring to the number of people engaged in it) is currently increasing, decreasing, or stabilizing?"

marginal differences. Clearly Bulgarians were slightly more optimistic than the other three groups about the state of affairs in their country (although it should be noted that by a very small margin, Hungary was the country in which the highest percentage of respondents believed that the scale of corruption was decreasing at the time of the survey). And as with the question discussed in the preceding paragraph, far fewer Hungarians had no view on the current status of corruption in their country than did Bulgarian, Polish, or Russian respondents.

Yet again, there is a remarkable similarity in some responses across the four countries. The very low percentages of respondents who assumed that there had been a decrease in the average sums of money or value of goods involved in corrupt acts over the ten-year period are almost identi-

TABLE 4.4.   Popular Perceptions of the Scale of Corruption (Sums of Money or Value of Goods Involved) since the Collapse of Communist Power, 2000 (in Percent)

	Increased	Decreased	Stayed about the same	Don't know
Bulgaria	60.9	1.7	10.0	27.5
Hungary	85.5	1.6	5.6	7.1
Poland	69.1	1.9	9.2	19.9
Russia	72.9	1.6	9.9	15.6

Note: The question read: "Where money or goods are involved, is it your impression that the average sums involved since 1989 [1991 for Russia] have increased, decreased, or stayed about the same?"

cal in all four, while the maximum difference in the proportion of repondents who believed that averages had remained about the same is well below 5 percent. On the other hand, considerably more Hungarians than Bulgarians believed there had been an increase in the average sums or value involved, whereas almost four times as many Bulgarians as Hungarians had no idea whether average sums or values had increased. In a sense, the "don't know" responses in table 4.4—other than the Hungarian figure—are the most surprising: since all post-communist states had very high levels of inflation in the early 1990s, and several did so beyond that period, it would have been reasonable to expect most citizens to assume that average sums and values had increased commensurately.[42]

Content Analysis While it cannot be assumed that there is a necessary correlation between the number of articles or reports on corruption in the mass media and how much corruption there really is, it is reasonable to infer some correlation between the amount of reporting and perceived levels of corruption.[43] A systematic sampling of mass media—content analysis—can therefore be helpful in inferring public attitudes, examining their origins, and providing circumstantial evidence of levels of legitimacy.[44]

Large-scale longitudinal content analysis (that is, analysis that covers several mass media outlets over several years) has until very recently been a highly resource-intensive exercise, and practical limitations meant that it was not possible to employ this method for this book (for our own content analysis of the reporting of corruption in the Soviet and Chinese press from the mid-1960s to the mid-1980s see L. Holmes 1993, 120–56). Małgorzata Fuszara was engaged during the 1990s in a comparative analysis of Bulgaria, Czechia, Poland, and Slovakia. But the scope of the analysis varied considerably from country to country when she published her initial findings (which at the time of this book's completion appeared to be the only comparative publication available), so that persuasive comparisons were not yet possible.[45] Even at the stage of research that she had reached in the late 1990s, however, Fuszara (1999, 3) was able to conclude that there were many more similarities than differences between cases and reporting of corruption across the four countries.

Another invaluable study is that undertaken by the Center for the Study of Democracy in Bulgaria. This study considers only the Bulgarian news media and, more recently, also western media reports on corruption in Bulgaria: it is not comparative. Nevertheless it is a longitudinal study, based on weekly reviews since February 1999, and has produced interesting results — as well as some fascinating quotations.[46] All articles, and more recently also broadcasts, are classified as primarily reports, analyses, or commentaries, and longitudinal analysis reveals that the weekly number of printed articles on corruption ranged between 81 and 1,087 from February 1999 to December 2001. Clearly corruption is a major issue in the Bulgarian media. Moreover, certain types of corruption have become far more salient in reports. For instance, clientelism became a particularly hot topic from June 2001 (all from "Coalition 2000" 2002, 59–60).[47]

Experiential (Proxy) Estimates

Surveys of Business Experiences   The TI CPI was a seminal development in the comparative analysis of corruption levels. Like most such developments, it was soon subjected to various criticisms (some of which were noted above), and commentators have suggested alternative ways of more accurately evaluating the level of various types of corruption within and across countries. Arguably the most influential method — at least within agencies that attempt to tackle the corruption problem in earnest — is to survey businesses operating within the countries being examined in terms of their own firsthand experiences of corruption, rather than their impressions (perceptions). While there have been some excellent surveys of this kind conducted by specialists within individual post-communist states (see for example Radaev 2002), the best-known exponent and implementer of this approach across several post-communist states is the World Bank. An early example of this kind of World Bank survey was one of two hundred Lithuanian businesspeople and foreign businesspeople active in Lithuania that was conducted in 1995. According to that survey, 54 percent of those operating within either Vilnius or Kaunas (the two largest cities) had paid bribes to officials in recent years, while some 80 percent of the foreign businesspeople claimed that they had been asked to pay bribes (all from Girnius 1995).

A far more comprehensive set of such surveys is the "Business Environment and Enterprise Performance Survey" (BEEPS). This is the largest subset of the World Business Environment Survey (WBES) initiated in 1999, which built on survey work carried out in connection with the *World Development Report 1997* (Thomas 2001, 241). It was initiated jointly by the World Bank and the Office of the Chief Economist at the European Bank for Reconstruction and Development, and has been conducted by means of face-to-face interviews with the owners and managers of firms in most post-communist states. As of mid-2004 two BEEPS had been completed—one conducted primarily in mid-1999 (BEEPS I), the second (BEEPS II) in 2002.[48]

Although the average number of interviewees in BEEPS I was 125–150 in each country, there were larger samples in two of the four CEE countries on which we are focusing: 250 in Poland and 550 in Russia. Since respondents were asked to report on activities that were in some cases clearly illegal, it was emphasized to them that all data would be kept strictly confidential and presented only in aggregated form from which it would be impossible for others to identify them. Moreover, as an additional method of encouraging respondents to reply openly without fear of identification or reprisal, several questions were framed indirectly (as when interviewees were asked about "firms in your line of business"). One can only surmise the extent to which these various precautionary measures were effective. But what seems highly probable is that the data yielded by these surveys are minimum ones: if fear on the part of respondents did distort the results, it would not have worsened but rather improved the picture of corruption, because some respondents were not reporting their experiences.[49]

How did our four countries fare in BEEPS I? Space limitations prevent detailed consideration of the results here (interested readers should consult the web site referred to in note 48). But a few observations can be made. One question invited respondents to estimate the expenditures (as a share of annual revenue) that they had to make as unofficial payments or gifts to public officials (so-called bribe taxes). The average for CIS countries was 3.7 percent, and for CEE countries 2.2 percent. Russia was below the CIS average, at 2.8 percent; the figure for Bulgaria was 2.1 percent, for Hungary 1.7 percent, and for Poland 1.6 percent. The post-communist countries in which firms paid proportionately the most in unofficial bribes — and which were thus, by one measure, the most corrupt — were, in descending order, Azerbaijan, Kyrgyzstan, Armenia, and Ukraine. At the other end of the spectrum, the countries in which there was the least corruption according to this variable were Croatia, Latvia, Slovenia, and Poland (Pradhan, Anderson, Hellman, Jones, Moore, Muller, Ryterman, and Sutch 2000, xvii–xviii).

BEEPS II surveyed the first twenty-two countries listed in note 48, plus Bosnia and Hercegovina, the Republic of Macedonia, Tajikistan, Yugoslavia, and, again as a transitional but not post-communist state, Turkey. For full results interested readers should visit the web site (http://info .worldbank.org/governance/beeps2002/) or see the detailed analysis published in 2004 (Gray, Hellman, and Ryterman 2004). Among the more interesting findings was this: whereas no Hungarian or Polish respondents believed that private payments or gifts to parliamentarians had had a major impact on their businesses, 4.9 percent of valid Russian responses (here meaning responses excluding "don't know") were affirmative, as were 2.2 percent of valid Bulgarian responses.[50] The method used in 2002 for calculating the "bribe tax" was slightly different from that used in 1999, so that no direct comparison of that variable can be made.[51] Over all, however, the analysts concluded that their results were "mixed but somewhat encouraging," and provide some — mostly assumed — reasons for guarded optimism (Gray, Hellman, and Ryterman 2004, xii, 5, 45).

Yet the reasons for their optimism were not entirely clear once the empirical results were scrutinized. For example, one finding was that state capture (see chapter 2) by firms appeared to have increased in post-communist states as marketization increased (Gray, Hellman, and Ryterman 2004, 27), whereas "corruption was seen as less problematic" to business than other obstacles in countries where there was still tight state control (Gray, Hellman, and Ryterman 2004, xii). This result could be interpreted as indicating that pro-market reforms encourage corruption, which is disappointing to advocates of reform.[52] Another general problem suggested by the results is that newer, smaller, private firms pay bribes more often than larger, established firms, and markedly more than state-run firms. While this might not be particularly surprising — new firms typically start small, and have to obtain a wide range of start-up permits from state authorities[53] — it is of concern if a solid bourgeois class relatively independent of the state is to develop (see chapters 6 and 7). Finally, an analysis of the BEEPS II data "confirms that many firms obtain net benefits from bribery," or at least perceive either a net benefit or no clear disadvantage (Gray, Hellman, and Ryterman 2004, xv, 46–47); as Gray and her coauthors (2004, 47) sensibly observe, firms in CEE and CIS are unlikely to play a major role in combating corruption until they are substantially disadvantaged by it. To make matters worse, state capture was seen by respondents as being a net cost in only one country surveyed, Croatia; in all the others, it was seen as either essentially costless or a net benefit (Gray, Hellman, and Ryterman 2004, 47–48). All this raises doubts about the appropriateness of even guarded optimism.

Regarding our selected states, the frequency with which bribes were paid had declined between BEEPS I and II in Hungary and Poland, but had risen somewhat in Bulgaria, and markedly so in Russia (Gray, Hellman, and Ryterman 2004, 17–19). Conversely, the percentage of captor firms had increased significantly in Hungary (threefold) and Bulgaria between 1999 and 2002, but only marginally in Poland and Russia (Gray, Hellman, and Ryterman 2004, 29–31). This said, judged by the extent to which corruption was seen as an obstacle to business, corruption had significantly diminished in Russia and worsened in Poland (Gray, Hellman, and Ryterman 2004, xii, 11–15). Using only this last variable, the BEEPS II results thus reflected similar trend lines to the TI assessments.

While BEEPS is probably the best-known of the business involvement surveys, mention should also be made of the International Crimes against Business Survey (ICBS), sponsored by the Interregional Crime and Justice Research Institute of the United Nations (UNICRI). The first of these was conducted during 1994 in ten countries, of which two were transition states. Another was conducted in 2000 in eight CEE capitals — including those of three of our countries (all but Poland) — and involved interviewing 520 businesspeople. Using the earlier surveys, it was possible to compare two overlapping periods (1993–97 and 1996–2000). One of the most interesting results was that whereas there was less victimization of citizens in the later period, business generally felt very much threatened by crime and corruption; this was especially true of smaller businesses (see http://www.unicri.it/Crimes %20against %20business.htm; http://www.hku.hk/crime/bsquest.doc for the questionnaire, visited March 2004; and Center for the Study of Democracy 2001, 37).

Surveys of Citizens' Experiences The previous method analyzed relates only to the business-state nexus. Moreover, as indicated above, TI CPIs focus overwhelmingly on the perceptions of the business sector and experts. Neither set of surveys tells us much about how ordinary citizens either perceive or experience corruption within their countries. Hence they provide only a partial picture — and like many incomplete images, they may distort the whole.

Indeed, an important point about comparative levels of corruption needs to be made; though obvious once highlighted, it is often overlooked. Other things being equal, higher levels of business-related corruption would be expected in countries where the state plays a significant role in the economy than in those where it plays a relatively minor role. There might be just as much business impropriety in more laissez-faire states, or even more, but since the corruption does not directly involve state officials, these states will usually be ranked as less corrupt.[54] Moreover, the state agencies with which foreign businesses deal tend to be limited in number; a foreign business executive is more likely to come into direct contact with officials from ministries of trade and privatization agencies than with judges, military officers, or traffic police (unless the executive lives in the country in question).

Hence in any attempt to understand corruption in all its forms, it is imperative to consider also the views and experiences of ordinary citizens. The World Bank commenced corruption-oriented household surveys in 1998 to complement its business surveys, and some of their results are considered below. But in this area, the best-known academic research has been conducted by a small team headed by Professor William Miller of the University of Glasgow. The team has produced a substantial number of articles in recent years (for example Koshechkina, Grødeland, and Miller 1997; Miller, Koshechkina, and Grødeland 1997; Grødeland, Koshechkina, and Miller 1998a; Grødeland, Koshechkina, and Miller 1998b; Miller, Grødeland, and Koshechkina 1998; Miller, Grødeland, and Koshechkina 1999; Miller, Grødeland, and Koshechkina 2001a), and published a book in 2001 (Miller, Grødeland, and Koshechkina 2001b). Many of their findings have to do with general perceptions on corruption, and so are more appropriately considered elsewhere. But it is worth summarizing some of their results in terms of experience of corruption. Only one of the countries on which they have concentrated, Bulgaria, is one of our four CEE countries.

When asked in late 1997 or early 1998 (depending on the country and location) whether they had been directly asked for a bribe (money or a gift) by a public official in the preceding four to five years, only 7 percent of Bulgarians, 2 percent of Czechs, 4 percent of Slovaks, and 11 percent of Ukrainians answered in the affirmative. However, it is important to remember the distinction drawn in chapter 2 between meat-eating and grass-eating corrupt officials. The relatively low positive response rates just cited refer only to meat eaters. Far higher proportions of citizens indicated that an official, while not demanding a bribe outright, "showed he was expecting something"; the proportion of respondents who indicated that they had experienced grass eaters was 39 percent in Bulgaria, 44 percent in Czechia, 64 percent in Slovakia, and 56 percent in Ukraine (Miller, Grødeland, and Koshechkina 1998, 14–16).[55] If the two figures are combined, a disturbingly high number of citizens either were directly asked for a bribe or else believed that they were expected to give one — 46 percent of Bulgarians, 46 percent of Czechs, and much higher and almost identical figures for Ukrainians (67 percent) and Slovaks (68 percent).[56]

The Glasgow team also asked respondents whether they had actually offered bribes in the previous four to five years. Again, the response is in many ways disturbing. Although a majority of Bulgarians (66 percent) and Czechs (76 percent) maintained that they had never offered bribes to officials during this period, 57 percent of Ukrainians and 58 percent of Slovaks claimed they had. Although some of the bribes were minor (chocolates or a bottle of cognac), many were more substantial, and included sums of money. While some respondents said that they gave the "bribes" after the fact and as a sign of gratitude, others were clearly annoyed that they had had to pay, even before the service to which they presumably were entitled was performed by the official (Miller, Grøde-land, and Koshechkina 1998, 19–22).

Like all statistics on crime — some would claim statistics on anything[57] — those produced by the Glasgow team must be treated with caution, especially if they are to be used for drawing general conclusions. Their officials included medical personnel, and many analysts, myself included, would exclude this group for reasons given later in this chapter. For the purposes of this study, it is unfortunate that there are no data drawn from the most reformist post-communist states, notably Poland during the 1990s or Estonia (by the late 1990s, it was clear that much of Czechia's putatively radical reformism of the early to-mid-1990s had existed more on paper than in reality). But again, as long as they are not fetishized, these data provide a valuable insight into the scale of corruption in post-communist states, and can certainly be used to make interesting comparisons across the four countries surveyed by the Glasgow team.[58]

As of mid-2003 World Bank household surveys specifically on corruption had been conducted in six post-communist countries. These include data on citizens' experience of corruption. Only one of the six (Russia) was one of the four CEE and CIS states analyzed in this book — and that was the only one for which the full results had not yet been published in English. However, some of the results from the five other states, plus some of the Russian ones that were published in Russian, are considered later in the chapter.

Tracking Methods (Before-and-After Assessments)

In chapter 5 there is brief consideration of the role of the shadow economy in the economic activity of states. But discussions of shadow economies are based on guesstimates, and these guesstimates refer to all questionable economic activity, not just economic corruption. A more specific approach, admittedly difficult to organize, is to compare official revenues, prices, or both in a given unit (such as a city or hospital) before and after very specific anticorruption measures have been taken. There do not appear to be any such studies for the CEE or CIS states.[59] But the approach offers potentially yet another method for assessing corruption rates, and particularly the effectiveness of different anticorruption measures, in the future.

A related approach is to use public expenditure tracking surveys

(PETS), in which funds allocated to projects are monitored at each tier or level between the original source of the funds and the intended end user; if sums appear to go missing between levels, investigations can be initiated to determine whether a major cause is corruption. Again, this method does not appear to have been used yet in the post-communist world, but it has been effective elsewhere and could well be applied to CEE and CIS countries in the future.[60]

MAIN AREAS OF CORRUPTION

It appears that some groups are far more prone than others to corruption, even though it is difficult to obtain much detail on this apparent difference, and the balance of the groups does vary from state to state. The discussion here begins with just a few examples of the limited official statistics available. They are followed by an analysis of various groups' perceptions, primarily with reference to the perceived distributions in the CEE and CIS countries selected for this book, plus China.

Official Statistics

The data available on specific groups within the state apparatuses of post-communist states (and elsewhere) are patchy. Moreover, any attempt to provide reasonably full statistics on all the major groups for five countries over a fifteen-year period is beyond the scope of this book. Instead, just a few, essentially random data are provided here, largely to demonstrate that it is possible to find important parts of the jigsaw puzzle.

The official Russian Ministry of the Interior source cited earlier indicates that the total number of its officers (presumably, most of them police officers) charged with accepting bribes in 1996 was 420, representing a substantial decline of 13.0 percent from 1995 (Glavnyi Informatsionnyi Tsentr 1997, 34). A more recent source provides patchy data on the amount of corruption detected within the Russian police force. In the five-year period 1992–96, the number of criminal cases brought against law enforcement officers more than doubled, from 375 to 835. This number then rose still more dramatically, to 1,943 in 1998 (Altukhov 2001, 8). Polish data on police corruption are also difficult to track. However, forty-two police officers were dismissed for corruption in 1991 (*SWB/EE*, 29 April 1992), out of a total of approximately 94,000 officers. In 1997 eleven police officers were convicted of corruption in Hungary, and sixty-one citizens were convicted of attempting to bribe police officers (Ministry of the Interior [Hungary] 2000, 32–34; on Czech police corruption see Fric 1999). The chief Russian military prosecutor Valentin Panichev revealed in July 1996 that in the previous two years, law enforcement agencies had opened 267 criminal cases concerning possible military corruption; in 1995 thirty-six military officers were convicted of bribery in Russia. At the same meeting, it was claimed that the most corruption-prone sectors in Russia were the State Property Committee (the privatization agency), the Central Bank, the ministries of health, agriculture, defense, and the interior, the tax police, the state customs committee, and local power structures (*OMRI DD*, 9 July 1996). China also sometimes provides data on particular groups. For example, the number of party and government cadres arrested and convicted for corruption and bribery in 1996 was 13,530, while the number of justice officers was 4,471.

The difficulties involved in obtaining detailed figures on cases of officials from various agencies being investigated, prosecuted, and convicted do not prevent businesspeople and citizens from forming opinions on which groups are most and least corrupt; these perceptions can now be examined.

Various Groups' Perceptions

As mentioned in the introduction, four post-communist countries were chosen for survey analysis, with the same questionnaire distributed in each. Since the surveys were all conducted within three months of each other in 2000 using the same basic survey techniques, the results are as directly comparable as most cross-polity survey results. One set of questions was intended to determine which groups of officials were considered by respondents to be the most (and least) prone to corruption. Rather than rank-order from a long list, which survey lore indicates is likely to confuse respondents, the surveys invited respondents to classify each identified type of official as among "the most corrupt," "about average," or "the least corrupt," or to answer "don't know."[61] As a result, the response rate percentages should total 100 for each type of official, not across types of official. The taxonomy of officials presented was as follows:

The president
The prime minister
Ministers
Members of Parliament
Local elected representatives
Ministerial staff
Local council officials
Traffic police officers
Regular police officers
Customs officers and border guards
Judges
Members of the state procuracy (prosecutor's office)
Military officers
Ambassadors
University Rectors
Others (please specify)

With this listing in mind, the results of our four surveys can be analyzed and compared.

In Bulgaria, the reputation of the customs service appears to have improved little, despite government attempts since 1997 to clean it up. This group of state officials was identified by the highest percentage of respondents as among the most corrupt, at 58.1 percent; they were followed by traffic police officers (36.5 percent), Members of Parliament (27.4 percent), regular police officers (25.2 percent), ministers (25.1 percent), judges (23.5 percent), and prosecutors, or members of the State Prosecutor's Office (21.3 percent). At the other end of the spectrum, those officials seen as either least corrupt or not corrupt were the president (18.6 percent and 39.6 percent, for a total of 58.2 percent), military officers (22.4 percent and 25.9 percent, totaling 48.3 percent), the prime minister (15.0 percent and 14.0 percent, totaling 29 percent), and local council officials (18.1 percent and 6.4 percent, totaling 24.5 percent). Our findings on Bulgaria broadly resonate with those of other surveys, though there are some differences. In February 2000 the Bulgarian anticorruption organization Coalition 2000 published an assessment of corruption in the country during 1999 that contained survey data from two surveys, conducted in April and September 1999. These revealed that the customs service was considered the state agency most prone to corruption, followed by the tax service, the court system (including judges and prosecutors), the privatization agency, and the police. At the other end of the spectrum, the groups considered least prone to corruption were the president's administration, the National Statistical Office, and the military ("Coalition 2000" 2000, 8, 23).[62]

An earlier Bulgarian survey (conducted December 1997–January 1998) also provided some evidence on which groups of public officials were considered most and least corrupt, and, as far as it went, revealed very similar findings.[63] Respondents were asked, "Imagine a person who needs something that he [sic] is *entitled to by law*. Is it *likely* that this person would have to offer money, a present or a favor to get help from each of the following groups of officials?" (emphasis in original). Far and away the most "corrupt" group was "doctors in hospitals"; no less than 85.9 percent of interviewees responded that it was "likely" they would have to offer a bribe of some kind. However, since most comparative analyses of corruption would not include doctors as state officials, they will be discounted for the purposes of this analysis.[64] After doctors, the groups seen as most corruptible were customs officials (73.6 percent of respondents believed that they would have to offer a bribe), court officials (62.9 percent), municipal officials (61.5 percent), and police officers (56 percent). Elected officials were considered somewhat less susceptible to corruption, with members of parliament scoring 48.2 percent on this question, and elected municipal councilors 45.7 percent (all data from Center for the Study of Democracy 1998b).

In Hungary the group clearly perceived in our survey as the most prone to corruption was the traffic police, with 52.4 percent of all respondents including them in the most corrupt category. Some way behind were the regular police (39.1 percent) and customs officers (33.7 percent). At the other end of the spectrum were the president — 78.5 percent classified him as either in the least corrupt category (17.1 percent) or not at all corrupt (61.4 percent) — and the prime minister (74.9 percent, 25.2 percent, and 49.7 percent). Local elected representatives were considered less corrupt than they are in many other countries, with a quarter (24.9 percent) of respondents classifying them in the least corrupt (20.8 percent) or not at all corrupt (4.1 percent) categories.

The military were considered even less corrupt, with 41.4 percent of respondents classifying them as either not corrupt at all (14.2 percent) or among the least corrupt (27.2 percent),

It is interesting to compare our data with some of those generated in other surveys of Hungarian attitudes and beliefs relating to corruption. A poll conducted by a leading Czech survey organization in mid-2001 indicated that after the health services, the branch of the Hungarian state considered most corrupt, in terms of bribery, was the police;[65] this group was followed in order by ministries, state offices and bureaus ("red tape"), courts of law, customs officers, and the military (GfK 2001, 9, and second, unnumbered page of the "Introduction: Hungary" section). Although the categories used in the GfK survey are slightly different from and less comprehensive than our own (they do not refer to the president, for example, and there are fewer categories), there are considerable resonances between the two sets of results.[66] The main difference lies in the rating of customs officers, whom our respondents considered more corrupt than the GfK respondents did.[67]

Our Polish data suggest that customs officials and border guards are considered far and away the group most likely to engage in corruption, with almost three fifths (59.8 percent) of respondents considering them among those officials most prone to corruption. Next are local elected representatives (45.8 percent), traffic police officers (43.6 percent), and local council officials (41.6 percent). At 25.1 percent, regular police officers are considered rather more than half as likely as traffic cops to engage in corruption. At the other end of the spectrum, both the president and the prime minister were ranked among the least corrupt, at 73.3 percent and 59 percent. Military officers also fared well: only 4.5 percent of respondents ranked this group among the most prone to corruption, whereas 61 percent considered them among the least corrupt.

How do our Polish data compare with those generated by other surveys of Poland? A survey by CBOS in February 1994 related to the police was conducted at about the time when rumors of corruption in the police force in Poznan were rife and newspaper reports were just beginning to appear (see chapter 3). It is therefore not surprising that public perceptions of corruption among the police should have been rather negative. To the question "Do you believe that what the press reproaches the police for in Poznan is exceptional, an isolated case, or occurs frequently in the

Polish police?," 54 percent of respondents (N = 1198) answered that such occurrences were either rather frequent or very frequent (Centrum Badania Opinii Społecznej 1994a, 7).

A second survey by CBOS in 1994 focused on public perceptions of the judicial organs. It was conducted in April and involved 1,207 respondents, of whom 44 percent believed that there was about as much "dishonesty, bribery and corruption" in the judicial organs as everywhere else in Polish public life, while 12 percent believed there was more than elsewhere. Interestingly—and seemingly in contrast to the situation in Hungary—respondents perceived that judges were just as prone to corruption as police officers (Centrum Badania Opinii Społecznej 1994b, esp. 1–8).[68]

Like all survey data, the two sets just cited must be treated with caution. For instance, a comparison of the first with a survey using the same questions conducted in October 1993—just five months earlier—reveals that while public mistrust in the police had grown threefold in that period, trust in the administration and public service offices (*administracja i urzędy*) had improved: in March 1994 only 44 percent considered this one of the most corrupt areas of public life, in comparison with 58 percent in October 1993. It would therefore be unwise to draw too many specific conclusions about ongoing public perceptions of the state (Centrum Badania Opinii Społecznej 1994a, 5). This said, and even allowing for all the problems of surveying and the volatility of public opinion, there is a sufficiently clear outline of public attitudes here to be able to conclude that the Polish public did see a great deal of corruption in organs of the state which should be particularly trustworthy.[69]

A different approach to perceptions of which groups actually are most corrupt was revealed in the interviews of about a hundred Polish parliamentarians conducted in late 1998 and referred to above. These members of the political élite were asked which of six groups of officials (national politicians, local politicians, central public (civil) servants, local appointed officials, police, and customs officers)[70] presented the highest exposure to the risk of corruption. Customs officers were ranked first, followed by local politicians, local appointed officials, central public servants, the police, and national politicians. The question was then reversed, with respondents asked which of the same groups had the lowest exposure to the risk of corruption. National politicians were seen as having the lowest exposure, followed in ascending order by the police, local appointed officials, central public servants, local politicians, and customs officers (all data from Kurczewski 1999b, 2). (Although the two questions are mirror images, the reader will note that the ordering of groups in response to the second question is not a strict inversion of the ordering in response to the first question. Little should be made of changed ordering of local and central bureaucrats, however, since the difference in response rates was not statistically significant.)[71]

Finally, how do the Russian results compare? The surveys were conducted a few months after Vladimir Putin had been elected president, and it is not surprising that he should have been seen by only 8.8 percent of respondents as among the most corrupt state officials, whereas 46.0 percent saw him as among the least corrupt.[72] The prime minister (at the time, Mikhail Kasyanov) was also seen as one of the more honest state officials, with 11.6 percent classifying him among the most corrupt, and 35.4 percent among the least corrupt. The group seen as the most corrupt was traffic police officers (52.9 percent), followed by regular police officers (50.5 percent), and customs and border officers (46.5 percent).[73]

The GfK survey from 2001 mentioned earlier provides no data on perceived corruption levels among different groups of officials, although Russia is included in the comparative survey. But other surveys do provide such data. The INDEM Foundation produced a report in May 2002 (Satarov 2002), which aggregated and summarized findings of in-depth interviews with experts and two large-scale surveys (one of citizens, the other of entrepreneurs) conducted between late 1999 and 2001; since it was available only in Russian at the time of writing, there is slightly more coverage of it here than of an English-language survey conducted by the Public Opinion Foundation (POF), even though POF is also based in Russia. Table 2 in the INDEM report provides data on the corruptibility ranking of various organizations, and distinguishes the assessments of entrepreneurs and citizens. Twenty-nine organizations are listed; some are subdivisions of agencies included in our own surveys (for example, the Satarov team distinguishes between the upper and lower houses of parliament, and between courts at different levels), while others, such as trade unions, are not covered in our surveys at all. Conversely, our survey includes categories not explicitly covered by the INDEM survey, such as the prime minister. Therefore, only limited comparisons are possible.

The first observation about the INDEM findings is that the responses of entrepreneurs and citizens were remarkably similar. The only significant differences (that is, five or more rank-order positions) have to do with "private entrepreneurship" — unsurprisingly, entrepreneurs rated this group much less corrupt (ranking it thirteenth of twenty-nine groups, with those perceived as least corrupt ranked first) than ordinary citizens did (ranking it twenty-fifth) — the trade unions (ranked twelfth by entrepreneurs, only fifth by citizens), and the mass media (ranked twenty-second by entrepreneurs, seventeenth by citizens). If the agencies covered in our own survey are isolated, there is clearly similarity between the INDEM results and ours. Thus traffic police are seen in both as the most corrupt agency in this isolated group, followed by the regular police and parliamentarians in the INDEM summary.[74] The INDEM summary refers to the presidential administration, rather than just the president; because of this, and because the citizen survey may have been conducted while Yeltsin was still in power, it is not surprising that the INDEM rankings for presidential corruption are higher than ours; nevertheless, they are still toward the lower end.

The POF survey is closer to our own in terms of the classification of agencies. It has fourteen categories; while some, such as conscription stations and trade unions, have no functional equivalents in our survey, and other categories (such as "police, customs, law-enforcement agencies") are more aggregated than our own, there is considerable comparability. Another advantage of the POF findings is that they are time-series data; at the time of writing, results from three surveys were publicly available (July 1998, March 1999, and January 2002). One of the most obvious results from the three POF surveys is that the assessment of different groups is remarkably stable over the three-and-a-half-year period. Thus the "police, customs, and law-enforcement agencies" are consistently ranked the most corrupt of fourteen agencies (chosen by 55 percent of respondents in January 2002), followed by "the courts, prosecutors' offices" (37 percent) and "traffic police" (36 percent). The group ranked as the fourth-most corrupt in 2002, at 34 percent of responses, is "supreme federal power," a category too broad to permit direct comparison with our own findings.[75] But at the other end of the spectrum, the military ("army") is considered the least corrupt of the state organs, named in only 6 percent of responses (all data from Public Opinion Foundation 2002).[76] In short, to the extent that the INDEM and

TABLE 4.5. Officers and Agencies Perceived as Least and Most Corrupt, 2000

	Bulgaria	Hungary	Poland	Russia
President	1	1	1	1
Prime minister	3	2	3	2
Ministers	11	3		4 (tie)
Members of parliament	13		11	
Local elected representatives	5	11	14	
Ministerial staff				
Local council officials		12	12	11
Traffic police officers	14	15	13 ·	15
Regular police officers	12	14		14
Customs and border guards	15	13	15	13
Judges		4		
Members of the state procuracy		5		12
Military officers	2		2	
Ambassadors	4		4	3
University rectors			5	4 (tie)

Notes: Higher numbers indicate greater perceived corruption. Table excludes categories ranked 6 through 10. "Other" responses were too infrequent to be statistically significant.

POF survey results can be compared with our own, there appears to be a high degree of compatibility. Table 4.5 summarizes some of the salient data from our four countries in terms of which groups or offices are seen as most and least corrupt.

As noted earlier in the chapter, the World Bank has conducted a number of surveys on corruption in individual post-communist states. The categorization of public offices in these surveys differs not only from our own, but also from each other and from other World Bank surveys. On the other hand, it is worth maximizing comparison within these constraints. Tables 4.6 and 4.7 represent an attempt at such a maximization; for the sake of comparison with our own findings, the World Bank data have been reworked to conform to our fifteen categories. The method used is as follows.

The total list of categories for each country (including many not covered in our surveys, such as the mass media, schools, airlines, and

TABLE 4.6. Citizens' Perceptions of the Level of Corruption in Various Public Offices and Agencies in Seven Post-communist States, According to World Bank Surveys

	Bosnia-Hercegovina 2000	Georgia 1998
President[a]	M	
Prime minister[b]		
Ministers	M	
Members of parliament	M	
Local elected representatives		M
Ministerial staff		
Local council officials	H	M
Traffic police		H
Regular police[c]	M	H
Customs and border guards	H	H
Judges[d]	H	H
Members of state procuracy		
Military	L	
Ambassadors[e]		
University rectors[f]		

H = high, M = medium, L = low.

[a] Or presidential administration.

[b] Or prime minister's administration.

[c] Where "police" is not disaggregated into "regular" and "traffic" police, the ranking has been attributed to the regular police, and the assumption made that this includes the traffic police.

[d] Or courts; not clear whether this category includes members of the procuracy.

[e] Ambassadors not included in the World Bank surveys.

Kazakhstan 2001	Kyrgyzstan 2001	Latvia 1998	Romania 2000	Slovakia 1999
M	H		M	L
	H			
H			H	M
H	H		H	M
	M	M	M	M
H	H		H	H
M	M	M	M	M
		H		
H	H	H	H	H
		H	H	H
H	H	H	H	H
		H		
			L	L

ᶠ University rectors not included in the World Bank surveys (educational institutions often are included, but this is too broad a category for our purposes).

Notes: Some data on public perceptions of corruption are also included in a World Bank survey of public sector reforms in Armenia (see Armenian Democratic Forum 2001); however, these do not lend themselves to the exercise engaged in here.

Sources: Shkaratan 2001, 43; Anderson et al. 2000, 6; Anderson and Mukherjee 2002, x; Anderson 2002, 71; Anderson 1998, 12; Anderson et al. 2001, 5; Anderson 2000, 8.

TABLE 4.7. Combined Results of the World Bank and Holmes Surveys of Public Perceptions of the Level of Corruption in Various Public Offices and Agencies in Eleven Post-communist States

	Bosnia-Hercegovina 2000	Georgia 1998	Kazakhstan 2001	Kyrgyzstan 2001
President[a]	M		M	H
Prime minister[b]				H
Ministers	M		H	
Members of parliament	M		H	H
Local elected representatives		M		M
Ministerial staff			H	H
Local council officials	H	M	M	M
Traffic police		H		
Regular police[c]	M	H	H	H
Customs and border guards	H	H		
Judges[d]	H	H	H	H
Members of state procuracy				
Military	L			
Ambassadors[e]				
University rectors[f]				

H = high, M = medium, L = low.

[a] Or presidential administration.

[b] Or prime minister's administration.

[c] Where "police" is not disaggregated into "regular" and "traffic" police, the ranking has been attributed to the regular police, and the assumption made that this includes the traffic police.

[d] Or courts; not clear whether this category includes members of the procuracy.

[e] Ambassadors not included in the World Bank surveys.

[f] University rectors not included in the World Bank surveys (educational institutions often are included, but this is too broad a category for our purposes).

Note: For the last four columns, the valid responses to the question concerning which were perceived to be the most corrupt groups (here meaning responses excluding "don't know" and "other") were rank-ordered 1 to 15, because there are 15 types of office; the top 5 were ranked high, the next five medium, and the last five low.

It is important to note that the method used for determining least and medium in these last four columns is slightly different in this table from that used in table 4.5, which has

Latvia 1998	Romania 2000	Slovakia 1999	Bulgaria 2000	Hungary 2000	Poland 2000	Russia 2000
	M	L	L	L	L	L
			L	L	L	L
	H	M	H	L	M	L
	H	M	H	M	H	M
M	M	M	M	H	H	L
	H	H	M	M	M	M
M	M	M	M	H	H	H
H			H	H	H	H
H	H	H	H	H	M	H
H	H	H	H	H	H	H
H	H	H	M	M	M	M
H			M	M	M	H
	L	L	L	M	L	M
			L	L	L	L
			L	L	L	M

produced marginally different results; while this table rank-orders "most corrupt" only, table 4.5 uses the "most corrupt" responses to provide the higher numbers, and the "least corrupt" (plus "not corrupt" in the cases of Bulgaria and Hungary) to produce the lower rankings. This is why the medium cells were left blank in table 4.5; otherwise, it would have been necessary to produce two tables — one rank-ordering the "most corrupt" responses, the other the "least corrupt" — which would have rendered this exercise cumbersome and confusing. But a drawback of the method used in tables 4.5, 4.6, and 4.8 pertains here too, namely that the difference between agencies ranked at the bottom of one category and the top of the next can be marginal, while those between two offices within a given category can be much greater. Unfortunately, no method of presenting the rankings is without drawbacks.

Sources: Shkaratan 2001, 43; Anderson et al. 2000, 6; Anderson and Mukherjee 2002, x; Anderson 2002, 71; Anderson 1998, 12; Anderson et al. 2001, 5; Anderson 2000, 8; own surveys (last four columns).

utilities) has been divided into three, according to perceived level of corruption. Those offices or agencies perceived to be the most corrupt are ranked H; those in the middle are ranked M; and those in the bottom third are ranked L. In addition to the problem of classification identified in the middle of the preceding paragraph, another potential drawback is that the term "low" represented by "L" could be misleading: it must constantly be borne in mind that the categories are relative, and some agencies with an "L" rating would appear to have high levels of corruption in comparison with equivalent organizations in other countries. But it is emphasized throughout this chapter that none of the data should be fetishized: they are useful primarily for creating impressions, and to help better understand perceptions. Empty cells are those for which there are no discrete results. Once all agencies and offices were ranked, those more or less corresponding to the ones used in our own surveys were isolated, and their rankings inserted into the appropriate cells. It is because the fifteen offices and agencies in all cases constitute only a subset of the total list for each country that the distribution between H, M, and L is uneven in table 4.6; most of the Ls are to be found in those agencies not covered in our own survey and hence not included here.

The results of the World Bank surveys and our own — the latter presented in a different format to render them more directly comparable to the World Bank results — can now be combined in table 4.7. What emerges clearly from this exercise is that the police, together with customs and the border guards, are widely perceived as the most corrupt institutions; the police emerged worst of all, since they were rated highly corrupt in nine of the eleven countries surveyed, and fairly corrupt in the other two. Unlike our own surveys, most of the World Bank surveys have been administered to three groups: citizens, entrepreneurs, and public officials.[77] Because of space limitations, and because we have already considered some of the perceptions of the entrepreneurs elsewhere in this chapter, only the perceptions of officials will be summarized here.

Although our focus has been on four post-communist states, and to a lesser extent seven CEE and CIS countries surveyed by the World Bank, there is by now a considerable amount of additional survey data on the groups and officials that citizens in CEE and CIS countries believe are most prone to corruption. The GfK survey (2001, 8) reveals that when one averages across the ten countries surveyed on this variable, the health services were considered the most corrupt, followed in order by "red tape" (offices and bureaus), courts of law, customs officers, police, ministries, and the military.[78]

As indicated in chapter 1, it proved impossible to conduct our own surveys in China. Although there are still very few publicly available Chinese survey data on corruption, one published survey relevant to our purposes was conducted in 2001.[79] In this survey 121 local officials in Yunnan Province, surveyed in March, and 77 enterprise managers in Zhejiang Province, surveyed in April, were invited to rank twelve types of "official" in terms of their perceived level of corruption. Several of the categories, such as market managers and officials in the transportation system, do not correspond to any of those we have focused on for the CEE and CIS countries. But four do, and it is worth noting the results here. In table 4.9 only types of official identified elsewhere in this book as relevant to our methodology have been included, to maximize cross-polity comparability. This explains why there are only four rows, but the numerical rankings are on a scale of 1 to 12; to facilitate direct comparisons with table 4.8 (because this one is based on officials' and entrepreneurs' assessments, not the public's), the rankings have also been presented in terms of high, medium, and low levels of perceived corruption.

Comparing the various findings on CEE, the CIS, and China, and even allowing for the incompleteness, incompatibilities, and general softness of our data sets, it is incontrovertible that corruption among police officers, customs officials, and officers of the court is perceived as a serious problem in several states. Many citizens can no longer trust the state agencies upon which, in various ways, they should be able to depend for their protection and justice. This lack of trust unquestionably hinders the legitimation process of post-communist states, especially the need to create rule-of-law societies.[80] Conversely, this tendency is partly counteracted by the finding that presidents and prime ministers emerge as almost squeaky clean in all four of the CEE and CIS countries that are the focus of this book (though not in all the states surveyed by the World Bank, particularly Kyrgyzstan); at least the people at the very top of the system are widely perceived in some post-communist states to be above the enticements of corruption.[81] Yet it is of concern for those interested in the democratization project that parliamentarians are not seen as among the more trustworthy agents of the state — and indeed are ranked one of the least trustworthy groups by Bulgarians, Kazakhs, Kyrgyz, and Romanians.

TABLE 4.8. Public Officials' Perceptions of the Level of Corruption in Various Public Offices and Agencies in Seven Post-communist States, According to World Bank Surveys

	Bosnia-Hercegovina 2000	Georgia 1998
President[a]	H	L
Prime minister[b]		
Ministers	M	
Members of parliament	M	M
Local elected representatives		
Ministerial staff		M
Local council officials	H	M
Traffic police		H
Regular police[c]	L	H
Customs and border guards	H	H
Judges[d]	M	H
Members of state procuracy		
Military	L	
Ambassadors[e]		
University rectors[f]		

Notes: H = high, M = medium, L = low.

[a] Or presidential administration.

[b] Or prime minister's administration.

[c] Where "police" is not disaggregated into "regular" and "traffic" police, the ranking has been attributed to the regular police, and the assumption made that this includes the traffic police.

[d] Or courts; not clear whether this category includes members of the procuracy.

[e] Ambassadors not included in the World Bank surveys.

[f] University rectors not included in the World Bank surveys (educational institutions often are included, but this is too broad a category for our purposes).

Kazakhstan 2001	Kyrgyzstan 2001	Latvia 1998	Romania 2000	Slovakia 1999
L	H	L		L
	M			
		M	M	
M	H	H	M	
M	M	M	M	L
M	M	M	M	H
M	L	M	M	L
		H		
H	H	H	H	H
H	H	H	H	H
H	H	M	H	H
			L	L

Note: The World Bank reports on Georgia and Latvia provide household and enterprise perceptions of the level of corruption in identified groups of officials (agencies), but no directly comparable data on public officials' perceptions. For this reason, the data on public officials' "Ratings for Honesty and Integrity" that follow the data on household and enterprise perceptions of corruption in the World Bank documents have been used.

Sources: Shkaratan 2001, 43; Anderson et al. 2000, 7; Anderson and Mukherjee 2002, x; Anderson 2002, 71; Anderson 1998, 14; Anderson et al. 2001, 5; Anderson 2000, 8.

TABLE 4.9. Officers and Agencies Perceived as Least and Most Corrupt in China, 2002

	Local Government Officials' Ranking	Managers' Ranking	Local Government Officials' Ranking	Managers' Ranking
Customs	11	11	H	H
Judicial	9	8	H	M
Political leaders and officials in leading positions	5	7	M	M
Supervision and party discipline system	1	1	L	L

Note: Higher numbers indicate greater perceived corruption (12 = top of scale).

Source: Based on Yong Guo and Angang Hu 2002, table 4. (A very similar article was subsequently published but—interestingly—did not include these survey data; see Yong Guo and Angang Hu 2004.)

It would be unjustified to draw definitive causal inferences from a comparison of public perceptions and official responses. For instance, citizens may believe that a given group is particularly prone to corruption mainly because the government has taken actions suggesting that the group in question is unusually susceptible. Ultimately this is a sequencing (chicken-and-egg) question. Yet the tendency of so many citizens, entrepreneurs, and others to include in the most corrupt categories groups with which they come into most frequent and direct contact suggests that there is some correlation between perceptions and experiences, and hence between perceptions and reality.[82]

Direct Experiences

As already indicated, the World Bank conducted household surveys of experiences of corruption in Georgia and Latvia in 1998 (Kaufmann, Pradhan, and Ryterman 1998; Kaufmann, Pradhan, and Ryterman 1999), Slovakia in 1999, Bosnia-Hercegovina and Romania in 2000, and Kazakhstan and Kyrgyzstan in 2001.[83] One finding was that the officials to whom relevant citizens in the majority of these countries most frequently paid bribes were the traffic police;[84] in Georgia respondents indicated that they were expected to pay these officers seven out of ten times that they came into contact with them (Anderson 1998, 43; Anderson 2000, 16; Anderson, Cosmaciuc, Dininio, Spector, and Zoido-Lobaton 2000, 1:5–6; Anderson 2002, 4–5; Anderson and Mukherjee 2002, xii).[85] While the situation was better in Latvia, even there the figure was three times out of ten (Anderson 1998, 43); in Slovakia, almost 40 percent of car-owning citizens had paid a bribe to a traffic officer, while car-owning entrepreneurs revealed that they paid bribes at one in four such encounters (Anderson 2000, 16, 36–37).[86] In some countries more than 40 percent of citizens had encountered bribery during the previous twelve months (see for example Anderson, Cosmaciuc, Dininio, Spector, and Zoido-Lobaton 2001, viii; Anderson 2002, 15), although that figure is partly based on experience with agencies excluded from our analysis (such as health services). Even allowing for this distinction, it is clear that a large number of citizens had had direct experience of bribery in the court system, customs, and local councils.[87]

At the beginning of this chapter it was explained why no one can be certain of the scale of corruption in any country. This difficulty has led some long-term analysts of corruption to argue in their recent work that we should move away from attempts to produce overall classifications or rankings of corruption levels in individual countries, and instead focus on the level and types of corruption in individual agencies in individual countries, demonstrating how this is increasing or decreasing (Gray, Hellman, and Ryterman 2004, 6, 50). But many of the problems of measurement pertain at the micro-level as much as at the macro-level, so that even if a more targeted approach were really desirable, it would not necessarily be any better. Moreover, it is usually the general image of a country that attracts or discourages investors. Therefore if it is ac- cepted that corruption matters — and this entire book is based on such an assumption — then for all their methodological and hence epistemo- logical drawbacks, the various techniques and results discussed in this chapter are useful. Three golden rules apply in using them, however.

First, the data should never be fetishized. With the partial exception of official legal statistics — which may in many cases be more or less accu- rate, but provide an extremely incomplete picture of corruption — the data reproduced here are ultimately soft and patchy. The perception data are softer than the experiential data, but even the latter provide only partial snapshots of the overall corruption picture and are — as Kauf- mann, Kraay, and Mastruzzi (2003, 19) point out — to some extent subjective and perceptual themselves.[88] The results will also vary from time to time according to recent scandals or lack of them. But if the overall picture is of concern, this is what ultimately matters. And the various methods indicate that the general picture *is* of concern.

Second, the results generated by various methods should be compared and even combined whenever possible, if the ultimate aim is to seek an understanding of which countries and groups are more corrupt and which are less. Specialists on surveys, for instance, sometimes advocate "triangulation," here meaning that a more accurate picture of actual corruption is likely to be formed by comparing and combining the results of three types of survey — surveys of households, firms, and public offi- cials (see for example Kaufmann and Recanatini 2001, 10).[89] Others have gone further and proposed multiangular analysis and validation, which combines several methods of data collection (see for example Reinikka and Svensson 2003, 2; Lindelow 2003, 4). The point of triangulated and multiangular data collection and comparative analysis, and of other attempts to form as accurate a picture as possible, is not merely scholastic, but designed to assist in tailoring strategies appropriate to a particular time and place.

The third rule might initially appear contradictory in light of the first, which essentially constitutes a warning and could be seen as dismissive of the data. This is that the data should *not* be dismissed. Some analysts, such as the Hungarian legal specialist András Sajó, have in essence claimed that observers from outside CEE have largely created the "problem" of corruption through their own ethnocentric definitions and value judgments. He writes: "That the public's understanding of corruption is warped by Western categories does not mean that no corruption exists in Eastern Europe, only that how it is perceived is not always the result of genuine endogenous factors. Were it not for the drumbeat of external criticism, corruption would not be construed as an acute social problem, at least not in East Central Europe" (Sajó 1998, 37; repeated in Sajó 2002, 1).[90] In some cases, governments of countries that have fared poorly in the TI CPI and World Bank assessments have retaliated, either questioning the right of outsiders to evaluate their countries or rejecting the findings as inaccurate and biased. A report by the World Bank in 2000 ranked Azerbaijan the most corrupt of all postcommunist states — in line with many CPIs — and assessed the value of corruption-related activity in the country in 2000 at $1.4 billion. The reaction of the Azeri government was to dismiss the World Bank assessment as seriously flawed; in November 2000 the Azeri deputy finance minister retorted that the estimate was ridiculous, and that the real figure was closer to $100 million (RFE/RL, 20 November 2000).

While one might sympathize to some extent with Sajó's position, and with countries whose governments are accused of being particularly corrupt, it is indefensible to accept corruption, to see it as in some sense normal.[91] To do so can amount to acceptance of unjust inequalities[92] and the absence of the rule of law. And where there is élite legitimation of unjust inequalities, and scant regard for the rule of law, there is indifference toward democracy and hence at least implicit acceptance of tyranny. The motives of indigenous élites who dismiss criticisms of corruption within their countries must be questioned.[93]

But there is no need to mount moralistic objections to this kind of argument: universalist conceptions of morality are not only questionable but also currently unfashionable as a basis for academic argument. In an era in which rational choice and *homo economicus* thinking has tended to dominate in the Anglo-Celtic western world — and increasingly in the West as a whole — a more persuasive argument against defending or downplaying corruption is that it discourages investment and thus economic growth and development.[94] While it is difficult to prove this beyond any doubt — just as it is difficult to prove definitively that smoking causes cancer, or that global warming is a function of human activity — the circumstantial evidence is overwhelming (see chapter 5).

By this stage it will be obvious that assessing the scale of corruption in any country is difficult not merely from a technical point of view. Assessments are also a highly political activity, and it is crucial to be aware of this. But it is also important for those in CEE who dismiss or attack outsiders' efforts to measure corruption to acknowledge their own subjectivities and two important facts.[95] The first is that at least part of the reason why outsiders create an impression of a country is what its own citizens believe and tell others. These citizens' impressions are created partly — in many countries primarily — by their own media, which often play an irresponsible role by reporting allegations that have been inadequately researched and often prove groundless or untestable; examples were provided in chapter 3.

The second point develops from the first. Perceived high levels of corruption can deter investment in a country, which in turn is likely to render economic growth and development more difficult and increase poverty. Moreover, if the recent findings of Przeworski and Limongi (1997; see too Przeworski, Alvarez, Cheibub, and Limongi 2000) are correct — that while lower levels of economic development and per capita income do not necessarily make it less likely that a country will attempt to democratize, they do make it more difficult to sustain and consolidate democracy — then the potentially serious consequential effects of corruption on governance come sharply into focus. The onus is on those who believe that the problem of corruption in their country is exaggerated to demonstrate empirically that they are correct. Otherwise, their cynicism and rejection of dominant views could be interpreted as contributing to their countries' economic — and hence social and political — problems.

This all said, and even though professional differences are sometimes exaggerated, it is of concern that specialists working together, after years of refining their measurement methods, sometimes still cannot agree on whether corruption in post-communist states is improving or deteriorating (Kaufmann, Kraay, and Mastruzzi 2003, 31–32; Gray, Hellman, and Ryterman 2004, 45 n. 22).[96] Clearly much work remains to be done in the field of corruption measurement.

CHAPTER 5

The Impact of Corruption

The significance of corruption, and the likelihood that it will seriously undermine the state, varies from one country to the next. It is not possible to measure this significance with any precision. For instance, it is likely that the now relatively freer mass media in several countries exaggerate the extent of corruption, both to boost sales and because of partisan politics.[1] This might in turn imply that the impact of corruption is exaggerated. Conversely, in countries where corruption does not appear to analysts to be a major problem — perhaps because it is so well hidden — it is often perceived as such by citizens, and hence is of significance in numerous ways. Thus, despite severe problems of measurement, the ways in which corruption can make an impact can be identified. They are analyzed here in six categories: effects on individuals, environmental impact, economic impact, social impact, international impact, and political effects, including effects on legitimacy.

EFFECTS ON INDIVIDUALS

Corruption can directly affect the safety, well-being, and reputation of individuals in numerous ways. The two main ones pertain to those investigating it, and those who suffer because of accidents and other incidents arising from it. It is also worth considering the impact that corruption has on those involved in or accused of it.

Investigators and Reporters

Corruption can be literally a matter of life and death for both officials and ordinary citizens. Many have been murdered as a result of their involvement in or investigations into both organized crime and corruption. The editor of *Slava Sevastopola* in Ukraine, Vladimir Ivanov, was blown up in April 1995 after his newspaper published a series of articles on organized crime that included information on corruption. The Lithuanian journalist Vitas Lingys was shot to death in October 1993 after publishing a number of articles on organized crime in his country in the newspaper *Respublika*; although it was a local gangster, Boris Dekanidze, who was eventually sentenced to death for Lingys's murder, the dead journalist's own newspaper publicly stated on numerous occasions that his murder was the result of orders issued by "criminal structures and corrupt political forces" (*European*, 2–8 December 1994). There was widespread condemnation in Russia of the killers of Dmitrii Kholodov, journalist for *Moskovskii Komsomolets*, who was murdered in October 1994 while investigating corruption in the Russian military. He was blown up shortly before he was due to appear before a committee of the Duma at which he was to have made allegations against very senior officers, including the defense minister himself, General Pavel Grachev.[2] The murder of a journalist with *Novaya Gazeta* in 2001 was seen by many as linked to his exposé of corruption in the Kremlin (*EECR* 10, no. 1:36).[3] The newspaper *Novye Izvestiya* speculated that the assassination of the popular Russian parliamentarian Galina Starovoitova in St. Petersburg in November 1998 was linked to her campaign against organized crime and corruption (Whitmore 1999).[4] And the assassination of the mayor of Taganrog (Russia) in October 2002 has been linked to his anticorruption campaign.

Moving beyond the former Soviet Union, there have been allegations that journalists and researchers investigating so-called nomenklatura privatization in the former GDR may have been injured or even killed because of their "snooping" (J. Roth 1997, 191). In 1998 Jan Szul was appointed head of the leading Czech agency for combating corruption (the Council for the Protection of the Economic Interests of the Czech Republic), but resigned after just a few days because, according to the media, death threats were made against him and his family (Fuszara 1999, 8). And it is generally accepted that Bulgaria's last prime minister of the communist era, Andrey Lukanov, was assassinated in October 1996 partly in connection with his inquiries into corruption and organized crime.

At a less extreme level, journalists can be imprisoned apparently for investigating and reporting on corruption. Many believe this is why the

Xinhua journalist Gao Qinrong was arrested in December 1998 and sentenced in 1999 to thirteen years' imprisonment: he had reported on a major irrigation scam in Shanxi province that had embarrassed many local CCP officials (*Asiaweek* 26, no. 32). Less extreme still, investigative journalists can lose their jobs for probing too deeply into corruption allegations,[5] or seek asylum on the basis of threats received because of their investigations, as the Bulgarian journalist Eleonora Gountcheva did in 1997 (*RFE/RL*, 18 December 1997).

Losses Ultimately Arising from Corruption

Even ordinary citizens can be threatened by the ramifications of organized crime and, by implication (given their often close links), corruption. According to Viktor Ilyukhin, chairman of the Duma's Security Committee, the two bombs that exploded in Moscow in July 1996, injuring thirty-three people, were planted by organized-crime figures, allegedly in response to the decrees issued by the newly appointed national security advisor Aleksandr Lebed' and Mayor Yurii Luzhkov on fighting crime in Moscow (*OMRI DD*, 12 July 1996). The Russian prosecutor general Vladimir Ustinov claimed in September 2004 that the bombers who brought down two Russian airliners in August, killing ninety people, had paid (very small) bribes to an airline official to obtain their tickets (*MosNews.com*, 15 September 2004, visited September 2004).

While neither of these cases is strictly corruption in the way the term is used in this book, the overlap with it and the danger to citizens are clear.[6] But clearcut corruption appears to have been involved in the terrorist attacks on a school in Beslan (North Ossetia, southern Russia) in September 2004 in which approximately 330 people died — many of them children. Indeed, Ustinov acknowledged that the state's ability to prevent similar attacks in the future was unlikely to be as great as it should be because of widespread corruption in the police and military. Corruption was helping terrorists in two ways. First, they could pay bribes to acquire weapons and pass security checks. A survey in September 2004 by Yurii Levada's new independent survey company suggested that more than half the respondents blamed the Beslan tragedy on corrupt security officers (*Guardian Unlimited* online, 17 September 2004, visited September 2004). Second, support for the terrorists in the southern parts of Russia could grow because, according to Putin's advisor on Chechnya, corruption was preventing up to 80 percent of the state funding intended to improve the lot of the poor in those areas from reaching those for whom it was meant.

A very different way in which people may suffer physically because of corruption is that they can be injured or killed when substandard buildings, bridges, or other structures collapse. An example is the death of forty Chinese citizens in Chongqing municipality (Sichuan) in 1998 as a result of the collapse of a bridge; in January 1999 five senior officials were charged with corruption relating to this incident. The most serious punishments meted out in connection with the case were a death sentence (suspended for two years) for the former deputy secretary of Qijiang County Party Committee, for accepting bribes relating to the construction of the bridge, and life imprisonment for another senior official (*Transparency International Newsletter Corruption Reports*, June 1999; *CD*, 7 July 1999; *BR* 43, no. 21:14).

The psychological effects on citizens who lose their homes or life savings because of corruption can be profound. Much of the violent mass unrest in Albania in early 1997 was triggered by a failed pyramid scheme that many believed was related to the corruption of various government officials (*EECR* 6, no. 1:2–5). In 1987 some fifteen thousand people were left homeless in the village of Xilinji (China) because of a forest fire that destroyed their homes; it appears that many of the 3,600 houses lost might have been saved had it not been for the corrupt actions of the deputy director of the firefighting section of the Mohe County Public Security Bureau, who put protection of his own interests before those of the villagers (*CD*, 16 July 1987, and *BR* 31, no. 27:7). Finally, although the implications are less dramatic than in the cases just cited, a much larger number of ordinary Chinese citizens have been subjected to water rationing in recent years because of corruption relating to water projects (*International Herald Tribune*, 2 October 2000).

Allegations, Crimes, and Punishments

Corruption can also matter to people found guilty of it, in terms of fines and prison sentences; examples were cited in chapter 3. But even allegations or investigations can be more than some officials can handle. Thus the former president of the Georgian National Bank, Demur Dvalishvili, is alleged to have committed suicide in September 1994 at the

Georgian interior ministry, where he had been called to give evidence before a commission charged with investigating corruption (Anjaparidze 2001; RFE/RL, 29 July 2002). Another example is that of the deputy mayor of Beijing, Wang Baosen, who committed suicide in April 1995, apparently to avoid charges of serious corruption. In fact this has become a major phenomenon in China: according to the newspaper *Wen Wei Po* (Hong Kong), 1,252 Chinese officials committed suicide in 2003 because of investigations into corruption and abuse of power (*cbsnews online*, 30 January 2004).

Reactions and implications are not always so dramatic, but still serious. One not uncommon scenario is for a public figure against whom allegations have been made to resign before his or her case has been properly investigated. In this scenario, a public official is essentially being punished by feeling pressured to resign from office, and might suffer from the effects of public shaming even if not required to face the courts. What appeared to many to be an example of such a preemptive resignation is that of a former Czech chief public prosecutor, who resigned in September 1993 after he had been accused of improperly using his office to obtain housing privileges in Prague (*Keesings Record of World Events* 39, no. 9:39657). Yet another exit path adopted by some officials is to flee the country. In addition to several examples cited in chapter 3, it can be noted that according to a source based in Hong Kong, more than eight thousand Chinese officials fled the PRC in the first half of 2003 alone to avoid auditing and other kinds of corruption-related investigations (*cbsnews online*, 30 January 2004).

Finally, there are the potential vicarious effects of corruption allegations. Sometimes, politicians whose own reputations have not been sullied can be affected by allegations against their colleagues. A prime example is the Latvian prime minister Andris Šķēle (see chapter 3). Perhaps even more common are cases in which senior officials are forced or feel obliged to resign because of widespread corruption in the agencies that they head. Thus the Russian minister for foreign economic relations was allegedly pressured to resign in August 1993 because of widespread corruption in his ministry, while the Polish minister of justice resigned in March that year amid criticisms that he was too ineffectual in dealing with major corruption scandals.

Another form of vicarious impact occurs when allegations of corruption are made against officials in one country mainly, it appears, because

of attempts to sully the reputation of officials in another country. An example is the investigation in 1995 into the role of the former Lithuanian
defense minister, Audrius Butkevičius, in the building of housing units in
Kaliningrad for Russian troops withdrawing from Lithuania. According
to Butkevičius, the Lithuanian investigation was "a plot by certain political groups in Russia, who were seeking to undermine Russian Defence
Minister Pavel Grachev and Vladimir Shumeiko, the chairman of the
Russian Federation Assembly" (*Baltic Independent*, 21 July 1995).

ENVIRONMENTAL IMPACT

Although this is difficult to measure, there can be no doubt that the
environment in many post-communist states has been suffering as a
result of corruption. Officials often override or ignore environmental
planning guidelines in return for bribes or kickbacks from developers.
They can issue logging permits where this is inappropriate, or simply
disregard illegal logging and the smuggling of timber; this has been a
major problem in Siberia and the Russian Far East (*Johnson's Russia List*
8310, 2 August 2004). In other parts of the world (such as Bangladesh),
logging-related corruption has been a major factor in severe flooding
and, as a result, the loss of both lives and housing.[7] Since communist
states in general bequeathed a terrible environmental legacy (see for
example DeBardeleben 1991; Pryde 1991; Jancar-Webster ed. 1993; Carter and Turnock eds. 1996), anything that worsens the situation further
is a serious problem.[8] Some analysts have argued that environmental
conditions have even deterioriated in certain sectors since the collapse of
communism, as a direct result of corruption. Feiler (2002), for example,
cites a number of Romanian environmentalist NGOs that make such a
claim with respect to the administration of Romanian forests.

ECONOMIC IMPACT

It is impossible — and certainly beyond the capacity of this analyst! — to
determine with any precision how much economic effect corruption ex-
erts.[9] But if corruption is perceived to be significant in this way, then it *is*
significant: according to Frye (1998), "corruption has recently emerged

as perhaps the most important obstacle to economic reform [in post-communist states]," suggesting how significant some analysts perceive its economic impact to be.

There is no shortage of guesstimates as to the size of what are variously called the "shadow," "black," or "underground" economies of individual states.[10] Some of these are based on serious and sophisticated attempts at measurement, whereas others appear to have been virtually plucked out of the air by politicians and others whose principal aim is to highlight a real enough problem by sensationalizing its scale, rather than seek objectivity or accuracy. For our purposes, there is the additional problem that a great deal of what is covered by concepts such as the "shadow" and "black" economies has little or no direct relationship to corruption: much refers to the activities of organized crime, but the terms also cover petty crime and — of major significance throughout the post-communist world — the avoidance of tax payment. Thus guesstimates of the scale of the unreported economy have only tangential relevance to this book. Nevertheless, it is reasonable to infer that there is some connection between shadow economies and corruption. The increase of one may set the scene for, as well as reflect, an increase in the other; the two cultures often interact. Hence, while it is prudent to emphasize both the flimsy nature of most such assessments and the limited relationship between them and attempts to estimate the economic impact of corruption, brief consideration of some of the published figures is appropriate.

According to Zhilin (1995, 9), "the amount of 'shadow capital' in circulation in [Russia in late 1994] is roughly equivalent to that of legal government funds." A more recent estimate, by the Moscow office of the World Bank, was that 40–50 percent of the Russian economy was not reported in official statistics in 2002 (RFE/RL Newsline, 12 November 2002). Estimates of the size of the shadow economy in most other post-communist states tend to vary between 20 and 50 percent, depending on the country and the analyst.[11] For instance, Tsyganov (1996, 3) cites an estimate that 27 percent of the Chinese economy was by the mid-1990s in the "black market," though he also mentions that according to "some Western experts" the figure had already surpassed 50 percent. A more recent and conservative estimate is that of Hu Angang. He bases his calculations on what he calls four major types of corruption — rent seeking, the underground economy, tax evasion, and corruption in government investments and public expenditure — and argues that between them, they accounted for economic losses to the Chinese state of between 13.3 percent and 16.9 percent of GDP in the late 1990s (Hu Angang 2002, 44). Because the underground economy is only one of four related categories in this calculation, it is clear that Hu's assessment of its size is considerably lower than those of the narrower black market cited by Tsyganov. But because the Chinese economy is so large, even this very conservative estimate represents a considerable amount of economic activity. Even allowing for the very soft nature of all such data, and the fact that some cover all economic crime — not only crime involving officials — and often all undeclared economic activity, whether criminal or not, there can be little doubt that corruption is playing a major role in the economies of several post-communist countries.[12]

The potential impact of such relatively large shadow economies can now be considered. During a visit to Bangkok in May 1997, I had an informal discussion of corruption with a British engineer who worked for a traffic consultancy firm. He was at that time working in Thailand, having moved there from the Philippines, and informed me that corruption in his type of business (large-scale civil engineering projects, particularly highways) was rife in both countries. When pushed to suggest any important differences between the two, he immediately noted his clear impression that many Thai officials used at least some of their ill-gotten gains to invest in the Thai economy, whereas most Filipinos immediately moved their gains offshore.[13] It is not possible to check either the veracity of these allegations or the scale of the movements. But assuming that the distinction does apply in some parts of the world, which is hardly a controversial premise, it is possible that the final destination of corruptly acquired funds can be of major economic significance. Thailand has had a more impressive economic performance than the Philippines in recent years, and it may be that part of the reason is this domestic reinvestment. In the post-communist world, the precise scale on which reinvestment or overseas transfer occurs is similarly unknown. But it is clear that many Russians who have acquired funds through various forms of corruption have transferred these out of the country as soon as possible, rather than invest them in Russia (Tikhomirov 1997; Loungani and Mauro 2001). This is almost certainly an important part of the explanation for Russia's dramatic economic decline until the late 1990s. The problem of capital flight appears to have become less acute after the turn of the century, in part because of meetings between Putin and the so-called oligarchs that are considered in chapter 7. But it had intensified again by 2004 (CDPSP 56, no. 35:15–16), as fear spread that Putin might be intending to renationalize key parts of the economy, and as the solvency of parts of the banking sector was questioned.[14]

Certainly there are many who argue that corruption reduces economic growth and development (for example Murphy, Shleifer, and Vishny 1993; Shleifer and Vishny 1993; with reservations, Bardhan 1997, esp. 1327–30; Shelley 2003). Tanzi and Davoodi (1998) provide considerable evidence to demonstrate that while higher levels of corruption are associated with higher levels of public (state) investment, the productivity of that investment is lower than it would be if there were less corruption (see too Tanzi 2000, 154–70). Gray and Kaufmann (1998, esp. 24–25), citing a survey of global competitiveness conducted in 1997 by the World Economic Forum in fifty-nine countries, cite strong empirical evidence that managers have to spend more time with state officials in countries highly prone to bribery, which reduces efficiency and productivity. Various studies suggest that higher levels of corruption correlate strongly with lower operational expenditure by the state (as distinct from investment by the state). This reduction in expenditure has a negative impact on, for example, educational levels, which in turn hinders development and, apparently, citizens' reporting of corruption. Since poor economic performance increases legitimation problems, and since all post-communist states experienced severe economic problems in the early 1990s and several still do, anything that adds to these problems should be vigorously combated. In short, if corruption does hinder economic growth — and the evidence is strong that it does — then it matters in terms of consolidating the very fragile systems of post-communism.

Another way in which corruption can exert a bad influence on the economy is in permitting monopolization and oligopolization, with all their negative ramifications for the consumer and competition, notably higher prices and reduced choice. Although monopoly is still relatively distant in most parts of the post-communist world — though the dominance of natural resource monopolies such as Gazprom in the Russian economy has been seen by some as reflective of corrupt practices, as well as the legacy of communist monopolization — the constraining effects of the sometimes corrupt *chaebol* (conglomerates) in the South Korean economy have been widely noted (see for example *Business Week: Asian Edition*, 2 September 1996, 18–19; Kim 2002, 182–84). If small and medium-sized business is crowded out because of cartelization by large corporations and organized-crime gangs that succeed in their activities partly because of corruption, it is almost certain that the customer and the economy as a whole will suffer. Anyone who attempted to obtain a restaurant meal in Moscow at a reasonable price before the Russian economic crisis of August 1998 (see Tikhomirov ed. 1999) will be familiar with this problem; many Muscovites used to believe that the reason there were so few restaurants in their city, and that their average prices were so high, was that the so-called mafia were involved (through either direct ownership or demands for protection money).[15]

The theft of intellectual property is also a problem. Relatively lax rules on copyright in many countries, along with connivance by corrupt officials, permit and even encourage the production of imitation products that then undersell the genuine versions, with negative economic consequences for the original manufacturers. The production and sale of pirated tapes and discs — audio and video — in the PRC and Bulgaria (RFE/RL, 21 May 1997), for instance, have been a major problem for Western companies. But this is a two-edged sword. One of the reasons for the prolonged difficulties experienced by the PRC in gaining admission to the World Trade Organization — it was formally granted membership in November 2001, after some fifteen years of attempts — was precisely its inadequate control of media production and sales. Hence the PRC as a state was suffering economically, even as some of its citizens and officials benefited from the sales of imitation software and other products (Tsyganov 1996, 4–5).

From an economic perspective, one of the principal losers where there are high levels of corruption is the state itself, particularly in terms of reduced revenue. A major reason for the Russian government's difficulties under Yeltsin in reversing the decline of the economy was that the state had insufficient funds to implement necessary changes. Part of the explanation for this shortage was the severe problems experienced by the federal authorities in collecting taxes — from citizens, businesses, and the regional authorities. So serious did the problem become that in the view of one commentator this inability to raise taxes was by the late 1990s "rapidly becoming the greatest threat to economic and political stability" in Russia (Treisman 1998, 55).

Discouragement of Foreign Investment, Loans, and Trade

Corruption levels matter in terms of foreign perception. If businesspeople and international finance organizations (such as the IMF and the European Bank for Reconstruction and Development) lose confidence in a country because of perceived high levels of corruption, then they typically invest less or even refuse to provide loans. Paalo Mauro (1995) demonstrates fairly conclusively, on the basis of data gathered from almost seventy countries in the early 1980s, that investment levels in countries with high levels of corruption are up to 5 percent lower than in other countries, and that this reduced investment in turn lowers economic growth. More recent evidence is provided by a report published by the Control Risks Group in October 2002. According to that report, a survey of companies in Germany, Hong Kong, the Netherlands, Singapore, the United Kingdom, and the United States revealed that nearly 40 percent had decided not to invest in countries reputed to have high levels of corruption (TI Q, December 2002, 4). And in a survey in 2005 of 158 foreign companies either already operating in Russia or contemplating doing so, 71 percent identified corruption as the principal barrier to investment (*Moscow Times*, 5 March 2005).

The relevance of these general observations can now be considered vis-à-vis the post-communist world. While it is impossible to measure the impact of the FOZZ scandal of the early 1990s in Poland (see chapter 3), there can be little doubt that it had negative implications for Poland's standing among potential foreign investors. The economic and ultimately political implications are obvious. In this context it is worth recalling the CPIs discussed in chapter 4. While the tables are ultimately based on subjective judgements, perceptions are by definition largely subjective anyway — so that it does matter, in terms of investment decisions for example, how corrupt a particular country is believed to be.

While some appear unwilling to accept this,[16] many post-communist officials are aware that their country's reputation in terms of corruption is important to potential investors and official agencies in other countries, and that there are other bodies examining their business practices. For example, a survey by the World Bank in 1995 of foreign businesspeople engaged in economic activity with Lithuania revealed that approximately 90 percent indicated an unwillingness to invest any more in the country unless corruption was brought under control (Girnius

1995). And an article in the Latvian newspaper *Diena* in 1997 leaked the findings of a European Union report in which it was claimed that there was widespread corruption in the Latvian government.[17] The chairman of the Latvian parliament's European Affairs Committee, Edvins Inkens, downplayed the report by claiming that it was both exaggerated and somewhat outdated, in that it was designed particularly to encourage the Latvians to engage in a customs reform that was now under way. He saw it as partly the "work of forces trying to stop Latvia's EU integration." Nevertheless, he also acknowledged that news of the report was "unpleasant," and confirmed that his committee would draft a law on customs tariffs (*Baltic Times*, 9–15 January 1997). This case illustrates well that post-communist countries wishing to join western clubs such as the European Union have to play by those clubs' rules.

It is not merely the general perception of a country that has a negative impact on foreign investment and loans. Sometimes particular cases of corruption cause a major stir, with tangible secondary effects. In one of the most widely reported corruption scandals of 1999, it was alleged that a number of Russians — not only members of organized-crime gangs, but also senior officials — had been involved in laundering more than $15 billion worth of Russian funds through the Bank of New York. It was of particular concern that much of the money might have been IMF funds, which were intended for use in assisting the development of the Russian economy. Because of this scandal, the secretary of the U.S. Treasury, Lawrence Summers, indicated that IMF funds to Russia might be withheld until the situation was clarified (*Business Central Europe* 6, no. 65:13).[18]

Trade relations can also be negatively affected by corruption. In late 1997, for example, the Bulgarian and Ukrainian chambers of commerce urged their governments to end extortion by customs officers, which they claimed was a major reason for a marked decline in trade between the two countries in recent months (RFE/RL, 4 November 1997). Finally, an article in the weekly *168 Chasa* (21 May 1999 — cited in BPCWR, 15–21 May 1999) referred to a report by two Council of Europe monitors that criticized the high level of corruption in Bulgaria, and cited this as a significant reason why the country was not yet ready for membership in the major European structures. These structures would obviously include the European Union, so corruption could be seen as one reason why Bulgaria was not among the countries admitted in 2004 to this club, membership in which could have very positive economic effects for many of the poorer states of CEE.

SOCIAL IMPACT

In any society economic problems invariably have negative social conse-quences; unemployment, and all its ramifications, is perhaps the most obvious example. We now consider how corruption can create or exac-erbate social problems in the post-communist world.

According to the World Bank, corruption is the most significant cause of poverty in the contemporary world, particularly in developing coun-tries. The poor suffer in numerous ways as a result of corruption. One is that they are often expected to pay bribes to officials that they either cannot or can barely afford. Although it has been argued in this book that health services fall into a gray area of corruption, since doctors and other health workers are typically not state officials as the term is nor-mally understood, it would be precious not to note that many citizens in the post-communist world have paid large sums (relative to their in-comes) for medical goods and services that they should legally receive gratis. Another reason why corruption contributes to impoverishment is that funds intended for welfare projects of various kinds are often diverted by corrupt officials. For example, a report in the Chinese press (CD, 20 May 1997, 3, citing *Legal Daily*) revealed that twelve high-level officials of the Shaanxi Provincial Civil Affairs Department had been accused of misappropriating public funds designed for poverty relief and a major welfare project, as well as soliciting and accepting bribes, amounting to more than 11.7 million yuan (about $1.41 million at the time). This is a considerable sum in China. However, it almost pales into insignificance when compared with figures provided in the national audit for 1999. According to these, some 125 billion yuan (about $15 billion) allocated to poverty relief, water conservation projects, and housing resettlement were either misused or embezzled by officials (CD, 22 January 2000). The social impact of having such a large amount of money siphoned off should not be underestimated. Cases like this are not uncommon in China (see too CD, 27 May 1997, 3), and can also be found in post-communist Europe.[19]

It is not only the poor who can suffer, but also others who are entitled to compensation. In October 2000 the Ukrainian parliamentarian Viktor Zherdytskyy was arrested by German police in Hanover and charged with embezzlement. Zherdytskyy was under investigation at the time by the Ukrainian authorities for his possible role in the disappearance of some $38.4 million intended for Nazi victims in Ukraine; the funds had been provided by the German government (*EECR* 9, no. 4:41). In June 2004 a court in Hildesheim sentenced Zherdytskyy to almost six years' imprisonment for embezzlement of about $2.5 million; he announced his intention to appeal the verdict.

INTERNATIONAL IMPACT

The implications of widespread corruption in a country can be particularly serious if other countries believe that they are themselves being directly affected by it. Although the focus of this book is on corruption, it has also been pointed out that it is sometimes almost impossible to disentangle official corruption from organized crime. In this context, Gurov (1995, 283) has argued that "corruption is the driving force (*dvigatel'*) of organized crime." Much of the discussion that follows is based on that assumption.

Perhaps the most extreme example is the claim that nuclear material suitable for weapons use has been smuggled from Russia and Ukraine, partly because of corruption among military personnel. While fears about this possibility appear to have subsided in recent years (or at least did until 9/11), it was a cause of major concern from 1992 to 1994 in both western countries such as Germany, Austria, and France, and other post-communist states such as Bulgaria and Poland (see *Keesings Record of World Events* 1992, 38987, 39170, 39217; *Keesings Record of World Events* 1994, 40162–3, 40210, 40259; on the dangers and status of nuclear smuggling from the former Soviet Union see Ford 1996; Lee 1997; Webster ed. 1997, esp. 19–23, 61–63; Lee 1998; and Nelson 2000). While there appears to be little publicly available hard evidence to support the claim, the director of the FSB, Nikolai Patrushev, has suggested that some of the fruits of Boris Berezovskii's alleged corruption have provided funds to Chechen terrorists (*EECR* 11, nos. 1–2:40). Such allegations highlight once again some of the potentially deadly ramifications of corruption.

The impact of Russian organized crime has been felt around the world. In the words of Raymond Kendall, then the head of Interpol, "I don't want to give the impression that the Russian mafia is taking over in the West. But the amount of money they have is a threat to our societies. They are a danger for western businessmen in that they offer parallel channels of doing things. And unlike western mafias, they resort immediately to violence" (cited in Tillier 1996). Once again, to the extent that organized crime is as successful as it is in some post-communist states because of overt or implicit assistance or involvement by corrupt officials, the indirect effects of corruption make themselves felt.

There is increasing evidence that citizens beyond the post-communist world are being directly affected by members of organized-crime groups from Russia, and perhaps elsewhere. At its most extreme, they are being murdered (see Sweeney et al. 1996). Although the impact of the Russian mafia is—probably justifiably—the one most frequently mentioned in the world's press, other countries suffer from the activities of organized-crime gangs and corrupt officials in most post-communist and quasi-post-communist states. For instance, Tsyganov (1996, 4) cites an article published in *Guangming Ribao* in 1990 that referred to the corrupt production and smuggling of arms from Xiamen in Fujian Province (PRC) to Taiwan. The smuggling of arms and narcotics into non-post-communist states, and of stolen cars and other stolen goods into the post-communist states has become a major problem (Minchev et al. 2000). In addition, gangs from the post-communist world are involved in a major way in people smuggling, human trafficking and prostitution,[20] illegal gambling, protection rackets, and even the smuggling of human body parts in much of the globe, affecting ordinary people throughout the world.[21] The frequently close connections between organized crime and corrupt officials bring into focus the potentially global—and cruel—indirect effects of post-communist corruption.[22]

POLITICAL AND LEGITIMATION EFFECTS

It will be recalled from chapter 1 that one of the principal theoretical foci of this book is the nexus between corruption and legitimation. Primarily because of this focus, the following discussion treats the subject at some length.

Domestic Public Attitudes

A major theoretical concern of this book is the possible impact that corruption has been having on public attitudes toward attempts to further democracy, free markets, and privatize in the post-communist world. This is another aspect of corruption that is notoriously difficult to measure, and even detailed survey evidence on mass perceptions of a linkage between corruption and democratization remains scarce. However, it is possible to examine the limited and mostly circumstantial evidence available, and draw inferences from it. This entails examining the evidence relating directly to legitimation, which can be combined with related attitudinal evidence from which it is reasonable to draw inferences, such as evidence on privatization (see Frentzel-Zagórska and Zagórski 1993 on Poland; DeBardeleben 1999 on Russia) and organized crime (see Frisby 1998 on Russia). In chapter 4 there was consideration of cross-polity public perceptions of the scale of corruption, and how likely particular groups of officials within countries were to engage in it. Here we take up the broader question of the potential effects of corruption on attitudes toward the legitimacy of CEE and CIS transition states.

Public opinion and attitude survey data have long indicated that corruption and related crimes are perceived as a major problem in post-communist countries. A survey in Ukraine in 1993 revealed that the population's main concern was the mafia (Sajó 1994a, 44), while many Slovak opinion polls during the 1990s placed corruption among the three most significant concerns of citizens (Transparency International 1996b, 9). Despite the official figures on corruption in Czechia cited in chapter 4, Kettle (1995, 39) pointed out in the mid-1990s that according to surveys many Czechs believed both that corruption was widespread and that they could do little or nothing about it.

Of the countries focused on in this book, Poland and Bulgaria are the ones in which the most detailed surveys into attitudes toward corruption have been conducted; since these appear to have started earlier in Poland, some of them will be considered first. A 1995 survey revealed that no less than 93.4 percent of Poles considered corruption either an important or a very important issue;[23] this percentage was virtually unchanged by the end of 2003 (Centrum Badania Opinii Społecznej 2004a, 2) and even slightly higher by May 2004 (Centrum Badania

Opinii Społecznej 2004b, 2); all these figures were much higher than those of the early 1990s (Centrum Badania Opinii Społecznej 2004b, 2).

A number of specialized surveys help to produce a more detailed picture. For example, CBOS has conducted numerous surveys on particular aspects of corruption (see chapter 4). One conducted in February 1994 focused on public perceptions of the linkages between the sponsoring of state institutions and corruption. It was clear from the survey that in the view of most respondents, public institutions (a group that included the police) should not, except for medical services, accept private sponsorship — though a higher proportion (84 percent) adopted this position vis-à-vis the "sejm [parliament], government and ministries" than about the police (57 percent) or political parties (73 percent) (Centrum Badania Opinii Społecznej 1994a, esp. 1–7).[24]

The focus of a CBOS survey of 1,223 respondents in February 1995 was on politicians and public servants. It revealed the belief of 51 percent of those surveyed that many high-ranking officials allowed themselves to profit personally from their public functions, while a further 36 percent believed that some, but not many, politicians and public servants benefited in this way; only 2 percent of respondents believed that their politicians and senior public servants were completely honest. Interestingly, respondents perceived almost no difference between the levels of corruption in the "Solidarity period" (to 1993) and the "socialist (post-communist) period" (since 1993). Clear majorities of respondents believed that senior political figures in the regime at that time would "quite often" or "very often" collude with relatives, friends, and acquaintances in the placing of publicly funded orders (68 percent) and "quite often" or "very often" nominate relatives, friends, or acquaintances to positions in public administration, private firms, and banks (77 percent). Finally, 61 percent of respondents believed that senior members of the regime would use public funds to assist their political party (another 26 percent did not know) (Centrum Badania Opinii Społecznej 1995, esp. 1–14).

If these findings are combined with the earlier surveys on the police and the judiciary mentioned in chapter 4, it becomes clear that the Polish system had legitimacy problems in the mid-1990s, and a major reason emerges for the low levels of citizens' trust, noted by other analysts, in political institutions (see Mishler and Rose 1995). The findings were buttressed by the response to the question in our Polish survey on government legitimacy in June 2000. Of the 1,066 respondents, 715 (67.1 percent) expressed the opinion that corruption was undermining the legitimacy (authority) of the government "very much," while another 203 (19.0 percent) answered "yes, a little." Thus, some 86 percent of respondents were of the opinion that corruption was undermining the legitimation process, which is clearly a concern.

What of the other three countries? At a meeting in April 1997, the head of the best-known social survey organization in Russia, Yurii Levada of VTSIOM, indicated that relatively few data had been collected to that point on Russian attitudes toward corruption. However, those available paint an interesting picture. A survey of 3,000 respondents in 1994 revealed that the "growth of corruption and anarchy" was considered the third-most important change in the previous five years (since the end of communist rule and into the early post-communist period), marginally below "the growth of unemployment" and "the impoverishment of people," which were tied for first (Levada 2000a, 394). A survey in May 1995 revealed that approximately one quarter of those surveyed, and about one third of those with at least some higher education, saw corruption and bribe taking as a serious problem (EiSP 4 (1995):57); approximately one year later, Russians appear to have believed that corruption, and the crisis of morality more generally, had dramatically worsened (EiSP 4 (1996):59). Moreover, in a survey of 1,600 Russians in March 1996, 86 percent of respondents indicated that they were either "very concerned" (69.6 percent) or "somewhat concerned" (17.1 percent) about "corruption among high-ranking officials" (*sredi vysshikh dolzhnostnykh lits*).[25] Since these figures are much higher than the more general response to corruption, it appears that Russians were even more concerned about corruption at the top of the state system (what is sometimes called "grand" or "political" corruption) than at the lower levels.

The (possibly misguided) notion that the post-communist period in Russia is much more corrupt than the Soviet era is suggested by a survey conducted in 1998 by VTSIOM ($N = 1,500$) revealing that in the view of 68 percent of respondents who voted for Zyuganov (the leader of the communists) the current power élite was corrupt, whereas only 4 percent of the group believed that the Soviet power holders were corrupt. Since communist supporters would be *expected* to have a relatively positive image of the past, it is interesting to note that the comparable figures among respondents who voted for Yeltsin were 55 percent and 19 percent (Levada 2000a, 330). That this matters in terms of legitimacy is suggested by the sixth-most popular response to a question in the same survey about the rights and values that respondents associated to a significant extent with the concept of democracy: "A reduction of corruption and *blat*" (the latter term is defined in chapter 2); some 47 percent of respondents considered this a key feature of democracy, compared with only 37 percent opting for "a multiparty system," for example. In concluding this part of the analysis, it is worth pointing out that the most frequently cited answer to this question was "Equality of all citizens before the law"; that this might also have implications for corruption should be obvious (all data from Levada 2000a, 334–35).

One other "Russian" survey deserves special mention, even though, strictly speaking, it was conducted shortly before the collapse of the USSR and the Soviet communist system, in both Russia and what was at that time one of the fourteen other republics of the Soviet Union. In addition, it focused on attitudes toward organized crime rather than corruption per se. However, among the countries examined in depth in this book, it appears to be the only survey until recently of people who have been convicted of corruption; it is certainly described as unique in the Russian source in which it has been reproduced (Gurov 1995, 285–86).[26] It was considered too interesting to omit, the more so because it appears to be available only in Russian, a language that many readers of this book will not read. The survey was conducted among approximately nine hundred prisoners (former officials or *chinovniki*) convicted of corruption who were serving sentences in Irkutsk, Sverdlovsk, and the Kazakh Soviet Republic; the report on the survey was filed in January 1990.

Most of the prisoners (87 percent) were interested in following reports on crime in the media and in discussing these. A somewhat smaller majority (64 percent) expected that the struggle against organized crime would be intensified, and that therefore they would be less likely to be released early. Already by the time of this survey, a sizeable minority of the respondents (43 percent) believed that the state authorities would be unable to control the so-called mafia. Of the officials who had previously worked either in soviet (council) or Communist Party bodies, 64.5 percent believed that the measures being taken by the state against organized crime would at best only contain or marginally reduce its growth.

Finally, only a small minority (7.5 percent) approved of the work of the police in its struggle with organized crime and offered their help.

These findings suggest that many officials who were themselves convicted of corruption had lost faith, even before the collapse of the USSR, in the ability of their own state to control organized crime. Since most analysts would agree that the post-Soviet Russian state has in many ways been even weaker than its immediate predecessor — certainly until Putin came to power in 2000 — the depressing picture painted by this survey is of greater concern than it might otherwise have been.[27] The survey also reveals a high level of alienation from the police. While this is not particularly surprising among people who have been arrested and imprisoned, it might indicate, in more extreme form, a problem for the police with maintaining their popular image, which would make their work against crime even more difficult. The low levels of trust in law enforcement agencies demonstrated in chapter 4 have negative effects for the legitimacy of the system in any country.

Hungary appears to have conducted relatively few surveys explicitly into popular attitudes toward corruption, and data are scarcer than for Russia. However, a general survey of attitudes in 1995 revealed that 83 percent of Hungarians polled considered corruption either an important or a very important issue.[28] While this figure is somewhat lower than the Polish figure for 1995 cited above, it is similar to the Russian one, and still very high. In late 1999 and early 2000, focus group and survey research into Hungarian attitudes toward corruption was conducted by Gallup Hungary. While the detailed results do not appear to be generally available in English, very similar analyses by Manchin (2000) and Hankiss (2002) demonstrate that most Hungarians perceived corruption as more of a problem than they actually experienced themselves. The comparative survey conducted by GfK in 2001 and referred to in chapter 4 revealed the view of 64 percent of Hungarian respondents that they lived in a corrupt state (GfK 2001, 10); while this figure is not as high as the earlier one just cited (and is on a slightly different issue), that almost two thirds of Hungarians might have held this view as recently as 2001 must be of concern to those interested in the legitimacy of this post-communist state.

In contrast to Hungary, there has been a considerable amount of research into public attitudes toward corruption in Bulgaria. A survey conducted in Sofia by the AGORA 22 Agency in March 1994 revealed the view of some 74 percent of those interviewed that public servants would accept a bribe of 1,000 leva (approximately one fifth of the average monthly salary at the time) in return for providing a document or service more quickly than they would otherwise (Verheijen and Dimitrova 1996, 217). Several recent Bulgarian studies have been more detailed than those for most post-communist states. There are so many Bulgarian surveys that references here must be selective, starting with a group of polls conducted in 1997–98 that provide some indication of the scale of concern. The findings of these surveys will then be compared with some abbreviated findings for other countries recently summarized and published.

The Bulgarian studies were conducted by Vitosha Research, the survey research unit of the CSD (details of the surveys are in the bibliography under Center for the Study of Democracy 1998a and 1998b), and comprised three surveys over a ten-month period, focused on attitudes toward corruption.[29] The first was conducted in March 1997 and involved 1,185 respondents, the second in September 1997 and involved 1,032 respondents, and the third in December 1997 and January 1998 and involved 1,519 respondents. The polls revealed, first, that Bulgarians were critical of all forms of corruption among elected officials — though, unsurprisingly, much less critical of the acceptance of free meals than of free holidays, money, or gifts. Second, respondents tended to be more critical of corruption among civil servants than among elected officials, though the difference was not substantial. Third, and of particular relevance to this part of our argument, the results indicated that official campaigns against corruption can increase popular indignation, but perhaps only in the short term. The new government that came to power after the elections of April 1997 made the fight against corruption a top priority, and sought to raise public awareness and disapproval of it. That it succeeded in this objective was reflected in the uniformly higher levels of condemnation in the responses collected in September than in those collected in March. However, the results from January 1998 were remarkably similar to those from March 1997. Interviews conducted by me in Sofia in February 1998 indicated that the campaign had lost little impetus by then; this and the survey results suggest that the public was becoming immune or indifferent to government exhortations.[30]

The third of the Bulgarian surveys was conducted by CSD as part of an international project led by the Glasgow-based team referred to in chapter 4, and used that team's questions.[31] It was concerned with popular attitudes toward state officials, and provides further evidence of how widespread Bulgarians considered corruption to be.[32] The survey, of people aged eighteen and over interviewed face to face, revealed that 84.5 percent of respondents considered it either "bad" (53.5 percent) or "bad, but unavoidable" (31 percent) that one might have to give money or gifts or do favors to influence public administrators.[33]

Data cited in chapter 4 reveal that far fewer Bulgarians have actually been asked for a bribe, or believe that a bribe was expected, than, for instance, Ukrainians or Slovaks. But whether or not popular perceptions have exaggerated the scale of corruption in Bulgaria, it is clear that many citizens have been irritated by corruption and, as in Russia, that far more citizens are irritated by corruption at the top (so-called grand or political corruption) than at lower levels of the political system. In response to the question, "Which annoys you more — corruption amongst . . . ," 47.9 percent answered "top public officials" and 20.7 percent answered "lower-ranking public officials"; most of the other respondents answered "it depends" or "don't know."

More recent Bulgarian surveys reveal that corruption was considered by the end of the 1990s to be the third-worst problem in society (after unemployment and low incomes — "Coalition 2000" 2000, 4). Finally, in response to the question in our own survey in 2000 concerning the extent to which corruption was perceived to be undermining the legitimacy of the government, 69.9 percent of respondents answered that it was doing so "to a great extent," while a further 9.6 percent believed it was doing so "to a small extent"; hence almost 80 percent of Bulgarians indicated that corruption was undermining the legitimacy of their state and system. For the record, 17.7 percent responded that they did not know — leaving a paltry 2.8 percent who definitely did not believe that corruption was undermining the government. These results can be compared with those for the other three countries in our four-country survey, as summarized in table 5.1.

Thus the vast majority of respondents in all four countries saw the government's authority as being undermined by corruption, which could be taken to mean that corruption was delegitimizing the state. However, the precise significance of these data is difficult to assess, and could easily be exaggerated. Although I have been unable to discover

TABLE 5.1. Popular Perceptions of the Extent to Which Official Corruption Is
Undermining the Legitimacy of the Government, 2000 (in Percent)

	To a large extent	To a small extent	Not at all	Don't know
Bulgaria	69.9	9.6	2.8	17.7
Hungary	63.6	27.0	3.9	4.6
Poland	67.0	19.1	5.3	8.4
Russia	79.1	12.6	3.9	4.4

Note: The question read: "In your opinion, is corruption undermining the legitimacy
(authority) of the government?" The original question referred only to legitimacy, not to
authority, and to the state rather than to the government; but the wording was changed
when pilot studies in two of the countries indicated some confusion concerning the
meanings of "legitimacy" and "the state."

comparable data for a small number of western states for which I sought
similar survey questions, it is possible, and probably likely, that results
would not be so dissimilar in countries experiencing or having recently
experienced major corruption scandals at the time of the surveys (for
example the United States during or shortly after Watergate; the United
Kingdom around the time of the election of 1997, when "sleaze" in
politics was a major issue; or Germany in the late 1990s). However, it is
also likely that time-series survey data would highlight a difference between these consolidated democracies and our four transitional states,
with the latter manifesting greater long-term cynicism. This must remain speculation. What can be noted here is that the Global Corruption
Barometer for 2003 (based on surveys conducted in July 2002) included
a question that focused directly on the linkage between corruption and
legitimacy, and in some ways permits synchronic comparison of western
and post-communist states. Respondents were asked to assess the extent
to which they believed that corruption affected political life; the results
for six countries (recalling that the barometer did not include Hungary)
are summarized in table 5.2.

Clearly the odd one out here is the United States (though see below
on Bulgaria). On one level this might not be surprising, since Watergate
happened some three decades earlier. On the other hand, the so-called
Whitewater affair might have been expected to have a more recent im-

TABLE 5.2. Popular Perceptions of the Extent to Which Corruption Affects
Political Life, 2002 (in Percent; Valid Responses Only)

	Not significantly	Somewhat significantly	Very significantly
Bulgaria	20.3	39.7	40.0
Poland	5.3	28.7	66.0
Russia	6.8	30.8	62.3
Germany	10.7	34.4	54.9
United Kingdom	11.6	49.0	39.5
United States	59.8	33.1	7.1

Source: Based on Galtung et al. 2003, 23–24.

pact on attitudes. Perhaps its having been investigated, even if the investigation came to nothing, inspired popular confidence in the system.
Conversely, Germans were still reeling from the scandal embroiling
Chancellor Helmut Kohl and the CDU that first surfaced in November
1999, which was followed by another party financing scandal focused on
the Cologne branch of the other major party, the Social Democrats
(SPD), that broke shortly before the survey. Britons had experienced a
string of corruption scandals in the 1990s, and had not yet forgotten
them. Nevertheless, the percentage opting for "very significantly" was
still well below comparable figures for Poland and Russia.

Among post-communist states, Bulgaria appears to be the odd one
out vis-à-vis not only the other two states in our table, but all other post-
communist states (a total of eight) covered in the barometer. Apart
from Bulgaria, the percentage of respondents opting for the "very significantly" response exceeded 60 percent in all cases, peaking at 81.4 percent in Bosnia and Hercegovina. However, there is an important point
to be made about the Bulgarian results: there appears to have been a far
higher percentage of nonresponses (presumably "don't know" or no
reply) in Bulgaria than in any of the other countries in table 5.2; only
Russia comes anywhere near the Bulgarian percentage. This nonre-
sponse rate could seriously affect the results, and means that Bulgarians
might not have been as sanguine about corruption and politics in their
country as table 5.2 suggests; this is why the table's heading consciously
includes the phrase "valid responses only."[34]

Although China is still very secretive concerning sociopolitical public opinion survey data — there are no private and independent sociopolitical survey organizations in the PRC to compare with VTSIOM or CBOS, for instance — this does not mean that surveys are not conducted. Many are, in particular by bodies at the ministerial level and local authorities. General findings — usually the more innocuous ones — are sometimes published in the press.[35] There was a reference in the Chinese press in 1995 to a survey conducted by the Chinese Academy of Social Sciences, which revealed that corruption was considered one of the country's top three problems, along with crime and inflation (*http://www.transparency .org/newsletters/95.2/june95.html#aspac* — visited December 2002). A survey conducted by Horizon Market Research in 1999 revealed that more respondents identified "a clean government" as their top priority than any other issue (*CD*, 4 November 2002), while corruption remained "one of the top concerns" of the public according to a survey conducted in 2002 by the Chinese Academy of Social Sciences (*People's Daily*, online English-language edition, 13 March 2002, visited 18 September 2003).

But detailed data on attitudes toward corruption appear not to have been published until after the turn of the century.[36] During a visit to China in May–June 1997, however, I was able to ascertain from one of China's leading survey specialists that Beijing residents' attitudes toward corruption had been examined (as part of more general surveys) on several occasions since 1992, and that the results reflected serious concern. It appears that at the time surveys were being conducted under two rubrics: the Research Centre attached to the State Commission on Economic Restructuring, and local authorities. But even though quasi-private survey organizations such as the Research Centre for Contemporary China at Beijing University sometimes conduct surveys on behalf of local authorities, they have in the past been forbidden to publish or cite any of the data.[37] However, the reader is referred to the comparative survey data cited in chapter 8, which suggest that corruption has sometimes been perceived as even more of a problem by Chinese citizens than by many of their European post-communist counterparts, including the Russians (a point seemingly supported by the very general reports on the surveys conducted by the Chinese Academy of Social Sciences cited above). It is also worth noting a remark by the Chinese president himself at the Second Plenary of the Central Discipline Inspection Commission in mid-1993: "If we lower our guard and let corruption run wild, our party will be ruined, the people's power will be lost, and the great cause of socialist modernization will be forced off track" (Jiang Zemin in BR 36, no. 36:5). While the Chinese leadership may have become marginally less concerned with this issue than it was, one of the key items on the agenda at the plenum of the CCP's Central Committee in September 2004 was governance, including the need to keep up the struggle against corruption (*People's Daily*, on-line English-language edition, 26 September 2004, visited October 2004). Statements such as Jiang's, and the priorities of September 2004, have clear implications for legitimacy.

The kinds of survey data cited above from Europe have been borne out by the findings of the Glasgow team. These suggest that in the 1990s, while Ukrainians were more concerned and angry about it than the Czechs were, with the Slovaks and Bulgarians falling in between, corruption was a major issue for all four of these post-communist populations, despite their different cultural backgrounds, levels of economic development and difficulties, and other variables. One more specific finding of the research is that whereas many of the Ukrainians interviewed had had direct experience of low-level corruption, most Czechs had not, and were making assumptions largely on the basis of second-hand reports (including in the mass media — all information here from Koshechkina, Grødeland, and Miller 1997, though see too Miller, Grødeland, and Koshechkina 2001b, 82–87). That the Czechs were concerned about corruption despite limited direct experience supports the argument in this book that perceptions matter more than reality when considering the issue of legitimacy. This said, the relatively low proportion of Czechs with direct experience may simply reflect corruption that is worse at higher levels — with which ordinary members of the public would have less direct contact — rather than pervasive at all levels, as in Ukraine.[38]

Before concluding this discussion of surveys, it is worth considering some of the deeper issues raised by them, since if their methodology is flawed or potentially flawed, their use becomes questionable. In a brief but insightful essay, Juliet Gole (1999) has highlighted eight possible disadvantages (as well as five possible advantages) of public opinion surveys on corruption. Several of these are purely practical (polls are expensive; they are less useful as one-offs than if longitudinal; they are difficult to administer in countries with relatively few telephones), and there are usually solutions to them (larger research grants solve the first two, face-to-face interviews solve the third, and so on). But some of her objections are more epistemologically substantive and should be addressed.

One problem identified by Gole is that citizens often focus either on the corruption they experience in their own lives or on high-profile cases. This is probably true, and would be more or less consistent with our own findings (see especially table 4.5 and related text). It could also help to explain why the military is typically perceived as much less corrupt than other institutions; official statistics, at least, suggest that public opinion in this area might be particularly misguided. What is clear, however, is that even if Gole's point is valid, it in no way undermines our argument about the possible delegitimizing aspects of perceived systemic corruption in law enforcement agencies and among elected representatives, since both groups are, according to Gole, among those that citizens focus on. A second objection raised by Gole is that governments may not be prepared to act on survey results. This is also often true. But then it is up to a government to explain why it is not responding. If it provides either an inadequate answer or none at all, it is then up to nongovernment agencies to challenge the government. Even if there are few challenges, citizens will draw their own conclusions about the government's inaction. In short, such behavior by governments can be delegitimizing—and is thus of relevance to, and supportive of, our argument. Finally, Gole points out that surveys focusing on corruption may provide skewed results, because respondents are being asked to concentrate on something on which they do not usually focus. This too is a potentially valid criticism. But many surveys invite respondents to indicate the issues that concern them most, where corruption is just one among many possibilities. Since, as demonstrated elsewhere in this book, corruption typically figures so prominently in these broader surveys (in that it is highly ranked), it is appropriate to focus on it in more specialized surveys. These surveys can be a useful tool, along with others, for devising optimal strategies to combat corruption, or even as a starting point for correcting what the authorities believe to be seriously flawed perceptions.

In sum, Gole has raised several important points in her article; but all can be addressed, and none undermines arguments for the careful use of well-conceived surveys as one method among others for ascertaining popular perceptions of corruption and its potentially delegitimizing effects. Moreover, it is argued in this book that as many methods as possible should be used for measuring and forming impressions of corruption in a given country or group of countries.

To conclude this discussion of the delegitimizing aspects of corruption, it is worth citing the conclusions drawn by Richard Rose, William Mishler, and Christian Haerpfer (1998, 188), which are based on John Reed's comparative assessments of corruption (1995): "The presence or absence of the rule of law, as measured by the corruption index, shows a significant correlation with regime support. The higher the level of corruption in a new democracy, the less likely individuals are to support the new regime (−.24) and the higher the current level of corruption, the less likely individuals are to reject undemocratic alternatives (−.21)."

Certainly many post-communist politicians and officials have argued that the public is seriously concerned about corruption. For instance, the former commander of the Estonian defense forces, Aleksander Einseln, argued in an interview in 1996 that corruption was the most pressing issue on the Estonian political agenda (*Baltic Times*, 25 April–1 May 1996). A number of senior politicians have made the fight against it one of their principal foci during election campaigns; examples include the presidential candidates Aleksandr Lukashenka (Belarus, 1994), Emil Constantinescu (Romania, 1996), Boris Yeltsin (Russia, 1996), Mikhail Saakashvili (Georgia, 2003–4), and Viktor Yushchenko (Ukraine, 2004); and former King Simeon II in the Bulgarian parliamentary election of 2001.[39] Some politicans continue to emphasize the significance of corruption even after they have won a recent election: President Kwaśniewski stated on Polish television shortly after his resounding victory in the elections of October 2000 that corruption was a serious problem.[40]

Considering this subject from a different angle, the perceived inability to deal with corruption has sometimes been cited by leading politicians as the reason for their failures. In November 1994 the Albanian government held a referendum on a draft constitution, which was rejected; President Sali Berisha, who had strongly urged Albanians to vote in favor of the draft, admitted that the defeat was in part because the citizenry was protesting against his government's inability to control corruption, which was a major concern (Zanga 1995, 12). President

Emil Constantinescu of Romania apparently saw his failure to make serious inroads into the corruption problem as a reason not to contest the presidency again in 2000 (see chapter 7).

One potential danger of widespread public concern about corruption is that demagogues who promise to eradicate it, or merely bring it under control, may look increasingly attractive to voters if the more mainstream politicians appear incapable of tackling it. Although comparative analysis reveals that authoritarian leaders are not necessarily any better equipped to deal with corruption than their more democratic counterparts, this is not always as widely appreciated by desperate and sometimes poorly educated citizens as it should be. In short, a perception that corruption is a serious problem and that mainstream politicians are doing too little to combat it may result in more extremist politics.[41] Obviously extremism has serious negative consequences for democratization. In Russia, in particular, expansionist traditions suggest that a reinvigorated extremist movement would be of serious concern not only for Russia's own citizens but also for other countries.

Even if many voters are not attracted to extremists, their disappointment can result in political apathy and indifference. This too has negative implications for both the development of a democratic political culture and the legitimacy of the political system. That corruption can seriously affect the legitimacy of a regime is borne out by two observations relating to communist states, though the point could be made about other kinds of state. The first, by Tarkowski (1995, 35), is that "a widespread conviction of corruption inside the Gierek administration and of the growing role of 'connections' were a significant component of the growing frustration that resulted in the outburst of August 1980." The second, by Gordon White (1996, 161–62), is that Chinese student activists were able to mobilize more general support in 1989 by focusing on the regime's corruption. This point is further elaborated in chapter 8, when we go beyond considering the dangers merely to regimes and take up the much broader issue of dangers to systems.

The impact of corruption has been examined from a range of perspectives in this chapter. All of them matter, though some are of primary concern to particular groups, and others to different groups. Nevertheless, that corruption is a serious problem for transition states of CEE and the CIS cannot be questioned. Even if the problem is sometimes exaggerated by leaders, who use corruption and organized crime as scape-goats for other problems, it is no less true that perceptions — however formed, and however accurate or inaccurate — matter in politics, and are directly related to legitimacy. This in turn means that leaders who focus on corruption either believe it to be a serious problem, or, if they use it as a scapegoat, are aware of other very serious problems that are endangering the regime or system. The focus of our analysis will shortly move to what is being done, and what can be done, to deal with the problem. But if tactics and strategies are to be effective, it is necessary to understand how and why corruption has become such a serious problem in the first place. This is the focus of the next chapter.

CHAPTER 6

Causes of Corruption

In my earlier book on corruption (1993, 157–201), the reasons for it were classified under three principal headings — psychological, cultural, and system-related. To a large extent, that division still seems appropriate.[1] However, since many of the psychological and cultural factors transcend system changes, it would be tautologous to consider here in detail causes that have already been analyzed elsewhere. It would also be inappropriate to repeat here the explanations for Chinese corruption, since there have been few major fundamental changes in the PRC since my earlier book was completed;[2] the most significant may have been the formal legalization of privately owned production facilities — and this change is covered in the more general analysis of the corruption-related aspects of privatization in post-communism. Overall, the focus in this chapter is on factors relating to the changed circumstances of post-communism; these are essentially system-related. But some of the psychological and cultural factors are also briefly outlined, to avoid creating the impression that only system-related factors explain corruption in post-communist states.[3]

Ideally, large numbers of officials who have been found guilty of corruption would be surveyed to determine their motives. This would present enormous practical difficulties. In addition, so few officials charged with corruption are found guilty that it would be impossible in most countries to find samples large enough to be statistically significant. Finally, criminals are often not clear themselves about their own primary motivations. Hence most of this chapter is based on inference; while some parts are based on (mostly indirect) empirical evidence, others are derived from the views and statements of numerous observers. The conclusions do refer to our own survey evidence, however.

PSYCHOLOGICAL FACTORS

At the simplest and most intuitive level, corruption is often a manifestation of one of the seven deadly sins, greed. In a rare survey of Russian prisoners convicted of corruption, material interest was cited by more than 60 percent of the 347 respondents as encouraging "ongoing relations with criminal structures," while almost 70 percent cited money as the basis for mutual relations between bribe givers and corrupters (Repetskaya 2000, 81, 83).[4] Although selfishness will be considered in depth later in the chapter when the ramifications of neoliberalism are explored, it would be absurd to suggest that greed suddenly appeared in 1979 (the significance of this date will emerge below). Moreover, there is a cause-and-effect issue here: since neoliberals have been elected in "genuine" democracies — here meaning the closest we have in the real world to the ideals of most democratic theorists — it is far from clear whether neoliberal ideology has become dominant because of clever political marketing (or propaganda, to use a dated term) or because it resonates with the inherent selfishness of many voters.[5]

One reason why greed plays such a prominent role may be the emphasis in so many societies on material success. If Francis Fukuyama (1992, esp. 162–91) is correct in his view that one of the main driving forces of human development is the individual's desire for recognition by others — *thymos* — then the assumption that greater respect and status accrue to those having greater wealth can help to explain corruption that brings about pecuniary gain. It can also explain some of the grayer forms of corruption that are an outgrowth of patronage and cronyism. While corrupt behavior is often motivated by expectations of future paybacks of various kinds, one should not disregard the "feel-good" effect on the patron: patronage can make the donor (patron) feel more powerful and influential, thus increasing his or her *thymos*. Another common reason for corruption is that antisocial behavior simply appeals to some people. As the Polish mobster Marian Klepacki openly acknowledged, "Even if I had plenty of money, I would not go straight. It's because of my temperament" (*European*, 30 September–6 October 1994). Some people simply enjoy beating the system, or attempting to beat the system — including even officials who work for it.

People often find themselves involved in corruption because of peer (horizontal) or superior (vertical) pressure. While it is tempting to describe succumbing to such influence as a weakness, the pressure is sometimes strong. For instance, a refusal to collude with colleagues may result in being ostracized, while refusing to yield to pressure from above can result in decreased promotion prospects or even the loss of one's job. In such circumstances, especially in countries with high levels of unemployment or strong disincentives to whistleblowing, it would be more appropriate to describe resistance to such pressure as a sign of strength. Fear of unemployment can be heightened by one of the most important psychological causes of corruption: insecurity. The deeply psychological roots of personal insecurity, like the other psychological factors considered here, are not the domain of a mere political scientist, and will in any case be largely peculiar to each person. Conversely, much insecurity relates to an individual's relationship to the system, and is therefore considered later in the chapter.

One psychological factor that needs to be acknowledged is a sensitive issue. That factor is the motivation of people who become officers of the state's coercive branches (mainly the police and the military) or politicians. Many — probably most — seek out these positions for admirable reasons, including a desire to help others, a sense of public duty, and a commitment to improve society. But there are also those in any society who have more self-centered and questionable reasons, such as egotism, opportunism, or even a desire to gain access to and make legitimate use of weapons. For officials who have chosen their professions for ethically dubious reasons, their willingness to engage in corruption is compatible with their more cynical approach to life and society. This point about the psychological traits of officials has been explored from a different perspective by Tarkowski (1995, 38), who draws an interesting distinction between the approaches of politicians, whom he sees as much more strongly oriented toward unconventional and creative solutions, and bureaucrats, who tend to focus more on observing and enforcing rules. Many politicians are also more concerned with results (outputs, ends) than procedures (means), and thus more likely to bend the rules than they should in an ideal Weberian rule-of-law state.[6] This willingness to bend rules has immediately obvious implications for what are called penumbra types of corruption in this book, although the ramifications of the politicians' Weltanschauung sometimes extend to unambiguous corruption as well.

While psychological factors need to be incorporated into any reasonably comprehensive analysis of the causes of corruption (see Roldan 1989), they are of limited value in explaining why rates and types of corruption apparently vary so much from country to country and region to region. Those who believe that greed is the basic cause of corruption, for example, need to explain why corruption looks so different in Finland and Denmark from that in Bangladesh or Nigeria. For some, the answer to this question is simple: cultural differences, to which we now turn.

CULTURAL FACTORS

The legacies of both precommunist and communist political culture are often cited to explain contemporary corruption in post-communist states. For example, Glinkina (1998, 18, 21) explains Russian corruption partly in terms of three "aspects of the national mentality" that contribute to it: the influence of Asian culture, which emphasizes relationships with family and friends; the communist system, which did the same because of the demands that it imposed; and a low level of respect for the letter of the law, dating from the feudal period (for further cultural explanations, with reference to other post-communist societies, see Mungiu-Pippidi 1997, 85–86; Zon 1999, esp. 4–7; Kanin 2003 on the tradition of Big Men in South Eastern Europe; more generally on political culture in post-communist states see Pollack, Jacobs, Müller, and Pickel eds. 2003). In this book culture is understood in a broad sense, to include political and social values and traditions that are best understood as legacies of the past. Since my book on corruption in the late communist era, the communist legacy has become a new force to consider in understanding the post-communist world. But since this is addressed later, only cultural factors stemming from precommunist traditions are considered here, even if they continued into the communist era.

A cursory glance at the various TI CPIs since 1995 (see chapter 4) reveals that the countries perceived as the least corrupt are the Nordic states and New Zealand. Various hypotheses have been posited as to why these countries seem so much better able to keep corruption under control than other states. Two of the most popular are size and the social values associated with the dominant religion. Size is widely believed to be relevant because, as suggested in interviews with New Zealand public servants, it is more difficult to be corrupt in compact societies in which people tend to know more about each other's affairs than in larger, more anonymous societies (Pearse 2001: New Zealand's population is less than four million). This is not the place to assess the validity of these perceptions as they pertain to New Zealand. But it is appropriate to consider here the issue of size and corruption levels in the context of the post-communist states.

If one knew only that Estonia and Slovenia (whose populations are each less than two million) were perceived as the least corrupt of the post-communist countries, while Russia (about 147 million) and Ukraine (about 50 million) were among the most corrupt, then it would be tempting to correlate size with corruption levels. But this simple correlation does not hold up well if the latest TI CPIs are scrutinized. Among the most corrupt post-communist states are several small ones, including Albania (population about 3.4 million), Azerbaijan (8 million), Georgia (5.5 million), and Yugoslavia, that is, Serbia and Montenegro (10.8 million). China, with a population of 1.3 billion, appears to be less corrupt than not only Russia and Ukraine but also many of these small countries. And the relatively large Poland (almost 39 million) is still perceived to be one of the less corrupt post-communist countries, even though a Polish report in early 2004 pointed out that according to the TI CPI for 2003, the country would be the most corrupt state in the European Union once it joined in May 2004 (Centrum Badania Opinii Społecznej 2004a, 1). It might be suggested that the point would hold if a distinction were drawn between small and very small, the latter meaning with a population of less than two million. But even this division is questionable, since there are too few cases to produce persuasive evidence. Hence the size hypothesis is not robust.

Whereas size is an unreliable indicator of likely levels of corruption, a country's religious orientation, and in particular the dominant social values related to it, might appear to be a better guide.[7] Of the five post-communist states perceived as most corrupt in the TI CPI for 1999, for instance, four — Azerbaijan, Kazakhstan, Kyrgyzstan, and Uzbekistan — are predominantly Islamic,[8] while five of the six perceived as least corrupt all have Christian traditions (Czechia, Estonia, Hungary, Poland, and Slovenia; the odd one out is Mongolia — which, however, is not a Muslim society either, being predominantly Buddhist). But the TI CPI for 2002, for instance, paints a less tidy picture. Of the five most corrupt post-communist states, two are Islamic (Azerbaijan and Kazakhstan), two are predominantly Orthodox Christian (Georgia and Moldova), while the fifth is mainly Orthodox, with a substantial Catholic minority (Ukraine). At the other end of the scale, the ten least corrupt post-communist states in the CPI are all predominantly Christian.[9]

At a meeting with me in Warsaw, a leading Polish sociologist, Jolanta Babiuch-Luxmoore, referred to recent focus group research in Poland suggesting that while most Poles strongly condemned bribery, they were more tolerant of patronage and clientelism, which they associated with friendship and mutual loyalty. Dr. Babiuch-Luxmoore interpreted this apparent contradiction partly in terms of Catholic values, which placed loyalty to the family above loyalty to the state. She also suggested that these values were why Nordic and Germanic countries, which are predominantly Protestant, were less prone to systemic corruption than countries such as Poland and Italy. Protestant cultures tend to be less family-oriented than Catholic ones, to place greater emphasis on individual responsibility (they cannot expiate guilt through the confessional in the same way that Catholics can), and to have higher regard for the state.[10] But once again, it is important not to confuse apparent correlations with causal relationships. For instance, while Estonia (with Protestant traditions) appears to be one of the very least corrupt of the post-communist states, so does Slovenia — a country with strong Catholic traditions. As touched upon in chapter 4, the fact that both countries have much higher standards of living than any of the Islamic states referred to earlier might explain differing levels of corruption much better than religious traditions do.[11] Indeed, statistical correlations could be used to argue that it is less the religious tradition of a country than its average daily temperature that will indicate the level of corruption!

The values connected with modernity and premodernity are a cultural factor mentioned by Zon (1999, 5–6), with reference to Ukrainian corruption. These values are often related to religion, but should be treated discretely. According to this argument, one of the key differences between premodern and modern values is that the modern are oriented toward problem solving, whereas the premodern encourage people to learn to tolerate or live with problems. Another is that premodern values draw a sharper distinction between what Zon (1999, 6) calls "inside and outside morals." By this he means that the individual's code of behavior and loyalties within small groups on the one hand and toward much larger entities, especially society and the state, on the other are often more sharply differentiated in premodern societies than in modern ones. Zon maintains that both factors can be related to Ukraine's level of socioeconomic development, and its impact on attitudes toward the state, the market, networks, and corruption. Kanin (2003, esp. 497–501) makes a rather similar point about the former Yugoslavia.

So far the focus has been on what are in essence macrocultural factors, since they apply to large sections of society. But microcultural factors pertaining to particular groups are also relevant. For instance, microcultures within particular agencies of the state can help to explain differing rates of corruption. An enduring bureaucratic culture that emphasizes loyalty to the state and due process is sometimes cited as part of the explanation for the relatively low levels of corruption in New Zealand already noted. But individual officers of the state sometimes have a greater loyalty to their colleagues and agency than to the state and society more generally. This loyalty can be part of an individual's bonding and managing mechanism, especially when the world around is highly volatile, as it was in the early post-communist states. An example will clarify this. Reference was made in earlier chapters to the widespread concern in Bulgaria about corruption in the customs services. This corruption was investigated in the mid-1990s by an ad hoc committee established by parliament. It transpired that public servants from the Ministry of Finance felt an obligation (from a sense of loyalty) to protect their colleagues in customs, who in turn expected their colleagues in the Ministry of Finance to "turn a blind eye" (Verheijen and Dimitrova 1996, 205, 216).

SYSTEM-RELATED FACTORS

Various analysts (for example Frye 1998) argue that systemic factors rather than culture provide the best explanation of corruption in post-communist societies. An enormous number of system-related factors help to explain this corruption, and a comprehensive analysis would require a book in its own right.[12] Rather than attempt to enumerate every factor here — and in response to a reviewer of my first book who criticized me for listing explanatory factors but not identifying which were most important — what appear to be the four main categories more or less peculiar to post-communism have been isolated here. Although separated in this chapter solely to disentangle a complex phenomenon, it cannot be emphasized too strongly that most of these factors are closely interrelated or overlap, and are ultimately the ramifications of just one factor: the nature and context of post-communism itself. But the disaggregation undertaken here is an artificial process, and once the various factors have been identified — once the complex phenomenon has been deconstructed — the reader should remerge them.

The Legacy of Communism and Path Dependency

The legacy of communism overlaps with path dependency (as well as with culture); both factors are complex. Nine dimensions of the first can be highlighted. One is that the strictly hierarchical nature of the communist system meant that neither initiative nor personal responsibility was greatly encouraged. Although the management within enterprises in most communist countries tended to be highly centralized, more or less in line with the Soviet concept of "one-person management" (*edinonachalie*), even managers were severely constrained by plan targets to which their enterprises were subject and over which they had limited control. There were various economic reforms in most CEE countries and the USSR during the 1960s, starting with the New Economic System in the GDR in January 1963 and reaching their most radical form with the Hungarian New Economic Mechanism of 1968. These reforms were intended to increase management autonomy and raise initiative levels. But none was very successful.[13] The culture of dependency and low levels of initiative encouraged by the old system proved highly conducive to corruption when that system was suddenly transformed. This is because both officials and managers who are suddenly expected to assume far greater responsibility and take more risks can seek to cushion themselves by forming cozy relations with others in a similar position. Moreover, if bonuses used to be quasi-automatic in the old system, officials can compensate for lost bonus income in a new, more performance-based environment through bribe taking and other forms of rent seeking.

This underdevelopment of personal initiative for people who might otherwise have been expected to shoulder more responsibilities applied also in the moral or ethical sphere. While religion was only ever formally banned in one communist state (Albania, 1967), authorities throughout the communist world discouraged religious belief in various ways, albeit to differing levels in different countries and at different times. They claimed that communism provided answers to all existential questions, including appropriate ethics. Hence there was a moral void once communist power collapsed and many of its basic premises were discredited.

Second, there was considerable institutional blurring in the communist era. The most obvious example was the blurring of lines between the communist party and the formal state apparatus. In practice the demarcation between these entities was frequently hazy, so that the two virtually constituted a bicephalous but single unit, the party-state complex. At a broader level, even the distinction between society and this party-state complex — the state in a broad sense — was hazy. It is true that most citizens had a clearly defined conception of "them" (the party and state authorities) and "us" (fellow citizens); for these people the distinction between state and society was not blurred. But at the same time, because so much of the economy was formally owned and managed by the state, most people were state employees. Moreover, considering the situation from the official communist theoretical perspective, the state was — depending on the time and place — a workers' state, a dictatorship of the proletariat and poor peasantry, or an all-people's state. In all three conceptions there was in theory an identification of the state with either most or all of society. A practical ramification of this identification was that many citizens who would never contemplate stealing from their fellow citizens had far less compunction about helping themselves to state property that in a sense they had been told was theirs anyway.[14]

It is therefore not surprising that the relatively clear distinction traditionally drawn in most western countries between state and society or, just as important, between public and private should be less sharp in most post-communist countries, in which there is often confusion between the public and private sectors. This fuzziness manifests itself in the genuine difficulty that many post-communist politicians have experienced in understanding the concepts of private abuse of public office and conflict of interest (Colloudon 1997, 76), which in turn renders it more difficult to reduce high-level political corruption.[15]

Third, partly as a result of this institutional blurring, several post-communist states have been slow to privatize functions that are not typically performed by developed states. Perhaps counterintuitively, the state apparatus has substantially expanded in some states, such as Russia, since the collapse of communism.[16] On deliberation, this expansion should not be surprising in many cases. In addition to the need to establish new (and presumably temporary) state agencies to implement the privatization process, for example,[17] many of the states that have emerged from the dissolution of federalized communist states have had to establish their own ministries for foreign affairs, foreign trade, and defense, as well as military forces and a diplomatic corps, as a result of gaining sovereignty. This said, it appears that part of the expansion is sometimes due to the reluctance of former communist officials to give up their power bases, and even to their attempts to strengthen their bases by creating larger and more dependent teams; this is a situation ripe for patronage. Despite the various reasons, one point seems incontrovertible: other things being equal, there is greater scope for corruption where there is a higher proportion of state officials in the workforce.[18]

Fourth, it needs to be borne in mind not only that most communist states were either de jure or de facto one-party states, but that even within the ruling parties dissent was essentially forbidden, a legacy of Lenin's ban on factionalism in 1921. Although there was some movement toward a form of pluralism by the 1980s in countries such as Hungary and Poland, this was atypical; even in these progressive communist states, the changes were limited. One implication of this ideological conformity was that there was no established culture of compromise. Consequently it became even more difficult than it was already going to be to reach agreement on optimal restructuring and development paths in the post-communist era. The delays in agreeing on policies and legislation created confusion and despair, both of which can be conducive to increased corruption.

The fifth point is that the decision-making process in communist states was in general highly secretive. This absence of transparency has all too often been emulated in the post-communist era (see Coulloudon 2002, 198–200, who provides 1990s examples from Russia), and is highly conducive to corruption. A sixth dimension of the legacy is the high levels of patronage (clientelism) in the communist era (Eisenstadt and Roniger 1981; Rigby and Harasymiw eds. 1983; Willerton 1992). This practice, which in many situations becomes a form of corruption, has continued into the new era (Coulloudon 1992; McAuley 1997, 86–108; Coulloudon 1999). While the levels vary from one country to the next and from one ruling party or coalition to the next, clientelism continues to be a feature of many CEE and CIS states.

Seventh, whereas communist economies tended to have impressive growth rates in their early years,[19] these had in most cases substantially decelerated by the 1980s and fallen below those of their capitalist competitors. This was an embarrassment to leaderships such as those of the Soviet Union and Bulgaria, who in the 1960s had boasted of surpassing western states within two decades. Accompanying the decline was an increase in poverty in some communist states; Romania is a prime example.[20] According to Kaufmann, Kraay, and Zoido-Lobaton (1999a 6), "There is by now considerable evidence that governance on average tends to be better in richer countries." If their conclusion is correct, then the sorry state of the early post-communist economies that was a legacy of communism helps to explain poor governance and, as a corollary, higher levels of corruption.[21] Indeed, corruption can be seen from this perspective as a manifestation of the coping mechanisms that so many ordinary citizens have had to employ for survival during both the communist and post-communist eras, and which in the latter period are largely a cultural legacy of the former (Kneen 2000).

Eighth, communist states tended to legitimize themselves in terms of goal achievement (goal rationality, or teleologism), as distinct from, for example, the rule of law broadly understood (legal rationality — see Rigby 1982, esp. 10). Typically, the ends of plan fulfilment were more important than the means (that is, adhering to the rules in fulfilling the plan). This goal orientation encouraged a lack of respect for formal, rule-based procedures and the law more generally.

Finally but importantly, the impact of the communist legacy on civil society should not be overlooked. Communist authorities did not encourage a genuinely autonomous civil society, Gorbachev's major political reforms notwithstanding. Moreover, most cases in which the masses played a significant role in overthrowing communist power should be seen as examples of protest politics, not the power of civil society. Civil society has been a minor political actor in most post-communist countries; even the news media, while generally much freer than in the 1980s, have often played a questionable role. The underdeveloped culture of self-motivated political participation, largely a legacy of the communist era, has meant that a major potential source of control over corrupt officials has been a disappointment in most countries.

Whereas cultural determinist arguments focus on the effects of values and practices that are transmitted from generation to generation (albeit subject to mutation), path-dependent approaches pay more attention to structural constraints and possibilities, including institutional capacities. In rejecting many of the basic tenets of communism, CEE and CIS politicians in the transition period have forsworn certain options as politically infeasible. A good example is the reluctance of many politicians and state officials to use what they consider excessively draconian measures for combating corruption, on the grounds that doing so would be too reminiscent of the authoritarian past. Another consideration, often overlooked, is that there was a wide network of informers in most communist states. Many post-communist politicians have been anxious to distance themselves from this type of activity, which in turn means that there is one less watchdog or control in society and state agencies. Even in countries in which the former communists still constitute a significant political force — such as Moldova, Mongolia, and Russia — their parties have generally sought to distance themselves from the more coercive and clandestine dimensions of their pasts.

Path dependency refers to much more than simply the constraints (such as institutional and attitudinal ones) that limit decision makers.[22] At the most general level, it applies to all the parameters within which decision makers operate. In this sense, much of the analysis of the next three factors could be subsumed under path dependency. However, each is important enough in its own right to warrant discrete consideration.

Ramifications of the Multiple and Simultaneous Transition

The second major factor is a function of the unique situation of the post-communist countries. With the collapse of communist power, what are often referred to as the new democracies of CEE and the CIS attempted far more radical change than transition countries did in Latin America, Southern Europe, and elsewhere.[23] Like them, the post-communist countries of CEE and the CIS sought fundamental and comprehensive restructuring of the political system. But in addition, and at the same time, the post-communist countries were attempting economic restructuring of a type and on a scale previously unknown; redefining boundaries and identities; forging new international allegiances (political, economic, and military); creating new legal and educational systems; and seeking new ideological and ethical orientations. In sum, they were embarking on an unprecedented multiple and simultaneous transition in what was originally intended to be a short period. The implications for corruption were several.

Considering first some of the implications of the political transition, the fragility of the early stages of post-communism — exemplified by the electoral success in 1993 of the communist successor parties in the traditionally very anticommunist Poland, or by the violent conflict between the Russian president and parliament in the same year — meant that many politicians sought to build up their own power bases and weaken those of their rivals as a form of self-protection in uncertain times. These actions had major implications for corruption. They help to explain why so many exaggerated or unfounded allegations of corruption were made against politicians, and against public servants closely allied to particular politicians; many of those making the allegations hoped to strengthen their own position by undermining potential or actual competitors. They also help to explain the proclivity to patronage referred to above, which may have been partly due to the heritage of communism, but also played a more instrumental role in the post-communist political context.

A closely related feature of the political landscape of early post-communism has been the fluidity of political parties. In many post-communist countries new parties sprang up like mushrooms after the rain in the period following the collapse of communism. Even those parties that were not new typically revamped themselves dramatically, changing their names, orientations, policies, and leaders. Once formed or reconstituted, many then either subdivided or else merged with other parties to create even newer parties and coalitions. In addition to the political uncertainty that this fluidity caused, the scope for corruption connected to the financing of political parties a priori increased. Party financing laws were in most countries ambiguous or nonexistent; and there were very limited funds available anyway. Yet if parties were to crystallize and emerge as major political actors, they needed to advertise themselves. Advertising has become much more expensive almost everywhere in recent years, as the technological revolution in communications has resulted in far more outlets for political advertising than there used to be (and, accordingly, the need to advertise in as many of these outlets as possible), and as, in some cases, the number of elections has increased.[24] There was thus a significant stimulus to party-related corruption.

The legal transition often overlaps with the political. The sheer scale of the transitions, and the absence of relevant models for democratization, meant that there was bound to be legal and political confusion and disagreement over the way forward. Old laws were often treated as irrelevant even before new ones could be adopted. Constant political bickering compounded the problem. All this resulted in the major problem of legislative lag. The legal confusion symbolized by this lag, and to which it contributed, was ripe for exploitation by corrupt-minded officials, since it permitted them to take advantage of ambiguities and loopholes.[25] In fairness, some of what was subsequently called corruption resulted less from deliberate malfeasance than from genuine ignorance as to what did and did not constitute acceptable behavior. It will be recalled from chapter 2 that our fourth variable for identifying corrupt acts was clandestine behavior, and a tendency by officials to refrain from finding out whether dubious official conduct is in fact corrupt. But what happens if the authorities themselves are confused as to whether a given act constitutes corruption? In some cases, the authorities will disagree among themselves. Their confusion, plus the simultaneous near-breakdown of traditional values and moral codes, make the rise in corruption levels unsurprising. While countries such as Poland had reasonably clear alternative sources of "new" morality and values in the form of a re-energized church, religion was not a feasible or attractive alternative source of ethical guidance for many citizens in most countries. And the point about confusion among what were supposed to be authoritative agencies of the state applied to Poland as elsewhere. Despite this caveat, one ramification of the legislative lag is that officials have often enjoyed much wider scope for discretionary decision making than they would have had in a more codified and norm-based system. Again, ceteris paribus, the potential for corruption is greater where individual officials enjoy broader scope for more or less arbitrary decision making.[26] Political and legal confusion both reflects and contributes to a weak state, a theme explored below. At this point, some of the implications of the economic transition for corruption can be considered.

Numerous dimensions of the economic transition have affected corruption levels in post-communist countries. Massive privatization programs have created new opportunities, as already noted. But the relationship is complex, and not unidirectional. One of the most interesting questions in this context is a chicken-and-egg issue — or, in social science terminology, an issue of causal directionality. In an appeal to the Russian citizenry, the Organizing Committee of the National Salvation Front in Russia claimed that "crime, speculation, corruption and lawlessness" were a result of Yeltsin's and Gaidar's policies of privatization (*Sovetskaya Rossiya*, 1 October 1992, 1). But while some blame privatization for corruption, and suggest that the proponents of radical privatization and marketization policies at least condone if not actually encourage corruption, the proponents themselves often maintain that the privatization process is being hindered by corruption. For instance, Ella Pamfilova, then minister for social security in Russia, argued in 1993 that corruption was the obstacle against which market reforms "constantly stumble" (cited in *Financial Times*, 18 June 1993, 15). Thus the relationship between corruption and privatization is interactive and bidirectional, and it is clear that the state's regulatory powers during the marketization and privatization process often provide new opportunities for corruption. This all said, Kaufmann and Siegelbaum (1997) have argued convincingly that some approaches to privatization in transition states encourage corruption much more than others; this important differentiation should be borne in mind when considering the impact of privatization on corruption levels.[27]

Another problem related to the economic and legal transition is that property laws in most post-communist states have been vague and ambiguous. This is not the place to rehearse these in detail. But one area of property law that has discouraged investment, and in many cases increased opportunities for corruption, is restitution. An indication that this restitution has been an ongoing problem in some countries is that the Polish Law on Restitution had still not been finalized by mid-2001 — more than a decade after the collapse of communist power — mainly because of fundamental disagreements in both parliamentary chambers, and between parliament and the president (*EECR* 10, nos. 2–3:34).

Two other economic problems of early post-communism have had serious implications for morale among state officials, and thus for their propensity to engage in corruption. One has already been briefly mentioned — rapidly rising unemployment rates. Not only was systemic unemployment itself almost unknown in the communist world, but the poorly developed welfare states in early post-communism only increased the general sense of insecurity (Deacon et al. 1992: for an update and analyses of the diversities of CEE welfare states see Wagener 2002; J. Kovács 2002). The second was the extremely high rates of inflation in early post-communism (tabulated data through 1995 are in L. Holmes 1997b, 220–21), at a time when many officials' salaries were either not being increased at a commensurate rate, or in extreme cases not being paid at all.[28]

The Near-Absence of a Bourgeoisie

It was argued above that the scale and nature of attempted restructuring in CEE and the CIS over the past ten to fifteen years has been unprecedented. One important social aspect of the economic revolution, often overlooked, is crucial to understanding many of the problems of post-communism, including corruption. During the communist era most property, including the means of production, was owned and controlled by the state. There was no large-scale capital-owning class. On one level, this near-absence of a bourgeoisie[29] represents another aspect of the communist legacy and path dependency, as well as another dimension — a social and class one — of the multiple and simultaneous transition. But it is a sufficiently important factor to warrant being considered on its own.

If a state wishes to privatize its assets, it can do so in various ways. One is to sell to foreign investors. While this was an option for post-communist states, there were limits to its utility and feasibility. On the one hand, the West had limited funds to invest in the post-communist countries, and arguably less political will than it might have had,[30] for several reasons. One was the West's own economic problems, in particular the recession of the late 1980s and early 1990s. In addition, since so many countries overthrew the communist system more or less simultaneously — by the early 1990s, there were twenty-seven such countries in CEE and the CIS — there was far more demand on limited western funds than there would have been had, say, only three countries started a transition, as was the case with the southern European states of Greece, Portugal, and Spain during the mid-1970s. Third, the confused legislation on property ownership in all early post-communist states meant that many westerners were reluctant to purchase enterprises or make other investments until they could be certain that they would continue to be formally recognized as the legal owners. Something else contributed to western caution: whereas states such as Hungary welcomed foreign investment, others such as Czechia were initially reluctant to become overly dependent on western capital anyway (Pehe 1998, 40–41; Reed 2002, 276).[31]

All this suggested that investment would have to be generated primarily from within the individual countries. But in the absence of a wealthy capital-owning class, it was unclear how this investment would occur. This is not the place to examine the numerous methods — some of them ingenious — used by post-communist states to privatize their assets and attract investment (see for example Frydman and Rapaczynski 1994; Lavigne 1995, 155–90). It is sufficient to note that many members of the former nomenklatura (the various élites from the communist era)[32] were in a particularly advantageous position to benefit from some of the unusual privatization processes, albeit to differing extents in different countries.[33] Many were directly involved in the sell-off of state assets, benefiting from bribes and kickbacks paid by those to whom they sold assets at knock-down prices, and sometimes becoming shareholders themselves. Most post-communist states initially had little if any conflict-of-interest legislation; in the few that did, it was ambiguous and poorly implemented. Thus was created a situation ripe for corruption.

The need to encourage investment in countries with little or no indigenous bourgeoisie, in a situation where very high levels of foreign investment were either an unrealistic aspiration or unwanted, meant that several post-communist governments deliberately overlooked the source of investments. Thus Prime Minister Klaus in Czechia "brushed aside such objections [that "dirty money" was funding much of the Czech privatization process], saying that the origin of funds invested in the country's economic transformation was irrelevant, and that the only important matter was that the process begin quickly and not be delayed by such quibbles" (Kettle 1995, 39).[34] All too often, cash-strapped governments refused to investigate what were clearly questionable (and probably criminally acquired) funds.

The absence of clear guidelines or legislation on the privatization process was in many cases a result not merely of the legislative lag referred to earlier, but also of the desire to maximize investment funds — however generated — and, if need be, encourage market forces that included ethically questionable ones. Hence actions that would normally be considered at least improper, in some cases illegal, in most western states have often not been treated as such by post-communist authorities. In the absence of detailed and unambiguous regulations on conflicts of interest, for example, many officials have been legally able to profit from the privatization process. Antoni Kamiński cites two interesting examples from Poland. The first concerns a man who was deputy minister in charge of joint ventures in 1989–92. At the same time as he fulfilled his government role, he established a consulting firm that specialized in joint ventures. When Prime Minister Mazowiecki issued a decree in mid-1990 forbidding senior government officials to own or operate consultancy firms, the deputy minister apparently transferred the ownership of his company to his wife. The second case is that of the film director Janusz Zaorski. He was nominated head of the state television and radio network in 1991 — after which, allegedly, his wife founded a company specializing in the production of television programs; Zaorski's brother was apparently also a partner in the firm (Kamiński 1996, 11–12).[35]

The rapid and often questionable creation of a bourgeoisie, in the broader context of a confused legal framework and an undermining of social norms, has had further effects. One has been to exacerbate the sense of inequality and inequity in many post-communist states. The divide between "them" and "us" that was typical of the communist era has not faded, and in some countries has deepened. Demonstrable — often flaunted — wealth (in the form of Mercedeses, BMWs, and large sport utility vehicles) has replaced being on the nomenklatura list and having access to élite party shops as the status symbol in many post-communist countries. Typically this ostentation leads to at least as much resentment among the have-nots against the nouveaux riches as there was against the party élites in the past. This is especially so when ordinary citizens and lower-ranking state officials — who can be just as alienated from the state and its élites as anyone else — believe that the wealth was acquired improperly; they then perceive themselves as the losers of transition, and the nouveaux riches as the unfair winners. The problem is compounded by the apparent de facto (and occasionally de jure) immunity of so many high-level corrupt officials and members of organized-crime gangs, which annoys and frustrates many lower-level officials and ordinary citizens. In some cases this frustration transmutes into a sense of "if you can't beat 'em, join 'em," which exacerbates the problem of corruption.

Before finishing this discussion, it is worth considering the special situation of China. Ding (2000) has argued convincingly that a new, peculiar form of nomenklatura privatization has been occurring in China in recent years. He calls this variously illicit, informal, or prerogative privatization. It essentially involves officials becoming improperly involved in private ventures overseas, and profiting from them; Ding explains how and why opportunities for this sort of "entrepreneurship" often arise for officials and their relatives, but for few others. The relevance of this trend to our argument is that the core of what could become a "postsocialist grand bourgeoisie" (Ding 2000, 146) has been forming in still putatively communist China. Thus when the communist system is eventually replaced there, many of the problems faced by CEE and CIS post-communist states in recent years either will not be experienced by fully post-communist China, or else should be much less serious and of a different nature.

The International and Ideological Context

In an earlier analysis of post-communism (L. Holmes 1997b, esp. 21), it was argued that a salient feature of post-communism was unfortunate timing: so many countries became post-communist at about the same time, just as the West was entering a recession. One result was that the newly forming systems experienced greater difficulties in securing foreign investment than they might have done had the transition occurred piecemeal and in a more buoyant international financial climate. That it did not exacerbated the economic problems of post-communist states, which in turn rendered many officials more susceptible to supplementing their salary illicitly. But there was another crucial way in which the transitions toward market economies occurred at an unfortunate moment. Briefly stated, the argument is that enthusiasm in the West for neoliberalism (or economic rationalism, as it is better known in Oceania) was intensifying in the late 1980s, and that this made it more difficult to establish a market with clear rules in the post-communist world. This requires elaboration.

Margaret Thatcher came to power in the United Kingdom in 1979 — hence the earlier reference to the significance of that year — and soon began to establish a radically new version of capitalism there. Keynesian and neo-Keynesian approaches were discarded, and the old-fashioned if patronizing *noblesse oblige* form of conservatism was replaced by a hard-nosed neoliberalism. On one level, this change was intended to uncouple the state from the economy, so that privatization, outsourcing, downsizing, and deregulation became key policy orientations. The implications of these policies for state officials were profound. In the process of uncoupling, the British government had to develop an ideological justification for dismissing hundreds of thousands of state employees.[36] Suddenly there was a breakdown in the traditional tradeoff between on the one hand lower average incomes and greater security in state-sector jobs and on the other hand higher average incomes and less security in the private sector. Previously there had been a discreet notion of mutual loyalty between the state and its employees. Officials were sometimes dismissed, of course; but still there was a greater sense of security for state employees, and hence loyalty, than there was in the new era of neoliberalism. Those lucky enough to retain their posts in the new circumstances often found life much harder, as putative efficiency measures typically demanded longer hours, "multi-skilling," and sometimes salary freezes. The new policy, essentially one of divide and rule, undermined the traditional esprit de corps and morale of the public service.

Neoliberalism — whether in the form of Thatcherism in Britain, Reaganomics in the United States, Rogernomics in New Zealand, or any other variation on the theme — encourages a commercial ethos in everything, including areas where it has traditionally been absent. The basic tenets of public choice theory have permeated both public administration and the study of it, so that policy studies have largely replaced more traditional subjects in public administration. The implication of this shift for the new generation of public servants is that they have a different perspective on the role of the state. Citing Haque (1996, 518), "policy studies, policy analysis, and similar subfields, through their theoretical framework of public choice theory (which is also a framework for privatization), tend to infuse market norms, such as individual self-interest, utility, productivity, and efficiency into public administration and gradually replace its public norms, such as accountability, representativeness, equality and responsiveness."[37]

While the new approach in the United States was not so different from the previous ones, it was radically different from those of the countries of continental Western Europe and Australasia, which were more strongly oriented toward the welfare state. By the 1980s, according to Pirie (1988, 3), the ethos in favor of privatizing former state functions and enterprises, and the ramifications of doing so, had spread to more than one hundred countries. The paramount objectives now often appeared to be maximizing organizations' profitability and minimizing responsibility, while staff loyalty, whether to the state or to a company, meant little. Suddenly state officials discovered that they could be dismissed even when performing well in a post in which they had served for many years. While the esprit de corps of many branches of the public service was deeply engrained, it was not encouraged by the new rugged conservatives, for whom such subjectivities were at least anachronistic, if not anathema. Indeed the new breed of neoliberal politicians tended to undermine the legitimacy of the very concept of public service.

This shift toward the market ethos in every aspect of life, including politics and the state bureaucracy, has been seen by Della Porta and Mény (Della Porta and Mény eds. 1995c, esp.166–68; see too Hawley 2000) as a major factor in the apparent growth of corruption in Western Europe. If they are correct, as I believe they are, then one of the major reasons for corruption in post-communist states comes more sharply into focus, as does the reason why it is more extreme in these states.

The rejection of the old system was much more radical in the post-communist states than in the western states, which in a sense were modifying, albeit significantly, long-established arrangements. In CEE and the CIS, the notion of loyalty to a state or even an enterprise in the heady atmosphere of post-1989 would have been absurd: how can one continue to be loyal to something that no longer exists? However, had the new politicians managed to develop rapidly a sense of loyalty to a new system, and a system that was loyal to its employees, there might have been less of a problem with corruption in the 1990s. But the new systems were being developed in chaotic and egotistical times. Since the post-communist states were entering the capitalist world at this stage, and at a time when the "communications revolution" was accelerating, they were almost bound to be influenced by the type of thinking that by the end of the 1980s had begun to spread from the Anglo-Celtic world into continental Europe.

Many people interviewed in CEE and the CIS for this book argued that one of the reasons for so much corruption in so many post-communist countries is that the populations of these countries have for the most part not understood certain important realities of established market economies, including that they operate according to many rules and norms, both formal and informal. In this view, if post-communist states had a more sophisticated understanding of real-life market economics, instead of a simplistic notion that borders on economic anarchy, then the problem of corruption would be significantly reduced.[38] Perhaps these commentators are correct. But they may be inadvertently harking back to the pre-Thatcher era, when capitalism in Europe was more closely controlled by the state. In those days, many economists distinguished between the Nordic or Rhineland model and the North American or transatlantic model. But the transatlantic model clearly dominated in the 1990s. While the victory of the transatlantic model might suit Americans, who are by and large used to it, the result has been confusion and misery in many parts of Europe, as more and more governments have sought to deal with fiscal problems through privatization and by reducing the scale of the welfare state.[39] In this atmosphere, the old notions of a caring and responsible state become, like the public service ethos, anachronistic and anathema.

One way of reducing corruption is by developing a greater sense of loyalty and duty to the state—by building bureaucratic social capital. But when states themselves are still only forming and hence have no established legitimacy, doing this is difficult. If one notes in addition that the post-communist states cannot help being affected by the current dominant approach within established capitalist states, in which the state itself sometimes appears to be for sale and has increasingly yielded a separate identity to the market, it is hardly surprising that corruption should be such a problem. By now it should be clear that the emergence of post-communism was unfortunately timed because of more than just the commonly cited western economic recession.

It will be recalled that one of the legacies of communism was a blurring between institutions, and even between the state and society. This confusion between the private and public domains has been continued into post-communism partly because of the pervasive influence of neoliberal ideology. Whereas the traditional European model of the capitalist welfare state drew a reasonably sharp distinction between these two sectors, neoliberalism deliberately blurs them. Ironically, communism and neoliberal capitalism have much in common vis-à-vis this key variable. However, there is for our purposes one vital difference, and it is important to emphasize this difference in any analysis of post-communist corruption. The difference lies in attitudes toward the loyalty of state staffs. As already emphasized, neoliberalism is a rugged and unsentimental ideology, and well-performing and loyal state officials should not be surprised if they are suddenly made redundant.[40] This point leads to what is here called the transition gap thesis.

For the sake of clarity, just two models of capitalism have been identified here. One is a predominantly social democratic or social welfare version that was common for decades in Western Europe. In terms of attitudes toward the role of the state, the differences between this Scandinavian or Rhineland model and the communist model of CEE were fewer than the differences between the transatlantic model and the communist.[41] Expressing this another way, the communist East European model was separated by a smaller gap from the traditional west European model than from that which prevailed in the United Kingdom and the United States. Since the latter was beginning to spread throughout Western Europe too by the time of the collapse of the communist systems, the gap between the old systems and the intended new systems in CEE was greater than it would have been had the West European countries — particularly the Nordic and Germanic ones — largely retained the systems they had had for decades.[42] Thus the trauma of change was greater for state officials and citizens in CEE and the CIS than it would have been had post-communist politicians sought to replace the communist system with one less radically different from its predecessor. The principal implication of the transition gap thesis for corruption is that levels of confusion and insecurity were higher than they might otherwise have been; as argued earlier, confusion and a sense of job insecurity can be fertile soils for corruption.

It might appear by this stage that the argument here is simply against a particular form of capitalism, namely neoliberalism. While my own predilections are not toward this uncaring form of capitalism, the objective here is not normative but analytical: a better understanding of the phenomenon of corruption. In attempting to assess the role of neoliberalism, it is important to probe one level deeper, and ask why it has become so dominant an ideology in the contemporary western world. By doing so, the future of both it and corruption can be assessed from a more informed perspective.

It is no mere coincidence that the neoliberal wave started where and when it did. In the United Kingdom, two of the salient features of the 1970s were the oil crisis and some of the most serious challenges ever to the state from the blue-collar working classes, as symbolized by the various miners' strikes. Thatcher came to power with a promise to break the power of the trade unions, which she largely fulfilled. But the oil crisis and the strike wave were indicative of an even deeper process under way, of which these two phenomena were symptoms. That process was what is nowadays called globalization.

Despite the arguments of some dependency and world-systems theorists of the late 1960s and 1970s (Frank 1969; Wallerstein 1974; Cardoso and Faletto 1979), it was becoming obvious to many observers by the mid-1970s that some underdeveloped or developing countries might be able to overcome their late starts in the global race to economic development. As the oil crisis of 1973 had demonstrated, the chances that an underdeveloped country would catch up depended partly on what natural resources it had. If these were materials that the West desperately needed, countries possessing them could accelerate their development. At about the same time, Japan was developing rapidly while the "little dragons" of East Asia were beginning their liftoffs, suggesting that even countries with few natural resources might be able to break out of the vicious circle of underdevelopment and asymmetry if they possessed cheap, disciplined, and willing workforces or adopted policies friendly to investors. Finally, the growth rates of the second world — the communist states — still appeared at that stage to be impressive, yet again supporting the notion that nonwestern countries might be able to catch up with the West.

But the pressure on western states was not merely from international economic competition. Domestically, changing demographics were also a major factor. Ever more sophisticated and expensive medical treatment was contributing to a graying of populations. At the same time, consumerism and increased access to tertiary education, as well as changing attitudes toward the family, contraception, and women in the workforce, all helped to explain declining birth rates. With growing postemployment populations and proportionately shrinking workforces, most western states were experiencing rapidly increasing structural pressure on their welfare services, pension schemes, and other services. In this situation of growing international competition plus demographic pressures at home, many western governments felt obliged to seek radical solutions and change. This was the context in which neoliberalism became such a dominant force.

It has been argued that the spinoff effects of neoliberal ideology have contributed to the apparent increase in corruption in so many parts of the post-communist world, but that the fragility of states has exacerbated the problem. Another important point has so far been only alluded to: it is related to the discreteness of democratization and marketization, which are sometimes treated as two dimensions of essentially one process (often called modernization). In an article on corruption in China, Gordon White (1996, 150) points out that in the view of many neoliberal economists "reducing the economic role of the state through privatization and deregulation can be instrumental in reducing corruption and, second, democratization of the polity can be similarly effective by introducing more competition, transparency, and accountability into the political process." He goes on to argue that both India and China have liberalized economically and apparently experienced an increase in corruption, while South Korea and the Philippines have democratized and experienced either no lessening of corruption (Korea) or an outright increase (Philippines). Although White does not pursue this argument much further, he has touched on a vital aspect of corruption in transitional societies, including the post-communist ones.

White's clear separation of economic and political liberalization is appropriate. It does appear that in the transition to neoliberal economics, there may be an increase in corruption unless the economic liberalization is tied to a real democratization of politics, including a dramatic increase in transparency and the rule of law. The reason is simple. The process of privatization increases the amount of potentially high-stakes interaction between businesspeople and state officials. If the interaction occurs at the same time as the state itself is weak, or is encouraging selfishness and the ending of mutual loyalty between it and its employees, the likelihood of corruption increases, unless the democratic process acts as a counterweight. After all, economic reform itself is likely to prompt the state in the future to consider superfluous many of those charged with the privatizing process. Because of this, it might well be rational for officials to act corruptly, both in immediate terms (kickbacks in the privatization process) and for their futures (developing ties with possible future employers in the private sector). This is particularly true if a system of checks and balances has not yet emerged, or else appears largely unable to control corruption; both scenarios are common while democracy is still being established.

Much of this argument applies in principle to the West as well as to the post-communist states. However, three significant differences between the western and the post-communist processes help to explain why the argument of Della Porta and Mény concerning Western Europe, although possibly correct, could with modifications be even more useful as a starting point for explaining increased corruption in CEE and the CIS. First, while many western states have been enthusiastic about privatization, the process has been considerably more gradual and small-scale than in the post-communist world. Western countries have not been attempting rapid privatization of almost entire economies, as many CEE and CIS countries have more or less sought to do. Citing World Bank data, Kaufmann and Siegelbaum (1997, 419) have pointed out that there were only some 6,000 privatizations worldwide during the whole of the 1980s, whereas more than 50,000 medium- and large-scale enterprises were privatized by post-communist states in the first half of the 1990s alone. The East German privatization agency Treuhandanstalt alone privatized approximately 15,000 state-owned enterprises between 1990 and the end of 1994 (*Bundesministerium der Finanzen* web site, visited March 2003).

Second, the privatization process has for the most part been conducted in the West with established corporations and existing property-owning (capitalist) groupings that have more or less established ethical codes. Moreover, laws on property are in most cases much clearer and more stable, and the functioning of market principles more regularized, than in post-communist states. In contrast, the capitalist classes are still being formed in CEE and the CIS, and have had few agreed-on rules or established modi operandis. That so many so-called businesspeople in the post-communist states engage in questionable activities, sometimes including blatant gangsterism and other forms of criminality, obviously affects the whole privatization process.

Finally, the western process has been occurring in societies that are more stable, and that constitute consolidated democracies. There are also more established traditions of loyalty and responsibility in most western states. One manifestation of this is that responsible investigative journalism is generally more common than in transition states. Another is that there are still remnants of esprit de corps in many western state agencies, while the levels of transparency and accountability tend to be much higher than in post-communist states. This helps to explain the apparent conundrum (or counterfactual, in terms of the argument made here) that the highly neoliberal New Zealand appears to be among the world's least corrupt states (it consistently emerges in CPIs as one of the three or four least corrupt countries in the world); *inter alia*, it has some of the most transparent political practices in the world (Cangiano 1996; see too Sutch 1999).[43]

In short, the contrasts with western countries bring us back to the very nature of post-communism: a communist legacy and the implications of multiple transitions. Western states that have adopted neoliberalism have themselves had to introduce profound ideological change, to justify the state's significant uncoupling not only from the economy but even from protective functions that it has traditionally performed, such as managing prisons and policing.[44] But in comparison with what has been happening in CEE and the CIS, the changes are modest and the context conducive.

At the start of this chapter, I referred to the desirability of surveying corrupt officials and explained why doing so is not feasible. But citizens can be surveyed to determine what they believe are the principal causes of corruption in their countries. This issue was addressed in the four-country survey conducted in mid-2000 as part of the research for this book. Respondents were asked to select three factors from a list of fifteen (the last of which was open-ended, allowing them to name factors not already identified). These factors were:

1. Authorities have inadequate resources to deal with the problem
2. Communist legacy (patterns of behavior established before 1989 [1991 in the case of Russia], some of which have continued since then)
3. Competitive politics
4. Disrespect for or lack of faith in the authorities
5. A general sense of insecurity in society
6. Greater interaction with the West
7. High rates of inflation
8. Less authoritarianism generally, or a more lenient attitude by the authorities toward corruption in particular

9. Low salaries
10. Lower ethical standards
11. Marketization
12. Privatization
13. Unclear legislation
14. Unemployment
15. Other (please specify)[45]

The results were interesting, and in some cases, at least at first glance, unexpected. In Bulgaria the three causes most frequently cited were (in descending order of frequency) unemployment (15.8 percent of all responses), low salaries (14.4 percent), and unclear legislation (11.8 percent). The factor cited by the fewest respondents was greater interaction with the West (a mere 0.9 percent), while the communist legacy was identified by only 2.7 percent as the primary factor. The Hungarian responses revealed some overlap with the Bulgarian ones, but also significant differences. The most frequently cited reason for corruption was high inflation (17.1 percent), followed by low salaries (16.0 percent) and more lenient attitudes (10.6 percent). As in Bulgaria, interaction with the West was seen as the least important explanatory factor (1.9 percent), followed by competitive politics (2.2 percent) and a sense of insecurity (2.9 percent). The Polish results were identical to the Bulgarian ones in terms of the three most commonly cited causes; only the percentages differed. Thus the three most frequently cited causes were unemployment (19.7 percent), low salaries (15.8 percent), and unclear legislation (12.5 percent). At the other end of the spectrum, the least-cited causes were greater interaction with the West (2.6 percent) and the communist legacy (2.7 percent).

Finally, Russians agreed with the Hungarians that high inflation rates were the single most significant cause of corruption (10.9 percent);[46] interestingly, Bulgarian and Polish respondents considered these among the least important causes.[47] The second- and third-most frequently cited factors by Russians were low salaries (10.8 percent) and insufficient resources allocated to the authorities for seriously addressing problems (10.5 percent). This last factor did not figure in the top four in any of the other countries, and probably reflects the widespread feeling in Russia at the time that the state was weak; if so, Putin's recent accession to power at the time of the survey suggests that those who elected him because he promised to strengthen the state believed that he had not yet had time or the resources to do so. Like their neighbors in all three CEE countries surveyed, the Russians considered greater interaction with the West one of the two least significant factors explaining corruption (2.9 percent). Perhaps counterintuitively, they did not consider marketization an important factor either (2.9 percent). On the other hand, like the Bulgarians and Poles, Russian respondents also considered the communist legacy relatively unimportant in explaining corruption (4.5 percent). The rank-ordering of factors across all four countries can be quickly compared in table 6.1.

These results require interpretation, especially in light of the arguments in this chapter concerning the impact of neoliberalism and the communist legacy; at first glance, the data could appear fundamentally to undermine those arguments. But what appears to be obvious often is not.

As just indicated, respondents in all four countries agreed that greater interaction with the West was the least significant explanation of corruption among their officials. In Bulgaria, Hungary, and Poland, many citizens probably believed that their governments would be forced as a result of their attempts to join the European Union to act more vigorously to combat corruption — so that greater interaction with the West would be seen as a method for reducing corruption. Joining the European Union became such a concrete telos in many parts of CEE by the turn of the millennium that this view of the West in all likelihood dominated more abstract concepts such as globalization or neoliberalism. Indeed most CEE and CIS citizens, like their western counterparts, probably had (and have) little if any understanding of the term "neoliberalism." The teleological factor would not pertain in the case of Russia. There most citizens probably do not believe that the West plays any significant role in their country's internal affairs. But in Russia too, low levels of awareness of the concepts and impact of globalization and neoliberalism almost certainly pertain.

That the communist legacy is also ranked so low can be interpreted in various ways. One is that since the surveys were conducted in mid-2000, many citizens will not have identified much influence from something that collapsed almost a decade earlier (in Russia's case) or even longer ago than that (in the case of the other three countries); many younger respondents would have had only hazy recollections of the communist

TABLE 6.1.   Rank-Ordered Perceived Causes of Corruption, 2000

	Bulgaria	Hungary	Poland	Russia
Authorities have inadequate resources	12			3
Communist legacy	11		13	12
Competitive politics		13		
Disrespect for or lack of faith in the authorities				
A general sense of insecurity in society		12		
Greater interaction with the West	14	14	14	13 (tie)
High rates of inflation	13	1	12	1
Less authoritarianism		3		4
Low salaries	2	2	2	2
Lower ethical standards	4	4		
Marketization		11	11	13 (tie)
Privatization			4	11
Unclear legislation	3		3	
Unemployment	1		1	

Notes: Lower numbers indicate greater perceived significance. "Other" responses were too infrequent to be statistically significant.

era anyway. A second is that by the time of the surveys, many citizens were either overtly nostalgic for the past, or had selective memories, forgetting some of the worse aspects of the communist era. When the current situation is far from optimal, such selective memory is well known to social psychologists as a coping mechanism for overcoming cognitive dissonance. A number of recent studies have identified this, even for Hungary and Poland (Lampland 2002; Pine 2002), where one might expect less nostalgia than in the more troubled Bulgaria and Russia.[48] Finally, many citizens were either unaware of how widespread corruption was during the communist era — particularly at the higher levels — or else had forgotten (on Russia compare the data in Levada 2000a, 330, 564). In short, the survey data neither prove nor disprove our hypotheses about the communist legacy; but the results do require interpretation, as just provided.

Clearly there are numerous causes of corruption in post-communist countries. Some can be found in many other kinds of system, although the focus here has been on factors that are either peculiar to, or else far more salient in, the post-communist world. But in terms of systemic factors, the two most significant are the communist legacy, and the inadequacy and fragility of the systems themselves, which result largely from the scope of multiple and simultaneous transitions. The communist legacy has already been considered at length; here we can explore the issue of fragile systems, which can be subsumed under the concept of the weak state.

It is tempting to argue that the major systemic problem of the post-communist state has been that there is no system; such a statement is punchy and simple. Yet such a conclusion would not only be sensationalist and unscholarly, but also untrue and increasingly outdated. Furthermore, it would be insulting to the many honest and committed people in the post-communist world who have been making strenuous efforts to build new and better societies on the ruins of their communist pasts. But it would be fair to say that probably the single most important explanation for corruption in the post-communist world is that the system is still crystallizing and consolidating, and that most post-communist states are ultimately weak states.[49] Among the numerous ramifications of this instability and weakness are the absence or ambiguity of rules and regulations; high levels of insecurity in the public sector; the poorly developed nature of a new set of rules of the game; and the poor capacity of the state to implement policies, including tax collection.[50] These are ideal systemic factors for an increase in corruption; the last can be explored to make the point.

Daniel Tarschys (2003, esp. 367) has focused on the severe problem of the double extraction burden on businesses in CEE and CIS states. To operate, many businesses have to pay both official levies (state taxes) and unofficial or shadow ones (bribes to corrupt officials; protection money to either crime syndicates or semi-legitimate but private security agencies). If the state is too weak and too corrupt to protect businesses from shadow taxes (bribes, protection payments), then it is understandable that businesspeople should resent having to pay more than the law requires just to be able to operate.

This double extraction burden has various negative spinoff effects. First, businesses that attempt to work within the law, paying only official taxes, run the risk of being targeted by meat-eating officials or violent criminals, and may have to close down. Second, businesses that de facto pay the double "taxation" either have to charge higher prices (the extrac-

tion burden is passed on to the consumer, with inflationary implications)
or discover that they cannot afford to continue operating. Double "taxation" is likely to be part of the reason why, as Albats points out, the
number of people employed in small and medium-sized businesses in
Russia declined some 30 percent between 1995 and 2001, although this
must remain speculative (*Johnson's Russia List* 8268, 25 June 2004).

In any event, it is clear that the state is likely to remain weak unless it
can break out of a vicious spiral. At one level, it loses — or at least does
not increase — income from what should be a major source of revenue.
At a broader level, economic growth suffers, inflation and unemployment can both increase, and systemic legitimacy declines. While the
state authorities may attempt to compensate for the lost revenue by
increasing taxes, this is likely to exacerbate the problem, as remaining
businesses find themselves in the same vicious spiral as their weaker or
more honest erstwhile competitors who have already exited the market.
As Tarschys (2003, 367) reminds us, raising taxes too far creates a disin-
centive to economic activity, typically generating less revenue for the
state than the taxing authorities predicted. And less income means a
weaker state (on this whole issue see too Friedman, Johnson, Kaufmann, and Zoido-Lobaton 2000; Svensson 2003).

There are many other explanations for the weakness of most post-
communist states. One is that their fragility is yet another byproduct of
the unprecedented scale of the attempts at multiple, simultaneous transitions. There was, after all, no blueprint for the changes, and no vicarious experience on which to draw. This uniqueness of the post-communist transitions is undoubtedly a major part of the explanation. But there
is also another dimension, intimately related to corruption, that Joel
Hellman (1998) calls the "partial reform equilibrium" of many post-
communist states. Expressed crudely, Hellman's argument is that many
of those who provided the driving force for change in the early stages
of post-communism had a personal interest in introducing various reforms, but only to a certain point. Once they themselves had taken
advantage of the new arrangements, they sought to apply the brakes to
further reform, so as to consolidate their privileged positions. Many of
these people had benefited — often through questionable means, sometimes through overtly improper ones — from the confusion of the early
days of post-communism, and in doing so had simultaneously contributed to a general atmosphere of corruption and rule bending. Once their

positions were consolidated, they sought to ensure that no future legislation could deprive them of their ill-gotten gains. Nor were they enthusiastic about subjecting themselves to competition from powerful
agents, such as western companies.[51]

Hellman's argument applies more in some countries than in others.
Thus, whereas states such as Russia and Ukraine started reform but soon
either halted or severely hindered further progress, other countries
maintained the momentum through the 1990s. Interestingly, as Hellman notes, there is a close correlation between the level of reform introduced in a post-communist state and economic performance. In general,
countries that have continued to push ahead with major reform — those
least subject to the problem of partial reform equilibrium — are also
those that have sustained high growth rates.[52] It will be recalled that
according to the TI CPIs and various other assessments, countries such
as Estonia, Slovenia, and Poland until recently (countries that soon
opted for more radical, and in many ways more neoliberal reforms than
their neighbors) have made more progress against corruption than less
radically reformist countries such as the Central Asian states, Russia, and
Ukraine.[53] All this is compatible with both Hellman's thesis and the
neoliberalism argument posited here.

But there is a double sting in the tail of our argument. First, while the
spread of neoliberalism can help to explain the perceived rise of corruption levels in so many western states, the relationship is more complex in
post-communist states. There the apparent relationship between perceived levels of corruption and the extent to which radical reform has
been introduced strongly suggests that the communist legacy is a more
powerful explicator of corruption than neoliberalism is. In fact, if properly implemented, neoliberalism undermines cozy networks and embed-
ded cliques, and can thus help to overcome the communist legacy. It also
tends to improve economic performance, by removing or reducing subsidies of inefficient enterprises and allowing market forces far greater
play. Intuitively, it would seem that where economies are clearly improving, there is less sense of despair and perhaps less insecurity than in
a formerly communist system that appears unable to lift itself off the
floor. Therefore for the purposes of battling corruption, it is preferable
to opt for a system in which the former communists have their grip
weakened by neoliberalism than one in which they can continue to
exercise power and to own many of society's resources. Everything is

relative, and neoliberalism emerges as clearly preferable to the communist legacy.

Russia's special situation needs to be addressed.[54] While Gaidar's neoliberal reforms essentially went on hold by late 1993, the same was not true of all forms of privatization—a key aspect of economic reform. Moreover, whereas the earliest stages of Russian privatization were heavily dominated by the former nomenklatura (and therefore were stages during which the issue of the communist legacy clearly pertained), the two later stages—voucher privatization and the loans-for-shares schemes—were not to any meaningful extent. Voucher privatization was by most criteria a failure anyway, and citizens were soon selling off their shares to pay for basics; the story need not detain us. But Janine Wedel is correct to argue that the loans-for-shares scheme, which occurred primarily in 1995 and was a highly significant aspect of Russian privatization, was not dominated by the former communist nomenklatura. At first sight, this might appear to undermine our position. However, we fully concur with the argument of Coulloudon (2002, 195–98) that while many of the people involved might not have had communist pasts, the way privatization was handled in 1995 was very much reminiscent of the communist era. It also lent support to the argument that reform had stalled. Yeltsin had once been a member of the Politburo, and while he had clearly moved on from communism in several important ways, remnants of the past cronyistic methods were still evident. The concept of communist legacy in our argument refers not only to people, but also to behavior and attitudes.

The second sting in the tail of our argument, which must not be overlooked, is that the options available to post-communist states in the 1990s were limited. Even had they wanted to, it was simply unrealistic to expect the states to move swiftly from communism to a social-welfare version of capitalism. Long-established, more generous versions of the welfare state have proved too expensive even for most Nordic countries and Germany, so any suggestion that the impoverished early post-communist states should have sought to reduce the gap between the old system and the new must be dismissed as wishful thinking. High levels of insecurity and of related corruption were virtually inevitable.

One final point needs to be made before proceeding to the next chapter. The references above to relativism constitute a major part of the answer to possible charges that the earlier argument concerning the impact of neoliberalism on post-communist corruption is undermined by examples such as Estonia, Poland, and Slovenia.[55] It must not be forgotten that the post-communist states as a whole are still among the more corrupt parts of the world, and even the best performing CEE states emerge as considerably more corrupt than the best-performing West European states in comparative perception analyses. Given that all the post-communist states need to lift their game in the fight against corruption, we turn now to consider what they — and other agencies — can do and are doing.

CHAPTER 7

Measures against Corruption

There are numerous methods for tackling corruption (for general introductions see Eigen 1996; Transparency International and International Bank for Reconstruction and Development 1998; Williams and Doig eds. 2000). Some are primarily the responsibility of the state, while others place the onus more on civil society or on agencies beyond a particular country. This chapter outlines methods that have been used in post-communist states, as well as some that do not yet appear to have been used, but have been effective elsewhere. In assessing the various methods, both potential advantages and possible drawbacks will be considered.

THE ROLE OF THE POST-COMMUNIST STATE

Surveys suggest that most people living in the post-communist world believe that the onus in combating corruption is primarily on the state. For instance, in a survey of ten post-communist states in 2001 (GfK 2001, 20), the percentage of respondents indicating that they either totally or quite agreed with the statement "the state and not people should fight against corruption and bribery" amounted to 83 in Russia, 74 in Hungary, and 70 in Bulgaria; only in Poland, which had by far the lowest score and was the glaring exception among the ten states, did this figure drop below 50 (at 48). In the following pages we consider the vast arsenal of weapons at the state's disposal if it wants to tackle corruption. To the extent that there is any logic to the sequencing, it is that the first six methods can broadly be described as legal or punitive, the next six as structural, the next two as educational, and the last five as "other" (three of which are described as radical).

Use of the Legal System

One obvious but important method for dealing with corruption is for post-communist states to use the weight of the law. Ultimately the legal system can play a major role in addressing corruption from what is essentially a rational-choice perspective; it can be used to ensure that potential costs greatly outweigh potential benefits.

Some countries are attempting to deal with the corruption problem partly by specifying more clearly what constitutes corruption and by increasing the potential penalties for engaging in it. In March 1997, for instance, China's legislature, the National People's Congress, adopted a revised version of the Criminal Law; this was the first major revision since the PRC's adoption of the original Criminal Law in 1979. The new law specified a number of new crimes that can relate to corruption (including computer crime and various "new economic crimes"), and increased the number of articles dealing with corruption and bribery by state functionaries from three to seventeen. It also increased certain maximum sentences: whereas the previous maximum sentence for "abuse of power" was five years' imprisonment, it now became seven years' (all details from Wu Naitao 1997). Similarly, Poland increased the penalties for corruption in June 2003 (Pitera with Brennek, Kochanowski, Kojder, and Lęski 2004, 242–43).

But not all states have been tightening up like China or Poland. In earlier chapters, it was demonstrated that officials have been tried in courts of law and sentenced to terms of imprisonment. But many of those found guilty of corruption are subject to lenient punishments, such as fines and suspended sentences. For instance, 756 of the 1,191 prison sentences handed down for fraud in Hungary in 1996 were suspended. Of 183 people convicted of bribery in 1997, 88 received suspended prison sentences, 63 were fined, and only 18 — less than 10 percent — were actually imprisoned (Ministry of the Interior 2000, 33). It is reasonable to infer that this leniency sends the wrong message if the authorities are genuinely committed to substantially reducing corruption and strengthening the rule of law.

Symbolically, it is of particular concern when parliamentarians appear to be protecting their own, by refusing to lift parliamentary immunity. In recent years there have been various attempts in the five countries that are the focus of this book to constrain parliamentary abuse by alleged criminals.[1] But many of these attempts have been frustrated. It was unfortunate when the Polish Sejm for a long time refused to lift the immunity of the former head of the customs service, Ireneusz Sekuła, in 1995 when he was being investigated for alleged corruption (Kamiński 1996, 13), and when the Senate refused to lift the immunity of Senator Aleksander Gawronik in April 1994 (*SWB/EE*, 3 May 1994), meaning that he could not be charged with embezzlement.[2] It appears, however, that political parties in Poland have become much less willing since the late 1990s to protect deputies accused of corruption, and more cooperative in moves to lift their immunity (*Warsaw Voice*, 25 June 2000).[3]

But in 1997 Hungary adopted constitutional amendments that were designed to extend immunity, by providing it to ministers who were not parliamentarians — while the Hungarian Constitutional Court ruled that parliamentary immunity is in most circumstances permanent (*EECR* 6, nos. 2–3:17, 19).[4] While perhaps not going quite as far as the Hungarians, Russian deputies opted in September 2000 not to limit their own immunity, even though there was strong evidence that citizens wanted them to do so (*Izvestiya*, 21 September 2000, 3; *Trud*, 4 February 2000, 1).

It is also of concern how few cases of alleged corruption in postcommunist states that have been investigated have resulted in prosecution, let alone conviction.[5] The reader is reminded of the observation by Luneev (1997, 277–78) that in Russia conviction results from only one in eleven registered cases of the three main types of corruption (embezzlement, bribery, and abuse of office). The picture is slightly better for bribery than for official embezzlement. Luneev provides (unsourced) data indicating that there were 6,562 cases of official bribery recorded in Russia in 1986, and 3,454 convictions, a ratio of some 1.9:1.[6] However, the ratio had more than doubled in just eight years to approximately 4.4:1 by 1994 (the most recent year for which Luneev provides full data). The ratios for official embezzlement are far worse. In 1994 34,904 cases of official embezzlement were recorded in Russia, while there were only 2,747 convictions — yielding a ratio of registrations to convictions of almost 13:1.

There are at least three explanations for this sorry situation. One is that because of the very nature of corruption, it can be difficult to obtain prosecution witnesses. In a corrupt bilateral relationship, normally both sides (donor and recipient) have an interest in denying any wrongdoing to the authorities. Sometimes, especially if the corruption is of the meat-eating variety, one side that has felt unfairly and unduly pressured to enter into a corrupt exchange — possibly even threatened or coerced — will feel sufficiently incensed to cooperate fully with the investigating authorities (possibly in return for a promise of leniency, exemption, or even protection). But this is not as common as it might be, which renders the work of the prosecution much more difficult. Another reason, closely related to the first, is that some post-communist states appear genuinely concerned to respect the principle that a person is innocent until proven guilty, and in adhering to the letter of the law they make it more difficult for themselves to secure convictions. While such respect for the rule of law is not a salient feature of countries such as Belarus and Turkmenistan, it could help to explain the relatively low rates of conviction in countries such as Czechia, Hungary, and Poland. The third reason is that corruption itself can help to explain low conviction rates. Sometimes, good contacts in the procuracies can ensure that investigations are either closed or put on hold; this applies particularly to investigations of senior officials, including politicians and high-ranking law-enforcement officials. At other times, investigating personnel can themselves be bribed to drop investigations, or to file false reports in which they mendaciously claim not to have found any incriminating evidence.

CEE and CIS states are often relatively lenient even with officials who have been found guilty of corruption. It has already been mentioned (see chapter 3) that Jaroslav Lizner had his prison sentence reduced from seven years to six on appeal; the shorter sentence was subsequently in essence halved.[7] Moreover, some political leaderships have decided that use of the legal system is not a particularly effective way to combat corruption. According to one of President Yeltsin's advisers, the Russian presidential team had by the latter half of the 1990s decided that "attempts to prosecute officials for corruption had no future" (Satarov 2001, 6).[8]

This view may be exaggerated, however, or at least based on the assumption that the legal system will continue to operate in the way it previously has. One way in which the system could be better utilized is through the encouragement of autonomous activity by the judiciary and prosecutors. In Italy, for example, much of the drive in the Tangentopoli or *mani pulite* campaign of the early 1990s emanated from judges and prosecutors themselves (Nelken 1996; for a slightly different interpretation see Alberti 1997), while French judges have also become more assertive in recent years in combating political corruption. The communist legacy did not encourage such self-initiated activity by the judiciary. Although most post-communist states claim to be democracies or in transition to democracy, much of the focus in institution building has been on presidencies and parliaments, and to a lesser extent political parties. But some observers, such as the Russian legal specialist Valerii Savitskii (1996, esp. 417–18), have argued that a consolidated democracy is also a rule-of-law state, which in turn requires an independent and vocal judiciary.

In concluding this discussion, it is worth noting that the legal system can be used in questionable ways to combat corruption, and that a stand against corruption can sometimes conflict with commitments to strengthen the rule of law and better respect civil liberties and human rights. One obvious example is the use of undercover informers, either people already working within an organization or "spies" planted by the authorities. Another is entrapment (also known as provocation or the use of sting operations), in which the state sets a trap to catch officials suspected of corruption. One of the best-known examples of entrapment was the operation mounted against the privatization head Lizner in Czechia (see chapter 3 and above). It emerged after his arrest that the police had been fully aware of their actions, since they had set a trap; the money in the suitcase had been provided by the interior ministry's anticorruption department. But other countries have used this system too. For example, the Poles have for some time been using undercover agents to infiltrate suspicious groups, including of state officials suspected of corruption (*SWB/EE*, 12 September 1997). In September 1992 the government agreed to accept the concept of a "controlled bribe" (*zakup kontrolny*) or police provocation in the Penal Code, although this was to be used only in cases of suspected large-scale bribery (in excess of 130,000 złoty — Golik 1999).[9] In late 2000 the Polish authorities broadened the scope of this legislation.

Sometimes sting operations can go seriously awry. Although we have not encountered examples specifically in the context of corruption, as distinct from crime more generally, a Polish case highlights how missteps can occur. In what looked like a sting operation out of *Fawlty Towers*, police in Wrocław set a trap for a drug dealer, and arrested a man.[10] But he turned out to be an officer of the State Security Agency, which was apparently also trying to catch people involved in the sale and purchase of illicit drugs. Unfortunately this officer remained in custody at the time this incident was reported, since the State Security Agency has a policy of not publicly recognizing its own officers (all from DONOSY *Liberal Digest*, 15 January 2000).

Not all post-communist states — or agencies of the state — accept that surveillance and the potential abuse of civil rights are justified even if the objective is to combat crime and corruption. Thus the Hungarian Constitutional Court ruled against the tax office in July 2001, declaring that some of its surveillance work constituted an unjustified invasion of privacy (*EECR* 10, no. 4:20). As in established western states, there is often a tension in post-communist states between the desires to enforce the law and to enhance the rule of law; the two are sometimes incompatible. Another potential abuse of civil and human rights occurs when laws are changed in such a way as to undermine the rule-of-law tenet that a person is presumed innocent until proven guilty. Shortly after the turn of the century the Indonesian authorities announced that those accused of corruption would in the future have to prove their innocence, rather than be proven guilty by the prosecutors. The communist legacy makes it likely that such presumptions persist in parts of the post-communist world.

Finally, a particularly questionable use of the state's power is the execution of those found guilty of corruption. Of the countries on which we have focused, the one most likely to abuse its power in this way is China.[11] The PRC is one of few countries in the communist and post-communist world to employ capital punishment for crimes other than treason and causing the death of others; there the death penalty is not uncommon for more serious cases of corruption.[12] For example, the former chief of the financial section of Xuanwu Hospital was sentenced to death in 1997 for having embezzled public funds worth 848,000 yuan, or some $102,000 (*CD*, 28 May 1997, 3). In late July 2000 the death sentence was passed on the highest-ranking Chinese official to date to have been found guilty of corruption. The former vice-chairman of the Standing Committee of the National People's Congress (the legislature), Cheng Kejie, was given ten days to appeal the sentence, which was passed down for Cheng's acceptance of approximately 41 million yuan (almost $5 million) worth of bribes between 1992 and 1998, when he was chairman of Guangxi provincial government (*CD*, 1 August 2000). His appeal failed, and he was executed in September 2000 (*CD*,

23 August and 15 September 2000). Shortly after, in what has been described as "the biggest corruption trial in the history of Communist China" (*Berliner Morgenpost*, 14 September 2000, 8), almost one hundred government officials in Fujian province, primarily in the city of Xiamen, were tried for allegedly accepting bribes in connection with an organized large-scale smuggling operation. Among the many state functionaries were customs, police (including the deputy head of the Fujian police force), state security, and military officers. Of the several hundred people charged in connection with the smuggling operation, eleven officials were sentenced to death for accepting bribes worth approximately five million yuan (c. $600,000). Curiously for a state that seems intent on setting examples, the trial was not initially reported in the official Chinese press, only in the Hong Kong media. However, once the sentences had been announced in November 2000, the Chinese news media provided widespread coverage. Subsequent trials in connection with this case, including that of the former deputy minister of public security Li Jizhou in 2001, were also publicized; Li was sentenced to death, but the sentence was suspended for two years after he returned some of his illegally acquired wealth and informed on others (BR 44, no. 47:5–6).[13] More recently, the former vice-governor of Anhui Province, Wang Huaizhong, was executed in February 2004 for large-scale bribe taking.

In conclusion, while the state can and should use the legal system to deal with corruption, it also needs to be sensitive to fundamental human rights. In a sense, and perhaps ironically, this is particularly true of transition states claiming to be building democracy and the rule of law.

Public Shaming

Shaming is a practice used with both individuals and organizations; each form will be considered separately. Shaming of individuals is the practice whereby authorities seek to embarrass (shame) a person found guilty of a relatively minor crime or misdemeanor by widely publicizing that person's transgression among colleagues, co-residents, extended family, and others. Hence shaming consists of publicly naming and blaming. The idea behind shaming is that criminals or transgressors will be more embarrassed if their misdemeanors are broadcast to people with whom they have to deal day to day rather than to total strangers with whom they will never come into contact. Shaming is also considered a useful deterrent to *potential* miscreants. While it can be used to punish and deter many lesser crimes and misdemeanors, it can certainly be an appropriate method for dealing with some cases of corruption as well. The concept is common enough in several East and Southeast Asian cultures; both Singapore and China use it, for instance. It is sometimes argued that shaming only works in such cultures, since the concept of "face" is so important in them. But the differences between cultures can be exaggerated, as is so often the case, and are often a matter of degree rather than kind. While the concept of face does not in general find much resonance in Anglo-Celtic cultures, most English-speaking people are familiar with the concept of "saving face." Perhaps even more relevant is the concept of "letting down the side." Although the notion of face focuses on the individual and "the side" on the collective,[14] there is considerable overlap between these concepts.

Hence the suggestion that shaming can work only in Asian cultures must be challenged. Western cultures are becoming more multicultural anyway, so that what might once have appeared very different, "other," and alien no longer seems that way.[15] But many European societies have had experience with shaming anyway. This is certainly true of the post-communist states. In many of these, during the communist era, children in schools or adults in the workplace who had performed poorly would often find their photograph and some accompanying explanatory text posted on the school or workplace noticeboard.

So far, the notion of shaming has been considered with reference to individual corrupt officials. But an important development in the fight against corruption has been the public shaming of companies found guilty of offering bribes to officials. The best known example is from Singapore, which in 1996 named five foreign corporations for allegedly having paid bribes worth $9.8 million to one of its officials (who was convicted and sentenced to fourteen years' imprisonment—*Asiaweek*, 15 March 1996). In fact the shaming was reinforced by a potentially very effective measure, which deserves discrete attention and is considered below.

In all events, shaming has been included in the arsenals of some post-communist states. In 1998, for example, the Bulgarian minister for industry announced publicly that the Ministry of Finance was about to produce a list of individuals and companies that had cheated on their taxes (*Sofia Independent*, 30 January–5 February 1998, 6). There could be much more of this kind of sanction in the future (see Hall 1999, 542), although the increasing trend everywhere toward litigation, including actions for libel and slander, is likely to act as a restraining force.

Blacklisting

In the Singaporean case just cited, the five companies were not merely shamed but also forbidden to tender for contracts in Singapore for five years. While a direct connection cannot be proved, it is interesting to note that one of the companies, Siemens, joined the German branch of Transparency International shortly after being blacklisted; to be charitable, it looked as if the company had learned a lesson and was seeking to make amends.[16] It is also worth noting that Germany itself had engaged in blacklisting by 1995. In that year the state of Hessen barred sixty companies from public tenders, while Bavaria barred fourteen, in each case because of those companies' previous involvement in corrupt practices (*TI Newsletter*, September 1996, 5).[17]

Strengthening or Establishing Bodies to Combat Corruption

Another approach is to strengthen existing bodies, or else establish new ones, to combat corruption and related activities. An example of strengthening was the announcement in Russia in July 1996 that the number of interior ministry troops was to be increased by ten thousand, explicitly to make the force more effective in combating organized crime and the black economy (*OMRI DD*, 12 July 1996; see too *Segodnya*, 20 July 1996, 2).

The establishment of new bodies has been a popular method in many post-communist countries. For instance, a Bulgarian parliamentary standing committee to combat corruption was established in September 2002 (*EECR*, 11, no. 4–12, no. 1:11; *TI Q*, September 2002, 12). The Hungarians established a fraud squad in 1993 (*RFE/RL*, 22 March 1993); they then set up a special task force in 1996, attached to the parliament and headed by Dr. Jozsef Bencze, with the particular brief of tackling the problem of corruption. In Russia an anticorruption quick-response group was established under First Deputy Prime Minister Yegor Gaidar in early 1992 (*Izvestiya*, 24 March 1992, 2). In November 1995 the relatively new Russian interior minister Anatolii Kulikov announced the establishment of a new department, directly subordinate to him, to investigate personnel within his own ministry. The level of corruption he had discovered since coming to office in July, both in his own ministry and in the state apparatus generally, had shocked him. On announcing the new department Kulikov stated that the fight against organized crime would be superficial unless he put his own house in order (*OMRI DD*, 9 November 1995). There is also a Presidential Security Service in Russia, which announced in February 1996 that it had been investigating the large-scale smuggling of jewels purchased with embezzled funds. That case appears to have involved officers in the military, the KGB successor organs, or both (*OMRI DD*, 29 February 1996). Yet another example was the establishment of a National Anticorruption Committee (NAK) in Russia in 1999 (*Izvestiya*, 6 October 2000).

In China moves since the 1990s to target "tigers" (high-ranking officials) rather than "flies" (lower-ranking officials) have resulted in the establishment of new organs. The most important appears to be the Special Case Investigation Section (SCIS), established in 1997. According to an official at the Supreme People's Procuracy (in *BR* 40, no. 5:6), the SCIS was established to target "extremely severe legal cases and disciplinary offenses by officials at or above the ministry level in central government offices, and those above the vice-governor level in local areas," and to guide or coordinate anticorruption groups in provincial procuracies, particularly in cases of major corruption or cases that spread across different local authorities' jurisdictions. The establishment of bodies such as some of those mentioned above is in line with Heidenheimer's argument that the relative success of Hong Kong and Singapore in minimizing corruption is partly due to their having "taken the anti-corruption duties away from the police department and placed them with an agency directly under a high-level government official" (Heidenheimer ed. 1994, 18; see too Quah 1995, 408).

Although many post-communist states have been either establishing new agencies or else strengthening existing ones, such bodies are occasionally shut down, often for financial reasons or because they are regarded as having become redundant. A third common reason is essentially political: incoming governments sometimes want to abolish agencies established by their predecessors, from whose policies the new government wishes to distance itself. An example of closure is Poland's abolition of its Economic Crime Department within the Ministry of the

Interior in 1991. In this case, however, Prime Minister Cimoszewicz acknowledged in March 1996 that the dismantling had been a mistake, and vowed to adopt various measures to correct it (*SWB/EE*, 1 April 1996). Accordingly, a new post of commissioner for fighting organized crime was established and filled in May 1996, while it was also announced in July 1996 that the security police were to establish a new unit to combat organized crime.[18] For what *may* have been an example of the political abolition referred to above, Jozsef Bencze's agency in Hungary was also shut down in the late 1990s.

Some bodies related to but not directly involved in the fight against corruption might appear to outsiders to be using excessive measures. For instance, the Poles announced in mid-1996 their intention to establish an élite team of *armed* tax inspectors (at the same time as they increased the powers of treasury officials to work on the shadow economy — all from *Business Central Europe*, July–August 1996, 13); however, they subsequently shelved this plan. The Russians had armed — and scary! — tax inspectors until March 2003. Given the serious problems that several post-communist states have experienced in collecting taxes, which then increase the pressure on social welfare services because of inadequate revenue, such hard-line approaches could become more common in the region, unless either human rights concerns override the revenue-collecting imperative or changes to the tax system substantially reduce the problems of tax collection.

A final office that could be either established or strengthened, depending on the country, is that of the ombudsperson. This office was rare in the communist world, the first country to have established it being communist Poland in 1988.[19] During the 1990s several more formerly communist countries (including Hungary and Russia) provided citizens with this channel through which to air concerns.[20] But there is scope for more development in this area. In April 1999, for instance, an article in *Baltic Times* (22–28 April) bemoaned the absence of an ombudsperson in Latvia, which it claimed was unusual in Europe. Bulgaria too has been late in introducing the office. Its first ombudsperson was due to commence work in January 2004, after the promulgation of a law in May 2003; but because of disagreements over who should fill the office, it was still not occupied by May 2004.

In concluding this discussion, it is worth noting the forceful argument of Anechiarico and Jacobs (1996), with reference to the United

States, that the creation of more state controls to combat corruption can be counterproductive. For instance, increased controls can blur lines of responsibility, make state agencies less effective, reduce trust, and even create new opportunities for patronage and other forms of corruption. By now it will be obvious that many techniques intended to combat corruption can be two-edged swords.

Improving Legislation

The state can improve legislation in an endeavor to plug loopholes that facilitate corruption. Ambiguous laws can be rendered more precise, and new laws introduced to address issues that were not considered problems during the communist era. In July 1995 a research organization called "profile" published the findings of a survey of 980 Poles, conducted by the Center for Public Opinion Research, or OBOP, on behalf of the Office of Public Procurements, designed to determine popular attitudes toward and knowledge of recent (January 1995) legislation on tendering processes, which had been introduced partly to reduce corruption. The survey revealed that the method most commonly cited by respondents (44 percent of responses) as the best for combating corruption in public tendering processes was the introduction of "clear, stable legal provisions that are easy to implement" (Grobelna 1995, esp. 4).[21] While it would be absurd to draw any general conclusions on the basis of just one survey, the results of our own surveys in 2000 (see table 6.1) — and common sense — suggest that many citizens in post-communist states do regard less ambiguous legislation as helping to reduce corruption.

Perhaps the most obvious type of legislation to consider first is that aimed explicitly at defining and combating corruption. The Poles introduced such an anticorruption law in 1997, while the Russian Duma passed a draft law at its first reading in November 2002. Much of this sort of legislation includes income disclosure requirements of state officials.[22] But there have been various problems associated with these and closely related laws. One is serious delays. For instance, the Russian draft law had taken some ten years to reach its first reading, in part because President Yeltsin was publicly critical of an earlier version, produced by a working committee of the Duma's Security Committee, for being too harsh and wide-ranging (Nomokonov 2000, 126–28).[23] Such criticism sends the wrong message if a leadership is serious about wanting to reduce corruption. This wrong message was compounded in Russia when the law then floundered yet again; it had still not been adopted by late 2004 (see chapter 2).[24]

Another problem that usually creates a bad impression is adopting new anticorruption legislation that is more lenient than the law it replaces. In 1993 the Estonians introduced a law reducing the penalties for accepting or offering a bribe below those provided for in the 1990 legislation that it replaced (Raun 1997, 366); particularly since corruption appeared to be on the rise at the time, this was a strange move. Similarly, the Polish Ministry of Internal Affairs and Administration presented a report in April 1999 that had been commissioned by the Sejm, in which the authors criticized a recent liberalization of the Polish Penal Code that substantially reduced the penalties for various types of bribery and nepotism (Golik 1999).

One of the most important areas of legislation, from both symbolic and practical perspectives, is conflict-of-interest laws, particularly as they apply to politicians and officers of the law. For instance, Albania adopted a new anticorruption law in January 1996 that required all state officials to declare all property exceeding one million lek (approximately $10,000 at the time) and its origins. Within days President Berisha had set an example by publicly declaring his assets (he appeared to be a very frugal person — *OMRI DD*, 29 January 1996). In April 1994 Slovakia announced plans to introduce a new law on conflict of interest that was aimed explicitly at state officials (*Keesings Record of World Events* 1994, 39973). Hungary was debating a law on conflicts of interest throughout 1996 (*OMRI DD*, 4 June 1996); this finally went into effect in April 1997, and was expected immediately to affect some 40 of Hungary's 386 MPs (*Budapest Sun*, 10–16 April 1997, 2). Thereafter Hungarian members of parliament were obliged to choose between their roles as parliamentarians and as board members of companies that were either partly or fully state-owned.[25] Latvia introduced a new law in mid-1996 that forbade public servants to hold positions in private business (*Baltic Times*, 19–25 September 1996). In 2000 the Bulgarian parliament began debating a Law on the Public Register, designed to encourage public servants to declare all sources of income (*EECR* 9, no. 3:9).[26] And in August 2002 President Putin signed a decree intended to reform the state bureaucracy by increasing transparency; the decree provided new guidelines on conflicts of interest, integrity, and related ethical issues (on earlier Russian — and Belarusian — legislation relating to conflicts of interest see Ukhmanov 1999).

New conflict-of-interest legislation has in practice been perceived in some post-communist states as too weak and ambiguous. For example, in early 1992 Poland adopted what the former justice minister Jerzy Jaskiernia (1994, 61) called a "very strict" anticorruption law for parliamentarians and public servants; but this evidently did not deal adequately with the conflicts of interest, and Jaskiernia subsequently called for a proper law on this issue.[27] In fact the weaknesses of the 1992 law were recognized by Włodzimierz Cimoszewicz, deputy prime minister and justice minister, in October 1994, when he acknowledged both that the 1992 law was coexisting with one from 1981 (during the communist era), and that neither specified any sanctions for noncompliance (SWB/EE, 28 October 1994). It was then announced by a Ministry of Justice spokesperson, Andrzej Cubala, in December 1994 that his ministry was already working on changes to the 1992 law (SWB/EE, 30 December 1994), while the Polish Constitutional Tribunal finally removed one ambiguity in the law when it ruled in January 1995 that state officials were not to receive more than one salary even if they served on the board of companies co-owned by the State Treasury (SWB/EE, 13 January 1995). The ruling still did not resolve many gray areas of potential conflict of interest.

Similarly, the Czech law on conflicts of interest enacted in April 1992 (including one for parliamentary deputies) has been described as "vague and toothless" (Kettle 1995, 36). It was with a view to tightening it that the Czech cabinet agreed in January 1995 to amend this law for ministers and parliamentarians — though still not for public servants. One parliamentarian in Estonia considered the proposed anticorruption law there so weak that he suggested calling it the "corruption enhancement law" (in Sonumileht, 22 April 1996 — cited in Baltic Times, 25 April–1 May 1996). Already by 1999 the Hungarian minister of justice was publicly arguing that her country's conflict-of-interest law needed to be revised (Dávid 2000, 18). Yeltsin's presidential decree no. 361 of April 1992, which encouraged public servants to declare all sources of income, was soon criticized by the news media for being too vague; it lacked any detail on either deadlines or monitoring mechanisms (Coulloudon 2002, 202–3). The conflict-of-interest law introduced in Slovakia in October 2004 has serious shortcomings, according to Slovak anticorruption activists

(*TI Q*, December 2004, 14). And Putin's decree, mentioned above, was not binding, only advisory; tougher, follow-up legislation is required in Russia.

Although conflict-of-interest laws should be as unambiguous as possible, it is unrealistic to expect politicians not to hold shares in companies, for instance. The political lot of politicians in post-communist states is often precarious, and they may not serve in political office for very long. It is naïve in the contemporary world to expect politicians to perform their tasks selflessly — exclusively or even primarily out of concern for the public interest. But it is realistic to expect them to be honest about their financial holdings, and to declare how any public issue affects their private interests; they can then withdraw from deliberation on that issue and perhaps nominate someone else to substitute for them. In addition or alternatively, politicians can place their shares in a blind trust while in office, meaning that they do not participate in any way in the affairs of companies in which they have an ownership interest.

Along with conflict-of-interest laws, post-communist states need to introduce proper codes of ethics for all public officials. Many of the codes of behavior in the past were grounded in the communist system, and are thus totally inappropriate in current conditions; neither the concept of *partiinost'* (loyalty to the communist party) nor a morality based on the notion of the "new socialist person" is relevant nowadays. At the time of writing, more progress had been made in developing conflict-of-interest laws than codes of ethics. This is partly because producing generic versions of codes of ethics is more difficult. Nevertheless, the state could require various types of organization to produce their own codes by specified dates — rather than attempting to produce a generic code itself, which because of its difficulty can simply delay the clarification process.[28]

Another important branch of legislation that can be amended so as to facilitate the investigation of suspicious persons and activities is tax laws. Where the state has few powers to investigate private bank accounts, for example, it is easier for corrupt individuals to hide their ill-gotten gains. In this context it is worth noting that Poland introduced legislation in early 1996 (though its implementation was delayed) that would make it easier for tax officials to access individuals' bank accounts (*SWB/EE*, 22 February 1996). While the motivation behind the law appears to have been primarily to reduce income tax evasion and bring Polish tax regulations into line with those typical of OECD countries, one important ramification of the law is that it can alert taxation officials to abnormal accounts (especially ones that are unexpectedly large, relative to declared income), including the accounts of other state officials.[29]

There are other ways in which the state can monitor suspicious banking activities. The most obvious is to require banks to report unusual activities, notably cases of customers making large deposits unexpectedly, which may indicate attempted money laundering. Under Czech legislation that became effective on 1 July 1996, all financial institutions, including casinos and betting shops, were required to report unusual large-scale transactions to the Ministry of Finance, and to register all transactions in excess of 500,000 Crowns (about $18,520 as of March 1996 — EECR 5, no. 1:8; *Business Central Europe* 4, no. 29:30).[30] Yet several post-communist states still did not have laws against money laundering in the early years of the century; Shelley (2002, 62) points out that Russia had not had one, for example — although Moscow did adopt new laws in 2001 under pressure from the OECD's Financial Action Task Force.

Public procurement is another area in which new or improved legislation can play a positive role in countering corruption. For example, the Polish government adopted a public orders bill early in 1994 aimed at preventing corruption among public servants by introducing greater transparency into tendering processes for state contracts (SWB/EE, 5 March 1994). Bulgaria has required since January 2001 that all public procurement tenders be published in a register that is freely accessible on the internet (Economic Crime Division 2002, 16), and introduced a new public procurement act that took effect in October 2004 (TI Q, September 2004, 14).[31] And China tightened and standardized its rules on public procurement in July 2002 (*Renmin Ribao*, 10 July 2002). Yet another area ripe for substantial improvement is the regulation of political party financing. If the funding of parties is not highly transparent and the rules on funding are relatively ambiguous, then the likelihood of enhancing the popular legitimacy of what should be key institutions of the transformational states — and achieving positive secondary effects for democracy and the rule of law generally — will be considerably reduced.[32]

Finally, the laws governing the immunity of officials, notably parliamentarians, need substantial improvement in many post-communist states. Although moves in this direction have been mooted (for example that by Prime Minister Ivan Kostov of Bulgaria in May 1999 — see *Standart* 25 May 1999, summarized in BPCWR, 22–28 May 1999) and sometimes taken (see the point about regional governors in Russia in note 1), the changes have usually been piecemeal, and in response to particular problems. It is rare for there to be legislation in this field that ranges widely across most types of public office. Yet weakness or ambiguity in this area fosters cynicism among the citizenry about the commitment of states to eradicating or reducing corruption.

Before concluding this discussion, it is worth noting that legislators can sometimes resist proposals for tighter legislation, on the grounds that the proposed changes potentially affect civil rights. For example, during the first reading in the Sejm in September 1992 of legislation designed to counter money laundering, several Polish members of parliament resisted proposals to reduce the secrecy of banking, allegedly because of concerns about privacy (SWB/EE, 29 September 1992). Of course some of the legislators may have been protecting their own financial interests; it is often impossible to disentangle motives. But this point underscores that democracy and the fight against corruption sometimes interfere with each other.

Promotion and Protection of Whistleblowers and Witnesses

All too often, whistleblowers in post-communist states as elsewhere have suffered for having done the right thing. An example was the dismissal early in 1993 of the editor of *Armiya Rossii*, Lt. Colonel Aleksandr Zhilin, partly, it seems, for having reported on corruption in the armed forces (*Independent*, 20 February 1993, 9). Cases from China include those of Zhou Wei, whose whistleblowing in Shenyang landed him in a Chinese labor camp for two years from May 1999 for allegedly "disrupting public order" (*Economist*, 24–30 November 2001, 32–33); and the journalist Jiang Weiping, who in January 2002 was sentenced to nine years' imprisonment for writing articles on Chinese corruption for a Hong Kong periodical (TI Q, September 2002, 2).

Far from punishing such people, states serious about reducing corruption will have to provide protection for both whistleblowers and witnesses. Greater use of anonymous whistleblowing "hotlines" — of the sort already introduced in some post-communist countries such as

Belarus and Bulgaria — will have to be made. In January 1996 the Belarusian authorities announced the opening of a confidential hotline for whistleblowing on all kinds of crime, including corruption (*OMRI DD*, 26 January 1996). In Bulgaria hotlines were introduced in January 2000 specifically regarding the customs service (Todorov, Shentov, and Stoyanov eds. 2000, 39) — once again indicating how serious the problem of corruption among customs officers is perceived as being.

There are at least two more radical approaches. One is to grant immunity to citizens who have themselves broken the law by paying bribes, if they report their bribery to the authorities and are prepared to testify against corrupt officials. In June 2003 Poland introduced several amendments to its penal code designed to combat corruption; one introduced immunity for whistleblowing bribe payers (Pitera with Brennek, Kochanowski, Kojder, and Lęski 2004, 243). The other approach is to oblige public officials to blow the whistle if they suspect wrongdoing by a colleague. Although this policy does not yet appear to have been legislated in the post-communist world, the European Commission introduced such a requirement for European Union officials with effect from May 2004 (*TI Q*, September 2004, 5), which could well be emulated by individual states in the future. Some states only appear to be encouraging whistleblowing: they are unwilling or unable to support their stated commitments adequately in concrete ways. For example, soon after its establishment in Russia in 1999, the NAK established a number of Public Reception Centres for whistleblowers (among other purposes), but these were closed less than a year later because of inadequate funding (*Izvestiya*, 6 October 2000).

A number of senior police officials in CEE have recognized the need to improve witness protection if the fight against corruption and organized crime is to become more effective,[33] and some states have had appropriate legislation in place for many years (since at least 1973 in Hungary, for example — Ministry of the Interior 2000, 36). Better protection of witnesses would have to include witness relocation programs. These programs are expensive, however, and little progress has been made on them in the post-communist world. For instance, the first witness protection program in Russia was established in Moscow as recently as February 2002 (*RFE/RL Crime and Corruption Watch*, 28 February 2002, citing Russian television), while federal (pan-Russian) legislation was passed by the Duma only in late July 2004.

As elsewhere, one of the problems of providing greater protection for whistleblowers, notably in the form of guaranteed anonymity, is that of civil liberties. If whistleblowers can hide their identities, there is scope for mischief making: an employee who has had a disagreement with a superior may make groundless allegations simply as a form of revenge. While there is no completely satisfactory solution to this potential problem, investigations into alleged malfeasance that adhere to the rules of obtaining proper (convincing) evidence should not per se constitute a threat to civil liberties.

Changing Practices

Sometimes simply changing the way something is done can have a major impact on corruption. Since so many observers (for example Klitgaard 1988; Rose-Ackerman 1999) argue that a major cause of corruption is the excessive discretionary powers of some state officials, it is worth noting ways in which governments can and do reduce these powers.

A prime example is the administration of traffic fines. A number of post-communist states have sought to reduce corruption among the traffic police by altering the way fines are collected. In the past, traffic police in Hungary (Kosztolanyi 1999), Latvia, and elsewhere were able to fine traffic offenders (real and imagined!) on the spot, with the amount of the penalty often subject to their own somewhat arbitrary discretion. Monitoring the police was very difficult, and the system was highly conducive to corruption. In one scenario, citizens could be encouraged to pay an officer less than the stipulated fine; an exemption "fee" then went straight into the officer's own pocket. In another scenario, the citizen is told to pay a fine higher than the amount that the officer reports to his or her office; the officer pockets the difference. Under the new arrangements, there is a far more detailed set of criteria for determining appropriate fines. Even more important is that fines are no longer collected on the spot; rather, the citizen is required to go to a police station or another office (such as a post office) to pay. Poland introduced this sort of system in November 2000. Such a change should eradicate the second scenario described above, but it does not per se address the first: law-breaking drivers in post-communist states will continue to offer bribes to police officers in return for their not imposing a fine at all, just as they do in other countries.[34] Nevertheless, merely changing the legislation and publicizing the changes sends a clear message to citizens and traffic police officers alike that the state disapproves of — and is taking concrete measures to address — corruption, and in this sense can exert a positive effect even on the first type of case.

A more significant area in which the discretionary powers of officials have been reduced is taxation. It was pointed out in chapter 3 that several post-communist states have introduced flat-rate personal income tax schemes in recent years. While flat rates are in many ways socially regressive, since they often increase gini coefficients (that is, income inequality), they can be beneficial in reducing corruption.[35] Also of importance is the introduction of flat or low corporate income tax rates. Bulgaria introduced a flat and low (15 percent) corporate income tax rate in 2002, the same year as Russia reduced its corporate rate from 35 percent to 24 percent; the perception that taxes are unfairly high can encourage companies to circumvent them through bribery. That Estonia was the first country in the region to introduce flat-tax regimes for both personal income and businesses is probably one of many reasons for its apparently low corruption rates (among post-communist states).

There are many other ways in which practices can be changed with a view to reducing corruption. One affects the interaction between state functions and the private sector. In a way that would delight most neoliberals, Poland introduced private sponsorship of the police in 1992. In practical terms, this mainly meant that some police cars were provided by private motorcar manufacturing and sales companies. The potentially corrupting implications of this arrangement should be obvious (the police might treat owners or employees of the sponsoring companies who broke the law more leniently than other citizens). The Polish authorities soon learned the folly of their ways. In March 1994 the minister of internal affairs (responsible for the police) issued a draft decision designed to limit severely the types of state agencies that could be privately sponsored and the private entities that could be sponsors, and to subject all sponsorship to greater scrutiny by his ministry (SWB/EE, 24 March 1994).[36]

Another method used to better separate the state and market, specifically as a way of reducing corruption, is to prohibit state agencies from engaging in entrepreneurial activities. In 1998 the Chinese authorities banned the army and the police from engaging in commercial activities, after it was concluded that too many military and police officers and units were placing their private money-making interests ahead of their official duties (BR 41, no. 33:5). A different approach sometimes mooted is to encourage greater teamwork, so that employees can better monitor each other. While this approach can be effective, it is not invariably so; the peer (horizontal) and superior (vertical) pressures identified in chapter 6 as potential sources of corruption help to explain why. Moreover, employees can be more responsible when trusted to work on their own; if it is accepted that building trust as a component of social capital is a potentially powerful long-term means of combating corruption, then the use of greater mutual monitoring can be counterproductive.

Rotation of Offices

A method used in various parts of the world with some success is the rotation or transfer principle. Under this principle public officials are moved from office to office fairly regularly, on the assumption that they will be less able to develop cozy niches and clientelistic networks. Rotation has been advocated, and in some cases introduced, in several of the countries that are subjects of this book. A ministerial proposal to introduce such a system into the Hungarian customs service — but on a sudden, random basis — was made in 1995, with the intention of reducing illegal capital transfers abroad (SWB/EE, 1 April 1995). A Chinese ministry announced in July 1996 that it was introducing a rotation policy precisely to combat corruption; no member of staff was to remain in the same office for more than five years (CD, cited in TI Newsletter, September 1996, 2). Bulgaria has also introduced this practice in its endeavors to reduce the apparently very high levels of corruption among its customs officers (Todorov, Shentov, and Stoyanov eds. 2000, 39). And the Polish police commander Papala was by 1997 deliberately filling many of his most senior posts with officials from various parts of Poland so as to reduce the likelihood that excessively cozy — corrupt — relations would develop at that level between officers who had been working together for a long time (SWB/EE, 12 September 1997).

Unfortunately, research by Frank de Zwart (1996) on the use of rotation for combating corruption in the Indian public service reveals that it is not always without problems. For instance, rotation can create new opportunities for patronage, and for collusion between heads of different departments. In addition, overly rapid rotation may mean that occupants of offices have insufficient time to master their new job or develop much sense of commitment to it (*Baltic Times*, 20–26 May 1999, 4). Shelley (2000, 71) has argued that rotation can actually increase the costs of corruption for bribe givers, since they sometimes have to bribe replacement officials to ensure the continuation of projects corruptly approved by those officials' predecessors. Finally, one potentially serious problem of rotation is that corrupt officials from one agency can introduce their bad practices into others to which they are moved and that were previously incorrupt; there have been cases of this in Albania. Nevertheless, post-communist states can learn vicariously from the experiences of others, including the Chinese and Bulgarians, and a sensitive and refined version of rotation can sometimes assist in the fight against corruption.

The transfer system just described is basically a regularized, ongoing one. But governments in post-communist states have occasionally judged a situation to be so severely out of hand as to warrant drastic one-off measures that constitute an extreme and irregular version of rotation. Thus the provisional government appointed in Bulgaria in February 1997 considered the customs and border guard services so corrupt that they temporarily transferred the control of border crossings to the military (Manolova 1997). Our survey of Bulgarians in 2000 suggests that this measure did not produce the desired results — or that if it did, the positive outcomes were very short-lived.

Improving Officials' Conditions

A ninth method is to improve officials' conditions. One obvious area is pay. Although there is at present limited empirical evidence, one research project — focusing on Madagascar — demonstrated a strong negative correlation between the level of corruption and state employees' wages (cited in Tarschys 2003, 378). Quoting Heidenheimer (Heidenheimer ed. 1994, 18) once again, "In Singapore, salary levels, higher than those of American cabinet heads, help to insulate its public officials from corruption." Heidenheimer goes on to acknowledge that this approach is one that the post-communist countries cannot yet afford to implement.[37] But the situation may be changing. A reform of the customs service in Hungary shortly after the turn of the century, which provided for salary increases for customs officers, may have contributed to a marked reduction in corruption in the customs service (for another possible explanation for the drop, one not mutually exclusive with the one just posited, see the discussion below).

However, others have pointed out that low salaries are in some cases supplemented by government perquisites of one kind or another, and clearly feel that increasing salaries would only further privilege an already privileged group. While acknowledging that the salaries of Polish officials were in general very low, for instance, Blazej Torański argued (1994, 8) that "high level bureaucrats today get almost as many privileges as [their] communist predecessors" — the main difference being that the communists used to hide their privileges, whereas those of the current officers of the state are well-publicized.[38]

A method that might backfire is one that local governments in four Chinese provinces began trying in 2003. Each month, public servants working for these governments now have 5 percent deducted from their pay that goes into a retirement fund, together with a contribution from their employer. If individual public servants are found to have broken the law or violated regulations before retirement, they can lose part or all of the sum saved (TI Q, December 2003, 13). The danger here is that some public servants, particularly younger ones on lower incomes, might conclude that a reduction now in an already modest salary for a reward decades off is reason enough to succumb to the temptation of corruption, should an opportunity arise.

In Poland — though this is a common problem elsewhere in the post-communist world — poor conditions specifically affect one group that is supposed to play a major role in fighting crime: the police. In a report to the government submitted in March 1996, the head of the Polish police force, Jerzy Stanczyk, pointed out that the number of crimes of all sorts registered in Poland in 1990 was 547,000, and that there was at that time a force of 115,000 officers to contend with these. In contrast, there were only 100,000 police officers to investigate the 975,000 crimes registered in 1995 (SWB/EE, 27 March 1996).[39] Expressing this another way, the average number of crimes to be investigated by each member of the Polish police force had more than doubled in five years. Although the government claimed that it had increased funding for the police force during 1995, the chief of police perceived the increase as inadequate. Similar, even stronger complaints were being made by the Hungarian minister of the interior at about the same time (*SWB/EE*, 6 January 1995). Obviously the ability of the state to contain corruption will depend partly on its commitment and capacity adequately to fund the agencies charged with investigating allegations of official malfeasance.[40]

One way to improve the financial position of individual officials would be to streamline many government agencies and work more according to the old Leninist precept of "better fewer, but better." Doing so will often be difficult in countries that already have relatively high levels of unemployment. However, states will have to engage in cost-benefit analyses, and may often conclude that it is better in terms of legitimacy to have a leaner but more efficient and less corrupt (because better paid and more satisfied) officialdom. The Russian authorities appear to have thought along these lines; in November 2001 the deputy minister of internal affairs announced that there would be a 15–20 percent reduction in the number of traffic police, but that those remaining would be better paid (*RFE/RL*, 28 November 2001).[41]

Pecuniary reward is not the only working condition that needs to be improved. As argued in chapter 6, the very fragility of post-communism has meant that many public officials now have a sense of insecurity that was not typical of the communist era.[42] If the uncertainty of early post-communism is added to the commitment of some governments to a form of neoliberalism in economic policy, it becomes obvious why so many officials feel insecure: it is because they *are* insecure in their posts. Even if they manage to retain their positions until retirement, they cannot be confident that the state will then provide them with an adequate retirement pension. This uncertainty is not conducive to loyalty to the state. If governments were to introduce more job security into the public sector, the result would almost certainly be a positive effect on bureaucratic social capital and hence corruption rates. In this connection, Verheijen and Dimitrova (1996, esp. 202–3, 210–11) are justified in emphasizing the need for legislation that distinguishes the positions of public servants from those of private employees, particularly through civil service laws. Countries such as Hungary, Latvia, and Slovenia have introduced such legislation. But others — including Bulgaria, Poland, Slovakia, and Romania — were dragging their heels in the mid-1990s, despite in some cases having publicly acknowledged the importance and urgency of civil service legislation (Verheijen and Dimitrova 1996, 211). It appears that in some cases there has been delay because politicians find congenial a situation in which they can influence the administration of government with relative impunity; understandably, this often leads to resentment among the public servants themselves.

Neoliberals might balk at proposals for greater job security for public officials and a clearer demarcation of their functions. However, it must be remembered that theorists often develop their arguments — whether consciously or not — with regard to hypothetical worlds, not real worlds in which there are emotions, "irrationalities," and multiple rationalities. Even the notion of rationality itself is to some extent culturally determined, which renders the application of an essentially singular basic formula problematic. In particular, economic rationalist ideas have limited applicability to transitional societies, in which "ground rules" and institutional arrangements are still flimsy. In such circumstances, it must be acknowledged that the adoption of neoliberal policies will almost certainly have high costs, including possibly increased levels of corruption. As argued elsewhere in this book, the tradeoff might well be acceptable in countries attempting to overcome an entrenched communist legacy. But it needs to be acknowledged openly.

Finally, another measure that should help to reduce corruption, but that would be discounted by many neoliberals, is to increase the status and respect accorded to public officials, especially public servants. Although Fukuyama (1992) may have overstated his case, there is much truth in his argument that people need respect and recognition (*thymos* — see chapter 6). It would be culturally parochial or arrogant not to acknowledge that many societies place more emphasis on the collective than on the individual, but the issue is a relative one. In other words, these societies place less emphasis on the individual; they do not place no emphasis at all on the individual. Moreover, many of the European societies considered for this book have traditionally placed much emphasis on the individual anyway — albeit less than in Anglo-Celtic cultures, and their communist phases notwithstanding. The tendency of many cases of corruption to involve individuals rather than groups is itself an indication that measures to combat corruption must consider individually oriented reasons for it as well as cultural, structural, and systemic reasons. If others, particularly politicians and perhaps the news media, were to treat officials with greater respect, those officials would then develop greater *self*-respect, which in turn should have beneficial effects on corruption levels.[43]

Rewarding Officials

Instead of increasing all officials' salaries, government can financially reward individual officials for reporting citizens who offer them bribes, or for reporting crimes that in a different context might have encouraged them to seek a bribe in return for not reporting the crimes. For example, one element of the reform of Hungarian customs referred to above was the introduction of a bonus scheme for detecting and reporting customs offenses (particularly smuggling).[44] Unless most officials claim bonuses, this method is much cheaper than raising salaries across the board. It is thus more appropriate for many transition states, which typically experience severe economic problems in their early years and do not have the resources enjoyed by a relatively affluent country like Singapore.

Increased Use of Technology

There are several ways that technology can assist in the fight against corruption. Perhaps the most obvious is greater use of computers for storing, monitoring, and transferring data that might be relevant to the tracking of corrupt behavior and individuals. Shelley (2000, 73) points out that judicial corruption in St. Petersburg is believed to have decreased after the introduction of new computer technology in 1995. Judges now had better access to details of cases closely related to those they were presiding over themselves, and could therefore more readily identify colleagues whose rulings appeared to be much more lenient than the norm. Such marked differences can alert members of the judiciary to possibly corrupt behavior by their peers.

But computers are not the only form of control technology that can assist the state in combating corruption. In October 1992 the Polish National Inspection of Environmental Protection provided funding to purchase and install a radiation detection machine at the Lubieszyn border checkpoint, since it was suspected that the crossing was being used to smuggle radiation isotopes from Eastern Europe to the West (SWB/EE, 23 October 1992). And the potential advantages of automatic speed cameras have already been noted.

Changing the Gender Balance

On leaving Moscow (Sheremetyevo) airport on one occasion in the early 1990s, I asked the immigration official if he would stamp my passport as a souvenir; at that time, officials usually only stamped the visitor's visa, which was loose rather than permanently attached to the passport. The young man informed me that he would be happy to, in return for a $10 "fee." This was a blatant example of bribe seeking, and I did not receive a stamp in my passport. But during a visit in December 2000, I was standing in line at Sheremetyevo 2 airport ready to show my passport and visa to the immigration officials when I noticed that they were exclusively women. On leaving Moscow a few days later, I again noticed that all the officials checking the passports and paperwork of departing passengers were women. Knowing that Mexico City had recently attempted to deal with a serious problem of corruption among traffic police by making the force an all-female one (*Sunday Age*, 1 August 1999, 12), I asked the woman checking my passport whether there was a conscious policy. She smiled broadly and confirmed that there was — and was surprised that I had noticed. Her acknowledgment does not constitute proof that such a policy was in place. But if the experience of Mexico can be replicated, it seems that one way for the authorities to address corruption is by changing the gender balance in corrupt agencies.

Of course the change of gender balance might not be the actual or primary cause of reduced rates of malfeasance; while intuition, overall crime statistics, and limited empirical research suggest that women are in general less dishonest than men,[45] it may be the "new team" variable at work here rather than any innate gender difference. In other words, the real explanation might be that corruption had increased and become engrained among a long-standing group that happened to be predominantly male. This hypothesis appears to be partly supported by recent cross-polity research. Mukherjee and Gokcekus (2004) studied the relationship between gender balance and perceived corruption in public sector organizations in six countries — two of them post-communist (Bulgaria and Moldova) — and concluded that the optimal situation for minimizing corruption, based on empirical evidence, was one in which the balance of males and females in an organization was roughly equal. They discovered that a predominance of either men or women in a public sector organization, if they had been in office for some time, was associated with higher levels of corruption than where there were approximately even numbers. Since many public sector organizations in post-communist states are dominated by either men or women, it appears that making them more reflective of the overall gender distribution in society should reduce corruption levels.

Anti-Corruption Campaigns

A popular approach is to mount public campaigns against corruption. Poland in August 1994 and Slovakia in March 1995 mounted anti-corruption campaigns using the same name — Clean Hands — as that of the Italian anticorruption campaign initiated in 1992. Other post-communist countries to have mounted similarly named campaigns include Bulgaria, Czechia, the Republic of Macedonia, Russia, and Ukraine, while Hungary devised an interesting alternative: Transparent Pockets.

Political leaders often make anticorruption campaigns a prominent part of their programs. In his first public television broadcast to the nation, the new Polish premier Włodzimierz Cimoszewicz announced on 30 March 1996 that the fight against crime (of all sorts, but including corruption) was a top priority of the new government (SWB/EE, 1 April 1996). Similarly, President Boris Yeltsin gave a televised state-of-the-nation speech to parliament in February 1996 in which he announced a major attack on corruption among state officials (Rossiiskaya Gazeta, 24 February 1996, 2). The speech was followed by a presidential decree in June (Nezavisimaya Gazeta, 7 June 1996, 1) and formal legislation in July, to give the campaign bite (OMRI DD, 12 July 1996). Sali Berisha became the Albanian president in 1992 and soon declared war on corruption. In December 1994 he claimed that corruption was primarily a legacy of communism but acknowledged it as a serious problem that he would fight more resolutely. He then dismissed some of his ministers; although none was charged with corruption, it was made clear that this was why they had been relieved of their posts (Zanga 1995, 13). Finally, a remarkably honest approach was adopted by the Serbian leadership. In his New Year address in 1996, President Slobodan Milošević announced that the fight against crime would now become one of the government's top priorities. The prosecutor general Dragan Petković then made it clear that the campaign would focus on economic crime. He further acknowledged that while there had been international sanctions against Serbia, economic crime had actually been encouraged by the authorities; with the ending of sanctions, economic crime was now considered contrary to the interests of the state (*OMRI DD*, 23 January 1996).

The history of anticorruption campaigns in China is a long one; according to Ting Gong (1994, xv), the PRC has had more anticorruption campaigns than any other country. In 1994 the Chinese authorities published a special edition of documents concerned with the fight against corruption; it covered the years 1921–93 (Tsyganov 1996, 1). The publication of this collection was in line with what Gordon White (1996, 161–64) has seen as a marked intensification of the anticorruption campaign since 1989, which accelerated after 1992. White correctly points out that one of the reasons why the student activists of Tiananmen in 1989 initially found such resonance among broader sections of the population was precisely that they focused on the problem of corruption. Although the CCP leadership managed to bring the rebels to heel, it was also aware that their anticorruption message still reverberated, and that something would have to appear to have been done to deal with this serious problem.

Where White can be challenged is with regard to his suggestion (1996, 168 n.34) that the statements as cited in the Chinese press outside the PRC by President Jiang Zemin, who was also the communist general secretary, were more alarmist than those within the Chinese press itself.[46] In August 1993 Jiang stated clearly in the Chinese press that corruption was now undermining the very foundations of communist rule in his country (see chapter 1), and used this as a reason for clamping down still further on corruption. It was at about this time too that the leadership vowed to tackle more thoroughly the problem of corruption in the higher echelons of the party-state. In claiming that the important task now was to target the "tigers," not just the "flies" as in the past, the CCP leadership was declaring its war on corruption among more senior officials. This said, it appears that the campaign has not reached the very highest levels, since the highest-ranking officials to be caught to date have been Chen Xitong, head of the communist party in Beijing and member of the Politburo (see chapter 3), and Cheng Kejie (see above). Unlike so many of the fully post-communist countries, China has seen no prime ministers or presidents publicly implicated in recent times. Whether this reflects a less corrupt leadership in the CCP

than in other countries, or merely the country's much tighter censorship, might only be revealed once the communist political system has
gone the way of its counterparts in other formerly communist countries.

Although campaigns such as those just cited have some symbolic
importance — in that they demonstrate the commitment of the state to
overcome corruption — in practical terms they are often more successful
if they target particular government departments in which reasonably
high levels of corruption may a priori be expected, such as immigration
and customs. Heidenheimer (Heidenheimer ed. 1994, 18) claims that
this is another reason why Singapore has apparently been very successful
in tackling corruption. While the Bulgarian evidence relating to the
customs service suggests that even targeted programs can be less effective than intended, a few do appear to have scored some success. But
the evidence strongly suggests that general campaigns are often not only
relatively ineffectual, but can even be counterproductive. Citizens become cynical if leaders keep proclaiming new or renewed commitment
to the fight against corruption, but appear to be doing very little. Cohen
(1995, 40) has pointed out that President Yeltsin launched no fewer
than seven anticrime campaigns (against both corruption and organized
crime) in the relatively short period 1991 to mid-1994; since there was
relatively little to show for all the rhetoric, widespread cynicism is understandable. Political leaders run the risk of crying wolf once too often;
if there is to be any chance of their being effective, campaigns must be
short, targeted, and few in number.[47]

Some leaders in CEE and the CIS have publicly recognized the essen-
tial worthlessness of particular anticorruption campaigns. President
Lech Wałęsa of Poland claimed in late 1994 (SWB/EE, 28 October
1994) that the Clean Hands campaign was actually an "empty hands"
one — a charge that could be laid in many other countries. But possibly
the most damning point about general campaigns is that if the conclusions reached by Krastev and Ganev (2003) are valid, they sometimes
fail to improve mass perceptions even when there is evidence that they
have reduced corruption levels; this possibility is clearly of concern to
governments that attempt to enhance their legitimacy partly by waging
war on corruption.

Ethical Education

As noted by Rose-Ackerman (1978, 234), one of the potentially most effective weapons against corruption may be people's internalized sense of morality. According to focus group research conducted in Hungary in 1999–2000, many Hungarians apparently believe that improving morality should be the primary weapon in the fight against corruption (Hankiss 2002, 254). And to cite one of the choicer wordplays encountered in the research for this book, some argue that a key method for reducing corruption is "ethic cleansing" (Bardhan 1997, 1335).

In many countries, and certainly in most post-communist transitional ones, there has been something of a moral vacuum since the collapse of communism. For some citizens, this collapse meant that they could at last pursue their religious beliefs openly; and the moral vacuum meant that others, seeking a new ethical code, joined them. But as noted in chapter 6, religion has not filled the gap for many citizens, and unless both states and civil society provide new codes, the problem of corruption will continue to be a serious one.[48] Education here refers to instilling and developing new moral and social codes. The process should be started in the schools and reinforced at home.[49] But it is an ongoing process, and socialization agencies including the mass media have an important role to play.[50] To some extent the educational approach, which seeks to develop social capital, can be seen as an alternative to both the legal and the incentive-based approaches, which are based largely on cost-benefit principles. But it is preferable to see the two sets of approaches as complementary rather than in competition; often, the best approach is to use both carrot and stick. Adherents of rational-choice theory may dismiss this argument as wishful thinking; but the onus is then on them to prove the validity of their position empirically.

Linkages with External Governments and Agencies

Yet another method is to develop linkages with foreign agencies experienced in tackling various kinds of corruption and economic crime. To promote multilateral international cooperation, several post-communist countries joined Interpol in the 1990s, while others have strengthened their ties with it.[51] Such linkages can have tangible effects. For instance, the Russian interior ministry received some 2,500 notifications from various foreign law-enforcement agencies during 1991 (channeled through Interpol), and more than 3,000 in the first six months of 1992 (Glukhovsky 1992, 14).

International cooperation can also be predominantly or exclusively bilateral. Many post-communist states have increased their collaboration with each other, for instance by agreeing to exchange databases on known organized-crime gangs, to establish joint investigative teams, and to pursue people in one country who have committed crimes in the other; Poland and Russia reached such an agreement in March 1996. Conversely, the often tense relationship between the Baltic states and Russia in the early years of post-communism sometimes made the development of such linkages problematic (Tillier 1996).

With regard to Russia in particular, some western states have become so concerned about the spread of organized crime beyond its borders that they have had their relevant agencies establish formal ties with the Russian authorities. The best-known example is the FBI, which opened an office in Moscow. The London metropolitan police force also has a special arrangement with its Moscow counterpart. However, the problem of organized crime elsewhere in the post-communist world, both Russian and indigenous, has become so serious that western agencies have begun to look beyond Russia in their endeavors to contain it. It was announced in August 1996 that the FBI was intending to open an office in Warsaw, for instance; after its establishment in October 1996, this office was formally opened in February 1997 (*Życie Warszawy*, 21 February 1997, 2). This followed a visit to the United States in March 1996 by the Polish interior minister Z. Siemiatkowski, during which he met with the director of the FBI, Louis Freeh, primarily to discuss methods of combating organized crime. During the visit the United States agreed to assist Poland in developing computer technology and policing methods. Moreover, the United States agreed to train Polish police officers (as well as those from many other CEE countries) at the new International Police Academy that was to be opened in Budapest in April 1996 (*SWB/EE*, 14 and 21 March 1996). Although these measures were primarily designed to fight organized crime, particularly drug smuggling (which is a major reason for Washington's interest in collaboration), the frequent overlap of organized crime and corruption in the post-communist world means that such developments should help to lower the incidence of corruption as well.[52] Some post-communist countries have not gone so far as to establish FBI offices, but have sought FBI assistance in other ways. A typical example is Lithuania, which in the late 1990s invited the FBI into the country to train some of its law enforcement officers (*Baltic Times*, 19–25 November 1998).

For all the advantages of cooperation, post-communist states occasionally discover that foreign governments, whether themselves transitional or not, are less willing to assist in investigations than might be expected. The principal reason appears to be the fear of foreign states that their own role in the matter being examined will not bear close scrutiny. The Polish authorities discovered this during their investigation into the FOZZ scandal of the early 1990s, for example (*SWB/EE*, 7 December 1992). Another area that can cause problems is incompatible or nonexistent legislation, such as on extradition: appropriate treaties take time to negotiate and conclude, and problems of cooperation can arise in the meantime. Finally, cultural differences, in terms of attitudes toward private property and privacy, for instance, can hinder international cooperation.[53]

Norm Setting and Risk Assessments

Post-communist states can assist foreign agencies and companies interested in investing in their countries by engaging in norm setting and risk assessments.[54] Norm setting is the process of gathering and publishing the range of realistic costs for different types of project within a country —for instance, a mile of four-lane freeway, or a one-story warehouse with 100,000 square feet of space. If a potential investor then calls for tenders to construct a freeway or storage facilities, the bids can be compared with these average prices. Tenders well outside these parameters, whether much higher or lower, should encourage the investor to be cautious, and to investigate the tenderer and the pricing more thoroughly than the investor might otherwise do (see Kaufman 1998, 3). For instance, a tenderer might seek to charge above the norm because it will be able to secure all the necessary building permits much more quickly than other bidders: this should set alarm bells ringing in the investor's head, since the "fast tracking" might be made possible by bribing local officials. Not only will the investor be expected to pay a premium, but he or she may well find that the project encounters serious problems when it is discovered that the paperwork is not in order.[55]

Risk assessment is the practice of identifying and specifying the situations in which corrupt practices are particularly likely to emerge. The assessment can be based on the state's own experience, vicarious experience, or a priori assumptions (intuition). Having identified an area, such as customs, as a likely candidate for corruption, the state can then take steps to monitor a process or group particularly closely.

A Radical Approach: Purges

Reference was made earlier to the experiment in Mexico City that consisted of replacing male traffic police officers with female officers, and one possible way of attacking corruption is to purge entire state agencies. Unfortunately such an approach is quite likely to harm noncorrupt as well as corrupt officials, and raises serious issues of civil liberties and the rule of law. But where the communist legacy — including a tradition of corruption — is deeply ingrained, purges might be advisable, subject to safeguards. Perhaps the most important is that dismissed officials should be offered alternative employment — albeit employment that disperses them among various agencies to minimize the likelihood of their continuing to collude as a group — in the absence of hard evidence of their corruption.

Another method of purging is lustration (see chapter 3), which is piecemeal, not wholesale: according to this method a post-communist state removes officials from their posts only after examining the communist pasts of each. This policy was used widely in early post-communist Czechia and the former GDR. There is always the danger that the policy can become a political weapon — a form of revenge, for instance — and it should therefore be used with extreme caution if at all.

A Second Radical Approach: "If You Can't Beat 'Em . . ."

One of the few types of military corruption about which there appears to be a reasonably high level of public awareness in many post-communist states is in the area of conscription. In many countries young people have been able to avoid compulsory military service by having themselves declared unfit for service. Doing so sometimes involves the collusion of doctors, at other times corrupt conscription officers. Some post-communist states (such as Romania) have declared their intentions to move away from conscription and toward fully professional militaries.

But until this process is complete, or in countries in which there is no such intention, the state can think and act laterally by legalizing conscription buy-out. This has a triple beneficial effect. Simultaneously, the state removes one source of corruption, increases its income, and reduces alienation levels in one of its branches that can on occasion be threatening to the rest of the system. Colleagues in Serbia and Romania have informed me that legalized buy-out was adopted in their countries soon after the turn of the century, though I have been unable to verify this. In Russia the Union of Right Forces proposed legislation to this effect in June 2002. Legalizing something like a conscription buy-out so as to control it better merits consideration — though the experience of the United States during the Civil War warns that doing so can backfire.

A Final Radical Approach: Amnesties

In some post-communist states corruption has become so pervasive that it might now be best for governments to cut their losses and declare an amnesty on questionably acquired private wealth. There are certainly major problems with doing this, particularly in terms of the message it can send. For instance, it could appear that governments are sanctioning corruption (and economic crime more generally), and that they look after the interests of criminals or quasi-criminals better than those of honest citizens. Perhaps even more problematic are the implications for the development of a rule-of-law culture. In a real sense, governments should be seen as dealing with improprieties through the efficient, regular, and equal (impartial) application of the law if they are to foster respect for rules, and for the legal-rational state more generally.

But in situations where a weak state has in essence lost control, one-off radical and questionable solutions may be better in the long term than constantly fighting a losing battle. Popperian, piecemeal social engineering is often suitable for consolidated systems, but sometimes less appropriate in transition states than Rortyan relativism — a lesser-of-two-evils approach. In post-communist transition states, the argument in chapter 6 about the near-absence of an indigenous bourgeoisie is germane. Transition states need to develop bourgeoisies quickly, in part because of the key role that they appear to play in consolidating democracy (Moore 1967); if amnesties are one effective way of bringing this about, then the longer-term good may justify the questionable means.

In fact, some post-communist states with particularly serious corruption problems have already considered the possibility of amnesties. For example, shortly after Vladimir Putin was first elected in Russia a leading politician, Boris Nemtsov, proposed a meeting between the new president and Russia's so-called oligarchs.[56] This meeting, with twenty-one oligarchs in attendance, took place in late July 2000 (*Izvestiya*, 29 July 2000, 1), and apparently saw the president offer to terminate investigations into the origins of these men's fortunes, if the oligarchs would in turn guarantee to pay their companies' taxes in full and on time, invest in Russia (rather than send their capital abroad), and stay out of politics. The precise extent to which the president actually followed through on his offer is disputed (Dikun 2000; Jensen 2000; Lambroschini 2000; Tsipko 2000), but there is no question that Putin was widely interpreted as having offered to end investigations into dubious privatizations in the period 1994–98. In all events, in October 2000 Deputy Procurator General Yurii Biryukov confirmed to the Duma that investigations into the questionable "loans for shares" privatization of major Russia companies such as Sibneft' and Norilsk Nickel had ceased (*EECR* 9, no. 4:34). In January 2001 Putin again confirmed to the oligarchs that there would be no investigation of questionable privatizations. This time, however, there was an additional price attached to the deal: the oligarchs were to contribute 1.5 billion roubles to a fund for the families of Russian soldiers killed or wounded in Chechnya (*EECR* 10, no. 1:36).[57]

This was not Putin's first amnesty. In May 2000 he had declared an amnesty for many of Russia's prisoners. Unfortunately for the fight against corruption, it appears that among those able to take advantage of this amnesty were some of the very few corrupt officials actually serving prison sentences at the time, including a former defense minister and a provincial governor (*Kommersant*, 29 June 2000, 2). Even better known was the amnesty Putin granted to Boris Yeltsin on the day he took office from his predecessor (the decree is in *Rossiiskaya Gazeta*, 5 January 2000, 3).[58]

Along somewhat similar lines, the Bulgarian interior minister Bogomil Bonev held talks with organized-crime chiefs in the late 1990s and is said to have in essence offered them an ultimatum: either convert to legitimate business practices, or face a serious clampdown; by 2000 most had either converted or else been squeezed out of business (Fish and Brooks 2000, 68). President Rexhep Mejdani of Albania urged the legalization of the shadow economy in July 1999 (*RFE/RL*, 28 July 1999), while in Ukraine President Leonid Kuchma proposed a similar new law in mid-2000 (*Business Central Europe* 7, no. 74, September 2000, 46–47). And in March 2001 a law granting a moratorium on all shadow capital, effective from June, was passed by the Kazakh parliament (*RFE/RL*, 15 June 2001). Clearly such laws would have implications for corrupt officials.

But these states were not the trailblazers. In 1997 the government in Romania, having been newly elected in November 1996, was already contemplating a turning of the page on the suspicious privatizations and other sources of substantial wealth of recent years. According to Rob Whitford (1997), citing a rumor circulating in Bucharest, the government summoned some of those who had made fortunes in recent years through questionable means and told them "in effect, that they'd had their fun, that the past wouldn't be scrutinised too closely, but that from now on they would have to act like good capitalists, obeying all the rules and playing a straight game." And as early as September 1992, the Polish government adopted the concept of state's evidence in the Penal Code, whereby those who confessed to their own role in organized crime or corruption, or revealed the role of anyone else, were ensured either leniency or impunity (*SWB/EE*, 26 September 1992).

Although it is neither fully post-communist nor, apparently, as weak as many post-communist states,[59] China has also introduced a form of amnesty in recent years. This can be seen from its use of so-called 581 accounts. Under this scheme, which has been introduced piecemeal since 2000 in various cities, officials are encouraged to deposit within a specified time funds equal to those that they have acquired through bribe taking into accounts numbered 581; if they do so, they are eligible for receipts guaranteeing them certain types of impunity. Many Chinese legal experts have criticized this experiment, however, arguing that it looks as if the state is either condoning corruption or else losing its resolve to reduce it (*BR* 44, no. 33:23–25).

THE ROLE OF WESTERN STATES

There can be no question that the primary responsibility for dealing with corruption within their countries rests with post-communist governments and citizenries themselves. However, some western states could and should do much more to help overcome the problem. For example, one must criticize the policy pursued until recently by Australia, France, Germany, the Netherlands, and several other countries of allowing tax deductions to companies that offer bribes to foreign businesspeople and state officials, a policy that promotes corruption. It was thus encouraging that in 1996 the twenty-eight states that were then members of the OECD agreed to amend domestic laws so as to outlaw this practice — although it must be noted that many European countries were reluctant to follow the American lead in pushing for this agreement (*New York Times*, 28 November 1996).

Perhaps even more reprehensible than the tax deductibility laws have been laws in Switzerland, Luxembourg, Nauru, the Cook Islands, and elsewhere that permit "secret" bank accounts and opaque banking practices generally.[60] Such practices are highly conducive to money laundering. If corrupt officials and those engaged in organized crime did not find it so relatively simple to hide the money they had misappropriated, the scale of both corruption and organized crime in the post-communist world would surely be reduced.[61] At the other end of the scale, the United States is to be praised for having introduced legislation as early as 1977 (the Foreign Corrupt Practices Act, or FCPA) that explicitly prohibits American companies from offering bribes to foreign companies and public officials; the legislation was introduced in the wake of the Watergate and Lockheed scandals.[62] Indeed it appears that some of the recent actions of organizations such as the OECD and the IMF against corruption (see below) are partly due to American corporations' complaints about losing billions of dollars' worth of business each year because of the legislation, of which no other country had an equivalent until the late 1990s. According to an estimate by the U.S. trade representative Mickey Kantor, based on data from the CIA, American firms lost $45 billion worth of overseas contracts in 1995 because of the bribery ban (*New York Times*, 28 November 1996).

THE ROLE OF INTERNATIONAL ORGANIZATIONS

International and supranational organizations also have a role to play in combating corruption, including in the post-communist states (Klitgaard 1998). Yet it must be noted that only recently have many of these organizations begun to take corruption seriously. Thus when the OECD issued its "Recommendations on Bribery in International Business Transactions" in May 1994, these were described as "the first multilateral agreement among governments to combat the bribery of foreign officials" (Transparency International 1996c, 15). TI further claims that the European Union started to focus on the problem only in 1995.[63]

But the anticorruption bandwagon is now clearly on the move. In addition to introducing the agreement to outlaw tax deductibility for bribery in 1996, the OECD has made the bribing of foreign officials a crime through the Convention on Combating Bribery of Foreign Public Officials, adopted in 1997 and effective in February 1999. By late 1999 this convention had been signed by thirty-four states, including a number of post-communist ones. In 2000 the OECD produced report cards on the twenty-one states that had deposited their instruments of ratification of the convention; of these, four were post-communist states (Bulgaria, Czechia, Hungary, and Slovakia).[64] The first round of report cards focused on national legislation, while a follow-up assessed how it was being implemented.[65]

One concrete way in which the international community of states has sought to address the problem of hiding the proceeds of corruption has been through the OECD's Financial Action Task Force (FATF) on Money Laundering, established in 1989 at the Paris summit of the G-7.[66] It regularly updates a blacklist of tax-haven countries whose banking practices are considered insufficiently transparent and hence are conducive to money laundering. Some countries have been very responsive to pressure from the FATF. For instance, Austria was criticized for permitting anonymous savings passbook accounts, and in February 2000 was threatened with suspension from the FATF; within months it had introduced legislation banning such accounts. But some of the other miscreant states, including Liechtenstein, Nauru, and Russia, had as of 2000 been reluctant to address the criticisms made by the FATF. Russia has improved under Putin, however, and was not only removed from the FATF's List of Non-Cooperative Countries and Territories in October 2002 but even granted full membership in the FATF in June 2003. Conversely, Ukraine was identified in 2002 as one of the world's worst offenders for money laundering (though it was removed from FATF's blacklist in March 2004).

The Council of Europe has also taken steps in recent years to combat corruption. For example, its Committee of Ministers adopted Guiding

Principles for the Fight against Corruption in November 1997, which were followed in November 1998 by a Criminal Law Convention on Corruption and in September 1999 by a Civil Law Convention. The International Chamber of Commerce is yet another agency that is seeking to reduce corruption at the international level. It approved a set of rules — Extortion and Bribery in International Business Transactions: Rules and Recommendations — in 1996 (revised in 1999) that prohibits bribery. And in mid-1996 the World Bank introduced tough new anticorruption guidelines making clear that it was henceforth committed to canceling any project in which it was involved if it discovered evidence of official corruption in either the procurement or the implementation stage of the project. Élites that have in the past used western credits and aid to line their own pockets have in recent years found that it is more difficult to do so, and that any gains could prove to be short term.

Many other organizations could be listed (for example the United Nations and the IMF),[67] as could other programs and policies (including shaming and blacklisting, a practice that was carried out by the World Bank against three companies from the United Kingdom in early 1999);[68] interested readers should visit the web sites of the relevant agencies for up-to-date details. But it can be noted that the basic thrust of the measures outlined so far is punitive. International organizations sometimes use the carrot as well as the stick, however. Thus the World Bank occasionally names and praises countries that it believes are making serious efforts to reduce corruption. Latvia was congratulated in 1999 on its official anticorruption program, which was seen by the World Bank as a model in CEE (*Baltic Times*, 8–14 April 1999), while Romania's judicial reform so strongly impressed the World Bank that in June 2002 it announced its decision to provide, in recognition of the achievement, a grant of $250,000 and a loan of $18 million specifically to fight corruption (Jovic 2003, 192). Bulgaria's Coalition 2000 has also been praised by the bank as a model of cooperation between the state and civil society.

All the guidelines referred to in the previous paragraphs can affect but are not specifically directed at the countries of CEE and the CIS. But the Council of Europe has in addition taken measures designed explicitly to address the problems of organized crime and corruption in the European post-communist states. In June 1996, together with the Phare program of the European Union, it established the Octopus project, in which no fewer than sixteen CEE and CIS countries agreed to participate (Albania, Bulgaria, Croatia, Czechia, Estonia, Hungary, Latvia, Lithuania, Republic of Macedonia, Moldova, Poland, Romania, Russia, Slovakia, Slovenia, and Ukraine). The project ran for eighteen months and primarily involved introducing measures designed to facilitate greater cooperation between countries in their mutual fight against crime. The measures included harmonizing legislation, increasing information exchanges, and establishing proper monitoring services. A conference was held in Strasbourg in December 1997 to conclude the project, at which a number of specific measures were recommended to particular post-communist states.[69] A follow-up project, Octopus II, was officially launched in February 1999 and completed in December 2000. One of its principal objectives was to combat organized crime and corruption in CEE as part of the preparations for accession to the European Union of the ten CEE states that had applied for membership and were likely to be admitted in or after 2004 (although a total of sixteen post-communist states participated in the program; for an official assessment of Octopus II see Economic Crime Division 2002).

The European Union is also playing a role in combating corruption in these countries. In addition to cooperative work with the OECD through the SIGMA project, the EU has exerted considerable pressure in recent years on the states that have applied to join it; they include Bulgaria, Hungary, and Poland. For instance, under the auspices of Agenda 2000, the EU produced a series of Commission Opinions — one for each applicant country — in 1997, specifying the issues that applicants would have to address if they were to qualify for membership. Each report included an analysis of the four main sets of criteria to be met if countries were to be fully eligible (political; economic; ability to assume the obligations of membership; administrative capacity to apply the *acquis communautaire* — that is, the body of European laws, rulings, and regulations that all member states must agree to abide by and enforce). In the first category only one variable was mentioned in all ten general evaluations: the need to combat corruption more effectively. While other variables, such as better treatment of minorities, appeared in several assessments, the call to reduce corruption was universal (see for example European Commission 1997a, 20, and 1997b, 20).[70] According to the Open Society Institute (2002), this pressure by the European Union to tackle corruption brought positive results in several applicant states.

Another way to refine anticorruption efforts is to focus on particular groups within the state apparatus. For instance, the UN General Assembly adopted a Code of Conduct for Law Enforcement Officers as early as December 1979, with a recommendation that it be considered by national governments when producing their own codes and laws on such officers; one of its articles, article 7, deals explicitly with corruption.

In concluding this discussion, five points should be noted. First, post-communist governments themselves often submit requests to international organizations to investigate the corruption situation in their country. For example, the World Bank report on Poland that was published in March 2000 had been commissioned in May 1999 by the minister of finance, Leszek Balcerowicz (Sutch with Dybula and Wojciechowicz 2000; *Warsaw Voice*, 25 June 2000). In 1999 the Latvian government also asked the World Bank to produce a report, after it had been ranked the most corrupt of the Baltic states; although the bank initially produced the report secretly, it appears that it did so largely to maximize the likelihood that the investigations would be effective. Thus it should not be assumed that critical reports by external agencies are invariably perceived by post-communist governments as signs of interference or cultural imperialism: such assessments are often both requested and considered helpful.

Second, international organizations should sometimes be more realistic and culturally sensitive, the first point notwithstanding. For instance, rather than ban all gifts, it would be more sensible to suggest the maximum acceptable value of gifts from a particular person or agency over a specified time (for example, not to exceed $100 in any twelve-month period). The limits should be kept low enough that permitted gifts are unlikely to influence anyone or any decisions, but high enough to permit Christmas gifts (western cultures often engage in legitimate, business-related gift giving too!), traditional gifts exchanged upon meeting, and so on. Although some countries and organizations do draw a distinction between gifts and bribes, too many still do not. But overly rigid and insensitive zero-tolerance approaches can make normal social intercourse appear corrupt, and excessive inflexibility can desensitize people to real corruption by applying the term too broadly; more common sense on the part of large organizations would be welcome.

Third, international organizations need to work more closely with civil society, rather than fund states to police themselves. This is sometimes formally difficult, because the organizations' charters and rules require them to fund only states and not interfere in domestic politics.[71] But creative application of the rules — or even amending them to suit changed conditions — is possible and often desirable. Thus the World Bank began early in the new century to consider granting more funds directly to local governments, and in May 2004, in Paris, it signed its first ever collaboration agreement with a local government organization. This was in part a result and symbol of its endeavors to reduce the opportunities for national élites to cream funds off for their own benefit.

Fourth, international organizations should constantly seek to ensure that their actual practices are in line with their professed objectives. For instance, the World Bank has overtly committed itself to reducing corruption, as well as to increased environmental sensitivity and transparency. Yet while it is beyond the scope of this book to assess the validity of those claims, it is worth noting that in the view of a number of Romanian environmentalists, some of the bank's practices in developing infrastructure in Romanian forests are actually conducive to corruption, harmful to the environment, and insufficiently transparent (Feiler 2002).[72]

Finally, while most international organizations at least pay lip service to the notion of combating corruption, there are a few that apparently still do not even recognize the issue as a major one. Arguably the highest-profile example is the World Trade Organization, which has been criticized by TI for its apparent indifference (Eigen 2003).

THE ROLE OF TRANSNATIONAL CORPORATIONS AND INTERNATIONAL BANKING ORGANIZATIONS

Setting an Example

The case of Siemens — which, as mentioned above, was blacklisted by Singapore but soon sought to improve its image — exemplifies the important role that transnational corporations (TNCs) can play in setting examples. Often, simply establishing a presence in relatively corrupt countries can introduce new standards of what is and is not acceptable behavior, which can have secondary effects way beyond the direct reach of the individual TNCs. A number of major international corporations — among them British Petroleum, General Electric, Royal Dutch Shell, and Texaco — have set an example by introducing codes of ethics or conduct for their own staff, which make it clear that offering bribes is unacceptable, even in countries where bribes are considered normal (or at least more common than in western states).

However, it appears that even companies with ethical codes cannot and do not guarantee that they will always abide by their spirit. Allegations of Siemens's continuing attempts in the twenty-first century to use bribery to secure foreign contracts were noted above. Shell, which adopted its code in March 1997, was heavily criticized by some elements of the Bulgarian news media in early 1998 for concluding a distribution deal with the Bulgarian company LITEX Commerce. Shell's network manager for CEE allegedly decided against investigating LITEX too closely, even though the company's rapid growth was exceptional and perhaps cause for suspicion. At about the time the deal was concluded, it was announced that LITEX was under investigation for possible financial improprieties involving gas smuggling and unpaid taxes (*Sofia Independent*, 30 January–5 February 1998, 6–7). TNCs that are serious about presenting a clean image should seek to avoid questionable linkages to other companies. Finally, Cirtautas (2001, 81) argues that it was hypocritical and incongruous of Microsoft to promote a "clean hands" campaign in Czechia at the same time as it was facing antitrust charges in the United States. If TNCs are to be heeded seriously by transition states, they must practice what they preach. Just as there can be international state-to-state cooperation in fighting corruption, so can there be either state-to-business or business-to-business cooperation. An example of state-to-business cooperation is provided by Poland. It was reported in 1994 (*SWB/EE*, 4 May 1994) that a Polish provincial prosecutor's office was collaborating with a foundation established by several German insurance companies, in its endeavors to crack down on gangs stealing cars in Germany for sale in Poland.

As a relatively extreme measure, TNCs can demonstrate their opposition to corruption by withdrawing from states in which they believe that there is an inadequate commitment to combating it. The American corporation Motorola threatened to do this in Ukraine in 1997 (Shelley 1998, 655), while the Anglo-Dutch corporation Unilever withdrew from Bulgaria in 1999 on the grounds that it was too difficult to operate in the country without constantly paying bribes (*Economist* 350, 1999, 3). However, several American companies have been reluctant to name states where their refusal to pay bribes has cost them contracts, for fear of losing future business in those countries. This is an issue that urgently needs addressing.

Another practice that needs rectification is the adoption of an arm's length approach by many TNCs through the use of local so-called facilitators. Some major corporations have sought to circumvent the OECD's and national governments' ban on paying bribes to foreign officials by paying "speed money" to third parties in the countries in which the companies are doing business, or wanting to do business, as a way of facilitating or accelerating their operations or bids (Bray 2004, 317). All too often, the facilitators pay bribes on behalf of the TNCs — who then claim ignorance, but deliberately do not enquire too closely into expense claims made by the facilitators.[73] Private banks also have a role to play in combating corruption; once again, most of the activity in this area is relatively recent. In October 2000 a group of some of the world's largest banks announced their agreement on a set of guidelines, known as the Wolfsberg Anti–Money Laundering Principles, which they suggested should be adopted by all international private banks as part of the effort to counter international money laundering; these were supplemented in November 2002 by a set of principles for correspondent banking (TI Newsletter, March 2001, 3; TI Q, December 2002, 4; U. Roth 2003, 8).

Quadruple Bottom-Lining and Reputational Risk

An important measure that could be taken by both TNCs and corporations generally, and is already being discussed in some quarters, is known as quadruple bottom lining. In recent years a number of corporations have been "triple bottom-lining" by presenting their annual performance figures and contributions in terms of three variables: economic (profit and loss), environmental, and social (Schilizzi 2002). They are now being encouraged to report on their governance performance as well. The reporting could include information on any ethical codes that the companies have introduced. But more importantly, it would indicate the practical measures that they have adopted to implement their putative commitment to ethical issues, such as, for example, improving the conditions of their workers, or pressuring governments of states in which they have invested or expressed interest in investing to improve their record on human rights or combating corruption. It might be argued that overtly pressuring governments to respect human rights or fight corruption is too much a political a function for TNCs. But such an argument is naïve. TNCs are by their very nature political, and they frequently attempt to influence governments to protect their own interests. Many contribute funds to political parties. Under the different approach being advocated here, the companies would be attempting to pressure governments for reasons less directly and narrowly related to their own interests. This said, and as figures on ethical investment indicate (Socially Responsible Investment or SRI — see Sparkes 2002), corporations could actually benefit financially, since an increasing number of investors will move their funds from less ethical to more ethical companies. Adding a fourth bottom line could swell the first, and thus be a "rational choice."

A closely related approach that can also combine being a better citizen with concern for profitability is to focus on reputational risk. If it can be demonstrated that companies lose business because of besmirched reputations, then they have an interest in minimizing activities likely to harm their image. Being accused of offering bribes to officials is precisely the kind of activity that can affect a corporate image negatively.[74]

Encouraging Private Litigation

Although this has apparently yet to occur vis-à-vis the awarding of CEE or CIS supply contracts, one potentially powerful weapon against corruption between private businesses and state officials is private litigation.[75] Legal action has already occurred in the context of privatization. For example, when the Bulgarian privatization agency announced in August 2002 that it was awarding the contract of sale of Bulgartabac (Bulgaria's tobacco monopoly) to a German-backed consortium, two losing bidders initiated proceedings against the award in the Bulgarian Supreme Administrative Court, leading to a suspension of the privatization process. The court eventually ruled that Bulgartabac should have been sold for a higher price, and required the originally successful bidders to submit a higher bid.

This Bulgarian case demonstrates the sorts of problems that attempts at litigation can raise. The delays caused by the Bulgarian litigation, and the view in some quarters that the court had interfered in a matter beyond its purview, led to proposals to prevent the courts from becoming involved in some of the most sensitive and high-profile privatizations.

These proposals resulted in the introduction in parliament in February 2003 of a change to the privatization act — which was promptly rejected by President Georgi Parvanov on the grounds that it could increase corruption and scare off potential foreign investors. After further disputes on this issue between the president, parliament, and the Constitutional Court, the Bulgartabac privatization process was suspended. One of the ironies of this case is that a Russian businessman believed by many Bulgarians to have close links to Bulgarian organized-crime syndicates was a major supporter of one of the unsuccessful bidding groups that originally took the matter to court (all details from EECR 12, nos. 2–3:11–12).

One can imagine other cases in which companies may have considered litigation. If, for example, other oil companies were to bring a lawsuit against Elf Aquitaine Petroleum for compensation against losses that they incurred because of the contract that Elf improperly won in the former GDR in the early 1990s, a message would be sent to other companies that seek to win competitive bidding processes by offering bribes.[76] This might be an even more powerful weapon against corruption than most of the state's possible methods already elaborated.[77] But since the laws regarding this type of compensation are in some postcommunist states nonexistent, and in others still too malleable — as demonstrated clearly by the Bulgarian case just cited — practical considerations suggest that such claims should be made through an international tribunal, perhaps attached to the International Court of Justice.[78] Using a single agency of this kind might also lead to standardized formulas for dealing with cases between different types of company and different countries. This said, the proposal here would apply only to international bidding processes. Purely domestic competitive bidding processes could be subject to judicial control within individual countries. Many postcommunist countries, including Poland and Hungary, would probably use the international regulations and practices as a guideline for their own legislation in this area anyway.

CIVIL SOCIETY, DOMESTIC AND INTERNATIONAL

So far the focus has been primarily on initiatives from the top — from the state and international organizations. But with the collapse of communism, there are in most countries better opportunities for citizen and nonstate initiatives against corruption than there were during the communist period. Trang (1994, 9) identifies two such channels: the news media; and private groups that both monitor corruption and engage in whistleblowing, and initiate or lobby for new legislation.

The News Media

The media became a major source of exposure of corruption in the 1990s, with Polish newspapers such as *Prawo i Życie*, *Życie Warszawy*, *Życie*, and the more racy *Nie* making a reputation for themselves as experts in investigative journalism. The scandal concerning the Hungarian privatization board in late 1996 initially broke with the publication in September of an article in the economic weekly *Figyelő*, while *Népszabadság* and *Élet és Irodalom* have also established good reputations in Hungary for their investigations of corruption. And *Novaya Gazeta* in Russia became noted in the 1990s for serious and responsible investigative journalism (Shelley 2000, 73).

But the media's role is not invariably positive. If serious investigative journalism is replaced by what is essentially partisan mud slinging, both the political system and the media themselves are discredited and compromised. In this context it is worth citing further data from our four-country survey conducted in 2000; the results of the question on the role of the media in publicizing corruption are summarized in table 7.1.

Even allowing for the slightly different approach adopted in the Russian survey (see note below the table), a number of observations can be made about the data in table 7.1. First, more than half the Polish respondents believed that their news media were for the most part reporting corruption in a responsible way. This is in marked contrast to the situation in Russia, where a mere 3 percent believed that their media played a mostly responsible role; approximately thirteen times as many Russians held the opposite view.[79] The Hungarian ranking was similar to the Russian, but with a dramatically reduced ratio. Conversely, the Bulgarian ranking was the same as the Polish, but again with a much smaller ratio. As with many other questions in our survey, far more Bulgarians were unwilling to commit themselves to a definite answer than any other set of respondents; and once again, Hungarians were the least likely to provide a noncommittal answer.

TABLE 7.1.   Perceptions of the Role of the Media in Publicizing Corruption, 2000 (in Percent)

	Mostly responsible	Mostly irresponsible	Do not know
Bulgaria	26.3	23.2	50.6
Hungary	35.6	48.3	16.1
Poland	52.7	22.2	24.9
Russia	3.0	39.1	39.5

Notes: Russian responses do not sum to 100 percent because 18.3 percent of Russian respondents chose a fourth response: "necessary." These responses were excluded because the primary interest here is the ratio of "responsible" to "irresponsible" — and the Russian picture is very clear. In the original questionnaire a distinction was drawn between "Don't know" and "It is difficult to generalize," but pilot studies revealed that many respondents saw no meaningful difference between these two responses, so they were collapsed.

In an insightful analysis of the role of the media in reporting scandals and corruption in Australia, Rodney Tiffen (1999, esp. 206–39) outlines five canine models of the role of the media: the watchdog (which he sees as the highest aspiration for the media); the muzzled watchdog (the media are constrained by external forces, especially defamation laws); the lapdog (the media allow themselves to be manipulated by those in power); the wolf (in many ways the most dangerous model, in which the media are careless in investigating allegations, pervert priorities, and, by misleading their audiences, encourage mass cynicism toward politics); and the yapping pack (the media often follow each other, pick on easy prey, and make lots of noise but are not playing a serious, constructive role). Tiffen's set of models is as applicable to the post-communist world as it is to Australia. All too often the media's role has been that of the wolf, yapping pack, or lapdog. But if civil society is to develop in a healthy manner, the media must make strenuous efforts to become watchdogs. In many post-communist states the media in general need to become far more independent of the state, in terms of ownership, influence, and censorship. The reporting of corruption is one of the best areas for assessing to which of the five models particular newspapers, television channels, and other outlets most closely approximate, and how well civil society is developing.

Unfortunately, external assessments suggest that media reporting of corruption has been far from optimal in many post-communist countries, for various reasons. Thus the assessment by Freedom House in 1999 of the capacity of the local news media in four post-communist states — Bulgaria, Hungary, Romania, and Ukraine — found that there were serious problems in all but Hungary. In Bulgaria, for instance, it appeared that many government officials used corrupt practices to ensure favorable coverage, while some journalists allegedly threatened to start political scandals unless they were paid off by those whom they were contemplating targeting (all from Addis, Henderson, Lief, O'Rourke, and Denton 1999). The freedom of the Russian media has unquestionably been reduced since Putin came to power, and there have been disturbing developments in Poland.[80] Rendering the development of an independent investigative media culture more difficult in Russia and several other countries is the occasional closing down of newspapers and other outlets that seek to probe the dark recesses of state activity. This was the fate of the Ukrainian newspaper *Politika* in 1998, after it had published a series of articles alleging corruption in the office of President Kuchma (RFE/RL, 10 December 1998). Less extreme, but still of concern, is the arrest of individual journalists on questionable libel charges (as with two Bulgarian journalists from *Trud* and *24 Chasa* in February 1996 — OMRI, 21 February 1996).

Domestic NGOs

Many activists and analysts committed to reducing corruption have long argued in favor of whistleblowing.[81] Perhaps surprisingly, whistleblowing has been encouraged by the state even in some post-communist countries in which democratization and self-initiated political activity by citizens have not progressed very far, such as Belarus (see above). Several post-communist countries now have domestic NGOs devoted to fighting corruption. Some of these work very closely with or have eventually been transformed into the local TI chapter. This is true of the Centre for Anticorruption Research and Initiatives in Russia, headed by Elena Panfilova. In other cases, the agencies are wholly domestic, not intending to become the local branch of an international NGO. A Polish example is the Against Corruption Program, headed by Grażyna Kopińska and largely funded by the Stefan Batory Foundation and the Helsinki Human

Rights Association. In 2000 this NGO launched a campaign with the slogan "KorupcJA?" (which translates as "Corruption — ME?"), designed to raise public awareness of the unacceptability of corruption.

In the four CEE countries on which we are focusing, however, the best-known of such NGO initiatives internationally is Coalition 2000 in Bulgaria, established in 1997. This coalition of several NGOs has been highly active in combating corruption, through a variety of methods. One of the most important was an advertising campaign that made it clearer to Bulgarians, in simple language and cartoons, both what corruption was and that it was unacceptable (for further details on Coalition 2000 visit the web site at www.online.bg/coalition2000; for details of a Polish NGO's interesting attempts at raising public awareness of the unacceptability of corruption through media campaigns see Bąk, Kulawczuk, and Szcześniak n.d., 45–47).

Some NGOs referred to in the preceding paragraphs have worked closely with government agencies and been criticized for doing so, largely on the grounds that the collaboration might compromise their independence. This is true of Coalition 2000. But two important facts need to be borne in mind. First, civil society is still underdeveloped in almost all post-communist countries; private communication infrastructures are for the most part poorly developed. Hence if NGOs are better able to communicate their messages to the public through the use of state-run channels, then assuming minimal interference by the state, these organizations can be far more effective. Second, close collaboration between NGOs and state agencies can raise the state's awareness of the problem being addressed by the NGOs, and increase the NGOs' influence on relevant legislation.

Other Forms of Action

In addition to the relatively structured aspects of civil society's activities identified by Trang, mention must also be made of the role that more spontaneous actions can play. While mass demonstrations and protests explicitly demanding that the authorities curb corruption and organized crime occur infrequently in the post-communist world, there have been examples. One such was the closure of shops and businesses in the Old Town in Warsaw in mid-1994, in protest at the authorities' apparent indifference to rampant protectionism (in the criminal sense) in the area

(*Time*, 22 August 1994, 14). The protesters achieved some success; since the closure, the Old Town has been heavily and very visibly policed. In September 1993 up to five thousand people staged a protest in Bucharest, demanding that politicians deal more firmly with official corruption (RFE/RL *News Briefs* 2, no. 38:17). In September 2000 some thirteen hundred farmers in China publicly demonstrated against what they perceived as the embezzlement of public funds by local officials (Saich 2004, 331). But the best-known example of this sort of protest was in Beijing in 1989, leading up to the Tiananmen massacre; while the western media tended to focus on the demands for democracy, the demonstrators also made very clear their anger at the authorities' corruption.

In addition to overt demonstrations, citizens can engage in whistle-blowing, write letters to the press, or show support or displeasure at the polls. But it takes time to develop a participatory culture where a predominantly subject culture has long been the norm, and the observation by Sajó (1994b, 108) that in Hungary "there is neither a tradition of nor trust in public participation" could be applied to many post-communist countries; this legacy can only gradually be overcome. Moreover, while several post-communist states included provisions in their constitutions for freedom of information, it is only recently that many have introduced dedicated freedom-of-information acts. Hungary introduced one as early as 1992, followed by Russia in 1995; but Bulgaria adopted its Public Information Act only in June 2000, and Poland its Law on Access to Public Information in September 2001, after publication of its first draft freedom-of-information act (produced by the Adam Smith Research Center) as late as 2000. Such laws need not only to be passed, but to be tested in practice. This takes time. But it is a process that must be undertaken and consolidated if civil society is to become stronger and more confident vis-à-vis the state in CEE and the CIS.

Transparency International

In addition to domestic NGOs, there are international ones dedicated to the fight against corruption, to which both governments and the private sector turn for guidance and assistance. The principal example is Transparency International, or TI, which is based in Berlin. This was established in early 1993 as an international organization seeking to eliminate serious corruption in major international business transactions, especially those involving public funds (Eigen 1994; Galtung ed. 1994, esp. 113–23). After visits to Budapest, Warsaw, and Prague in February and March 1996, national chapters of TI had been "practically formed" already by September 1996. This meant that Hungary and Poland were, as in so many other aspects of transition, the trailblazers among the post-communist states.[82] In contrast to their Hungarian and Polish counterparts, the Czech authorities at that time apparently regarded the problem of corruption in their country as no worse than in other OECD countries, a problem that the authorities themselves and the market would handle with minimal outside interference. This reaction might have reflected, or at least been exaggerated by, the presence in Prague of the TI delegation in the run-up to an election, so that the ruling group wanted neither to appear too subservient to foreign organizations, nor to stir the water in such a way that their own management of the transitional process looked less impressive. Nevertheless, since Czechia's international reputation for corruption — according to the CPIS — was similar to that of Poland, its officials' attitudes toward TI did not enhance the country's image. Conversely, since TI had already established a good reputation for itself and was well respected by corporations and governments around the world (the visits in 1996 were sponsored by the PHARE Democracy Program of the European Union), word of the positive reaction from the authorities in Hungary and Poland soon spread, and may have helped these states to enjoy a generally better image than Czechia by the turn of the millennium.[83]

This chapter has outlined numerous measures for reducing the incidence of corruption. At the outset, it was pointed out that many citizens consider it primarily the state's responsibility to combat corruption. But there are problems with this view, so that Schloss (1998) is justified in advocating a multi-pronged or multi-agency approach. One of the drawbacks of an excessive focus on the state is that it presupposes the capacity of the state authorities to effect policies; in fact, as demonstrated in chapter 6, many post-communist states are still relatively weak, which limits their abilities. Another drawback is that this public focus on the state is ultimately based on an assumption of governmental self-control. Admittedly, the state comprises many agencies, and it can be argued that one agency should monitor another. In practice, however, and as demonstrated in chapter 2, agencies are often ordered hierarchically, and it is usually difficult for what is in practice a lower-ranking body to bring a higher-ranking one to heel. A clear example is the way President Yeltsin used to shut down agencies or dismiss their heads if they appeared to be coming too close to the presidency itself in their investigations. Aleksandr Rutskoi and Yurii Boldyrev in 1993, and the former prosecutor general Yurii Skuratov in 1999, all learned this at their careers' expense.[84]

Third, it appears that many states have been placed in a serious dilemma since September 11, with implications for their attitudes toward corruption. Just as states around the world are reassessing their policies on privacy, with national security now often considered more important than civil liberties, so corruption is now typically perceived as less of a danger than terrorism. A prime example, according to *Newsweek* (17 December 2001 — cited in the *Australian*, 18 December 2001, 7), is that the U.S. Congress unanimously but secretly agreed in late 2001 to allocate to intelligence agents a tenfold increase in funds for bribing foreign officials, especially those able to provide information relating to terrorism. If the U.S. government thus condones corruption, even when the reasons might be understandable, it is sending a message that corruption may be acceptable under certain circumstances. Given the global influence of the United States, many post-communist élites could emulate its position for their own benefit.[85]

Despite these problems, a state can adopt many measures that no other agency or group can. Hence, while it is unwise and even dangerous to place too much — let alone exclusive — emphasis on the state in fighting corruption, the state does have an important role to play. But what is not always clear is that all parties purportedly dissatisfied with corruption actually care as much about it as they claim to do. This point requires substantiation. In the West, big business is not invariably as disturbed by the ramifications of post-communist corruption as might be assumed. A good example is the response of many western business leaders to a rash of thefts during the 1990s of German cars, which were then smuggled into post-communist states. Although many of the leaders expressed concern, random, small-scale interviews conducted by me in Berlin in January 1997 revealed that in the view of many members of the public, German car manufacturers had perhaps not been entirely disappointed to see their (already-sold) products disappear from German streets, only to appear again in Moscow, Warsaw, or Prague. This was because the German owners could then claim insurance and purchase a replacement vehicle, boosting car sales. In addition, the increased presence of German brands on CEE and CIS streets can constitute a form of advertising. Often, the person whose car has been stolen is also happy with the arrangement, since depending on the type of insurance, it can mean that he or she acquires a brand-new car. There is a cost to all this, of course, in that insurance premiums have to rise. But the burden of extra costs is so widely dispersed that the increase is often marginal to the individual. It is thus close to an all-win — ultimately, a nonfinite version of the tragedy of the commons.[86] Another example of ambiguity — hypocrisy, even — is provided by various international organizations, which criticized the levels of immunity enjoyed by many states' officials, on the grounds that it was conducive to corruption, and then pushed hard to secure immunity for their own officials (Rooke 2004, 113).

Ambiguities such as those just identified constitute an important reason why a decade or more of anticorruption measures have been much less successful than they should have been, as has been argued by Naím (2005) and others — including even leading World Bank specialists on corruption such as Daniel Kaufmann (cited in Naím 2005, 96). But ambiguity, in the particular sense of double standards and mixed motives, is only part of the puzzle. To explore this point, it is worth considering the problems confronting attempts to rank-order anticorruption methods. Is it in fact possible to rank-order the potential effectiveness of different methods for combating corruption? To a large extent, anticorruption strategies must be customized; the optimal prioritization varies from country to country, and even over time, depending on circumstances. For instance, the choice and balance of methods will depend partly on which groups of officials are perceived as most corrupt, and the resources available to a state. Moreover, litigation against states and companies that may have been involved in corrupt privatization practices cannot be effective if legal processes and structures are inadequate or nonexistent in the relevant jurisdictions.

While it is thus impossible to provide a general, cross-polity template of the best ways to deal with corruption, there is a factor, as distinct from a method, that is all-important in all cases. Part of that factor is the political will of leaderships, especially where civil society is still weak and citizens look to the state to deal with social problems. The will of leadership affects attitudes, and the efficacy of the methods analyzed in this chapter. In the view of Jon Quah (1995, 408–9), the single most important reason for Singapore's success in bringing corruption under control was the will and genuine commitment of its leadership to reducing corruption to manageable levels, and to converting the problem from systemic to largely individual. Singapore's success is reflected in its long history of being rated among the least corrupt of all nations; it is the only nonwestern state to appear among the ten least corrupt states in every TI CPI since the first was published in 1995.[87] Some have made similar observations about the role of leadership will in other little dragons, notably Hong Kong and South Korea (*Businessweek: Asian Edition*, 2 September 1996, 18–19). Although South Korea still has a long way to go to catch up with Singapore in terms of reputation, Hong Kong does have a relatively clean image, being the only Asian country apart from Japan and Singapore to appear in TI's top twenty in 1996 (eighteenth, with a score of 7.01). While it might be argued that this reputation for rectitude is a reflection of British organizational culture, the fact is that Hong Kong was still ranking well among Asian states after the end of British rule — being sixteenth overall and second among Asian states, with an improved score of 8.0, in the CPI for 2004.[88] But is there enough political will among CEE leaders?

Some post-communist leaderships have publicly declared a serious commitment to eradicating corruption. Prime Minister Cimoszewicz of Poland did so on various occasions (see for example *SWB/EE*, 1 April 1996). Much more recently, Presidents Saakashvili (Georgia) and Yushchenko (Ukraine) have made similar commitments. And when he came to power in late 1996, President Constantinescu of Romania appeared to have the real will to bring corruption under control. Within a month or so of taking office, he had appointed a high-ranking adviser to oversee the fight against corruption. As an unsigned article in the *Economist* (3 May 1997, 36) put it, "No East European leader has come into office more determined to crush crime, especially the sort that involves the use of state privileges to defraud the public, than Romania's new president, Emil Constantinescu."

Constantinescu's ultimate inability to make much of an impression was arguably less a function of a weak will than of a weak state to implement it.[89] A leadership genuinely committed to reducing corruption can often do so. But this assumes that the leadership really has power; as argued in chapter 6, the weakness of the state in so many post-communist countries means that such an assumption is sometimes false. In light of this, leadership will is a necessary but insufficient condition. The leadership must also have a strong state at its disposal if its will is to bring about tangible outcomes. Too many post-communist leaders have lacked both the will and the capacity to mount a serious attack on corruption.

In addition to leadership will and state capacity, another important variable that has been mentioned at various points now needs to be highlighted. It is all too easy to accuse CEE and CIS politicians of being selfish, hypocritical, and even corrupt. Many are, as in other systems. But others are genuinely committed to clean governance, democracy, and the rule of law. Yet the use of some of the potentially most effective measures for combating corruption, such as the planting of undercover agents within organizations known or suspected to be highly corrupt, causes anguish for many well-intentioned post-communist politicians, for whom such techniques smack too much of the communist past. It must be acknowledged that different components of democracy and the rule of law can and do come into conflict with each other, sometimes fundamentally; numerous observers have made this point with reference to the French revolutionaries' advocacy of both liberty and equality. Most liberal democratic states have become more acutely aware since September 11 of the potential tensions between the individual's rights to civil liberties and privacy on the one hand, and both the individual's and the collective's rights to security on the other. Such conflicts and even contradictions have to be recognized, accepted, and managed. The same applies to the use of often highly effective anticorruption measures, such as networks of informers and sting operations. As long as there is appropriate management of these techniques and they are not used indiscriminately or arbitrarily, there is no inherent reason to consider them antithetical to democracy's basic tenets. The often arbitrary use of the state's powers during the communist era can explain why so many CEE and CIS politicians find it even more difficult than their counterparts in established democracies to acknowledge the legitimacy of the techniques, but it is time for them to move on from the past.[90] Once again, a Rortyan relativism is called for. If the potential harm to society of corruption is markedly greater than the potential drawbacks of the state's

TABLE 7.2. Popular Perceptions of the Probable Future of Corruption, 2000 (in Percent)

	Increase	Decrease	Stay at about same level	Difficult to predict
Bulgaria	30.1	9.1	17.6	43.1
Hungary	50.1	10.4	30.5	9.0
Poland	41.8	12.5	29.0	16.6
Russia	39.1	17.4	25.0	18.5

use of what can from some perspectives be seen as questionable anticorruption methods, then the anticorruption methods should be considered the lesser evil.

Leaders and other senior political actors who do not take corruption seriously, or who find it difficult to forget the past, are doing themselves and their systems long-term harm. Much of the public's mistrust of political institutions in post-communist states is the result of corruption. This brings us back to the issue of legitimacy, which will be a major theme in the concluding chapter. Before considering that theme, however, this is an appropriate point at which to report citizens' perceptions of the likelihood that corruption will be reduced in the future, as identified both in our own surveys and the TI Corruption Barometer for 2003.

A number of observations can be made about table 7.2. First, and somewhat surprisingly, Hungarians were much more likely than Bulgarians, Poles, or Russians to believe that corruption would increase in the future; they were also the most certain of their views, having the lowest score on "difficult to predict." The Bulgarian respondents were by far the most equivocal, being almost five times as likely as Hungarians to find it difficult to predict the likelihood of an increase or decrease in corruption. As argued at other points in this book, the most likely explanation for this is that at the time of the surveys, the Bulgarian government had strongly committed itself to combating corruption, but had achieved results that were less impressive than the rhetoric. One possible reading of this is that citizens do believe that political will might be able to reduce corruption; but it would be foolish to draw firm conclusions on the basis of just one survey result. That respondents who

TABLE 7.3. Expectations of Change in the Corruption Situation over the Next
Three Years, July 2002 (in Percent)

	Increase	Decrease	Stay at about same level	Don't know or no response
Bulgaria	18.1	22.1	33.7	26.1
Poland	38.2	9.5	35.5	16.7
Russia	46.0	8.0	29.2	16.8

Source: Galtung et al. 2003, 27–28

foresaw a decline in corruption were in a small minority in all four states
is a concern, and will be examined in chapter 8.

The dearth of longitudinal data on any aspect of corruption encourages creative comparison wherever possible and justifiable. Thus it is
worth presenting the findings of the Global Corruption Barometer of
2003 relating to future expectations about corruption, even though it is
not directly comparable with our own surveys because it does not include Hungary, and is more time-specific than our own question.

Several observations can be made about these data. Once again, Bulgarians emerge as the least confident respondents, although by a smaller
margin than in the survey that we conducted in 2000; the Russian figures in the two surveys are very close, while the Polish ones are almost
identical. There was no substantial difference between the percentages
in the three countries of respondents who expected the situation to
remain more or less as it was at the time they were surveyed. However,
there was a substantial difference in the percentages expecting an increase. Bulgarians were far more optimistic than Poles, let alone Russians. Equally, Bulgarians were far more likely than Poles or Russians to
expect a decrease. Interestingly, this more positive perception resonates
quite well with the perceived lessening of Bulgaria's corruption. Conversely, the findings analyzed in chapter 4 might suggest that Poles
should be even more concerned than the Russians are. Russian pessimism may have deepened further since the Barometer for 2003; according to a survey in late 2004, 82 percent of Russians believed that the
Russian authorities would be unable to reduce corruption in the coming
years, despite their optimism in other areas.

CHAPTER 8

Conclusions

Corruption is a serious problem in the post-communist world, both in its own right and because of its connections with organized crime and even terrorism. But is it more serious in post-communist states than elsewhere? Analysts such as Sajó (2002; 2003) and Krastev (2004) maintain that the West, as well as some of its compatriots, often exaggerates the problem, for reasons that are largely political.[1] There is unquestionably some weight to this argument. However, as argued in earlier chapters, we must be wary of replacing one oversimplification with another; corruption is indeed a problem for many CEE and CIS citizens. The seriousness of corruption is an issue to be addressed in this concluding chapter. But first, it is worth briefly and comparatively considering the five countries on which we have chosen to focus, and others where appropriate, in terms of the four variables identified in chapter 1.

SOME HYPOTHESES TESTED

It was argued in chapter 1 that the five countries were chosen partly to test a number of hypotheses concerning the variable rates of corruption in the post-communist world. By now, it is clear why it is impossible to be certain about our perceptions of differences in the relative scale of corruption in various countries. Moreover, five is too small a number of cases from which to be able to draw general conclusions with any degree of confidence. On the other hand, there is sufficient evidence to permit tentative conclusions, and it would be unnecessarily self-limiting not to interrogate our findings to the maximum permissible extent.

It will be recalled that the four variables to be tested against perceived levels of corruption were size, culture, ethnic homogeneity, and approaches to reform. Each will now be considered in turn. In doing so, the clusterings produced in chapter 4 on the basis of the TI rankings for 1999 and 2004, plus the scores provided in table 4.1, will be used. While this approach has its drawbacks, there appears to be no better method at present for evaluating overall and relative corruption levels, an assumption borne out by the relative closeness of the rankings to those produced by other methods. This approach also has the advantage of providing a greater range of countries for comparison than just our five.

But it is with the five that our analysis begins. Focusing only on them produces a complex picture with regard to the correlation of corruption and size. Thus while Bulgaria is much smaller than Poland and China, it was perceived in the late 1990s as slightly more corrupt than either. However, it has improved in recent years. Russia is territorially much larger than our three CEE states, though it has a much smaller population than China. But it too has improved. Hungary has a relatively small population, and has deteriorated slightly. Poland is a medium-sized state, but it appears by most methodologies to have become measurably more corrupt. And while China is very large, it appears not to have become any more or less corrupt than it was in the late 1990s. Our five countries do not support the hypothesis that there is a clear correlation between size and perceived levels of corruption.

Moving beyond our five, it emerges that while there might be some positive correlation between either population or territorial size and corruption levels, the correlation is at most weak. Thus all the countries in groups A and B in 1999 except Poland are relatively small, while the countries that are largest both by population (China, Russia, and Ukraine) and by territory (China, Kazakhstan, Russia, and Ukraine) are all in groups C and D. But group D also includes a number of small countries, among them Albania, Azerbaijan, Georgia, and Yugoslavia. Similarly, while the clusterings for 2004 are headed in group A by two very small states (Estonia and Slovenia), group E — most corrupt — also includes several small states (Azerbaijan, Georgia, and Moldova), while China, Russia, and Ukraine are spread over three groupings (C to E). Moreover, there are too few large states in our sample from which to be able to draw general conclusions.

There is a slightly stronger correlation between corruption levels and culture, at least in the sense of dominant religious traditions. Analyzing first the clusterings for 1999, predominantly Islamic states feature exclusively in group D and Orthodox Christian states exclusively in groups C and D, while mainly Catholic or Protestant countries are primarily in groups A and B — though there is a sprinkling of these in groups C and D as well.[2] The clusterings for 2004 are more persuasive, although Orthodox Bulgaria in group B is an outlier. While it is tempting to correlate religious culture and corruption levels, it should also be noted that the countries in group D (1999) and groups D and E (2004) are for the most part also the countries with the lowest per capita GDP figures. As noted in chapter 6, poverty might therefore be a better explanatory variable than religion. This argument is supported by Montinola and Jackman (2002, esp. 169), and Gray, Hellman, and Ryterman (2004, 42), who state bluntly that "richer countries have lower corruption levels." However, it must be also be acknowledged that there is a question of causal directionality here — assuming that there is any causal relationship at all — and it would be unwise to dismiss completely the notion that lower levels of economic development can be partly explained in terms of religious cultural values. For instance, material wealth may be less important to many Muslims or Orthodox Christians than religious devotion or other values.

All five of our selected countries have ethnically quite homogeneous populations, although the level of homogeneity is higher in Poland (94 percent Polish), Hungary (about 92 percent Hungarian) and China (about 92 percent Han Chinese) than in Russia (about 87 percent Russian) or Bulgaria (about 83 percent Bulgarian). Since these five span all four groups of nations in 1999, and three out of five groups in 2004, it would be difficult to sustain the argument that ethnically diverse post-communist societies are more prone to corruption than ethnically homogeneous ones. Indeed, Estonia is widely considered among the least corrupt of the post-communist states, although only 65 percent of its population is Estonian; conversely, Azerbaijan's population is some 89 percent Azeri, yet the country is regularly ranked by most measures as one of the most corrupt post-communist states. In sum, any correlation between ethnic homogeneity and perceived corruption levels is weak.

Our final variable is each country's approach to economic reform. It was argued in chapter 1 that the contrast drawn between the Polish and Hungarian approaches to restructuring is often exaggerated; it is simplistic to see Poland as exemplifying the shock therapy, or big bang, approach, and Hungary the gradualist approach. Poland's privatization process, for example, was slower and later than in many post-communist countries, while Hungary adopted what might be called a steady dynamism (in that the reform process maintained its momentum, even if there were few sudden, radical changes). In their different ways, both countries maintained the pressure for reform in the 1990s. And both countries performed relatively well in the comparative corruption rankings during most of the 1990s. But the situation has been changing in recent years. While Hungary has deteriorated a little, Poland has deteriorated markedly. In terms of our argument about reform and neoliberalism, this requires an explanation.

In both countries, communist successors have been elected to power on various occasions since 1989. In Poland they again came to power in 2001. While it would be quite inappropriate to argue that the SLD bears much resemblance to the Polish United Workers Party (PUWP) in terms of policies and approach, there may be just enough residual (and possibly unconscious) old thinking and old networks to have had an impact on corruption levels. But Poland's decline, though continuing since the turn of the century, appears to have started in the late 1990s, before the SLD returned to power; its TI score dropped from 5.08 to 4.1 between 1997 and 2000. Our hypothesis is that the bickering within the ruling Solidarity Electoral Action — which eventually collapsed — plus the tensions between it and the left-of-center president contributed to the uncertainty and aimlessness that were conducive to corruption. Compared with the early 1990s, the reform process slowed. Poland thus begins to appear more in line with Hellman's partial reform equilibrium argument than might initially be assumed, despite findings by Hanley (2000) that Poland was more effective even than Hungary in minimizing nomenklatura privatization.

Conversely, Russia and Bulgaria were for much of the 1990s more hesitant about economic reform. Both experienced periods of commitment to radicalism, but have also often applied the brakes; this is particularly true of Russia. But Bulgaria really began to reform once the Union of Democratic Forces (UDF) came to power in 1997. While the UDF was replaced in 2001, its replacement was not the communist successors but a new grouping that was as strongly committed to fighting corruption as the UDF had been. As argued in chapter 6, Russia did not entirely cease to reform after Gaidar's departure. But the loans-for-shares privatization was a distorted and largely illegitimate type of reform that smacked heavily of the old communist patronage and insider methods. While Putin can be criticized on many levels for his efforts to tighten up (such as his treatment of the news media), he also introduced important economic reforms during his first term, including reforms of land ownership, and appears committed to tidying up some of the mess created by the shady deals of the 1990s.[3]

Thus, while it would be wrong to argue that neoliberalism is part of the explanation for Russia's apparent (and still modest) improvement in recent times in controlling corruption, the argument about overcoming the communist legacy does to some extent apply. However, if Putin continues to move toward authoritarianism, it is possible that corruption levels will begin to rise again. There are three possible scenarios for avoiding this. Under the first, Putin becomes a Stalin-like dictator and the population lives in fear. This seems unlikely, in part because Putin is not the international isolationist that Stalin sought to be until the 1940s; the current Russian leader appears to care about international opinion. Under the second scenario, Putin develops into such a model of incorrupt leadership that he inspires others to emulate him. The problem with this is that Putin is already well into his second term — his last, according to the current Russian constitution — so the chances that this will occur appear slim. Under the third scenario, Putin's goal of doubling GDP is achieved, the country's wealth is spread more equitably than at present, and the result is a positive impact on corruption. But again, it is inconceivable that this could happen within Putin's term of office. If Putin extends his term, thus moving unambiguously from a fragile and partial democracy to some form of authoritarianism, then unless either the first or third scenario eventuates, the experience of dictatorships around the world suggests that corruption could increase (though see below).

China is a particularly interesting case in terms of reform. It has introduced radical economic reforms since the late 1970s, which received a renewed boost in the late 1990s. It performs better than Russia in the comparative corruption rankings, yet has a less autonomous civil society than any of our four states in CEE and the CIS. On the one hand, its experience proves that even relatively authoritarian communist states cannot avoid corruption.[4] On the other, precisely because China is not subject to as much societal control of corruption as more open societies are, its performance — on a par with Bulgaria — is better than might be expected.[5] But the system there is fragile, and is essentially dependent on impressive economic performance. Were this performance to falter in a significant way, the communist political system would collapse.

A pattern that emerges hazily from our comparison of just five countries crystallizes markedly when the full set of post-communist countries included in our clustering is considered. While a correlation does not equate to a causal relationship, clearly the post-communist states that have adopted the most radical economic reforms are perceived to have the lowest levels of corruption; countries that start to falter in their reforms often then begin to become more corrupt. But we have also seen that as with any detailed and honest comparison, generalities have to be disaggregated to explain individual cases.

There is one other point alluded to above but deliberately glossed over, though observant readers may have already picked up on it in our wording. This point is that while many dictatorships have unquestionably been highly corrupt, the relationship between corruption, democracy, and authoritarianism is complex. The authors of one cross-polity time-series analysis of the nature of this relationship have concluded that authoritarian systems can be less corrupt than troubled democratizing ones — but that the lowest corruption rates are to be found in consolidated democracies (Montinola and Jackman 2002). This finding resonates with many of our own tentative conclusions. It would be compatible with the apparent improvement in Russia, a troubled democracy that is currently heading toward authoritarianism, and with the experience of Poland (just a troubled democracy). It would be less convincing an explanation of Bulgaria, however, which does appear to have made progress in its fight against corruption, despite having a troubled democracy. Once again, our small sample means that it is not possible to determine whether Bulgaria is simply an exception to a general pattern or rather requires us to reconsider our generalizations. Much work still needs to be done.

THE SERIOUSNESS OF THE PROBLEM

A salient feature of post-communist states is that they are transitional.[6] But the scale and nature of their transitions are broader and more complex than those of Latin American or Southern European states, despite the claims of analysts such as Schmitter and Karl (1994). Because of the communist legacy and the range of transformations being attempted, it is not surprising that the post-communist states should have in general been so fragile — even more fragile than the other transitional states are or were (depending on the country). Precisely this fragility is one of the reasons for the apparent growth in corruption and organized crime; as Anatolii Chubais, then minister for privatization and deputy prime minister in Russia, argued in 1993, "crime and corruption are a function of a weak state" (quoted in *Financial Times*, 18 June 1993, 15). Advancing the argument while endeavoring to explain the weak state that makes corruption more likely, a leading Hungarian criminologist, Mariann Kránitz, has observed that the dislocation caused by the collapse of the old system is typical of the kind of situation in which corruption thrives: "Each war, revolution, change of regime, formation and development of a new class of property holders, and change in the society's distribution of wealth encourages the growth of corruption. During these periods of radical change, the state, the legislature, law enforcement bodies, and the criminal justice system simply do not have time to deal with corruption" (Kránitz 1994, 107).[7]

Yet it is precisely this vicious circle that creates even worse legitimation problems for the new states than corruption does for more established ones. Only if the new authorities can bring corruption under control might they be able to enhance their own popular legitimacy. This point emerges from the following quotation from István Hagelmeyer, then president of the Hungarian State Audit Office: "The fight against corruption is one of the most important undertakings in our new world. We must face this problem in order to eradicate it, as it causes not only economic damage, but also poisons public trust" (Hagelmeyer 1994, 11). Indeed, if ordinary citizens associate corruption with organized crime, and both of these with the whole privatization and marketization project, and if this project is in turn associated with the western model including democracy, then the prospects for post-communism appear bleak.

Yet another vicious circle — identified in chapter 7 as a problem — is observable here. Interviews that I have conducted reveal that many post-communist officials have been loath to use what they consider excessive state power in their fight against corruption, for fear that they will appear to be emulating the authoritarianism of their communist predecessors.[8] Having overthrown one form of excessive state control, they are anxious not to appear to be replacing it with another. Ironically, the louder the accusations that the communist successor parties are — when in power — only marginally different from their predecessors, the worse this problem can become.

This reluctance to appear overly authoritarian returns us to the issue of the weak state. A number of authors (for example S. Holmes 1996; L. Holmes 1998c; Gill 2000) have argued that in cases where civil society is weak and a major transformation is required, it is vital to have a strong state. There are unquestionably dangers in this, notably that the state can become overly powerful and increasingly authoritarian, at the expense of the democratization process. Nevertheless, it is possible to incorporate in-built safeguards to minimize the likelihood of such an outcome. These include (largely) uncensored mass media and an independent judiciary, as well as the more obvious prerequisite of regular, genuinely contested elections, the results of which are respected by all major players. The dangers are more marked in post-communist transitional states than in western states, since the transitional states are generally more fragile, and have democratic norms that are less well entrenched. The post-communist states do not have the bedrock of legal-rational legitimacy, based on the concept of rule of law broadly understood, to sustain them through hard times. If corruption plays a major role in hindering the development of such legal-rational legitimacy, it becomes clear why it is a more serious problem in the post-communist states than in western states (though not necessarily more serious than in developing states).[9]

It has been argued in this book that neoliberalism generally weakens the state, by reducing its rights and responsibilities. But since, as has also been argued, post-communist states that have gone further down the path of reform — usually in the direction of neoliberalism — typically have lower levels of corruption than the more hesitant states, there might appear to be a major contradiction or impasse in the claim that neoliberalism weakens the state. In fact there is no contradiction. It has been argued in earlier chapters that while the spread of neoliberal practices is probably a major explanation for the apparent increase in corruption in the West, the relationship between such practices and corruption in the post-communist states is more complex. In these states the communist legacy needs to be factored into the equation. It has also been pointed out that even the least corrupt of the post-communist states are still much more corrupt than many other states. Hence, to make an obvious point, everything is relative. Post-communist states need to be both strong and reformist simultaneously. This means that state institutions must be strengthened and cleansed (in other words, their corruption levels must be substantially reduced) at the same time as they need to maintain the pace of reform and overcome the communist legacy. Unfortunately this is often easier said than done.

A final point is that interpreting the emphasis placed by international financial institutions such as the IMF (and to a lesser extent the World Bank) on introducing basically neoliberal or Washington Consensus reforms in transitional states may also be more complex than it initially appears. It would be naïve to ignore the likelihood that ideology is a major reason for this emphasis, possibly the primary one. But it should not be overlooked that the introduction of such changes, including the requirement that economies open up to foreign investors, can be a powerful weapon in the fight against indigenous crony capitalism.[10] Hence the emphasis on the need for radical reforms can be seen on one level as part of the struggle against corruption, including the ramifications of nomenklatura privatization.

Just as the relationship between corruption and neoliberalism needs to be problematized, so corruption itself is better understood if considered from perspectives other than purely ethical ones. While corruption is rarely defensible from a moral standpoint, it is difficult to understand the ambiguous attitudes that so many citizens appear to have toward corruption if it is analyzed solely in ethical terms. If the struggle against corruption is to be effective, it is important to appreciate how corruption is sometimes seen as nothing more than the lesser of two evils, perhaps even something advantageous. This is the focus of the following discussion.

FUNCTIONALITIES OF CORRUPTION

While corruption is cause for concern in most post-communist states, it is a complex phenomenon that can be beneficial even as it does harm. There are several aspects to this.

Particularly during periods of major and potentially disruptive political conflict — which has typified many post-communist states — some forms of patronage can play a positive role by keeping political differences in check. The well-respected Russian analyst Lilia Shevtsova (2001, 101) has argued that the basis for relative stability in Russian society in recent years is patron-client relations.[11] Consistent with this general argument, and as mentioned in chapter 3, there have been allegations that pro-democratic forces have sometimes bribed Zhirinovskii's Liberal Democrats in the Russian parliament to vote with them on important issues, and that without this support, the communists and other nationalist and conservative forces would have been able to hinder the democratization and marketization processes even more than they have done (this point was made in several interviews conducted in Moscow, April–May 1997).[12]

Moreover, corruption can sometimes help to provide goods to citizens during difficult times, when the state is unable to supply them (see the reference to Serbia in chapter 7). This was true of the communist era, when standing in line, or queuing, symbolized the serious imbalance between supply and demand. In the post-communist era, queuing has become much less common than it was. But to some extent queuing has been replaced by overt inflation. Because of the marked rise in official poverty in most post-communist states in recent years, many citizens would find it hard to survive were they not able to overcome or reduce some of their problems through bribery and other ways of corrupting officials. Indeed, where officials themselves are not paid salaries for months on end, corruption can help them to survive.

Although most post-communist states claim to be attempting to reduce the role of the state in the economy, even short visits to many of them reveals that a number of the old bureaucratic practices remain well entrenched. Contemporary Russia, for example, does not have noticeably less red tape than the Soviet Union did.[13] In such circumstances, if corruption can accelerate or simplify processes (for instance, in terms of privatization, or new construction projects), then it can play a positive role in economic development. In addition, allegations of corruption in high places, as long as they are kept within reasonable bounds, can also play a useful scapegoating role for governments and states during hard times. Eudaemonism is not yet a viable source of legitimacy for many states, while legal rationality takes years to mature; at the same time, too much emphasis on official nationalism can exacerbate the problem of disintegrative unofficial nationalisms. In this situation, scapegoating — despite its resonances with the communist notion of enemies within — can play a legitimizing role in the short term.

In light of the well-publicized (though unproven) allegations of corruption against him in the past,[14] the resounding victories by Yurii Luzhkov in the mayoral elections of 1996, 1999, and 2003 in Moscow suggest that citizens might sometimes accept corruption in return for effective leadership and the anticipation of improved economic performance; the return to power of Fatos Nano in Albania (1997) and Ion Iliescu in Romania (2000) can also be interpreted partly in these terms of an expected tradeoff.[15] In short, the role and implications of corruption under post-communism are complex, just as they were during the communist era, and not invariably negative (for the classic cost-benefit analysis of corruption see Nye 1967).[16]

THE DYNAMISM OF POST-COMMUNIST CORRUPTION

Allowing for the complex role and occasional short-term functionality of corruption does not significantly detract from its overall and long-term negative effects. Yet despite the pessimism of many citizens suggested by tables 7.2 and 7.3, it is possible that corruption will be reduced to manageable levels in some of the post-communist states in which it is currently a serious problem; both corruption and the fight against it are dynamic and changing, and the outlook is not entirely bleak.

Earlier, an apparent vicious circle was identified: to reduce corruption, a strong and largely uncorrupted state is needed — yet the more corruption there is or is perceived to be, the less citizens trust the state, and the more they seek to avoid paying the taxes that are necessary to strengthen it. One of the many prerequisites for a strong state — adequate resources — is thus absent. Against this are some important changes that are or might be under way in many post-communist states. One of the most important is an irony of post-communism: the likelihood that many of those who break or bend the law in the early days of post-communism to generate personal wealth will subsequently want the law to protect and legitimize their gains and themselves. For many, such a tradeoff — future legitimacy in return for playing henceforth by the rules — already is or is likely to become an attractive proposition.

Another change is that the free fall experienced by so many economies after the collapse of communist power has now been either stopped or even reversed in most cases. According to the European Bank for Reconstruction and Development, even as late as 1999 only two post-communist economies (Poland and Slovenia) had surpassed their real GDP levels from 1989, while Slovakia had just reached it, and Hungary was poised to do so (Fries and Sanfey 2001, 15). But the turnarounds in many states by the end of the 1990s and in the early years of the new century give some reason for cautious optimism.[17] The stronger the economies become, the less desperate people will be about survival, and the greater the likelihood that some officials who currently engage in corrupt practices primarily to survive will think twice about continuing with their antisocial behavior. At the same time, strengthening economies will permit better payment of law enforcement officers, and indeed all state officials; this too should help to bring corruption down to more manageable levels. It will be recalled in this context that according to our own surveys from 2000 (table 6.1), ordinary citizens in all four countries considered low salaries the second-most significant cause of corruption.

Third, the quality of legislation is gradually improving in many countries, and legislative lag is slowly being overcome. There are signs in several states that a culture of compromise is emerging within the political system, which will contribute to this improvement.[18] Such a culture would enhance the possibilities for effective incremental decision making in the future; assuming that this happens once the legislative lag has been overcome, it would be another sign of democratic consolidation.[19] The simplification of taxation regimes and reduction of tax rates referred to in earlier chapters should both contribute to the economic improvement mentioned above and lead to higher revenues for the state.[20] Like the second and third areas of change, this should in time contribute to a strengthening of the state.

Another change that would strengthen the state is the regularization of politics. As this occurs in post-communist countries, there should be more time and energy for agreeing on ways to tackle corruption. It is relevant in this context that partly as a function of electoral laws and the passage of time, party systems are beginning to emerge in some post-communist countries. Hungary already has reasonably well-defined major parties and party identifications. Bulgaria until 2001 did have what appeared to be a relatively stable two-and-a-half-party system (Union of Democratic Forces; Bulgarian Socialist Party; Movement for Rights and Freedoms). The victory in the elections of June 2001 of a new political organization centered on the former king changed this, although the remaining parties are still forces within Bulgarian politics, and there is widespread disappointment with the movement led by Simeon II. Russia has what can be called a partly crystallized system, since there are well-established parties that have built up reasonably solid constituencies, even though these compete against many relatively new parties in most elections. Thus the Communists, Yabloko, and the Liberal Democrats reappear election after election — although some 60 percent of votes in the parliamentary elections of December 1999 went to parties that had been formed in the previous six months. Similarly, almost 38 percent of those Russians who took part in the parliamentary elections in December 2003 (turnout was almost 56 percent) voted for a party that was formally only two years old (Unified Russia), while a further 9 percent voted for an even newer party (Motherland — *Rodina*). Poland has the least consolidated party system, and by early 2005 many Poles were wondering about the left, centrist, and right-of-center options that they would have at the next election. As party systems do consolidate in some countries, often as a result of changed laws on political parties, so the rules of the game crystallize. Moreover, the very newness — and hence confusion — of the earliest stages of post-communism is in many cases being replaced by a familiarity with institutions and politicians. Among the many reasons for Yeltsin's success in the presidential election of 1996 was that he was a "devil" whom people knew. While familiarity sometimes breeds contempt, it can in other contexts reduce feelings of uncertainty and confusion.[21]

Sixth, there is the potential impact of personnel turnover. Although there are likely to be debates for many years to come over what proportion of putatively new élites are in fact members of the former élites (notably of the old nomenklatura), and while this proportion differs from one post-communist state to another (for details see for example Kryshtanovskaya and White 1996; Steen 1997; Higley, Pakulski and Wesolowski 1998; Lane and Ross 1999; Hanley 2000), the proportion must drop in all countries as existing officials resign, retire, or die. As argued at several points in this book, a major reason for the corruption in post-communist states is the legacy of the past. Although it was often less well documented than it should have been, there is evidence of high-level and widespread corruption before 1989 in virtually all the former communist states. As elaborated in chapter 6, the very nature of communism — a centrally planned economy, closely knit élitism, hypocrisy, and shortages, to name but four of a series of contributory factors — was highly conducive to corruption, and established behavioral patterns that have been carried over into post-communism by too many politicians and officials. Moreover, many of these former officials were determined not to miss out in the transition from communism, and engaged in highly questionable activities during the privatization process to ensure that their privileged lifestyles would continue under the new regime.[22] It would be naïve not to acknowledge that their thought and behavioral patterns are likely to be transmitted in part to their successors, many of whom they will train. Nevertheless, the younger generation is subject to at least as many contemporary influences as past ones, and the influence of communist methods is likely to decline at an accelerating rate.

It is not only the state that should become stronger. Civil society has the capacity to become more effective too. The news media, for instance, could play a positive and more significant role in bringing corruption to heel. There is no inherent reason why NGOs should not become more effective too in combating corruption. Although both the severe economic problems of early post-communism and the unpleasant memories from the communist era of state-run social organizations help to explain why social movements and civil society more generally have been less active and visible than many had hoped at the beginning of the 1990s (Pickvance 1999; Howard 2002; Howard 2003), it is an encouraging sign that the institutional and ideological frameworks are now in place in many post-communist states to permit more involvement by self-motivated citizens in the future.[23] It is also encouraging that many international organizations are committed to helping the post-communist NGOs to develop.

Related to the last point is a somewhat abstract one about the learning curve of doing business in societies in which private enterprise was for decades of marginal significance. The point concerns the potential for increasing trust and improving reliability as agents come to understand the implications of iterated exchanges. A hypothetical situation can help to clarify this. I check into a hotel, and pay a local laundry to wash my clothes. This is in a country with little regard for formalities, such as issuing receipts for clothes deposited. I am required to pay up front when I leave my dirty clothes. When I return a day later, the launderers claim not to have been paid, and I have to pay a second time if I want to retrieve my clothes. The launderers have assumed that I am only a one-off customer, like most of the hotel's guests. But in fact I am on a funded research trip of four weeks, and would have used the laundry twice a week—a total of eight times. Had they known this, the launderers might have thought twice about cheating me, because of the iterated nature of the business. Thus, in the real world, time and the desire to maintain regular income from a quite tightly defined constituency—to build up *trust* and thus social capital—can counter the improper pursuit of a quick buck.

Finally, there are the indirect and direct influences of external agents. For example, other countries can unintentionally act as models for transition states; Singapore is one such, its authoritarianism notwithstanding. The impact of globalizing communications, particularly on younger politicians and officials, should not be underestimated either. But there are also more direct influences. The most obvious for approximately one third of the post-communist states is the European Union. Of our five states, two—Hungary and Poland—were admitted in May 2004, while Bulgaria is hoping to join in 2007. In recent years membership of the European Union has become a new telos for a substantial number of citizens in several post-communist states. As they have learned how well Ireland and Spain, and to a lesser extent Portugal, have fared since admission, particularly in terms of economic development and living standards, they believe that they see light at the end of their own dark tunnels.[24] Since the European Union indicated clearly from 1997 on that applicant states had to strive to reduce corruption if they were to be admitted, it becomes obvious that this external agency can sometimes be influential in reducing corruption, and will seek to maintain its influence.[25]

It is also possible to break out of the other vicious circle—that of wanting to bring corruption under control, but being concerned that measures adopted will be perceived by others as moves toward authoritarianism. As argued in chapter 7, few if any conceptions of liberal democracy would deny that one of its salient features is the rule of law; democracy is not anarchy. As long as laws are clear, adequately publicized, applied fairly and universally, and adopted by democratically elected representatives, then their application cannot be seen as authoritarianism. On the contrary—tolerance of corruption, which implies disregard for the rule of law, is by most criteria far less democratic than the struggle to eradicate it. As time passes, and the complex relationship between democracy and legality is better understood in post-communist countries, so the fight against corruption should become more decisive and effective.

The more optimistic scenario of declining corruption outlined above is only a possible one, not a necessary one. Some countries—including Hungary, Poland, and Slovenia—are more likely to move to it in the foreseeable future than others. Conversely, the increasing repression and media censorship in countries such as Belarus, Kyrgyzstan, and now also Russia under Putin, bode ill for the responsible investigative watchdog journalism that can help to highlight the problem of corruption and encourage citizens to demand that it be brought under control;[26] countries such as Turkmenistan and Tajikistan made very little progress in this area to start with. While the research by Montinola and Jackman (2002) mentioned earlier suggests that moves toward authoritarianism might reduce corruption, the evidence from countries such as Indonesia, the Philippines, several African and Latin American states—and indeed the former communist systems—indicates the need for caution in too readily accepting this conclusion. Not only are there plenty of authoritarian systems that have worse corruption problems than the so-called troubled democracies—though authoritarian regimes are often better at hiding it—but, as already indicated, Montinola and Jackman also point out that consolidating democracy is the best way to reduce corruption over the long term.

The suggestion that new bourgeoisies will demand the regularization of property rights, with positive pipeline effects for a rule-of-law culture, can also be questioned. In a piece that to some extent resonates with and builds on Hellman's partial reform equilibrium thesis (1998), Hoff and Stiglitz (2002) have produced a powerful model-based argument to challenge the assumption that the early winners of post-communism will seek legal protection of the wealth acquired by so many through various forms of asset stripping. If this constituency continued to perceive that it was more advantageous to strip assets than to build value, there would be serious negative implications for the development of the rule of law. Assuming that the hypothesis of Hoff and Stiglitz proves correct, even if only in the short to medium term, high levels of corruption will continue to be a salient feature of many post-communist states for years to come. This is probably one reason why so many citizens in post-communist countries believe that corruption will continue to be a serious problem.

The still-fragile state of the economy in several post-communist countries does not suggest an imminent lessening of corruption either. Indeed, there could also be an unfortunate dialectic operating here. Dobel (1978, 961–62) has argued that inequality is the single most important source of corruption in any system, while Ward (1989), M. Johnston (1989), the World Bank, and others see corruption as a major source of inequality and poverty. If poverty and inequality both promote and are exacerbated by corruption, then the growing economic and social stratification in many post-communist countries (see for example Janos 2000, 403–4) augurs badly for the fight against corruption, at the same time as it is likely to be intensified by corruption.[27] Once again, a vicious circle can be created.

Another potentially disturbing development in some countries is the increase of state control over private organizations. In the mid-1990s TI expressed concern about this in the context of attempting to establish a Slovak chapter. A law passed in Slovakia in June 1996 required nonprofit civic foundations to register with the Ministry of the Interior, which could have made it easier for the state to stifle or incorporate elements within civil society that might otherwise independently seek to counter corruption (Transparency International 1996b, 12). At about the same time, Kamiński (1996, 5–10) expressed a similar concern vis-à-vis the adoption of a number of acts in Poland since 1993, including the misleadingly titled Industrial Self-Government Act. He argued that these acts blurred the division between the state and the private sector; inasmuch as so much corruption occurs at the interface of these two, the chances of corruption increase, at the same time as free enterprise is hindered by state interference. Russia also tightened its control over NGOs in 2004. All this is disappointing both for the fight against corruption and for the development of civil society generally in such states.

It has been argued that there is no inherent reason why corruption cannot be brought under control in post-communist states in the future, but also that various recent developments in several of these countries do not bode well. Ultimately the fate of the struggle against corruption will depend to a considerable extent on the will of post-communist governments; agency must overcome structure. At present it seems that too many post-communist politicians and senior officials are still improperly enriching themselves, benefiting from the uncertainties and opportunities of post-communism, so much so that it is as yet unclear whether the will to bring corruption under control exists. Nowhere is this more obvious than in the murky world of privatization. For this reason, arguments such as those of Hellman (1998) or Hoff and Stiglitz (2002) already outlined, and the application of the concept of state capture to the CEE and CIS states, provide useful theoretical insights into developments in the post-communist world over the past ten to fifteen years, the limitations of these concepts notwithstanding.

It has further been argued here that much of the apparent increase in corruption in the 1990s and the early years of the new century is a function of the very nature of post-communism; this point must now be examined more closely. As noted in chapter 6, post-communist states have been undergoing a whole series of simultaneous transformations and are having to establish new cultural patterns. These new patterns include a much greater capacity for political compromise, and an agreement on the rules of the game. But a salient feature of the rejection of communist power was a rejection of both teleology and the communist ethical code; even when citizens believed that they were rejecting communist values, their having been subjected to constant socialization in these values meant that they could not entirely avoid their insidious effects. While some have found hope in religion since the collapse of communism, others have found it difficult to create a new moral code for themselves. If the aggregated effects of this personal dilemma for millions of people are added to the problems of the weak state in so many countries, the so-called corruption eruption becomes much easier to understand.[28]

At the same time, the dynamism of post-communism means that this situation could change rapidly. In 1990 many analysts considered it inconceivable that the electorates in countries such as Lithuania, Hungary, and above all Poland should freely choose communist successors within three or four years; that the voters did so could be interpreted as revealing just how rapidly mass attitudes can change.[29] While it is not argued here that a powerful new morality is imminent, it must be acknowledged that prediction about societies undergoing such unprecedented changes is difficult, so that allowance should be made for possibilities that a priori appear improbable. As mentioned at the end of chapter 7, for instance, President Constantinescu of Romania made the fight against corruption a top priority — and (largely circumstantial) evidence suggests that he might have already been changing Romanians' attitudes toward their political institutions by mid-1997. In the words of the *Economist* (3 May 1997, 36), "The effect on public opinion has been electric. Seeing corrupt bankers and politicians thrown into jail or out of office is 'far better for the market economy than economic reform,' says one Romanian . . . Romanians, who have come to expect betrayal from their institutions, may be cautiously starting to trust them." That Romanians were subsequently disappointed does not diminish the initial widespread optimism; indeed, the high level of disappointment by 2000 probably reflects the high expectations.

LEGITIMACY PROBLEMS OF THE POST-COMMUNIST STATE

In an earlier article, I argued that there are at least six discernible theories of the crisis of the contemporary state (generally, not specifically post-communist), although there is overlap between some of them (L. Holmes 1997a). This earlier analysis will not be repeated here. Moreover, it is questionable whether the term "crisis" is still appropriate, given the chronic situation in so many states. But one earlier argument that remains relevant is that there is a seventh possible crisis of the state, that of public trust in the authorities.[30] In a real sense, this crisis is directly related to the crisis of legitimacy. But legitimacy issues constitute a more general problem of the state than, for instance, that identified by Jürgen Habermas (Habermas 1973a and 1973b), since it can apply to any kind of state. Moreover, the problems, which in some situations *can* constitute a crisis, do not necessarily proceed through the four stages identified by Habermas. In the approach advocated here, the principal cause of public mistrust of the state is corruption. Mistrust is thus a major dimension of legitimacy, to which we now return.

Legitimacy is a notoriously difficult concept to measure, but tentative steps can be taken. A starting point is to refer the reader back to table 5.2; that some western states performed poorly in the measures summarized in the table only testifies to the widespread delegitimization of the contemporary state. Lena Kolarska-Bobińska (2002) has collated much valuable — if

TABLE 8.1.   Popular Perceptions of the Connections between Official
Corruption and Organized Crime, 2000 (in Percent)

	Very close	Close	Not very close	Essentially nonexistent	Don't know
Bulgaria	24.3	32.0	10.2	4.1	29.5
Hungary	12.2	48.0	25.1	2.7	11.8
Poland	16.0	37.7	23.0	2.2	21.0
Russia	43.5	43.2	5.0	0.6	7.7

by necessity ultimately circumstantial — evidence on the connections between corruption and legitimacy in Poland. Our own four-country survey included one question that related directly to legitimacy (see table
5.1 and related text), and a second that almost certainly does too. The
second asked respondents to assess how close they believed the connections were between corruption and organized crime; it is assumed here
that there is a serious legitimacy problem for any state in which much of
the population perceives a close or very close connection.[31]

Table 8.1 reveals significant differences in the perceptions of respondents in the four countries surveyed. Almost 87 percent of Russians
believed that there were close or very close connections between corrupt
officials and organized crime; although the figure was lowest in Hungary (at approximately 60 percent), it is still very high for systems attempting to increase their legitimacy. Once again, Bulgarians were far
less sure of what to believe than the other three groups, though it is
worth noting that more than one fifth of Polish respondents also answered "don't know." Overall, the responses to this question suggest
that post-communist states have been experiencing a serious problem of
legitimacy, at least of the legal-rational variety.

In chapter 4 the obvious point was made that all survey data must be
treated with caution. In many of the more general surveys cited in chapter 5 (the Russian ones being the main exception), respondents were
asked either to focus on corruption, or else were not expected to rank-
order or choose between variables; in these circumstances, overwhelming majorities revealed their concerns about corruption. But let us assume that Gole (1999) is at least partly correct in assuming that seeking
respondents' attitudes toward corruption forces them to focus on some-

thing that they might not otherwise consider. If she is, then the sort of survey that invites respondents to choose from a long list the three or more issues that are of greatest concern to them might counter her objection. Such surveys have been conducted worldwide, and yield interesting results in terms of the perceived seriousness of corruption. One such can now be considered.

In 1995 (during spring in the Northern Hemisphere), respondents in thirty-six countries, embracing virtually all types of system, were asked to identify the three issues that most concerned them from a list of eight: criminality, unemployment, shortage of money, pollution of the environment, AIDS, corruption, inflation, and narcotics. Of the post-communist and quasi-post-communist states, China, Czechia, Hungary, Poland, and Russia were included in the survey. In only one of these, China, did corruption figure in the top three concerns; there it was second only to inflation.[32] However, criminality was the number one concern in Hungary, Poland, and Russia, and number two in Czechia (after inflation); in all countries in which it ranked number one, it did so by a substantial margin.[33] Since many citizens in post-communist states apparently see a close connection between corruption and organized crime, the less prominent ranking of corruption than might a priori have been expected begins to look less surprising. If respondents are permitted only three choices, it is reasonable to infer that many will opt for a broader category that can include corruption, rather than for a narrower one when they are also concerned about other types of criminality with which corruption is perceived to be linked. Hence this international comparative survey does not suggest that the widespread concerns about corruption identified in chapter 5 are exaggerated.

However, replies to the one direct question on legitimacy in our surveys (see chapter 5), and to that on the nexus between corruption and crime, should not be fetishized. In particular, they cannot really tell us about popular attitudes toward democracy as a concept, since other surveys and research methods indicate that many citizens in post-communist countries draw a fairly sharp distinction between the practices of their regimes and the democratic ideal (Dryzek and Holmes 2002). Nevertheless, our survey results do suggest that at the least, corruption is hindering the legitimation project in all four CEE and CIS states examined in this book.

Whether it is accepted that there is a corruption-related legitimacy crisis of the post-communist state depends to a considerable degree on what is understood by the term "crisis." Some of the more extreme statements by post-communist politicians would suggest that there is indeed a crisis. But politicians often make these statements to discredit competitors or protect their own reputations: if corruption is later brought under control, the politician who warned of a crisis will appear to have been a good crisis manager. During the more monolithic and teleological communist era, there could be a logical inconsistency in claims by the so-called political vanguard that a crisis had arisen — which it might subsequently claim to have solved — since the vanguard could not blame the crisis on anyone but itself.[34] In view of this contradiction, such statements were rare, and typically made only when there clearly was a serious problem. But in the post-communist era of competitive politics, this problem of illogic does not arise, so that warnings by post-communist politicians of a crisis cannot per se be taken as convincing evidence that they genuinely perceive a crisis. Such utterances can be merely a case of political mischief making and point scoring.

Moreover, while the problem appears to have manifested itself in new guises and to have become more salient in recent years, it is a long-term issue, not a new one. To refer to such an enduring phenomenon as a crisis is to debase or devalue the term. Rather, there is a chronic problem that might lead to crisis. Mikhail Gorbachev's concept of the pre-crisis (Gorbachev 1987, esp. 51) would be a more appropriate term. It follows that the apparent worldwide growth of corruption since the late 1980s should not yet, as a general matter, be described as a crisis — any more than the other long-term developments described by others as one or another form of the crisis of the state should be so described.[35] This is not to deny the validity of describing the situation in particular states at particular times as a crisis. Crises of states do occur, as was all too obvious throughout Eastern Europe and the USSR at the end of the 1980s and the beginning of the 1990s, in Russia in September–October 1993, in Bulgaria and Albania in early 1997, in Georgia in 2003, in Ukraine in late 2004, in Kyrgyzstan and Uzbekistan in 2005, and in several other cases.[36] Having made this point, the special and delicate situation of most post-communist states — the new member states of the European Union least of all — means that corruption is more likely to lead some of them to real crisis than their more robust western neighbors. But as argued above, even western states must be wary not to permit the cancer of corruption to undermine them.

If corruption does lead to crisis, there could be little popular support for any kind of state in light of the apparent loss of faith in all kinds of political system during recent years in so many post-communist countries.[37] In theory, this loss of support might be seen as desirable, since it could imply that civil society would largely run itself, in line with both the Marxist notion of a withering away of the state and radical democratic theories. But such a scenario is currently unrealistic. Civil society has not developed sufficiently for citizens to organize themselves in this way. Rather, despite some encouraging signs to the contrary, it remains a possibility that those who are currently undermining states through organized crime and corruption are precisely those who could take control.[38] As Skaperdas and Syropoulos (1995) have argued, organized-crime gangs can take control when states are weak and unable to fill power vacuums. Or, citing Putnam (1993, 183), "Palermo may represent the future of Moscow."[39] While it is sometimes argued that mafia-like organizations can bring order and structure to societies in which the state is weak or nonexistent (Hess 1998, 14–38), such a development would be retrograde, and should not be happening at the start of the twenty-first century.

ROTTEN STATES—OR ROTTEN SOCIETIES?

As noted in chapter 4, Vladimir Shlapentokh (2003) and others have argued that the political and economic élites in Russia (and elsewhere), as well as ordinary citizens, were becoming so used to corruption as to no longer see it as a major problem; corruption had become normal. This argument leads us to consideration of a very important issue: that corruption reflects the condition not only of the state and its officers, but also of society. While it can also be symptomatic of desperation, widespread corruption is all too often a reflection of rottenness, selfishness, and amorality. Does this suggest that neoliberalism is what most citizens really want? And are they willing to accept corruption in return for personal benefits?

In so many parts of the world, citizens in recent times appear to have

TABLE 8.2. Popular Attitudes toward the Acceptability of Corruption, 2000 (in Percent)

	Often acceptable	Occasionally acceptable	Never acceptable	Don't know
Bulgaria	0.4	6.1	76.7	16.8
Hungary	2.4	30.7	63.6	3.3
Poland	1.1	15.2	70.3	13.2
Russia	37.6	21.6	23.0	17.7

wanted to have their cake and eat it. They want clean and effective government that will defend their interests, but also lower taxes. They will often use corruption in the state as an excuse to avoid paying taxes, so that the state reduces services still further, which leads to a heightened sense of insecurity among public officials, whose loyalty then declines. It is a depressing vicious circle. Ironically, inasmuch as individuals are not merely complex but also ambiguous and contradictory, and since different groups within society have different objectives and values, these contradictions are often exacerbated precisely by the presence of a well-developed democracy.

The ambiguity of citizens, at least in our four selected CEE and CIS states, is exemplified well in two tables, which report responses to the questions, "In your opinion, is corruption ever acceptable?" (table 8.2) and "In your opinion, is corruption ever necessary?" (table 8.3). While a substantial number of respondents in all four countries see corruption as a serious problem, much lower percentages condemn corruption in all circumstances.

The results summarized in tables 8.2 and 8.3 were among the most interesting and disparate in our survey. Only the Bulgarian results were more or less consistent, in that approximately 80 percent of respondents saw corruption as never acceptable or necessary; elsewhere there were substantial differences between the percentage of respondents who believed that corruption was never acceptable and the percentage who believed it was never necessary. The difference between Bulgarian and Russian attitudes toward corruption was enormous: only 6.5 percent of Bulgarians demonstrated any acceptance of corruption, whereas almost 60 percent of Russian respondents did. The latter statistic might be seen

TABLE 8.3.   Popular Attitudes toward the Necessity of Corruption, 2000 (in Percent)

	Often necessary	Occasionally necessary	Never necessary	Don't know
Bulgaria	0.4	3.9	80.9	14.9
Hungary	10.7	33.4	47.5	8.3
Poland	16.7	18.5	46.2	18.5
Russia	64.4	14.8	7.2	13.5

as support for Shlapentokh's depressing argument — though our observations in chapter 4 about the meaning of the term "normal" are pertinent here — but also as evidence that Russian results cannot be considered typical of post-communism generally. Considered from another angle, less than one quarter of Russians believed that corruption was never acceptable, compared with more than three quarters of Bulgarian respondents. In terms of attitudes toward acceptability, the Poles were closer overall to the Bulgarians, and the Hungarians closer to the Russians — though there was still a significant difference between Hungarian and Russian attitudes. While almost 80 percent of Russian respondents believed that corruption was often or sometimes necessary, a mere 4.3 percent of Bulgarians shared this opinion; Hungarian and Polish respondents were much closer to each other (at 44.1 percent and 35.2 percent), although Poles were more likely than Hungarians to see corruption as necessary fairly regularly. As with so many other questions in the survey, the Hungarians were more confident in their attitudes and perceptions than any of the other three sets of respondents.

By the late 1990s there were signs that citizens in some countries — not only post-communist ones — might be beginning to change direction and attitudes again. Neoliberalism was being challenged. In the home of Thatcherism, a party whose leader advocated higher taxes in return for better social services (Paddy Ashdown of the Liberal Democrats) substantially increased its number of seats after the elections of May 1997, while a moderately left-of-center Labour Party whose leader (Tony Blair) was apparently interested in finding a "third way" put an end to eighteen years of Conservative rule.[40] In France, the elections of May–June 1997 also testified to a swing to the left, as did the German election of September 1998. Indeed, by the late 1990s the vast majority of states in the European Union had left-of-center governments. Ideological changes — a questioning of elements of neoliberal capitalism — were visible in parts of CEE too.

It remains to be seen whether the leftward shifts in Western Europe (and perhaps also in CEE) were merely short-term protest votes that testified above all to the poor performance of the parties in power or symptomatic of a more profound movement. Certainly the shift was not universal in the western world. At about the same time as Western Europe was allegedly moving leftward, a Democratic president in the United States was signing legislation (1996) that many saw at the time as the biggest single attack on the American welfare system since its introduction in the 1930s. Subsequently, albeit under questionable circumstances, a radically right-wing president (George W. Bush) came to power in the United States in 2000; the same man scored a second — more convincing — victory in 2004. And while British (June 2001 and May 2005) and German (September 2002) voters reelected putatively left-of-center governments, there were swings back to the right in Italy (May 2001) and France (June 2002).

But such volatility testifies at least to some questioning of the dominant ideological paradigm, and to the presence of healthy democratic politics. While most mainstream left-of-center parties have adopted elements of neoliberalism, many citizens are increasingly challenging the validity of the argument that the market always performs tasks better than the state. Even in the United States, the electricity blackouts in California and the major corporate scandals soon after the turn of the century raised questions about the optimal form of capitalism, and the role that the state should play in it. A symbolically significant sign of questioning was the publication in 2004 of an article by one of the leading American gurus of free trade and neoliberalism, Paul Samuelson, in which the man described by the *Berliner Zeitung* (25–26 September 2004, 11) as "the best-known living economist in the world" warned of the dangers of unlimited free trade and unquestioned globalization, thus abandoning some of his own most fundamental neoliberal tenets of previous decades (Samuelson 2004).[41]

Perhaps the increasing pace of globalization and medical scientific discoveries (which have the concomitant effect of "graying" populations) will force western countries to become accustomed to lower standards of state provision. Lower standards might decrease the opportunities for some types of corruption, but malfeasance and alienation can merely be transferred from the state to society and the corporate sector; there is no inherent reason why they should decrease overall, let alone disappear. This is a depressing scenario. It remains to be seen whether the will to combat corruption, and its close relative organized crime, really exists — or if, in fact, most people in most societies have now come to accept and live with criminality, despite their indications to the contrary when surveyed. If our argument about the influence on post-communist states of the West is correct, any growing rottenness in the West will have negative implications for the post-communist countries. This is why it is so important to deal properly with cases of corruption, particularly high-profile ones (such as the oil-for-food allegations about the United Nations that surfaced in 2003). There is, perhaps as never before, a need to ensure that international organizations, states, and societies all become cleaner; Palermo is a scary as well as attractive place, and may find resonances in far more capitals than just the Russian.

Yet the depressing tone of the last paragraph notwithstanding, the term "rotten," whether applied to states or societies, is ultimately inappropriate. It connotes irrevocability, or at the very least the need to excise rotten parts. While the evidence garnered for this book gives little cause for joy or optimism, the apparent lessening of corruption in Bulgaria, and perhaps in Russia under Putin, plus the achievements of Singapore and Hong Kong in fighting corruption, indicate that nothing is inevitable, and that societies may be able to heal or at least improve themselves. Unless one is a particular type of structural determinist and has no faith in agency, there is no reason to abandon all hope. Admittedly, the agents will have to be very determined, and both strengthen and cleanse the institutions of the state. Neoliberalism can play a very useful role in the post-communist states in overcoming the communist legacy and setting economies on the right path. Once those goals have been achieved, however, there will be a need for a clearer demarcation between states and markets — in short, institutionalization. Those who believe that neoliberalism and globalization cannot be modified and reined in need to explain why downsizing was replaced by right-sizing, and why someone as influential as Samuelson has shifted ground.

Notes

PREFACE

1   The terms former Soviet Union, East Central Europe, and South Eastern Europe are also used in this study. The former Soviet Union includes the post-communist Baltic States, which the CIS does not. East Central Europe refers to a subset of CEE countries — Czechia, Hungary, Poland, Slovakia, and Slovenia. The term South Eastern Europe, which is less politically loaded than the term Balkans, refers to Albania, Bulgaria, Romania, and all parts of former Yugoslavia excluding Slovenia. In this book, CEE refers to the Baltic States, East Central Europe, and South Eastern Europe combined, but does *not* include the Slavic states of the former Soviet Union.

2   It can with some justification be argued that the term "post-communism" is already redundant, especially given the considerable diversity of states usually embraced by the term (see Rupnik 1999). But I maintain that there remains just enough in common between these states in terms of communist legacy and international context to justify continued if cautious use of the term. The continuing divisions of various kinds between East and West Germany suggest that incorporation does not invariably and immediately erase all lines, which is why even those countries that joined the European Union in 2004 can for a while longer be labeled post-communist.

1: INTRODUCTION

1   In line with most academic analyses of the topic, the conception of corruption adopted here relates only to public officials. Hence the term "official corruption" is in a sense tautologous. However, since many journalists and others use the term "corruption" in a much broader sense — to refer, for instance, to bribe taking and bribe giving between businesspeople — the term "official corruption" has been used at the very start of this book to make clear to readers exactly which conception is being used. A much fuller analysis of the meaning(s) of corruption is provided in chapter 1.

2   There are two major additional meanings of post-communism. More broadly it refers to the political state of the world after the collapse of communist power and the end of the cold war. In its narrower sense, in which it is

often used within CEE, the term refers to periods since the collapse of communist power when communist successor parties have formed the government or been dominant within it. Our usage is the most common one, however. For further consideration of the concept of post-communism see Sakwa 1999.

3   See the results of the comparative survey by the World Bank (1999) of the major regions of the world from 1996 to 1999 and the accompanying analysis in Kaufmann, Kraay, and Zoido-Lobatan 1999a and 1999b. By 2002 some parts of South Eastern Europe were considered to have become in some ways even more corrupt than most of the CIS — see Gray, Hellman, and Ryterman 2004, esp. xii, 13, 19, 26, 28.

4   The CIS and CEE do not constitute the whole of the post-communist world, but there is no consideration here of countries such as Mongolia or Cambodia.

5   In a recent textbook on Chinese politics, Tony Saich identified corruption as the principal internal challenge facing the People's Republic of China in the early twenty-first century (Saich 2004, 329–37).

6   In August 1999 the Chinese authorities actually tightened the regulations relating to this: see the *Mercury* (Durban), 12 October 1999, 31. The new regulations were designed, *inter alia*, to "safeguard national security" (*People's Daily*, on-line English-language edition, 27 July 2000). On the rare occasions when the Chinese media do carry survey data relating to corruption, they tend to paint a much more flattering picture of Chinese attitudes than common sense, experience, and knowledge of other countries suggest is likely to be accurate or meaningful. For survey data on the putatively high levels of public support for the Chinese government's anticorruption policies see *People's Daily*, on-line English-language edition, 13 April 2002, visited January 2003. For a recent example of informally communicated survey data on Chinese attitudes towards corruption cited by a Sinologist based at Harvard — presumably because he too found it difficult to gain access to publicly available printed sources — see Saich 2004, 334. According to this source, a survey of more than two thousand respondents in 2000 indicated that some 40 percent had little or no confidence in the Chinese government's ability to combat corruption.

7   The modifier "essentially" is employed because of the special status of China's autonomous regions.

8   The other three are Turkey, Mexico, and Australia.

9   One country that wants to be recognized as "western" and European — but is also a late starter — is Bulgaria, which became a member of NATO in 2004 (whereas Hungary and Poland joined in 1999) and of the European Union in 2007 (which they joined in 2004).

10   For recent collections on corruption in the West generally see Wil-

liams, Moran, and Flanary eds. 2000, and in developing countries Williams and Theobald eds. 2000.

11   Originally Haughey was to stand trial for alleged corruption. But this was delayed in mid-2000 on the grounds that the deputy prime minister of Ireland had made comments in May that might have compromised a trial. Nevertheless, Haughey was required to face the Moriarty Tribunal, and later to pay several million pounds in tax. For recent analyses of Irish corruption see Collins and O'Shea 2001; Collins 2004, esp. 606–10.

12   See for example Andrew Rawnsley's article in the *Observer*, 17 February 2002. One of the best-known scandals related to a substantial contribution made to the Labour Party in 1997 by the head of Formula One racing, Bernie Ecclestone. After the donation Blair's Labour government exempted Formula One from what was supposed to be a pan-European ban on tobacco advertising at car races. Once knowledge of the donation became public the Labour Party returned the money. On European corruption generally, including in the United Kingdom, see Della Porta and Mény eds. 1995a and 1997; Bull and Newell eds. 2003. On political corruption in the United Kingdom, including the "Cash for Questions" scandal, see Doig 1996; Leigh and Vulliamy 1997; Doig 2003.

13   The third was Georgia, which is primarily Orthodox Christian.

14   The CPI is scaled from 0 to 10; the less corrupt a state is perceived to be, the higher its score.

15   Readers who infer, understandably but incorrectly, that I believe it legitimate to talk of *other* Huntingtonian dividing lines are encouraged to read my critique of the "clash of civilizations" thesis (L. Holmes 1998a). Huntington's argument can be found in Huntington 1993, 1996.

16   More generally on the timing of the "corruption eruption"—a term that Naím also uses for the title of a journal article (1995) — and for empirical evidence on the increased coverage of corruption in the serious western press since the 1980s, see McCoy and Heckel 2001.

17   In fairness it should be noted, as Nelken and Levi (1996, 1) have observed, that "before the 1990s, many in the West saw corruption as a problem limited to 'underdeveloped' countries . . . However, political scandals in most West European countries mean that there is now no escaping its systematic presence in developed democracies." A similar point has been made by Della Porta and Mény (Della Porta and Mény eds. 1995b, 10), although they distinguish the Mediterranean states (which have long been seen as having an ingrained tradition of corruption) from the more northerly states of Europe, and see the change of perspective on the latter beginning *during* the 1980s. Hence the views of Schöpflin and others writing before the 1990s, or certainly before the mid-1980s, are understandable.

18   I have discovered from discussions with American colleagues that neo-liberalism as a concept is not as familiar or unambiguous to them as it is to Europeans or Australasians. It is broadly coterminous with the term "Washington consensus."

19   Readers will discover from later chapters that the argument in this book favors elements of neoliberalism for post-communist states. However, the argument is couched very much in relative and dynamic terms. Neo-liberalism is seen to play a positive role in overcoming the communist legacy, but should then be tempered to permit the emergence and consolidation of both strong, legitimate democratic institutions and a resilient democratic political culture, in which social capital and trust can develop.

20   Valid responses are those that represent a choice of one of the options offered by the interiewer. As will be seen in the various tables, however, "don't know" answers are also classified in this book as valid, since one purpose of the surveys was to determine how many people had no clear view on a given issue. Many professional surveyors exclude "don't know" responses from published results—certainly if this category constitutes less than 10 percent of all responses. Since the total number (N) for each survey is given here, readers can recalculate the percentages presented in the tables to produce "valid" results according to this alternative, narrower meaning.

21   Ideally the method used would have been fully standardized and conducted more or less simultaneously. Unfortunately this would have required customized surveys, which are considerably more expensive and difficult to organize than omnibus ones; conducting them in four countries would have made the project prohibitively expensive. However, although the approach adopted here is suboptimal, the effect on results is marginal.

22   Hungary did have a three-round presidential election in June 2000, but the Hungarian president is elected by the National Assembly (parliament), not the citizenry.

2: DEFINITIONAL AND TAXONOMICAL ASPECTS

1   For a classic analysis of the cultural dimensions of gift-giving in traditional societies, including the notion of mutual obligation and reciprocity, see Mauss 1970. Mauss provides a history of the transition from the exchange of goods based on morality to a purely rational economic exchange. On the concept of the gift in China, and its relationship to politics, see Yang 1989.

2   For survey data on what Poles regard as corruption (as of 2000) see for example Osiak 2000. Whereas just over half the respondents (51 percent; N = 1000) considered it corruption if a doctor accepted a gift, nearly a third (31

percent) did not (Osiak 2000, 6, 9; Batory Foundation 2000, question 6) — revealing fundamental divisions within Polish society on this question. A small-scale (N = 102) Hungarian survey in 1999 providing evidence of divergent views on what constitutes corruption is summarized in Hungarian Gallup Institute 2000, esp. 51. For further empirical (survey-based) evidence that various groups within a society can have different perceptions of what constitutes corruption see Anderson 2002, 44–45; Anderson and Mukherjee 2002, 69–70.

3   The president of the Hungarian State Audit Office has argued that while some branches of social science use the concept of corruption, "substantive law cannot handle the term" (Kovács 2000, 21). For a stimulating theoretical analysis of the distinctions between legality and legitimacy, focusing on CEE, see Pribán 2002, while a broad and controversial theoretical discussion is Schmitt 2004.

4   Some analyses of rent seeking in communist and post-communist societies focus on the attempts *by* officials to obtain pecuniary benefit ("rent") for services that they are illegally or improperly "selling." Other analyses focus more on attempts by managers, owners, and others to gain pecuniary advantage *from* officials. Thus Glinkina (1998, 18) defines a rent-seeking situation as one "in which wealth is sought not through profits from market competition with other firms but through access to government subsidies and granting of monopoly status." However, the majority of analysts agree that the principal target of investigation should be the relationship between the market and the state. On rent seeking generally, including its various meanings, see Buchanan, Tollison, and Tullock eds. 1980; Rowley, Tollison, and Tullock eds. 1988. For a critique and rejection of the rent-seeking approach see Hutchcroft 2002, 117–20.

5   For classic comparative introductions see Lemarchand and Legg 1972; Eisenstadt and Lemarchand eds. 1981; Clapham ed. 1982; Eisenstadt and Roniger 1984. A useful overview and analysis of the much more recent so-called third wave of research into patronage and clientelism is Roniger 2004.

6   In fact there are significant differences. For instance, the old-boy network is permanently exclusive; those who did not attend the "right" schools can never make up for that. The Chinese concept is in one sense more open: it is based more on the gradual development of a relationship, and does not depend on past and immutable factors in the same way that the British concept does. Moreover, the Chinese concept more directly implies reciprocity. Nevertheless, there are important similarities between the two concepts, particularly in terms of mutual loyalty and privileging "insiders" over others.

7   In Russian *blat* is a system of obtaining goods or favors through connections (*svyazy*). For a scholarly, full-length analysis of the concept and its

practice see Ledeneva 1998; note that Ledeneva does not see blat as a form of corruption as such. A more recent edited collection is Lovell, Ledeneva, and Rogachevskii eds. 2000. One of the most obvious differences between blat and networking is that blat has often been related to overt shortages, whereas networking in the more affluent United States is less clearly so (although the perceived need to network does imply competition for limited resources). Moreover, blat operates at many more personal levels than the ultimately corporate networking. But there remain significant resonances between the two concepts and practices.

8   For a scholarly study of the history of bribery and its meanings from 3000 B.C. see Noonan 1984.

9   Though see below on business-to-business corruption. For a starting point on corporate crime see Clinard 1990; a fascinating recent study of corporate crime in the United States is O'Brien 2003.

10   The concept of a tip is another tricky and related issue. Being Anglo-Australian, I find it almost offensive that waiters — and many other service personnel — in the United States expect what seem to me to be very large tips, especially if their service has been decidedly average; Australian and European norms on tipping are very different from American ones. But the American waiters would — understandably, in view of predominant American attitudes and practices (culture) — find *my* behavior offensive if I were not to leave a 15 or 20 percent tip. This point illustrates two broader ones. One is that there can be marked attitudinal differences even between cultures that are in many ways similar. The other is that the concept of corruption is murky, and that it relates closely (and confusingly) to many other everyday practices that most of us rarely even question. If one subscribes to the notion that corruption can occur at the lowest levels and need not involve state officials, its boundaries become particularly blurred. For a fuller analysis of the distinctions and overlaps between the concepts of a gift and a bribe, and between both of them and a tip, see Rose-Ackerman 1999, esp. 99–110.

11   Note that Palmier's own preferred definition (1983, 208) is "the acquisition of forbidden benefits by officials or employees, so bringing into question their loyalty to their employers." For various reasons, including its broad reference to "employees" as well as officials, this definition is not used here.

12   A new Russian criminal code became effective in January 1997. One of the aims of replacing the version enacted in 1960 was to address economic crimes more explicitly. But the new code was still vague on corruption. The Russian Duma in March 2003 was to begin considering a number of amendments to the 1997 code (*Pravda*, 12 March 2003), but it had not completed this by the end of the year. Similarly, while a Russian draft bill on corruption

that included a number of specific definitions (for example of "bribery" and "corrupt relations") was accepted by the Duma on its first reading in November 2002, it was then delayed and had not been adopted by late 2004. V. N. Lopatin, writing in March 2003, reflected the frustration of many when he complained about the lack of a definition in Russian legislation (Lopatin 2003, 87).

13   The Chinese terms cited in the first set of parentheses are those most commonly used to translate corruption. The first means greed and dirt, while the second and third have a worse connotation, both referring to rottenness and decomposition. But in addition, *fubai* also refers to nonperformance (see Kwong 1997, 3) and according to some interpretations to a specific form of corruption, namely embezzlement. Several other terms are sometimes used to translate "corruption" into Chinese, and commentators often disagree on the precise meaning of Chinese terms (compare Kwong 1997, 3–27, and the various terms translated there with those in Johnston and Hao 1995, esp. 87). The first Thai term cited is quite obviously a borrowing from English; the second, more traditional term literally means "to cheat from the people and hide from the king" (Pasuk Phongpaichit and Sungsidh Piriyarangsan 1996, 9). I am indebted to Dr. Michael Connors for tracking down and transliterating the most suitable Thai terms for bribery.

14   Thus Kuz'minov (1999, thesis 5) distinguishes "corruption in its narrow sense" from bribery. He argues that "bribery is distinguished from corruption by the fact that an official is bought off not to violate his duties but to fulfil them."

15   In 2000 Transparency International broadened its definition to include B2B (business to business) activities. For instance, Pope (2000a, 13) defines corruption as "the misuse of entrusted power for private benefit," and goes on to specify, "be it by private economic agents or by government officials." This changed definition was intended to reflect the increased blurring between the state and the business sector, which fits well with the argument here about the nature and impact of neoliberalism. However, given both the normative rejection here of neoliberalism, and the confusion generated by the changed TI definition—which becomes even greater when it is borne in mind that TI still uses the original definition for the purposes of its CPI—the new definition is not adopted here. More persuasive is the suggestion by Offe (2004) that we should include business-to-business activities under the general term "corruption," and distinguish this from the narrower concept of political corruption (on which he concentrates), which would necessarily involve public (state) office. This is an initially tempting proposition. Once again, however, there is an inherent blurring between market and state in such an approach. Another problem is that many commentators use the term "political corrup-

tion" more narrowly than Offe, to refer only to corruption among politicians (thus excluding appointed officers of the state). For these reasons, the approach is unsuitable for the argument developed in this book, which assumes that all corruption is on one level necessarily "political" (in that it directly relates to the political system).

16   It is partly because of his focus on the necessity of *exchange* (of public decisions for money) or interactivity that the definition of corruption posited by Weingrod (1968), which has subsequently been accepted by Della Porta and Mény (1995c, 172), is rejected here as too narrow. The interesting approach of Gambetta (2002) — which assumes *three* agents (the truster, the fiduciary, and the corrupter) — is rejected for the same reason. For arguments by well-regarded analysts of corruption that it need not involve at least two active parties and can be engaged in by one alone see Ting Gong 1997, 287; Gray, Hellman, and Ryterman 2004, 7, 9.

17   Sajó (2002, 3) makes the initially persuasive point that especially in the case of party financing, officials may break rules out of a sense of loyalty and not for personal gain, and uses this as a reason for dismissing the definition of corruption advanced by LaPalombara (1994). However, such officials are still putting particular interests ahead of those of society and the law, and may well do so in the hope of future personal advantage (such as securing a — paid — seat in parliament). Thus the point is ultimately unconvincing.

18   For a summary of a Chinese conception (Yu Keping's) of white, gray, and black corruption, which is different from Heidenheimer's, see Yan Sun 2001, 249.

19   In an earlier analysis of corruption in communist states (L. Holmes 1993, esp. 69–70), I used a third approach, which was also soft and explicitly normative. If acts of a particular type (such as nepotism) had been condemned by Marx and Lenin, or appeared to be generally condemned in western value systems, then it was inferred that at least some and perhaps many citizens in the communist world would also see such acts as corrupt. This third method was devised to deal with the problems of researching what were relatively closed societies (glasnost in some of them at the very end notwithstanding); in the much freer atmosphere of post-communism, such inferential methods are less suitable or necessary than they were.

20   This said, the neoliberal model of capitalism blurs the distinction for different reasons; these, and the implications of this for corruption in the post-communist world, are examined in chapter 6.

21   Russia is in many ways an exception, however. The leading Russian politician Grigorii Yavlinskii argued in the late 1990s that under the peculiar Russian form of privatization up to 82 percent of enterprises were no longer owned by the state, but nor were many fully privately owned (a point that

resonates with Bowser's — see note 41 below); for citation details and an explanation of this apparent conundrum see Coulloudon 2002, 195–98.

22   One of the leading western analysts of the second economy in communist states is Gregory Grossman of the University of California, Berkeley. In addition to his own work on the subject (including his classic article from 1977 — see the bibliography), Grossman has produced a twenty-three-page bibliography of works in major western languages covering the period to the collapse of communist power — see Grossman 1996 (available from Professor Grossman).

23   The differences between the "gray" and "black" economies relate primarily to two variables, legality and reporting. Gray economic activity is generally legal but unreported — so that it might have illegal ramifications, such as failure to pay required transaction taxes. Black economic activity is clearly illegal, as well as unreported. For a recent Bulgarian introduction to the concepts see Center for the Study of Democracy 2003a.

24   However, Ariel Cohen (1995, 42) adopts an approach similar to this Polish one in defining the "post-Soviet *mafiya*" as "a highly capable and influential cadre of former party members and KGB officials."

25   Officials may be involved in such activity, however. If they are, but in a purely private capacity (in a way unrelated to their public office), they are not participating as officials. Conversely, if they do make use of their official position, their activities constitute collusion between corrupt officials and organized crime. Moreover, if improper actions are carried out exclusively by a "group" of officials, this constitutes corruption rather than organized-crime activity (it is practically inconceivable that such a group would exist and make no use of its members' official positions).

26   For one of the most authoritative analyses of organized crime and "the mafia" in Russia by a Russian see Gurov 1995; Gurov was writing about white-collar crime even in the Soviet period — see Gurov 1990. For an earlier study of the Russian and Soviet mafia, also by a Russian but available in English, see Vaksberg 1991. On the more traditional forms of organized crime in Russia, in particular the "thieves in law," see Razinkin 1995. And for an indigenous analysis of the connections between corruption and organized crime in Romania see Banciu and Radulescu 1994.

27   It is interesting to relate the tendency of so many Italian analysts to separate corruption from clientelism to the point made earlier about Polish attitudes toward bribery and clientelism; both countries have strong Catholic and familist traditions. But my point about the likelihood that similar views would be held in many cultures warns us against narrow and reductionist cultural determinism or even explanation.

28   See note 16, above.

29   Apparently the first formal (legal) recognition that sex could be used as a medium of exchange in corrupt acts was by a Japanese court in 1915; in most western courts, it is included in the concept of "non-property benefits" (BR 44, no. 32:23–25).

30   The unfortunate (messy) reference to "intending" and "aspiring" is to allow for corruption by officers and candidates of political parties, who may or may not occupy an elected state position (notably, parliamentarian) at the time of committing a corrupt act.

31   It will be recalled that our Nortistani official was pursuing his or her personal interests, and that society's interests were harmed, even if only marginally. The degree to which society's interests are negatively affected is irrelevant in defining or identifying a corrupt act; it can be of significance in attempting to understand or predict society's reactions, however. One other very interesting — and difficult! — question was put to me by a postgraduate student in Warsaw in 2001. He asked whether one should consider corrupt the acts of an official which are against the public interest (and which in other circumstances would unambiguously be classified as corrupt), but have been committed because of threats to that official or his or her family, say by an organized-crime gang. After long deliberation I decided that the act does formally constitute corruption, but that the state should be particularly lenient in dealing with the official, treating the case as one of "extenuating circumstances."

32   Yet again there is a problem of demarcation and identification, since determining "general interest" is fraught with difficulties. But there comes a point at which analysts have to drag themselves out of the quagmire of definition if they are to make any progress in combating negative social phenomena.

33   It might be objected that some corrupt officials enjoy flaunting the fruits of their improper activities, which raises questions about the concept of secrecy. But there is a significant difference between flaunting the results of corruption and bragging about the actions (or nonactions) that are the source of the results. More problematic are the cases of "corruption" in which officials did or did not do something that they did not consider improper at the time but that is later judged improper by others; the Greiner case cited earlier is a prime example. Some have argued that the so-called sunlight test is the ultimate determinant of whether an action or nonaction constitutes corruption. While it usually is a good test, the type of case just cited reveals its limitations. This is a highly pertinent issue in post-communist states, since both legislation and values in the early stages following the collapse of communist power were often ambiguous or essentially nonexistent. The approach adopted here is to include references to such problematic cases at appropriate junctures, but to avoid dependence on them for empirical sup-

port. In other words, and as argued in the text, there is greater flexibility in applying our fourth criterion than in applying the first three.

34 It must constantly be borne in mind that the term clientelism, as used in this book, implies at least the hope or possibility of some personal benefit to the patron, even if the benefit is unspecified and in the distant future. It is important to distinguish this situation from one in which a senior person openly appoints a junior person known to him or her to a post, with no expectation of any personal benefit; a well-qualified applicant for a post must not be disadvantaged simply because of being acquainted with the senior person. To those readers who regard my position as having shifted toward that of analysts who do not consider clientelism a form of corruption, the reply is that I would not use the term clientelism to describe the situation just outlined.

35 In August 2003 an Australian politician (Pauline Hanson) was sentenced to three years' imprisonment for electoral fraud. The sentencing judge argued that what she had done would undermine public faith in the political system, unless she was seen to have been adequately punished. In fact, some 95 percent of viewers sending e-mails to one of Australia's most popular television channels (Channel 9) the day after the sentence was announced indicated their belief that the punishment was quite unsuitable (too harsh) — and that the judge's statements and actions raised more doubts about the legitimacy of the judicial system than Ms. Hanson's actions did about the political system. This case is cited to highlight with a concrete example the need to question assumptions about how citizens will assess the actions of politicians and law enforcers. In this case there was clearly far more outrage about the judge's behavior than about the politician's. Ms. Hanson's conviction was reversed on appeal, and she was released from prison in November 2003.

36 By mixed systems is meant what are often called semi-presidential systems. The latter term is rejected here (other than when others' usage is directly cited), since it necessarily connotes more power in the hands of the president than of parliament, while the term semi-parliamentary connotes the opposite. The term mixed is free of such implicit loadings.

37 For a meandering analysis of *kompromat* in post-communist Russia see A. Szilágyi 2002.

38 Most of the fourteen categories here could be further disaggregated. For example, Todorov, Shentov, and Stoyanov eds. 2000, 13–14, identify no fewer than eleven types of smuggling and customs fraud by officials, and maintain that the list is not exhaustive — while the prime minister of Chandragupta, writing in the fourth century B.C., identified at least forty types of embezzlement (Klitgaard 1988, 7; Bardhan 1997, 1320).

39 The Russian language has in earlier centuries distinguished between accepting a bribe or "reward" for performing more quickly a function that one should do anyway (*mzdoimstvo*), and accepting a bribe for not performing a function that one should do, or even blatant extortion (*likhoimstvo*). These terms are now considered old-fashioned by many Russians, however; when they are used, they are often treated as synonyms for bribery or bribe taking. I have here given the most common interpretations of the terms; for a far more sophisticated and detailed analysis see Potter 2000, esp. 28–33; see too Kelly 2000, 74.

40 Our own a priori view — that most citizens would be more incensed by corruption engaged in purely for personal gain — was also held by Yves Mény (1996, 311). But TI Barometer findings suggest that this is another area in which intuition can mislead, and that we might have to reconsider our assumptions.

41 However, it can be noted that the very concept of state capture — defined as improper (offering private benefits) and nontransparent attempts to "influence the *formulation* of laws, regulations, decrees and other government policies" for the would-be captor's advantage (Gray, Hellman, and Ryterman 2004, 10; emphasis in original) — is problematic, especially if associated too strongly with former Soviet states. At a detailed application level, Taagepera (2002, 251–52) has asked how, according to World Bank analyses, Latvia can have such an extraordinarily bad score measuring the level of state capture of presidential decrees when the Latvian president cannot issue decrees! At a more general level, Bowser (2002, 85) argues that the application of the concept of state capture is inappropriate in most of the former Soviet Union because "there exists no truly independent private sector to capture the state. Social networks and 'clans' are the state, and have been since Soviet times." While he may have overstated his case, there is much to Bowser's general point. Similarly, Michael (2004, 20) makes a basically valid point when he criticizes the double standards of many observers. He maintains that the concept of state capture is applied pejoratively to transition states to describe what in most OECD countries are described approvingly as interest group politics, public-private partnerships, or synergy. Like Bowser's point, Michael's needs refining, since interest-group politics and the like would only be comparable to state capture if they involved covert activity and offers of private benefit to officials. But there is no question that lobbying in western states can and sometimes does look remarkably similar to state capture, especially when it is less open than it should be. Nor should it be overlooked that whereas lobbying is considered legitimate in some western states (notably the United States), it is formally unacceptable in others (such as France). Finally, it is difficult adequately to measure the level of administrative corruption —

distinguished from state capture primarily in that it focuses on improper attempts to influence the implementation rather than the formulation of rules and policies (Gray, Hellman, and Ryterman 2004, 10) — as Miller, Grøde-land, and Koshechkina (2001b) have demonstrated.

42   For a recent Russian attempt at creating a (five-category) typology — some elements of which would not be accepted by most analysts, such as "corruption" connected with show business and with the organization of sporting events — see Antonyan 2003. Offe (2004, 81–83) suggests a four-category typology that does focus on corruption as understood in this book, but excludes some phenomena that we would include.

3: ACTUAL, ALLEGED, AND ARGUABLE CORRUPTION

1   This situation changed when Constantinescu became president in 1996, although by 2000 he was widely perceived to have done less to combat corruption than he had promised. Apparently aware of this popular disappointment, he did not seek reelection in 2000.

2   A recent example of this from beyond the post-communist world is the reaction to Kofi Annan, secretary general of the United Nations, when his son Kojo was accused of being involved in the food-for-oil (also known as the oil-for-food) corruption scandal relating to Iraq. This scandal broke in 2003 and was ongoing at the time of writing.

3   In a sadly ironic twist, Lukanov was murdered in October 1996, according to some observers because he was about to make serious allegations to Parliament about corruption in the "highest echelons of power" (OMRI DD, 4 and 23 October 1996).

4   Both Balev and Zhivkov were acquitted in February 1996, however — SWB/EE, 12 February 1996.

5   In 1998 Aleksandr Lebed' acknowledged that he had used "gray" money to finance his election campaign for the governorship of Krasnoyarsk (Izves-tiya, 31 March 1998, 4). He might have been expected to act similarly for the Russian presidential electoral campaign in 2000, but contrary to expectations Lebed' did not compete for the presidency.

6   It will be recalled from chapter 2 that Remington classified Belarus as parliamentary in the early 1990s. But this classification has had to be revised since Lukashenka came to power in 1994.

7   On this problem in the major Latin states of the Mediterranean region see Pujas and Rhodes 1999.

8   The resignation had several causes, but most commentators see the Rywingate case as a major one.

9   In March 2000 a motion to override Putin's decree and lift Yeltsin's immunity was narrowly defeated in the Duma. For allegations concerning Putin's own involvement in corruption in the early 1990s (long before he became president), especially in the so-called food-for-metals scandal in St. Petersburg, see RFE/RL *Russian Political Weekly*, 10 September 2003.

10   However, shortly after the Yeltsin case was closed in February 2001, Putin signed a new law that would limit the scope of immunity for former presidents if serious crimes were alleged — see *EECR* 10, no. 1:37. It can also be noted that while Yeltsin himself was officially immune, some of those who had been close to him were not. Thus Pavel Borodin, the former head of the Presidential Administration Office who under Putin had been state secretary of the Russia-Belarus Union, was arrested in New York in January 2001, after the issuance in March 2000 of a Swiss warrant in connection with the Mabetex case and money laundering. He was extradited to Switzerland in April 2001 but later released. The Swiss authorities again summoned Borodin in August 2001 to appear in court in Geneva in September. Eventually, in March 2002, Borodin was found guilty of money laundering by a Swiss court and sentenced to a heavy fine.

11   It should be noted that there was almost certainly an element of "politics" and personal animosity underlying these allegations.

12   Meeting with Professor L. Csapó, December 1999. For an example of a highly loaded "smear article" about Prime Minister Dr. Péter Medgyessy, including allegations of corruption, see the Open Society Archives article of 4 October 2002 at http://www.osa.ceu.hu/kampanyarchiv/enx/01.html (visited May 2003). Shortly before the 2002 election, the Hungarian police did launch an investigation into Medgyessy's involvement in what some of the media had portrayed in November 2001 as the questionable sale and conversion of the Gresham Palace into a hotel (RFE/RL, 11 December 2001). However, Medgyessy successfully sued two newspapers in March 2002 for libel in connection with this case (RFE/RL, 27 March 2002).

13   The prime minister is alleged to have argued that Rywin needed to see a psychiatrist (from the Konrad Adenauer Stiftung: *http://www.kas.de/publikationen/2003/1290_dokument.html*, visited March 2003); but Miller was also criticized for not reporting Rywin's alleged attempt at securing a bribe, which led to speculation on the reasons for his silence (*Economist*, 1–7 March 2003, 45). According to reports in the American news media, Michnik delayed reporting the alleged malfeasance for fear of jeopardizing Poland's bid to join the European Union (*TI Q*, March 2003, 3).

14   Rutskoi appears never to have produced satisfactory evidence to support his most serious allegations either.

15   One of the reasons for suspicion is Chernomyrdin's enormous wealth.

According to an article in *Le Monde* (29 March 1997) that was based on reports made in April 1996 to the U.S. Congress by Louis Freeh, director of the Federal Bureau of Investigation, and John Deutch, former director of the Central Intelligence Agency, Chernomyrdin was worth $5 billion, making him wealthier than Rupert Murdoch. The article was translated into Russian and published in *Izvestiya*, 1 April 1997, 1. The *New York Times* had already made allegations about Chernomyrdin's corruption in 1995 (6 June and 3 July — cited in Reddaway and Glinski 2001, 487, 699). Fedorov had also made quite specific allegations about Chernomyrdin but again, according to Reddaway and Glinski (2001, 487, 699), he was not sued for libel.

16   Melniks was cleared after investigation. Nevertheless, someone else (Roberts Zile) was appointed finance minister at the end of February 1997.

17   The observant reader will have noticed that the allegations of impropriety made against Oleksy's wife were made at about the same time and concerning the same company as those against Kwaśniewski's wife.

18   This claim was published in mid-1997 in *Novaya Gazeta*, to which I did not have access while including this reference. However, the allegations were reissued in Russian on the internet by the Russian National News Service — *http://www.nns.ru/chronicle/article/3dnya.html* (visited March 2003). Despite the suspicions and cynicism, the book did get published, by Vagrius Press. But this has not stopped the media from attempting to smear Nemtsov — see for example the article by Yurii Vetrov in *Moskovskii Komsomolets*, 9 June 2003, in which Vetrov suggests that $100,000 was a very large sum for such a book.

19   Chubais was cleared in 2002 of allegations that he had improperly benefited from the privatization process.

20   This is a complicated case; for further details on the misleadingly named Oilgate scandal see Z. Szilagyi 1996a, 43.

21   Olechowski withdrew his resignation three days after tendering it, apparently having decided that his actions had not breached the regulations. His eventual resignation in January 1995, officially because of political differences with other members of the government, was just two days after the Constitutional Tribunal had resolved that there *had been* a conflict of interest. But the tribunal also acknowledged that there had been room for differing interpretations, and so announced that its reading of the legislation would be effective only from the time of the ruling, not retrospectively. This enabled Olechowski to claim that he had been vindicated.

22   The FSB (the Russian security service, successor to the KGB) discovered about $1 million in Yurkov's apartment, which he is alleged to have obtained in return for permitting large corporations to reduce their tax bills by reporting artifically low output and sales. According to the FSB in 1998, the losses to the state of illegally reduced tax bills amounted to "hundreds of

millions of dollars." Yurkov was found guilty in 2001 and sentenced to a long prison sentence (*Pravda*, 18 December 2001, citing a figure for losses to the state of a considerably lower order than suggested in *Izvestiya* on 10 June 1998). Note that at about the same time as Yurkov's arrest, a further twenty officials from the State Committee of Statistics were accused of being engaged in embezzlement between 1994 and 1998 (*Izvestiya*, 11 June 1998, 1).

23   Kovalev had been the center of a scandal in June 1997, when a video allegedly of him in a sauna was publicly broadcast; he was dismissed after this, in July 1997. The incident was serious not merely because he had been caught with several naked women: the sauna was said to be a well-known haunt of organized crime groups (RFE/RL, 23 June 1997). His dismissal and subsequent arrest have been linked by some observers to his investigation into corruption in the circles around Yeltsin (*Izvestiya*, 9 February 1999, 2).

24   For further allegations about Aksenenko, dating from the late 1990s, see Coulloudon 2002, 197–98. There were reports in March 2003 of new allegations against Aksenenko being investigated by the Procurator's Office; in October the office completed its investigations and sent its report to the courts, but some alleged that this action too was political (RFE/RL, 14 October 2003).

25   There were allegations during the Russian election campaigns in December 1999 that Zhirinovskii had improperly "forgotten" to disclose some of his major assets, including a number of apartments in Moscow. But for a very different perspective on Russia's Liberal Democratic Party see the survey results in *Izvestiya*, 6 October 2000.

26   For an argument that the allegations about Sobchak were essentially political mischief making see *Izvestiya*, 14 November 1997, 2. Sobchak died in February 2000.

27   All information on this Polish case has been obtained from SWB/EE, 12 March 1994 to 10 February 1995; a more detailed analysis is in L. Holmes 1997c, 140–41.

28   Widespread rumors of corruption in the Gdansk police force led to an investigation in 1994 but were found to be largely groundless. Nevertheless, three officers were discovered to have been involved with gangs smuggling in stolen cars from western countries — see SWB/EE, 4 May 1994.

29   For a detailed analysis of corruption in the Polish police force see Łajtar 2000.

30   The charges related particularly to the so-called Rocco case, the details of which are not relevant for our purposes. But readers interested in following it up could start with SWB/EE, April–May 1997.

31   Grachev soon acknowledged that he had indeed been involved in corruption — primarily in providing his accuser, Rokhlin, with an apartment and

medical treatment! (see his interview in Konstantinova 1996; see also OMRI DD, 8 July 1996).

32   In mid-2003 the same newspaper carried a list of generals and admirals who had been found to have broken the criminal code between 1992 and 2003 — many by committing corrupt acts; see *Komsomol'skaya Pravda*, 7, 8, 9, 11, and 14 July 2003.

33   Space limitations prevent an adequate analysis of this major case here. One of the many allegations was that General Ji had in 1996 been involved in offering funds for President Clinton's presidential campaign (see Newsmax .com, 27 January 2000); he was subsequently cleared of any impropriety in the matter (Mulvenon 2003, 30).

34   That is, it recalled "Monty Python's Flying Circus," the British television comedy series characterized by bizarre, almost surreal, humor, which also often had a sting in it.

35   Quentin Reed (2002, 279) gives a figure of 3.8 million Crowns, less than half that cited by Kettle. It was a large sum of money either way.

36   The bank chief made a similar offer in the following February, but on that occasion because of his claims about excessive interference from outside, not corruption (RFE/RL, 3 February 1993). For a less ambiguous example of bank-related corruption in Bulgaria see SWB/EE, 7 July 1997.

37   For another major Chinese banking scandal (from 2001) see BR 44, no. 46:6.

38   Once he had secured immunity, many expected Korzhakov to reveal unsavory aspects of Yeltsin's household and entourage. These expectations were not frustrated. In November 1998 Korzhakov alleged that the "oligarch" Boris Berezovskii had been trying to blackmail Yeltsin and his family over some foreign property deals, in an effort to stop the president and the Russian government from investigating him and his business.

39   There have been rumors within China that Chen did not in fact stay long in prison, soon being transferred to house arrest in a luxurious home. But I have been unable to verify this rumor. Another claim is that subsequently he was "quietly granted conditional release" in early 2004 (*Straits Times*, 26 January 2004) — although I have been unable to confirm this either. For a listing compiled in 2000 of senior Chinese officials sentenced to death or long prison sentences for corruption "in recent years" see BR 43, no. 21:12–17.

40   Modrow had originally been found guilty of the same offense in May 1993 but was released with a mere caution and a suspended fine. This led to criticism, and eventually the Federal Court ordered a retrial.

41   I am indebted to Ivan Krastev of the Centre for Liberal Strategies for providing me with a summary of the initial findings.

42   The man known as the chief architect of Polish economic reform after

the collapse of communism, Leszek Balcerowicz, unsuccessfully proposed the introduction of a low, flat personal income tax rate in Poland in 1998 when he was deputy prime minister (*EECR* 9, nos. 1–2:29). The newly established Civic Forum party also proposed a flat rate in January 2001 (*EECR* 10, no. 1:31), while Prime Minister Leszek Miller declared his support for such an arrangement in mid-2003 (*EECR* 12, nos. 2–3:37). But while the Poles have been toying with the idea, other countries have actually implemented it: Estonia (1994), Lithuania (1994), Latvia (1995), Russia (2001), Serbia (2003), Slovakia (2004), Ukraine (2004), Georgia (2005), and Romania (2005); for an overview see the *Economist*, 16 April 2005, 9, 63–65.

43   For details on the various taxes and high rates in Russia during the 1990s see Varese 1997, 585–87. The situation has improved somewhat under Putin; corporate tax rates were reduced from 35 to 24 percent in 2002, resulting in a substantial increase in net profitability.

44   On party financing in post-communist states see Gel'man 1998 (on Russia); Smilov 2002 (on Russia and Bulgaria); Walecki 2000a, 2000b, and 2000c (on Poland); P. Lewis 1998 (on East Central Europe); Walecki 2003 (on CEE and CIS). More generally on the connections between party financing and corruption see R. Williams ed. 2000a.

45   On the problem of low levels of trust in post-communist countries — especially in the state, and often relating to corruption — see Kornai and Rose-Ackerman eds. 2004; Kornai, Rothstein, and Rose-Ackerman eds. 2004.

46   For evidence, based on a survey conducted in 1995, that Russians acquire most of their political knowledge at election time from television — though not specifically about corruption — see Levada 2000a, 68–69.

47   This said, the text reveals that nearly 60 percent of Romanian respondents — presumably of all types — identified the media as their prime source, compared with only about half of this figure (29 percent) in Kyrgyzstan. For the record, the proportion of Kyrgyz respondents citing relatives and friends as their principal source was 37 percent; the percentage of Romanians identifying this source as their principal one is not reported. While the World Bank report on Kyrgyzstan is not entirely clear on this score, the text implies that the results are only those from household (citizen) surveys.

48   While there do not appear to be any directly comparable data on the impact of the Chinese media, a survey in 2000 (in *CD*, 25 December 2000) listed the ten domestic and ten international issues that Chinese citizens considered the most important, based on "the news" (and thus the media). One of the domestic issues was the government's crackdown on corruption, with citizens particularly interested in the Cheng Kejie case referred to earlier in this chapter. The survey was more representative than most, with an *N* of 58 million respondents.

4: ON THE SCALE AND MAIN AREAS OF CORRUPTION

1   Others have summarized the methods slightly differently. Thus Manchin (2000) refers to three methods: perception-based measurement; measurement based on "incidences of corruptive activities," which includes attempts or expectations, and is also known as the proxy method; and expert estimates.

2   See note 12 to chapter 2.

3   It is not only in CEE that general crime statistics are often questionable because of underreporting by the police or manipulation by politicians — on this phenomenon in the United Kingdom see *Guardian Weekly*, 8 November 1998, 5; *Independent* (London), 1 August 2000, 1; *Daily Express*, 12 October 2004, 24.

4   Britannica bases its figures on both Interpol's *International Crime Statistics* and various national sources. They mostly exclude minor traffic infringements, as well as civil offenses. Unfortunately attempts to check the original data were frustrated by restrictions on access to the statistics on the Interpol web site.

5   For evidence from the early 1990s that Russian and Hungarian citizens had little expectation of being treated fairly by the state authorities see Miller, Grødeland, and Koshechkina 2001b, 6–7. For empirical data from UNICRI's International Crime Victims Surveys suggesting that the vast majority of citizens in several CEE and CIS capitals (including Budapest, Moscow, Sofia, and Warsaw) had far more direct experience of corruption in the early twenty-first century than citizens in West European capital cities, see Alvazzi del Frate and van Kesteren 2004, 25; although the analysis of crime victimization is based on data from 2000, the survey of corruption experiences appears to have been conducted in 2001 and revealed remarkably similar levels in Moscow, Sofia, and Warsaw (Budapest was somewhat lower; for recent evidence that Budapest appears to be doing better at controlling corruption than neighboring post-communist capitals, including Warsaw, see Ortmann 2004). For our purposes the salient point is that it was the police who appeared most likely to accept or demand bribes (Alvazzi del Frate and van Kesteren 2004, 25–28). And for claims about police violence against ordinary citizens in Russia — which presumably would be yet another reason for many to minimize their contact with those who are supposed to protect them — see the article by Igor Rotar in *Izvestiya*, 1 September 1995, 3.

6   For a comparative analysis of general crime rates in several early post-communist states see Lotspeich 1995 and L. Holmes 2001, 196.

7   For evidence that the Russian police sometimes deliberately understate crime statistics see *Kommersant*, 12 October 2000, 3.

8   Between 1990 and 1995 the yearbooks contained two potentially relevant statistics. These were the percentage of crimes that were either economic
and official (*khozyaistvennye i dolzhnostnye*) or crimes against the administrative order. Unfortunately the meaning of these terms is not defined, nor are
the data further disaggregated. For the record, the first category dropped
from 4.8 percent of all crimes in 1990 to 2.9 percent in 1994, with the lowest
figure being 1.9 percent in 1993. Conversely, the second category increased
slightly over the same period, from 2.5 percent in 1990 to 2.8 percent, though
it had dropped in most years in between, with a low figure of 2.0 percent in
1994. All data from Goskomstat 1995, 107.

9   For further relatively modest figures on official corruption in Russia see
Kramer 1994, table II. One possible reason for the different impressions
formed by the various figures is that in some cases the lower ones refer to the
actual prosecution of officials, the higher ones to investigations. While this
distinction might help to explain some of the discrepancy, several of the data
clearly conflict with each other.

10   The source used for these data does not define "large-scale" or "particularly large-scale."

11   This last statistic is the same as the unreferenced one cited by Glinkina.

12   These data are very close but not identical to both the figures from the
Ministry of Justice provided to the Open Society Institute (2002, 85) for 1998
and 1999 (which seem to have been the only years for which data on these
crimes were made available to the institute), and the figures on the number of
persons suspected of engaging in bribery provided in the 2003 statistical
yearbook (436) — 138 in 1999, 55 in 2000, 60 in 2001, and 67 in 2002.

13   This is often translated in official sources as "papers crimes"; for supporting evidence that it does relate to corruption, and examples of its various
forms, see Center for the Study of Democracy 2002b, 9–11.

14   In line with the observation made in note 3 and the text here, the
police chief of Bulgaria (by then no longer Gatsov) made a similar comment
at a news conference in 1997, when he announced that the police deliberately
understate crime statistics (*SWB/EE*, 27 March 1997).

15   This is not a misprint — the statistical yearbooks have been double-
checked, and they indicate an enormous jump in the number of cases of fraud
between 1994 and 1995, and a subsequent drop in 1996. The 1995 figure is
from the 1995 yearbook (206), published in 1996; it is repeated in the 1997
yearbook (260), published in 1998.

16   For a more disaggregated version of these data see Ministry of the
Interior [Hungary] 2000, 32–35.

17   The word translated here as "economic" is *gospodarcze*. Until recently,

most official Polish sources also translated the word this way; but the trend now is to use "commercial."

18   The official Polish statistical yearbooks indicate that the higher figure for 1995 includes excise, and this point presumably applies to subsequent figures. There are no figures in the 1998 yearbook for 1991–94. Although there is no proper explanation for this change, a cryptic note in the 1998 edition states that "some data for the years 1990, 1995 and 1996 have been corrected in relation to (*w stosunku do*) those published in the previous edition of the yearbook." However, the reason for the dramatic change from 1999 is not clear.

19   Private communication to the author in Warsaw, 24 February 1997. My subsequent research and the data provided immediately after this sentence convince me that there was either a misunderstanding here or a simple error. But the communication was made through a Polish interpreter to minimize the possibilities of mistranslation. I indicated my surprise and asked whether the figure was correct, but the very low figure was repeated by the official.

20   The data for 1998 are not included here because they are incomplete. The data for 2001 are to be treated with caution, since some cases seemed likely to be appealed (so that the data were not finalized).

21   The point made in the preceding note about the tentative nature of the 2001 data also applies to these data.

22   The points made in note 20 about the incomplete data for 1998 and the provisionality of the 2001 data apply here too. That the data cited here from the Open Society Institute on different CEE states vary so much, in terms of the years covered and the types of corruption included, underscores our point about the substantial difficulties involved in obtaining and comparing official data on corruption.

23   I am deeply indebted to a leading professor of criminology at the China University of Political Science and Law for making these data available to me during a three-hour meeting in Beijing, 22 May 1997. I am also extremely grateful to my colleague Dr. Michael Dutton for acting as an interpreter at that meeting. For statistics on registered and investigated economic cases in China from 1979 to 1988 (unfortunately not disaggregated to permit consideration of corruption alone other than for 1982–88, as indicated in the text), see He Bingsong 1992, 247; these reveal that the "Great Leap Forward" in terms of the number of cases considered (as distinct from the number registered, which is usually much lower) occurred in the early stages of Deng's economic reform, with the number soaring from 784 in 1979 to 15,964 in 1980 and 45,247 in 1981. The rate of growth then slowed, peaking at 81,591 in 1986 and falling to 59,405 in 1987 and 66,300 in 1988.

24   The data for 1994 and subsequent years are not directly comparable with the earlier ones, since a new category of "cases of unidentified wealth" was introduced. The figure of 50,088 comprises 36,471 cases of bribery and corruption and 13,617 cases of unidentified wealth.

25   These changes correlate temporally with general political clampdowns and, more specifically, anticorruption campaigns.

26   This estimate is compatible with a report that 35,084 cases of "corruption, dereliction of duty and bribe-taking" were being investigated by Chinese prosecutors in 1998 (*CD*, 21 January 1999).

27   Further statistics on Chinese corruption can be found in, *inter alia*, *Beijing Review*, 1 April 1996, 17–19; and *CD*, 11 and 14 March 2000.

28   For official statistics on corruption in post-communist states that had applied for membership in the European Union see Open Society Institute 2002.

29   I have used the phrase "do not know" as the last response cited in the text, which is the phrase used in the English-language versions of Kurczewski's analysis; in his Polish version the response is "difficult to answer." It is assumed here that the two responses are essentially the same.

30   The word "élite" is in quotation marks here to highlight that several of the groups included by the Steen team would be considered staffs by other analysts, myself included. Having made the point once, however, I omit the quotation marks in subsequent references to Steen's valuable research.

31   Another useful source on the attitudes and beliefs of staffs toward corruption, specifically in Bulgaria, is the Corruption Monitoring System of Coalition 2000 — see for example the reference in Center for the Study of Democracy 2002a, 37–38. This group also publishes an annual survey of corruption in Bulgaria, which now includes data on public perceptions and experiences in Bulgaria and other states in South Eastern Europe — see for example "Koalitsiya 2000" 2003 (Bulgarian version) and "Coalition 2000" 2003 (English version). For a Hungarian analysis of public officials' views on corruption, based on focus group research rather than a large-scale survey, see Gallup Organization and the Hungarian Gallup Institute 2000.

32   The decision to separate the TI comparative surveys from the more detailed and mostly indigenous surveys is to some extent arbitrary, and reflects the need for a balance between the presentations of different methods in this chapter. But readers are urged to look also at the survey results in chapter 5.

33   According to Dollar, Fisman, and Gatti (1999, 2), the most commonly cited index in the economics-based literature on corruption is the Corruption Index of the International Country Risk Guide. This index, produced by the PRS Group, uses a scale of 0 to 6, in which zero represents the highest level of corruption. The index is not nearly as well known outside the economics profession as the CPI, however.

34   For the sake of transparency, I acknowledge that I have worked closely with TI on several occasions. However, I have also worked with TÁRKI (for which Endre Sík has worked part-time); notably, TÁRKI conducted the Hungarian survey commissioned for this book. My position is based solely on which of the two perspectives appears intellectually more convincing. Sík prefers the proxy (experiential) approach rather than perception-based approaches, but he appears to have been unaware that the World Bank had been conducting experiential surveys since the late 1990s. The point about fizzling out will be exemplified in chapter 5, with reference to Bulgaria.

35   TI itself acknowledges that this is permissible—see the Frequently Asked Questions concerning the 2004 CPI on the TI web site. In 2003, in conjunction with Gallup International, TI announced the new Global Corruption Barometer (briefly mentioned in chapter 2), specifically designed to measure changes over time in both the experience of bribery and attitudes toward corruption in individual countries (Galtung 2003). In July 2003 the first barometer was published; it provided data on forty-six countries, plus Hong Kong and the Palestinian Authority (Galtung, Smith, and Homel 2003; Kotalik and Garcia 2004, 23). Of these, eight (nine if Germany is included) were post-communist; three of the four states from CEE and the CIS studied in this book were analyzed, but Hungary was not, and no data on China were available "because of censorship" (Galtung, Smith, and Homel 2003, 18). The results of a question concerning the extent to which respondents' personal and family lives were affected by corruption are interesting, mainly because they are partly at odds with the image created by other methods. Thus 50.1 percent of Russian respondents stated that corruption did not significantly affect their personal and family lives, whereas 76.5 percent of Bulgarians stated that it affected them "very significantly"; Poles were apparently more strongly affected than Russians, with only 37.8 percent indicating that the effects of corruption were not significant (19–20). Attitudes revealed in this barometer were also at odds with the findings of most other methods on the effects of corruption on business. In response to a question concerning the extent to which respondents believed that the business environment was affected by corruption, only 48.7 percent of Russians answered "very significantly," compared with 59.7 percent of Poles and a remarkably high 81.8 percent of Bulgarians (21–22).

36   As a group the Nordic countries invariably emerge in the TI CPIS as the least corrupt in Europe, with Finland scoring 9.7, Denmark and Iceland 9.5, Sweden 9.2, and Norway 8.9 in the 2004 index; Switzerland also performed well, at 9.1. Twelve of the fifteen states then belonging to the European Union scored above 7.0 in the 2004 CPI; those that did not were Greece (4.3), Italy (4.8), and Portugal (6.3).

37   The TI data from the earlier periods do appear to treat the Czech Republic in isolation, even though it was at the time part of Czechoslovakia.

38   The differential between Estonia and Latvia had reduced slightly by the time of the 2004 CPI (Lithuania ranked in between these two), though it remained significant, at two percentage points (6.0 to 4.0).

39   For the 2004 assessments used here, Freedom House asked the specialists who produce its individual country reports to provide preliminary ratings, which were then evaluated by both American and CEE and CIS academic advisers. The final rating for each country was usually a compromise between all of these; in cases of insufficient agreement, the editors at Freedom House made the ultimate decision. The Freedom House ratings for 2004 are based partly on popular perceptions of the levels of corruption, and largely on an assessment of both the measures taken to fight corruption and media coverage.

40   Almost certainly for Poland, and probably for Hungary, the differences reflect the tendency of the Freedom House assessments to be strongly influenced by new laws and campaigns that are seen as indicating serious commitment in a country to combating corruption. For a brief overview of what Poland was doing in this area in 2002–3 see Pitera with Brennek, Kochanowski, Kojder, and Lęski 2004, 242–44.

41   It is also possible that many Bulgarians who answered "don't know" actually did not care, but were not given the option to say so. This possibility occurred to me when I received the results of a survey that I had organized in Bulgaria in October 2003 concerning the financing of political parties (see note 15 to chapter 8). Perhaps the response "don't care" should be made an option in many social surveys.

42   A useful source for further survey data on CEE and CIS countries is the web site http://www.nobribes.org/.

43   The findings in one recent piece of research urge caution in making such an inference. The (unnamed) authors of an analysis of the possible connections between media coverage and public attitudes concluded: "Comparing the intensity of the media coverage of corruption [in Bulgaria between 1999 and 2003] with the level of negative public attitudes disproves the theory that the debate on corruption . . . makes society more sensitive to the phenomenon." This conclusion is interesting and counterintuitive, but it must be treated warily. First, there need to be far more case studies to ensure that this is a typical pattern. Second, it might be that excessive coverage of corruption numbs people to it (which would appear to endorse our argument in chapter 7 that anticorruption campaigns can be counterproductive). But finally, the researchers themselves go on to argue — sensibly — that public

perceptions and attitudes are formed by a complex mixture of factors, one of which *is* exposure to the media ("Coalition 2000" 2004, 16–17).

44   The term content analysis is used here in its broader — and, it appears, increasingly popular — sense, to refer to any systematic analysis of media content. There is no assumption here that it refers only to sampling (only editorials published on Fridays, for example), rather than to a full run of a newspaper over a certain period. Given the search facility in so many software programs nowadays, and the rapidly increasing availability of newspapers and other periodicals on line, the latter type of analysis is becoming much easier than it was.

45   For an analysis of articles just in the Polish press (a total of 323 items during the 1990s from four leading publications — *Gazeta Wyborcza*, *Rzeczpospolita*, *Wprost*, and *Nie*), see Fuszara 2000. Fuszara identifies ten types of article on corruption, plus an "others" category — see esp. 49–54.

46   The reports for 1999 and early 2000 are available on line in English — see *http://www.anticorruption.bg/eng/mmonitoring/weekly.htm*. The reports for 2002 and 2003 were available only in Bulgarian at the time of writing. For more recent (from November 2002) English-language monthly surveys see *http://www.anticorruption.bg/eng/mmonitoring/monthly.htm*.

47   For recent Polish analysis of the coverage of corruption in 185 periodicals see Transparency International Polska (forthcoming). For a more quantitative than qualitative analysis of Russian press coverage of corruption from October to December 2000 see Kislinskaya 2000.

48   The original states were Albania, Armenia, Azerbaijan, Belarus, Bulgaria, Croatia, Czechia, Estonia, Georgia, Hungary, Kazakhstan, Kyrgyzstan, Latvia, Lithuania, Moldova, Poland, Romania, Russia, Slovakia, Slovenia, Ukraine, and Uzbekistan (Pradhan, Anderson, Hellman, Jones, Moore, Muller, Ryterman, and Sutch 2000, 5). The World Bank web site from which the full details for BEEPS 1 can be obtained — *http://info.worldbank.org/governance/beeps/* — is slightly confusing, in that parts of it indicate that the survey was conducted in mid-1999, while others indicate "1999–2000." Moreover, according to some parts the survey was of the twenty-two countries just listed, while according to others up to twenty-six took part. Of the additional countries, one (Turkey) is clearly not a post-communist state, though it might be considered transitional. The three additional post-communist "states" for the first BEEPS are all successor states or units of the former Yugoslavia — Bosnia, the Republic of Macedonia, and the Republic of Serbia. It is assumed here that extra surveys were conducted in late 1999 and 2000, and their results subsequently incorporated into BEEPS 1 (web site visited June 2003). In conclusion, the highest figure cited here (twenty-six) is more or less compatible with the figures produced by Gray, Hellman, and Ryterman (2004, 2), who state that BEEPS I was conducted in "24 transition countries (plus Turkey)"; if the Republic of Serbia — which is not currently a fully sovereign state — is added, the figures match.

49   For evidence that some Kyrgyz public officials, fearing reprisals, refused to answer certain questions in a survey by the World Bank in 2001 — including questions on corruption — see Anderson 2002, 2, 41. The possibility that some respondents exaggerate in their answers is acknowledged; but it is our firm belief that this tendency would be greatly outweighed by fear, which skews responses in the other direction.

50   Note that the number of valid responses to this question was relatively low in all cases, ranging from 24 in Hungary to 90 in Bulgaria (only 41 in Russia). The numbers are higher, but still not very high, if all responses are included (including "don't know"), ranging from 50 in Hungary to 114 in Bulgaria. The "don't know" category was in all cases significant, at 21.1 percent in Bulgaria, 43.8 percent in Poland, 52.0 percent in Hungary, and 52.3 percent in Russia. Website visited June 2003.

51   The question in the 1999 survey refers to revenue, while that in 2002 refers to sales (Gray, Hellman, and Ryterman 2004, esp. 55–56). The impact of this marginal change is difficult to assess, but it is a priori unlikely to be significant, at least in terms of country relativities. It is understandable that survey researchers should refine their questionnaires over time; but changes frustrate attempts at time-series analysis, and it is hoped that BEEPS III will be more directly comparable with BEEPS II than BEEPS II was with BEEPS I.

52   The authors' own reason for optimism was their belief that the impact of state capture may have declined across the region as a whole (Gray, Hellman, and Ryterman 2004, 31). But their ultimate uncertainty is highlighted by the use of the term "may."

53   For detailed and broadly supportive evidence from post-communist Russia see Radaev 2002, esp. 290–93.

54   The reader is reminded of TI's changed definition of corruption since 2000, which can include business-to-business activities. Were this approach to be adopted in the CPI, the point just made would be invalidated for CPI results since 2000. However, the 2004 CPI makes it quite clear that the definition of corruption used for its purposes remains "the abuse of public office for private gain," and that this focuses on, for example, "bribe-taking by public officials in public procurement" (see the FAQs about the CPI on the TI web site).

55   It is important to note that the Glasgow team's statistics are based exclusively on the conventional notion of valid responses — they exclude "don't know" and "mixed/depends" answers. This yields slightly higher per-

centages than if such responses had been included. To give the reader some idea of how *little the figures* would change if these replies were incorporated, the first cited Bulgarian figure of 7 percent drops to 6.5 percent if all responses are included, the second from 39 percent to 34.2 percent (Center for the Study of Democracy 1998a). Given that the figures cited by Miller, Grødeland, and Koshechkina are rounded, the differences might be even smaller. For the record, the total *N*s for each country in the Glasgow-based analysis were 1,519 in Bulgaria, 1,003 in Czechia, 1,056 in Slovakia, and 1,200 in Ukraine; in all cases samples were nationally representative (Miller, Grødeland, and Koshechkina 1998, 1).

56   For a somewhat comparable set of responses from a Russian survey conducted in July 2000, see Levada 2001, 54. However, it must be noted that the data in Levada's table can easily be misinterpreted unless one takes heed of the note below it. Unfortunately, Levada's table and accompanying text do not provide any indication of the percentage of all respondents who have been directly or indirectly solicited by officials for bribes or "gifts."

57   In addition to the reference cited in note 3, it is appropriate to recall the phrase "lies, damned lies, and statistics."

58   For the results of broadly comparable surveys conducted in Albania, Bulgaria, and the Republic of Macedonia in January 2000, which provide data on the percentages of citizens who had been asked for "money, gifts or services" when they approached officials during 1999, see *Monitor* (CSD, Bulgaria) 8, spring 2000, 17–18. The figures refer only to meat eating for both Bulgaria and Macedonia, but to both direct requests and inferences by citizens for Albania. In all three countries the figures pertain to specific groups of officials rather than to officials in a generic sense. In general the Bulgarian percentages cited are higher than those generated by the Glasgow team; but this is largely because the three-country comparison includes the responses only of citizens who had actually had contact with the particular group of officials.

59   For an example of research into the prices paid for similar goods before and after a crackdown on corruption in hospitals in Argentina, with the prices lowered by some 15 percent in the short term (first nine months of the crackdown) and 10 percent thereafter, see di Tella and Schargrodsky 2003.

60   On PETS, and the closely related QSDS or quantitative service delivery surveys, see Reinikka, Svensson, and Kurey 2002; Lindelow 2003; Reinikka and Svensson 2003. PETS have been organized in a number of developing and transition countries in Africa and Latin America, the first being Uganda in 1996.

61   Our Hungarian survey organization suggested that for Hungary there should be a fifth category, "not at all corrupt." Unfortunately this suggestion

— which was accepted — arrived after the survey organizations in Poland and Russia had finalized their questionnaires. It was therefore decided to collapse the "least corrupt" and "not at all corrupt" categories for all comparative observations, but to separate them where doing so seemed appropriate in making comments on Hungary or Bulgaria alone.

62   A more detailed English-language summary of the results of the three-country survey referred to in note 58 can be found in Coalition 2000's *Clean Future* (Bulgaria) 5, spring 2000, 8–9, which reveals that customs officers were perceived to be the most corrupt group of officials in all three countries. The judiciary continued in the early twenty-first century to be seen by most Bulgarians as highly corrupt — see Center for the Study of Democracy 2003b, 38.

63   Given the nature of the question, it is not surprising that the president and prime minister, for instance, were not included in the list of officials to assess.

64   This decision becomes even more justifiable when it is borne in mind that Bulgaria began introducing a controversial reform of health services in 1997, one element of which was to be greater privatization; the reform process was still incomplete at the time of writing.

65   For details of a citizen survey commissioned by the Hungarian Ministry of the Interior in October 1998, which revealed that 36 percent of the adult population considered police officers rather prone to bribery, see Ministry of the Interior [Hungary] 2000, 27–28.

66   The N for the GfK survey was 1,000 respondents per country, selected as a nationally representative sample; surveying was by face-to-face interview.

67   For further Hungarian perception-based data in English see Vásárhelyi 1999, and the summary of surveys conducted by G. Bognár, R. Gál, and M. Vásárhelyi (but published in Hungarian) provided in Sík 2002, 99–100. Vásárhelyi's research compared the views of high-ranking civil servants and the general public, and found that the public usually saw more corruption in specific situations than the civil servants did. Somewhat similar results, indicating that citizens often have a more stringent view of corruption than public servants do, are reported for Czechia, Hungary, Poland, and Slovakia in Ortmann 2004. However, there is some evidence that citizens' perceptions are often close to those of experts and entrepreneurs — see the INDEM and POF Russian results reported later in this chapter. This might in turn suggest that public servants prefer to have a better self-image than is warranted, though this possibility must remain speculation.

68   Apart from the GfK data cited, I am unaware of any survey data to support the contention here about Hungarian attitudes; the inference is based primarily on several interviews conducted in Budapest in September 1996 and July 2000.

69   When asked if either they themselves or anyone in their immediate entourage had ever encountered a case of bribery or other form of corruption, only 15 percent of respondents answered in the affirmative — while 82 percent reported that they never had (Centrum Badania Opinii Społecznej 1994b, 2). Part of the explanation for this might be that respondents were referring only to meat-eating corruption, not grass-eating situations in which they felt only that they might be expected to offer a bribe. Even allowing for this, there might be a serious mismatch between perceptions of corruption and the actual situation in Poland (and probably in many other countries). But in terms of legitimacy, perceptions matter more than "reality." Moreover, this apparent discrepancy could well mean that many Poles do not personally experience corruption because they are not involved with high-ranking officials; if they believe that corruption is worse higher up the state hierarchy than at lower levels, this too is bound to increase the legitimation problems of the state. For related but more recent CBOS data on all this see Centrum Badania Opinii Społecznej 2000. For further Polish survey data, generated by the Batory Foundation, see Osiak 2000, Kubiak 2002, and the web site *http://www.batory.org.pl/korupcja/pub.htm*. The survey from July 2000 referred to in Osiak revealed that Poles considered the police and the traffic police even more prone to corruption than public servants or doctors.

70   Two of the categories have been relabeled here to render them more consistent with the terminology used in this book and more familiar to English speakers. The third and fourth categories in this list were actually called "general public administration" and "self-government administration."

71   Readers who consult Kurczewski's book (1999a, 271) will find a table almost identical to the English-language version cited here, but they need to be alerted to a minor typographical error in it; the correct data are included in an errata sheet.

72   Had the survey been conducted in late 1999, by which time most Russians knew of the Mabetex corruption scandal surrounding President Yeltsin, the results would almost certainly have been very different.

73   For depressing survey evidence suggesting that many Russian police officers consider corruption justifiable in various circumstances see Beck and Lee 2002.

74   It is almost certain that the term used by INDEM for what I have interpreted as regular police — *pravookhranitel'nye organy*, or law enforcement agencies — includes customs officials and border guards, partly because this is the common meaning of the term in Russian, and partly because there is no other grouping that is likely to subsume these two agencies. If they are included, the resonances between the INDEM results and our own become even more pronounced.

75   This group was considered even more corrupt than judicial officials and the traffic police in 1999, second only to "the police, customs and law enforcement agencies."

76   The POF surveys also include tables of responses from experts on perceived levels of corruption in different agencies. Space limitations preclude the results from being summarized here. But they are very similar to the responses from the general public, with two exceptions. First; "supreme federal power" is considered much less corrupt by the experts than by the public. Second, the experts consider local authorities much more corrupt than ordinary citizens do.

77   To avert any misunderstanding, the World Bank methodology is superior to our own, since it is more comprehensive. Unfortunately, it is also considerably more expensive to undertake, which is why we could not use it.

78   References to the school system and banking have been omitted here, given our approach to corruption. For those interested, these two groups were considered the least corrupt after the military. Unfortunately for our purposes, the ten countries used to produce the averages include one (Austria) that is not post-communist; readers wishing to reconstruct the list omitting Austria would have to average and then rank-order the other nine using the individual country data provided in the (unpaginated) section "Introduction of All Countries."

79   Note that China was one of only three countries (the others being Brazil and Pakistan) in TI's Global Corruption Barometer for which there were no data concerning corruption (Kotalik and Garcia 2004, 23).

80   According to the *Far Eastern Economic Review* (20 August 1998, 12), corruption among the police and judiciary in China "probably stirs the greatest public anger." The same article (11) reminded readers that in his speech to the 15th Party Congress in September 1997, the party leader Jiang Zemin subtly implied that the CCP itself should acknowledge the supremacy of the law over the party, when he referred to the rule *of* law instead of the more customary (in the PRC) rule *by* law.

81   Though see note 72. Nevertheless, it is encouraging that Russians had not lost all faith in the office of the president, and that most believed their new head of state to be relatively untainted.

82   It appears that the other groups perceived by many citizens as corrupt are ones whose alleged corruption is often commented upon in the media, notably parliamentarians. However, table 4.7 suggests that this group is not believed to be quite as corrupt as the law-enforcing agencies.

83   The sources cited could give the impression that there was also a household survey of Albania in 1998 (Thomas 2001, 242–43); in fact, only surveys of public officials and entrepreneurs were conducted there. Moreover, at the time

of writing the full, final Albanian report was not publicly available. The World Bank had already been conducting household surveys of several post-communist states since the early 1990s; but these were general socioeconomic surveys, and did not directly address the issue of corruption. The two surveys from 1998 referred to here were not only of households; they also involved enterprise managers and public officials. More recently, the World Bank has conducted surveys of corruption that have been either full-scale (Bosnia and Hercegovina, mid-2000; Romania, April–May 2000) or partial, in that corruption was only one of several foci relating to governance (Armenia, 2001; Kazakhstan, winter–spring 2001; Kyrgyzstan, 2001); the reports are available on line through the World Bank web site under the heading "Governance and Anticorruption Diagnostics" (the address appears to change from time to time, but readers could try http://lnweb18.worldbank.org/ECA/ecspeExt.nsf/ExtECADocByUnid/1B 062B0DC8A543B485256C63005D49FD?Opendocument&Start=1&Count= 5). There was also a survey of Russian public attitudes; this was not publicly available at the time of writing (only a discursive introduction was on the World Bank web site as of October 2004), but it appears to be the same INDEM survey referred to earlier in this chapter (it is available in Russian).

84   By relevant is meant that in most of these surveys, only the bribery experiences of citizens who have come into direct contact with the group of officials in question are solicited, so that the sample sizes varied; for the traffic police, for example, only the experiences of drivers were sought. Unfortunately, the data on popular direct experiences of corruption in Bosnia and Hercegovina (Shkaratan 2001, 13) are not disaggregated in a way that isolates the relative levels of corruption among different groups of officials.

85   The health sector, the educational sector, or both emerged as even more corrupt than the traffic police in several countries; but given the bounded approach to corruption adopted in this book, they are excluded from our consideration.

86   Perhaps counterintuitively, the notable exception to this general finding was Romania, where "only" 15 percent of relevant respondents reported paying a bribe, compared with the 22 percent of relevant respondents who had paid bribes to judicial officials. However, the term "judicial officials" is somewhat problematic in the World Bank survey cited here, since it includes attorneys (all from Anderson, Cosmaciuc, Dininio, Spector, and Zoido-Lobaton 2001, xi, 16–17).

87   Another relevant survey of corruption experience is the UNICRI International Crime Victim Survey mentioned above — although this is based only on public opinion polls, not surveys of officials or entrepreneurs (http://www.unicri.it/icvs/).

88   Readers are reminded of surveyors' attempts to compensate for re-

spondents' fear in BEEPS; such attempts are legitimate and understandable, but increase the subjectivity of the findings.

89   According to Thomas (2001, 242), the triangulation method was first used in surveys of the post-communist world in 1998, when the World Bank conducted the surveys of Albania, Georgia, and Latvia cited above.

90   In a subsequent article, Sajó (2003, 172) endorses this theme by arguing that "international politics is, to a great extent, about the allocation of moral superiority or inferiority on the basis of the alleged levels of corruption."

91   For claims by two Russian analysts that corruption has become normal in post-communist Russia see Shlapentokh 2003, esp. 152–53, and Shevtsova 2003, 8; for a similar claim about Bulgaria see Marko Semov's remarks in *Novinar Daily*, 19 April 1999, cited in BPCWR, 17–23 April 1999, while Sajó (2002) makes a similar point about Hungary. But it is important to note that "normal" can have significantly diverse connotations. Thus the legitimacy-related implications of corruption that most citizens accept because they feel powerless to do anything about it (other than learning to live with it) are quite different from the implications of corruption that citizens are genuinely unconcerned about. For the results of the Demoskop survey of July 2000, according to which 66 percent of Poles believed that ordinary people could do nothing to counter corruption (that is, felt powerless), see *TI Newsletter*, September 2000. And although the evidence is still too incomplete to be persuasive, another indicator that many citizens do not simply accept corruption, but rather are frustrated by their inability to do anything about it, is the overwhelming number of calls received by TI Bosnia and Hercegovina (TI BiH) when it opened a free hotline to its Centre for Advocacy and Legal Advice in February 2004. In its first month of operation, the hotline received in excess of 900 calls, more than 520 of which related to corruption. Evidently many citizens were angry about corruption, but had previously not known what to do about it or else had been dismissed by the Bosnian authorities when they had attempted to voice their concerns (Press Release, TI BiH, 11 March 2004; see too *TI Q*, September 2004, 6). There is likely to be further such evidence from other TI national chapters in the future.

92   I have used the adjective "unjust" because I am a meritocrat and do not advocate equality of income. But meritocracy means higher rewards to those who perform best according to specified and known criteria, not inequality caused and reinforced by clandestine agreements, personal relationships, and similar considerations. Of course there is plenty of corruption in the West too. But most western governments and societies acknowledge that it is wrong, even though it exists. And although many CEE governments, societies, and analysts acknowledge this as well, many do not.

93   For a Bulgarian claim that there would be no point in trying to im-

prove the economies of the post-communist states of South Eastern Europe by pouring large amounts of western funding into them, since élites would immediately steal three quarters of the money, see the comments by B. Dimitrov in *Trud*, 27 April 1999, cited in *Bulgarian Media on Corruption Weekly Review*, 24–30 April 1999.

94   TI has sought to counter some of the anticipated criticism of an alleged western bias by producing a Bribe Payers' Index (BPI), details of which are in chapter 7.

95   Arguably the most sustained attacks on "western" attempts to measure corruption can be found in Kotkin and Sajó eds. 2002 — esp. in Sajó 2002, Sík 2002. For a more subdued and technical critique of TI's CPI — although the term "bootstrapping procedures" may sound emotive to nonstatisticians — see Kaufmann, Kraay, and Mastruzzi 2003, 32–39.

96   In a disturbing conclusion, Gray, Hellman, and Ryterman (2004, 45) suggest that "differences in findings among polls and surveys of various types raise interesting and important questions for further analysis." As already argued, according to our own reading of the data published by Gray, Hellman, and Ryterman the differences are less marked than they suggest, and some of their own optimistic interpretations represent wishful thinking, which in part accounts for the apparent discrepancies. If this is so, the differences between the various analyses become less pronounced.

5: THE IMPACT OF CORRUPTION

1   A Bulgarian analysis of the media conducted by the Center for Independent Journalism in Sofia in the late 1990s concluded that the treatment of corruption was very general and superficial in most articles and broadcasts primarily dealing with it, and that in 25 percent of them corruption was not analyzed at all — BPCWR, 15–21 May 1999.

2   For the record, the acting prosecutor general, Ilyushenko, stated publicly in December 1994 that based on investigations Grachev had not committed any crime. Doubts remained in some people's minds, however. In February 2000, six people, including four military intelligence officers, were charged with Kholodov's murder; they went on trial in November but were acquitted in June 2002 and — after reconsideration of the case — a second time in June 2004. Kholodov's father then declared his intention to appeal the decision in the European Court of Human Rights.

3   In July 2004 a report listed six journalists who had been murdered in Russia since 2000, all of whom had been investigating corruption and organized crime — *Johnson's Russia List* 8297, 19 July 2004.

4   Six people, including a military intelligence officer, were arrested in November 2002 and accused of involvement in Starovoitova's murder; another person was subsequently charged. Their trial began in January 2004 and was still ongoing as of February 2005; at least four other people were expected to have to stand trial too.

5   Unfortunately, this is not peculiar to transitional or developing countries. Thus a journalist based in Luxembourg was dismissed allegedly because of the investigations he had conducted into corruption in the European Union (*TI Newsletter*, June 1999, 4).

6   Note that a police officer was subsequently charged in connection with the terrorist attacks on the two aircraft, albeit for negligence rather than corruption — MosNews.com, 24 September 2004, visited September 2004.

7   For an example of Chinese concerns that specific cases of corruption were increasing the threat of floods in Nanjing see *South China Morning Post* (internet edition), 3 August 1998.

8   A small conference on the Environmental Impact of Corruption was held at the American University in April 2001. Unfortunately no papers were produced from that meeting.

9   For attempts to measure the economic effects of organized crime, though not explicitly with reference to post-communist countries, see various approaches in the edited volume by Fiorentini and Peltzman 1995 (some of which are highly technical).

10   For an analysis of these various terms and further references see L. Holmes 1993, 73–76. These related phenomena have in common that they refer to unreported or unregistered economic activity. Some is overtly illegal (the black economy), but much else either is not illegal or is legally ambiguous.

11   By way of comparison, a study by the Austrian economist Friedrich Schneider from 1997 suggests that the shadow economy accounts for more than 25 percent of GDP in Italy, more than 20 percent in Belgium and Spain, and perhaps one seventh of total output in the world's richest countries (*Economist*, 3 May 1997, 91–92). For a more thorough analysis, by the same analyst and a coauthor, see Schneider and Enste 2000.

12   One of the more creative methods for attempting to measure the size of the shadow economy as a percentage of GDP involves comparing key physical inputs, such as electricity, and current officially recorded demand. Using this method, Schneider and Enste (2000, esp. 80–81) estimated the shadow economy as between 20 and 28 percent of GDP in the period 1990–93 in Bulgaria, Hungary, and Poland, and between 20 and 27 percent in the same period in Russia. That four countries emerge with identical or nearly identical figures must cast suspicion on the efficacy of this method, however. More-

over, it is unclear how much allowance has been made for illegal "hooking up" by individuals and families to electricity grids for the purposes of private consumption. This is a common enough practice in some countries. But since it is often unrelated to any kind of production, it should not be considered part of the shadow economy in the specific sense of unrecorded productive economic activity. Finally, some parts of the shadow and black economies do not use power inputs on any meaningful scale, and so would escape this sort of investigation.

13 For corroborating, related evidence see Hutchcroft 2002, 119. Compare this observation with the comment about robber barons in the next note.

14 Several analysts, as well as politicians such as Boris Nemtsov, have argued that this issue of reinvestment constitutes one of the major differences between the nature and role of the so-called robber barons and others who "stole" public property in eighteenth- and nineteenth-century America and post-communist Russia's "oligarchs" and "mafia." On this see Lucky 1997. For recent Chinese government concern regarding capital flight see CD, 21 August 2002, and *Financial Times*, 24 August 2002, 7; these articles refer to a report on capital flight prepared by specialists from Beijing University, according to which almost $40 billion was sent out of China in 1998 and some $24 billion in 1999. See also Ding 2000, 141–42.

15 The restaurant situation improved markedly after 1998.

16 An example is the executive director of the Bulgarian Privatization Agency in May 1999 — see *BPCWR*, 22–28 May 1999.

17 The report had already been referred to on Latvian Radio in December (*OMRI DD*, 19 December 1996). In the radio report it was claimed that approximately 50 percent of profits generated from criminal activities in Latvia was being used to bribe state officials. I am indebted to Nicholas Redman for bringing this report to my attention.

18 In connection with this case a Russian émigré couple (plus another Russian) were formally charged with money laundering; the two were then arrested in October 1999 by authorities in New York. In February 2000 the couple pleaded guilty — at about the same time as the IMF shifted its attention to the corrupt misuse of funds it had provided to Ukraine. Despite the guilty plea, the two were not sentenced. While searching for further information on this affair, I discovered a reference to a book on it — *Redwash* (author unidentified). I failed to find this book — but see *http://www.moscowtelegraph.com/ redwash/foreward.htm* for the foreword to the book, and an announcement that it was expected to be published in both Russian and English by the end of 2003.

19 For example, a senior official at the United Nations was accused of

having siphoned off European Union funds intended to improve the electricity supply in Kosova — *TI Q*, March 2003, 5.

20   Of course these are also major social problems; their inclusion in this section, because of their international dimensions, does not detract from their serious social implications.

21   On smuggling (of people, drugs, and other contraband) and trafficking from CEE to the West see Center for the Study of Democracy 2002b; Hajdinjak 2002; Ciconte 2004. Freemantle (1995, 146–55) provides details on the smuggling and trade in human body parts.

22   For a sensationalist, exaggerated (one hopes), but nevertheless disturbing analysis of the globalization of organized crime, and in particular the role of Russian organized crime in bringing it about, see Sterling 1995.

23   Data kindly provided to the author by Professor András Sajó during an interview in Budapest, 24 September 1996.

24   I am deeply indebted to Professor Lena Kolarska-Bobińska, at that time (1997) director of CBOS, for having placed the results of this and the following two surveys at my disposal, and to Mr. Oliver Freeman for invaluable assistance in translating all the Polish surveys cited here into English (I studied Polish formally only from 2000).

25   Data kindly provided to the author by Yurii Levada in Moscow, 25 April 1997. It is noteworthy that the data are very close to the results of our own Polish question on legitimacy.

26   For a more recent Russian survey that provides information, *inter alia*, on motives of convicted corrupt officials see the reference to Repetzkaya's research in chapter 6.

27   In an effort to provide a more nuanced assessment of the early Putin leadership, a leading Russian political analyst, Lilia Shevtsova, has argued that weakness and amorphousness are also key features of Putin's personality and leadership — see Shevtsova 2001, esp. 99–101, 106.

28   Data kindly supplied to the author by Professor A. Sajó, Budapest, 11 April 1997; the survey was funded by the National Science Foundation.

29   I am indebted to the director of Vitosha Research, Aleksandr Stoyanov, for having kindly provided me with a copy of Center for the Study of Democracy 1998a during a visit that I made to Bulgaria in February 1998.

30   Another possible explanation: the government fight against corruption was already being so effective that public concern about the problem had declined. While the government was clearly making a serious effort to combat corruption, this explanation seems either farfetched or, more charitably, premature.

31   The Glasgow project was funded jointly by the Overseas Development

Administration (now the Department of International Development) and the (British) Economic and Social Research Council.

32   These results are very similar but not identical to those for Bulgaria cited in various analyses that have been produced by the Glasgow team — see esp. Miller, Grødeland, and Koshechkina 1998; Miller, Grødeland, and Koshechkina 1999; and Miller, Grødeland, and Koshechkina 2001b. The slight difference between the Vitosha figures and those provided by Miller, Grødeland, and Koshechkina are insignificant in terms of the argument here; they occur primarily because the Glasgow team has usually calculated percentages after omitting all mixed and "it depends" responses, whereas the Vitosha team has sometimes included mixed responses, and has specified where it has done so. Given my own preference for including indefinite responses (since this provides a fuller picture of attitudes, even though it is messier), and my having had access to the Bulgarian results first and translated the Bulgarian-language time-series responses (Center for the Study of Democracy 1998a), they are used for this part of the analysis. However, the figures produced by Miller, Grødeland, and Koshechkina have been used here for the summary of Czech, Slovak, and Ukrainian attitudes that follows the Bulgarian analysis.

33   The Vitosha percentages for this question are based exclusively on respondents who provided a definite answer (all "neither" and "don't know" responses are excluded).

34   Up to 1,072 Bulgarians were interviewed for the Barometer (based on appendix 5), whereas only 693 responses are recorded for the corruption/ politics question. Readers can see for themselves the differences in response rates for other countries by comparing the numbers in Appendices 3 and 5; basically, the differences are marginal for the three Western states listed in our table, a little greater for Poland, and larger still for Russia — though still much smaller than the Bulgarian gap.

35   See for example the survey of urban workers' concerns published in BR 40, no. 3: 21, or that on attitudes toward economic restructuring in BR 40, no. 6:22–23.

36   The reader is reminded of the pioneering survey cited by Saich (2004, 334) referred to in chapter 1, and cited as evidence of the difficulties in obtaining Chinese survey data on corruption; it is almost certainly the same survey as the one conducted by Horizon cited in the preceding sentence. While publicly available survey data are scarce, it is reasonable to infer that the anticorruption film To Be or Not to Be (2000) was as popular as it was in the PRC because it struck a chord with citizens; such culturally based evidence can be as persuasive and valuable as survey data.

37   I am grateful to a leading professor for providing all this information during a meeting in Beijing, 16 June 1997.

38   Surveys in other post-communist states reveal similar attitudes toward corruption. Nancy Lubin's survey-based research into attitudes in Kazakhstan and Uzbekistan in the early 1990s, for instance, indicates that many members of the public in both countries were of two minds about the political and economic reform process precisely because it was associated in their minds with corruption, which they perceived as having substantially increased since the Soviet period. Moreover, many respondents associated corruption with organized crime, and believed that both "local government officials" and "high-level government officials" belonged to "the mafia." As in so many other post-communist countries, the law-enforcement agencies (police, judiciary, procuracy) were seen to be riddled with corruption (Lubin 1995; for further analysis of corruption in the Central Asian post-communist states see Gleason 1995). The negative implications for legitimating a system are obvious.

39   Much of the success of the late Aleksandr Lebed' from 1996 until 2000 (when, contrary to expectations, he did not contest the presidential election) was due to his claims that he could bring order to Russia, in part by bringing crime under control. His popularity also owed something to his being perceived by many as the cleanest — least corrupt — politician at the top of Russian politics. It may well have been only a matter of time before serious attempts would be made to sully his reputation, which his premature death prevented. However, he did not help his own image in late 1996 by associating closely with the discredited former bodyguard to Yeltsin, Aleksandr Korzhakov. From the middle of 1999 his role and image were largely usurped anyway by Vladimir Putin. Lebed' died in a helicopter crash in April 2002.

40   On TVP 1, 14 December 2000. Much of the interview related to organized crime ("the mafia"), and it is worth noting Kwaśniewski's claim that the mafia was not a major problem in Poland, unlike in Russia. He could also have contrasted his country with Bulgaria: relatively soon after coming to office in early 1997, President Petar Stoyanov stated in a television interview that organized crime was the single biggest problem in his country (RFE/RL, 11 November 1997).

41   It is pertinent to refer here to the electoral successes of the communists in the parliamentary elections in Mongolia (July 2000) and Moldova (February 2001), and to the marked increase in their levels of electoral support in both Czechia and Slovakia during 2002.

6: CAUSES OF CORRUPTION

1   Others apparently agree — see Verheijen and Dimitrova 1996, esp. 204–11; Anusiewicz, Verheijen, and Dimitrova 2001, esp. 80–82.

2   However, for articles arguing that changing balances in both the polity (decentralization) and the economy (marketization) in the 1990s resulted in a change in the characteristics of transition China's corruption, see Ting Gong 1997; He Zengke 2000. According to several specialists within China, such as the political scientist He Zengke and the sociologist Deng Weizhi, the principal cause of corruption in the PRC is the monopolistic political system that largely forbids outsiders to control the power of party officials (*Far Eastern Economic Review*, 20 August 1998, 11).

3   For a wide-ranging introduction to the reasons for corruption generally see R. Williams 2000b.

4   The survey was conducted among prisoners — mainly former police officers, but also some former judges and other court officials — convicted of corruption and serving time in Irkutsk Special Colony for Former Officers of the Law. It appears to have been conducted in the late 1990s. Since the percentages in most tables total somewhat in excess of 100, it is assumed that respondents could provide multiple answers. Nevertheless, the responses cited here were far and away the most common ones.

5   These are not the only possible explanations. Another significant one is that growing relative poverty in the West has prompted many voters to elect politicians who promise low taxes simply because the voters hope that low taxes will improve their personal finances. It would be unfair to call this greed.

6   These differences in approach partly explain why there is sometimes a mutual lack of respect between politicians and public servants, which can also be conducive to corruption.

7   Rein Taagepera (2002, 256) makes the sensible point that cultural habits and values originally grounded in a common religion can survive the abolition (de facto as well as de jure) of that religion.

8   Tajikistan was first included in the CPI in October 2003 and Turkmenistan in October 2004, and both fared poorly — see chapter 4.

9   Taagepera (2002) has used data from the World Values Surveys, the World Bank, and TI to suggest a correlation between corruption and religious tradition, for which he has produced a visual summary (upper diagram, figure 3, p. 249).

10   Meeting with J. Babiuch-Luxmoore, Warsaw, 17 February 1997; as of 2002 the results of Dr. Babiuch-Luxmoore's research with focus groups had

not been published. Her fascinating cultural explanation of corruption is broadly in line with the nuclear "familist" argument produced by Banfield (1958, esp. 85, 116, 132, 135, 137), building on Max Weber and empirically studying a region of (Catholic) Italy. Banfield's argument is referred to by Lipset and Lenz (2000, 119–20), who empirically test the relationship between levels of familism and corruption, finding a high correlation.

11   The causality chain starts to look increasingly like a matrioshka doll, since one might ask why Islamic states tend to be much less economically developed than Christian states. But that question lies far beyond our remit here. For a highly technical analysis of how the culture of corruption is transmitted generationally, in general terms rather than specifically about post-communist societies, see Hauk and Sáez 1999.

12   For an overview of the systemic factors in Russia and Kazakhstan see Henderson 2000.

13   Distinctions drawn between the levels of autonomy enjoyed by managers in communist and capitalist systems are sometimes exaggerated. Western managers of larger firms are often subject to pressure from shareholders and boards of management. Nevertheless, they are encouraged to take risks in a way that was uncommon in the communist world. For an argument that risk taking by managers was much more of a feature of communism than is generally recognized — or accepted here — see Lampland 2002, 49.

14   The attitudinal ambiguity is plausible, however, because such citizens would normally only help themselves to items if they believed they could get away with it. For evidence of this attitude toward state property in the communist era see the quotation from 1971 by the Soviet minister of justice cited in L. Holmes 1993, 162.

15   An example of such blurring in the quasi-post-communist PRC is the increasing involvement of the military in economic enterprise from the late 1970s until the virtual reversal of the policy in 1998 (some military economic activity remained, but mainly to satisfy the military's own needs rather than as a commercial enterprise). Evidently many military officers and agencies had become more interested in running their businesses than in defending China, and the whole process appears to have generated considerable corruption (Mulvenon 2001).

16   According to Albats (*Johnson's Russia List* 8268, 25 June 2004), there is now one bureaucrat in Russia for every 49.6 citizens, compared with one for every 75.6 in the late Soviet era.

17   Many of the privatization agencies were dissolved during the 1990s on the grounds that their work was essentially complete; examples include the Treuhandanstalt in the former GDR (end of 1994) and the Czech privatization agency (July 1996).

18   The claim by many neoliberals that adoption of their approach will lead to reduced corruption initially appears obvious or tautologous: if the number of public officials declines because the state has offloaded many of its former tasks on to the private sector, then ceteris paribus and using our preferred definition of corruption as necessarily involving public office, the amount of corruption will also decline. But this apparently obvious point has to be challenged. If there is an increased number of opportunities for corruption (for example through outsourcing) and incentives for corruption, it is not mathematically obvious that a decrease in the number of officials will result in reduced levels of corruption. Montinola and Jackman (2002, esp. 154, 164, 168–69) provide empirical evidence that larger government does not necessarily mean more corruption, and may even mean less.

19   While apologists have often cited this fact as one of the advantages of communism, three points must be remembered. First, most types of economy enjoy impressive growth rates in postwar reconstruction periods. Second, the same is true of economies undergoing the transition from primarily agricultural to primarily industrial. Finally, some official statisticians from the communist world have in recent years admitted that they falsified — enhanced — growth rate data for political reasons (for evidence from the former USSR and Bulgaria see L. Holmes 1997b, 203), so that we shall never be certain that the growth rates reported by communist states were accurate. Given these three points, it becomes obvious why the apparently high growth rates in many communist states in the 1950s and 1960s may have been less impressive than they initially appear.

20   It is acknowledged that several post-communist states have seen further increases, often marked ones, both in poverty levels (the proportion of citizens below the poverty line) and in the gap between rich and poor — as seen in increasing gini coefficients, which reflect income inequality (see Milanovic 1998). A partial exception to this trend is Poland, where the increase in the gini coefficient has been modest (Keane and Prasad 2001).

21   A near complete set of annual GDP growth rates from 1989 to 2001 for each of the CEE and CIS countries can be found in Buiter, Lago, Fried, and Sanfey eds. 2001, 15. Another useful source for GDP statistics is the web site of the United Nations Development Programme.

22   For a pithy introduction to two interpretations of the concept of path dependency see Henderson and Robinson 1997, 30–31, 39. Beyer and Wielgohs (2001) highlight some of the limitations of the approach when applied to post-communist states.

23   The transition issue has been hotly debated — see Schmitter and Karl 1994; Bunce 1995a; Bunce 1995b; Karl and Schmitter 1995; Linz and Stepan 1996; Markwick 1996; Carothers 2002.

24   Both factors have also been linked to the apparent marked increase in funding-related political party scandals in the West in recent years.

25   For Prime Minister Jan Olszewski arguing this on Polish radio see *SWB/EE*, 13 January 1992; President Wałęsa also made this point publicly — *SWB/EE*, 14 October 1992 — as did the Bulgarian interior minister Viktor Mikhaylov in January 1994 — *SWB/EE*, 24 January 1994.

26   This point is strongly suggested by the correlation between corruption levels and bureaucratic arbitrariness (or regulatory discretion) identified in Hessel and Murphy 1998, esp. chart III.

27   An analysis of the Chinese economic reforms and their impact on corruption, which was a bestseller in the PRC itself, is a book by He Qinglian whose title could be translated as *The Pitfalls of Modernization* or *The Traps of Modernization* (1998). There is no English-language edition; for a summary of the argument and an analysis of the context in which the book was published see *Far Eastern Economic Review*, 22 October 1998, 12–14.

28   For example, the Vagnorius government in Lithuania announced in April 1992 that government and public service officials would not be paid until the country's debts had been paid off — *Express Chronicle*, 6 April 1992.

29   The reference here is to a conventional socioeconomic conception of a bourgeoisie (a capitalist class), not the cultural bourgeoisie referred to in Eyal, Szelényi, and Townsley 1998.

30   I have used the term "arguably," since some of the CEE and CIS students whom I taught in Poland in 2001 and 2002 contended that the West was simply not interested in their countries. One of them cited the Marshall Plan as evidence of how much could be achieved through political will, even when America's own economy was still shaky after the Second World War. Against this, I pointed out the argument of analysts such as Hannes Adomeit that in real terms, allowing for inflation and variable exchange rates, the German government pumped more funds into the former GDR in one year, 1992, than the United States did into all the European beneficiaries of Marshall aid in the five years from 1948 to 1952 (for some figures see *Pravda*, 9 September 1992, 2). Even so, the impact was perceived by many residents of the former GDR as minimal. There is categorically no intention here to belittle the substantial efforts made by either the Americans or the (West) Germans. Rather, the point is that the scale of investment or aid needed to make much difference in the post-communist world in the early 1990s was beyond even the capacities of the affluent West, however much political will there may have been.

31   There were various reasons for this reluctance. Perhaps the most important was that many CEE countries, having just escaped the claws of one major power (the USSR), were anxious not to become subordinate to another. Many Czechs, still remembering 1938 and its aftermath, were par-

ticularly apprehensive about potential German influence. Quite why Russia under Putin has been sending out mixed messages about foreign investment is less obvious, though Russia's ongoing identity problems are probably part of the answer.

32   The definition of the *nomenklatura* provided here is highly truncated and simplified, partly because I have assumed that most readers will be familiar with the concept. But for those who are not, or who want more detailed analyses, useful starting points include Harasymiw 1969, Burns 1987, and Rigby 1988.

33   Hanley (2000) provides persuasive evidence that nomenklatura privatization was far more widespread in Hungary than in Poland, for instance, which he explains primarily in terms of different privatization policies. It is generally accepted that Russia was particularly prone to this phenomenon — although it is difficult to believe that the rate would be much higher than the "more than 50 percent of state assets" allegedly transferred to members of the Bulgarian nomenklatura (this statistic is claimed to be an official one from the Bulgarian privatization agency — see *BPCWR*, 27 February to 5 March 1999). For further analyses see Frydman, Murphy, and Rapaczynski 1996; Kryshta-novskaya and White 1996; and, for a somewhat different perspective, Rigby 1999.

34   One of Klaus's best-known quotations in this context is his comment to Howard Golden: "Jay Gould and Vanderbilt were robber barons, but one generation later they were respected people" (cited in the *Age* (Melbourne), 5 December 1997, § B, 8).

35   Also private meetings with Professor Kamiński in Warsaw, 5 and 6 February 1997. Professor Kamiński was at one stage head of the Polish chapter of TI. For his recent arguments on post-communist corruption see Kamiński and Kamiński 2004.

36   According to Rees (1995, 20), between 1979 and 1995 Thatcher's government reduced the number of British public (civil) servants by almost 300,000 — from 732,000 to 440,000; it originally intended to reduce their numbers even more drastically, to a mere 200,000, by some time in the 1990s (Haque 1996, 514). Admittedly, the number of bureaucrats has increased in some post-communist states in comparison with the late communist era, as noted above. But there have been either actual or threatened severe cutbacks in other states, in which the point about insecurity is valid.

37   I disagree with Haque on one point. The level of accountability has generally increased under neoliberalism; it is responsibility as a public norm that suffers (see Gregory 1995).

38   In 1992 Viktor Chernomyrdin, later the Russian prime minister, argued that Russia needed a market, not a bazaar. On one level this comment

was about having organized capitalism rather than the small-scale and some-what chaotic arrangements of less developed economies.

39   One of the ironies of neoliberalism is that states have not in general reduced expenditure through privatization and outsourcing — for data on the percentage of GDP being spent by states on welfare see Castles 2002. Another irony is that in practice, regulation often increases rather than decreases as states seek to offload their responsibilities; this has certainly been the case in neoliberal Australia. It appears that the more the state seeks to reduce its responsibilities toward citizens, the more litigious society becomes. To give the appearance of helping citizens to look after themselves, judiciaries often award huge sums for accidents and the like. This practice leads to ridiculous situations in which the fear of litigation and an inability to obtain insurance results in the termination or severe curtailment of all sorts of legitimate and even necessary activities previously available to citizens (such as obstetrics). This in turn leads to pressure on states to do something. A typical reaction is to introduce more regulations, in an endeavor to delineate more clearly the responsibilities of each partner in all kinds of social interactions, and to police the observance of these regulations. Unfortunately, to quote a presenter at Vice President Al Gore's conference in February 1999 on fighting corruption among justice and security officials, "The more permits, licenses, quotas, concessions and allocations — the more there will be of corruption" ("Combating Corruption in Poland" 1999, 12). If it is true that more regulation leads to increased corruption (it can do so if the state monitors observance of its own regulations; and litigation against the state itself is likely to increase its proclivity to do so), then such developments may have an effect on corruption opposite from that putatively intended by almost all states and neo-liberals.

40   To those for whom late communist power remains essentially syn-onymous with Stalinism and totalitarianism, the arbitrariness and insecurity of neoliberalism may seem to have much in common with the communist approach. In fact, and perhaps in response to Stalinism, later communist leaderships typically granted high levels of security to their bureaucracies. This is exemplified well by Leonid Brezhnev's "stability of cadres" policy in the Soviet Union. This approach, which made state officials feel much more secure, is almost certainly one reason why the economic reforms of the 1960s were so ineffectual: those officials most directly responsible for implementing them were also those who had most to lose by them, so that they often obstructed policy changes.

41   For the sake of simplicity, I have in essence collapsed the Rhineland and Scandinavian welfare models here. For a sophisticated analysis of the

differences between them, as well as a detailed examination of how both differ from the American model, see Esping-Anderson 1990.

42   It is acknowledged that most of continental Europe did not travel down the neoliberal path as far as the United Kingdom did. That they did not is reflected in the German government's perceived need in 2003–4, and then the Italian government's in 2004, to introduce more radical (neoliberal) reform, which resulted in widespread protest and strikes in both countries. Nevertheless, major reformist steps were already taken in the 1980s and 1990s.

43   New Zealand's privatization process was also modest and gradual in comparison with that in most post-communist states. This — together with the aforementioned size variable, and the enduring effects of a tradition of responsible public service — helps to explain why such a neoliberal state can fare so well in CPIs. This said, New Zealand has had its share of corruption scandals in recent years; for a brief listing see L. Holmes 1998b, while a fuller and more up-to-date analysis is in Gregory 2002. In early 2001 no fewer than four members of the New Zealand cabinet had to resign because of allegations of corruption.

44   On the changing nature of policing in western states in recent years, including the rise of private policing, see for example Bayley and Shearing 1996; Shearing and Stenning eds. 1987; *Economist*, 19 April 1997, 19–22; and Button 2002. L. Johnston (1992), however, argues that there has always been private policing, and recent changes are less innovative than they appear, while Nalla and Newman (1991) even maintain that in recent years there has been a greater increase in public than private policing.

45   Observant readers will notice that this list is alphabetical. This is deliberate, as part of an attempt not to "steer" respondents. The actual sequence of factors varied in each of the four surveys, since the list (apart from the final factor) was alphabetical in each of the four languages.

46   A survey conducted by VTSIOM at more or less the same time as our own produced rather similar results (unsurprisingly). Admittedly the rankings were not identical with ours. Thus "the current economic and financial crisis" — which could be seen to overlap with our inflation response — was only the second-most often cited cause of Russian corruption; the first was lenient treatment by the authorities (Levada 2000b, esp.13), which was the fourth-most common response in our results. But the maximum percentage difference between the five most frequently cited causes in the VTSIOM survey was only six, suggesting that little should be made of the slight differences in rank ordering in the two sets of responses.

47   According to the European Bank for Reconstruction and Develop-

ment, the inflation rate in Bulgaria in 1999 (the last full year before our surveys were conducted) was 0.7 percent, while in Poland it was 7.3 percent. Conversely, it was 10.1 percent in Hungary and 86.1 percent in Russia — Buiter, Lago, Fris, and Sanfey eds. 2001, 16. Surprisingly, the rates for the whole of 2000 were rather similar for Bulgaria (10.4 percent), Hungary (9.7), and Poland (10.1); Russia's declined substantially, although it was still more than double the Polish rate, at 20.8 percent (International Monetary Fund 2001, 119). One possible explanation for the apparent discrepancy in Central Europe between our survey results and these inflation rates is that many respondents believed that corruption was not a particularly recent phenomenon, whereas changes in inflation rates — especially the increases in Bulgaria and Poland in 2000 — were recent, and therefore did not provide a particularly good explanation for official malfeasance. This is not the only possibility, of course; another obvious one is that respondents in Bulgaria and Poland simply saw other, more persuasive long-term explanations for corruption than the somewhat volatile inflation rates.

48   This said, it is worth recalling that many observers were surprised when Poland in 1993 and Hungary in 1994 elected communist successor parties to power. Poland did so again in 2001, while the communist successors in Hungary narrowly lost to the main opposition party in the same year. The nostalgia factor seems to have reached further back than the communist period in Bulgaria: in their elections in 2001, a new political party led by former King Simeon II topped the polls. In the Czech elections of June 2002, the largely unreformed communists were seen by many to have been the most successful party, even though they finished third, since they improved their performance so dramatically, securing some 20 percent of the vote. In Russia the communists were the largest single party in the legislature between 1995 and 2003, but they were relegated to second place in the parliamentary elections of December 2003.

49   Kuz'minov (1999, thesis 9) is just one of many analysts who have argued this. The results of the Bulgarian and Polish elections of 2001, and the Russian election of 2003, provide solid evidence of the still fragile nature of so-called party systems in CEE and the CIS, thus endorsing the point about crystallization.

50   Although China is not often seen as a weak state, some analysts maintain that it is. One such is Wang Shaoguang (2003), who measures China against six tasks that he believes must be fulfilled properly if a state is to qualify as effective. These are to monopolize the legitimate use of force; to extract resources; to shape national identity and mobilize consent; to regulate society and the economy; to maintain the internal coherence of state institutions; and to redistribute resources. According to Wang, China falls short on all six.

51   Hellman's argument is similar to, though more developed than, one made by a leading Russian specialist on corruption, Lev Timofeyev (1994). For an argument that CEE corruption is on one level a form of protectionism against foreign competition see Krastev 1998.

52   At least most of the time: Poland's economy hit problems in the early twenty-first century, having been identified as the "tiger" economy of CEE in the 1990s. By 2003 growth had picked up again, though high unemployment remained a serious problem.

53   There are always unique or customized explanations as well as generic ones for the different perceived rates of corruption in different countries. For instance, some Estonians have argued that two of the reasons why their country appears less corrupt than its Baltic neighbors are its greater proximity to the relatively incorrupt Nordic states and the commensurately greater influence that it receives from them, and the lesser cultural tendency of Estonians to wash their dirty linen in public. While it is difficult to test the latter argument empirically, it is worth noting that the electoral campaigns in the run-up to the elections of 1999 did not focus on political scandals, of which corruption is the most common source in many post-communist countries — see *Baltic Times* 5, no. 144 (1999). But note also the persuasive argument by Taagepera (2002) that the Baltic states remain much less Nordic in their attitudes, and far more strongly influenced by their Soviet past, than most of their citizens wish to believe.

54   I am indebted to Janine Wedel for raising this issue with me at a meeting in Warsaw in August 2004, and forcing me to address more overtly the peculiarities of the Russian case.

55   The reasons for Poland's recent deterioration in terms of corruption, and the relationship of this deterioration to our argument concerning neo-liberalism, are addressed in chapter 8.

7: MEASURES AGAINST CORRUPTION

1   In 2000, as part of Bulgaria's preparations for entering the European Union and its campaign against corruption, there was a proposal to amend the constitution so as to restrict immunity for both parliamentarians and judges. Unfortunately the Constitutional Court ruled in May 2001 that a provision granting immunity to parliamentary candidates during election campaigns must remain in force — thus limiting the potential effect of the amendments (*EECR* 9, no. 3:10; 10, nos. 2–3:11). Bulgaria was still being criticized by external agencies in mid-2002 for granting judges too much immunity (*EECR* 11, no. 4–12, no. 1:13). However, Bulgarian judges' immu-

nity was substantially reduced in September 2003, with the enactment of constitutional amendments that permitted dismissal for abuse of office; the European Union warmly welcomed these changes. The Central Electoral Commission in Russia refused to register a number of political parties in the lead-up to the elections in December 1999 because they included alleged criminals seeking to avoid prosecution by securing parliamentary immunity (*EECR* 9, nos. 1–2:35–36). However, Shelley (2000, 71) points out that a number of so-called oligarchs — whose fortunes had in many cases been made in questionable circumstances — were able to slip through this net and secure immunity. Certainly there have been allegations in the Russian press that it is possible to buy one's way onto a party electoral list; in an article entitled (in translation) "How Much Does a Seat in the Duma Cost?" (*Izvestiya*, 29 June 1995, 4), it is claimed that those seeking inclusion on a party list could often secure it through payment of 300–450 million roubles in November 1993, but would have had to offer approximately 1,000 times more than this by 1994. Another article from about the same time (*Izvestiya*, 6 April 1995, 4) actually included detailed data on the number of criminal deputies and the nature of their crimes. But the picture is not all bad for those seeking greater justice in Russia. For example, some of those who sought immunity in the mid-1990s by being elected to the Duma subsequently saw their immunity removed. An example is Sergei Mavrodi, who went on the run in 1996 and was caught and charged with large-scale fraud in February 2003. In July 2000 Russia adopted a new law, effective January 2002, stripping regional governors of their parliamentary immunity in the Russian upper house (details in *EECR* 9, no. 3:35; see too Ross 2003, 38). A final point is that some parliamentarians need to fear more than losing just their immunity. Shortly after the Russian parliamentarian and faction leader Vladimir Golovlev lost his immunity in July 2002, he was assassinated (in August) — according to some, because of his involvement in corrupt activities relating to privatization in the early 1990s. (see *Guardian*, 22 August 2002, and *Russia Reform Monitor* 961 — online at *http://www.afpc.org/rrm/rrm961.htm*, visited January 2003).

2   Eventually the allegations and evidence concerning Sekuła became so embarrassing that in November 1996 his immunity was lifted. He died in May 2000, after being shot three times in March; a two-year investigation failed to determine whether it was a case of murder or suicide. On Sekuła see also Roszkowski 1997, 100. Article 105 of the current (1997) Polish Constitution makes it clear that the Sejm can lift an MP's parliamentary immunity, which is not sacrosanct. In the early years of the twenty-first century at least one Polish politician, the populist Andrzej Lepper, came close to losing his immunity on more than one occasion (for destruction of Polish wheat in-

tended for the European Union, and for making apparently groundless allegations of corruption against fellow politicians).

3   Another group that has all too often escaped punishment because of immunity is judges; for an article criticizing this in the Russian context see *Izvestiya*, 10 March 1995, 5.

4   This means that while parliamentarians lose their immunity once they lose their parliamentary seat, they can never be tried for most actions committed while they were MPs.

5   For a complaint about this in the Russian media see *Izvestiya*, 19 August 1997, 5. On a claim by the Hungarian chief prosecutor in 1996 that only a small fraction of corruption cases were detected, and that of these a maximum of one in ten resulted in prosecution (let alone conviction), see *SWB/EE*, 24 December 1996.

6   Because of the time it takes to investigate crimes and bring them to court, it is not appropriate to argue that just over half of the cases recorded in 1986 resulted in convictions; the data cannot be sufficiently disaggregated to permit this kind of interrogation. But it is appropriate to compare cases recorded with cases resulting in convictions across different years.

7   In June 2002 Lizner's lawyer sought a retrial, claiming new evidence — *Prague Tribune* 83, 2002.

8   As the judicial branch of the state occasionally makes very clear, it believes that senior politicians often treat corrupt officials too leniently. Thus in November 1998 the Hungarian justice minister refused to endorse a pardon that President Göncz wanted to grant to a senior banker; this was apparently the first time a Hungarian minister had refused to countersign a presidential decision (*RFE/RL*, 11 November 1998).

9   On the methods used by Russian provocateurs to catch bribe takers see *Izvestiya*, 24 November 1995, 7.

10   *Fawlty Towers* was a British television comedy series; one of its salient (and most amusing) features was that things kept going wrong, despite brave attempts at good organization.

11   Another communist state tending toward post-communism, Vietnam, also sometimes executes officials for corruption.

12   There is now a small but vocal movement against the death penalty in China.

13   While we have criticized the general policy of being too lenient with those found guilty of corruption, we make an exception with regard to suspending (or revoking) the death penalty. Another recent example is that of the former mayor of Shenyang, Mu Suixin, who had his death sentence suspended for two years in October 2001 (*BR* 44 no. 43:6). Apparently he

died in prison of cancer in 2002 (PRC News on line at http://www.prcnews.com/archives/cat_chinas_legal_labyrinth.html, visited June 2004).

14   This indirectly highlights the point that those culturalists who argue that 'the West' focuses on the individual, while 'the East' focuses far more on the collective, may be oversimplifying.

15   It is worth recalling that Puritans used shaming as a form of punishment some three centuries ago. However, for Australians being shocked at a child shoplifter being publicly shamed see *The Australian*, 6 March 1998, 3.

16   However, it appears that the lesson may not have been learnt for very long, or at least not throughout the whole company. In August 2001, the Slovak finance ministry filed a lawsuit, following allegations that a Siemens employee had attempted to bribe the chair of the commission charged with nominating the successful bidder for a contract to provide a new information system for the Slovak state treasury (Brusis, Kempe, and van Meurs 2003, 185).

17   The Hessen ban on contracts lasted only six months (Hawley 2000, 3), suggesting a weaker commitment to blacklisting than might be desirable for real effectiveness. Another possible sign of the sometimes lukewarm approach to fighting corruption in Germany was the rejection in 2002 by the upper house (Bundesrat) of a bill designed to establish a public register of companies proven to have used corrupt or otherwise illegal means in bidding for public procurement contracts. Those opposed to the bill claimed that they were not rejecting its underlying principles and would produce a modified version for consideration (*TI* Q, September 2002, 12), though no such legislation has been passed yet.

18   There had been such a unit in the 1980s, but it was abolished shortly after the collapse of communist power in Poland.

19   The formal title of the office was Commissioner for Citizens' Rights, and its first occupant was Professor Ewa Letowska.

20   In many countries, including Hungary, there are several ombudspersons, dealing with different areas of citizen concern; the focus here is simply on whether the principle of an ombudsperson has been officially accepted.

21   I am indebted to Professor Andrzej Rzepliński of Warsaw University for making this report available to me and helping me with the translation of it into English.

22   On the problems of implementing the Polish legislation see Golik 2000.

23   For an analysis of post-communist Russian legislation relating to corruption, and attempts at legislation, see Chuklinov 2003.

24   According to Lopatin (2003, 85), the only part of Russia to have

passed (1994) and been applying a dedicated law on corruption was the Republic of Bashkortostan.

25   For a list of relevant Hungarian legislation see UNODCCP and UNICRI 2000, 16–17. The Hungarian legislation evidently still needs fine tuning and supplementation, however. Thus the head of the office of the prime minister was obliged to resign in March 2003 after it was discovered that a contract to audit state-run companies had been awarded to a law firm in which he was a partner. But Prime Minister Péter Medgyessy moved swiftly to address potential conflicts of interest among members of the government, ordering that a draft code of ethics for cabinet members be prepared, and encouraging his ministers publicly to declare all interests in state-run enterprises (EECR 12, nos. 2–3 (2003): 22).

26   For a list of Bulgarian anticorruption legislation to mid-1999 see *Demokratsiya*, 12 June 1999, as summarized in BPCWR, 12–18 June 1999.

27   Author's meeting with Jaskiernia in Warsaw, 27 March 1996; see also Jaskiernia 1995, 33–35, and SWB/EE, 8 June 1992.

28   The Hungarian Code of Ethics for Public Officials is produced by the Hungarian College of Public Officials and is on line at http://www.b-m.hu/kozszolgalat/etika/angol/aetika_21.htm, visited June 2004.

29   Three post-communist states — Czechia, Hungary, and Poland — were admitted to the OECD in 1995–96. Slovakia was admitted in 2000. These four are the only post-communist member states of the OECD.

30   For an overview of measures being taken in China to counter money laundering, plus data on the scale of this problem, see BR 45, no. 31 (2002): 16–19.

31   The new Bulgarian act does not extend to pharmaceuticals procurements, about which there has been considerable controversy.

32   Only one chapter (Sakwa 2000) in R. Williams ed. 2000a is on a post-communist state. In 2000 Bulgaria introduced draft new legislation on party financing, after a number of allegations in 1999 of corrupt funding of the UDF and other parties (EECR 9, nos. 1–2: 9).

33   For the head of the Bulgarian police acknowledging this see SWB/EE, 27 March 1997.

34   An even better solution than that described here is to introduce fully automated speed cameras. But the initial investment in these is expensive.

35   While they may often increase inequality, flat rates should have a beneficial effect on the development of a reasonably affluent middle class or bourgeoisie that is important, as argued below, to consolidating democracy in post-communist transition states. Moreover, the extent to which flat-tax regimes increase overall income inequality is contested; in some states, puta-

tively redistributive systems are so complex and permit so many concessions that the wealthy can virtually — and legally — avoid paying income tax at all.

36   It is usually assumed that transition states can and should learn vicariously from the experiences of established democracies. But there are times when the opposite also holds. Thus the United Kingdom introduced changes in the mid-1990s designed to encourage police forces to seek up to 1 percent of their annual income from private sponsorship (*Times*, 6 January 1997, 6); apparently the British authorities were either unaware of, or did not heed, the corruption-related experiences of countries such as Poland.

37   For further details on the Singaporean approach to corruption see Quah 1995, which also provides details (413) of the enormous salaries paid to top officials; these were in excess of $25,000 a month as long ago as 1989. For evidence that Russia was about to raise the salaries of various officials specifically to reduce corruption see *Izvestiya*, 23 June 2000; it did so again in 2004, the offices for which salaries were raised including that of president. An example of a senior Bulgarian official (the minister of state administration Mario Tagarinski) calling for higher official salaries to reduce corruption is in *Standart*, 17 June 1999, summarized in *Bulgarian Media on Corruption Weekly Review*, 12–18 June 1999. And for a Chinese debate on the advantages and disadvantages of raising salaries as part of the anticorruption struggle see *BR* 45, no. 29:26–27; China has substantially raised the incomes of some officials, including military officers, since the late 1990s (see for example *CD*, 15 March 2000).

38   It should be noted that many of the "privileges" identified by Torański would be seen as perfectly legitimate perquisites of the post in most western societies; on this see too Tarchalski 2000. At a presentation at the Kennan Institute in mid-2004, Professor Yevgenia Albats claimed that if various benefits are factored in, high-level Russian bureaucrats receive an annual salary equivalent to more than $500,000, which in her view helps to explain why so few Russian bureaucrats leave the public sector for the private sector. She also argued that the most successful post-communist transitions have been in countries that forced the previous communist bureaucrats out of office, and where lustration has played a significant role (which it did not in Russia: all from *Johnson's Russia List* 8268, 25 June 2004).

39   Stanczyk also pointed out that many officers were experiencing difficulties in obtaining fuel for their police cars, which is a clear indication of the resources problem faced by Poland and most other post-communist states during the 1990s.

40   The Polish interior minister informed the Polish Sejm at the end of March 1996 that the size of the Polish police force was to grow to 126,000 officers, which would have been a welcome development to Stanczyk (*SWB/EE*, 1 April 1996). Note also that according to a statement in September 1997 by Leszek Miller,

then the Polish minister of internal affairs and administration, increasing police salaries should result in less corruption in the force (*SWB/EE*, 12 September 1997).

41   At the time of the announcement, the deputy minister rejected the popular notion that traffic police are highly corrupt; but his actions may have spoken louder than his words.

42   In the late 1990s the Chinese authorities announced their intention substantially to reduce staffs — but with no increase in salaries to those still employed (*South China Morning Post*, 26 May 1998).

43   In this context, Verheijen and Dimitrova (1996, 214, 218) are justified in implicitly criticizing the Bulgarian authorities for giving so little public acknowledgment to a group of high-ranking officials from the ministry of finance, who successfully concluded an agreement with the London club of creditors that was likely to result in a much-needed increase in foreign investment in Bulgaria. The same authors, writing with Tomasz Anusiewicz (2001, 88), have more recently argued in a similar vein that a carrot approach — praising outstanding civil servants — is likely to be more effective in curbing corruption than the ultimately counterproductive approach of making false allegations of corruption.

44   Unfortunately, like so many of the methods considered here, this one can have unintended negative consequences. Some Hungarian customs officers have apparently been so successful that with their bonuses, they have been earning more than parliamentarians (private communication from TI, September 2004). This has led to some disgruntlement — and could conceivably even be used by some MPs as self-justification for corruption.

45   For statistical evidence, based on a sample of more than a hundred countries, that corruption levels are lower in countries in which female representation in parliament is higher see Dollar, Fisman, and Gatti 1999. See too Transparency International 2000b. Unfortunately, our point about corruption and affluence pertains here too: there is an issue of causal directionality.

46   It is true that some politically sensitive items published in Hong Kong are not published at all in the PRC's press, or else are published later. The point being made in the text here refers specifically to the top leadership's statements about the corrosive effects of corruption.

47   The reader is reminded of the Bulgarian survey data from 1997–98 cited in chapter 5, which appear to support this point. For an evaluation of what are called cleanup campaigns that is both cross-polity (twenty-five countries, mainly in the Middle East and North Africa) and time-series (seventeen years) see Gillespie and Okruhlik 1991; the authors conclude (92), frustratingly if honestly, that it remains unclear whether such campaigns "actually reduce the incidence of corrupt transactions."

48   For data from the World Values Survey indicating the comparatively low levels in post-communist states in the mid-1990s of membership in church and religious organizations see Howard 2002, 160, and Howard 2003, 64.

49   The Polish Ministry of Education was to begin teaching school-children about corruption and the fight against it in late 2003 — *Gazeta Wyborcza*, 11 August 2003.

50   China established its first Anti-Corruption School, based at Hunan University, in the early twenty-first century. It accepts both undergraduates and postgraduates (*TI Q*, March 2003, 14).

51   By early 1996 all former Soviet states except Kyrgyzstan, Tajikistan, and Turkmenistan were members of Interpol. On this and developing linkages between Interpol and Russia in the 1990s see Tillier 1996. For the record, Kyrgyzstan joined Interpol soon after Tillier's article was published; Tajikistan and Turkmenistan were still not members as of mid-2004.

52   Although they have in general been more reluctant than other CEE governments to seek foreign assistance in fighting corruption, even the Czech authorities sought help from the FBI in dealing with the banking scandals involving state officials that emerged in 1996 (Slay 1996, 43).

53   On cooperation between the United States and Russia, and why it tends to be closer and more successful on issues relating to organized crime than to high-level corruption, see Shelley 2002.

54   For a useful survey of various anticorruption laws and norms around the world (labeled best practices in the source), which can be used by countries seeking to learn from others' experiences and legislation, see Pope 2000, 305–36.

55   As part of the process described here, the state can involve professional experts from the private sector, which represents one form of cooperation between the state and civil society. An example of this occurred in the Russian city of Krasnoyarsk — see Kleshko 2001.

56   Two of the best-known and troublesome (to the state) oligarchs, Boris Berezovskii and Vladimir Gusinskii, were not invited to the July meeting; they were already in open conflict with Putin, whose administration had started a high profile clamp-down on them in May and June. On the Russian oligarchs see Freeland 2000; Klebnikov 2000; Tsyganov 2001; Hoffman 2002.

57   Some argue that Putin had reneged on this agreement by 2003. In fact, at the time of writing he still appeared to be attacking only those oligarchs who he believed had broken the agreement. This said, the situation was in flux, and some investigations had been reopened.

58   There have been rumors that Viktor Yushchenko, newly elected president of Ukraine in 2005, offered a similar immunity deal to his predecessor,

Leonid Kuchma; but these have been denied by Yushchenko (*Economist*, 19 March 2005, 54).

59   Though see the reference in chapter 6 to Wang Shaoguang's arguments.

60   Switzerland introduced progressively tougher laws on money laundering in 1990, 1992, and 1998, because of both external pressure and a very committed advocate within the country. However, it appears that the Swiss Bankers' Association continues to resist pressure to change its traditionally secretive methods — see the *Age* (Melbourne), 11 September 2002, "Business," 6. This claim is partly endorsed in a paper by the CEO of the Swiss Bankers' Association — U. Roth 2003, esp. 8–10. For a detailed analysis and critique of past Swiss practices in this area see Trepp 1996.

61   To give recipient countries and businesses in emerging market economies an opportunity to rank the countries and firms perceived as most likely to offer them bribes, TI introduced a second rank-ordered table in 1999. This was the Bribe Payers' Index, or BPI; an updated version was published in 2002. Since it focuses on countries that are major investors or donors in other countries, the list is much shorter than the CPI: it ranked only nineteen countries in 1999 and twenty-one in 2002. The concept of the BPI is fair enough; it can be likened to legislation and policing methods that target sex workers' clients as well as the sex workers themselves. This said, some of those who had been critics of the CPI — and had performed relatively poorly in it — performed poorly in the BPI too. Of the countries targeted in this study, only one was included in the BPI in 1999. This was the PRC, which was ranked as the most likely of the nineteen countries in the survey to offer bribes to foreign officials. In 2002 the BPI included two of our five states, the PRC and Russia; they enjoyed the dubious honour of being ranked twentieth and twenty-first.

62   The BPIs referred to in the previous note suggest that American companies are more likely than Australian, Dutch, French, or German companies to offer bribes in "emerging market economies," the point in the previous paragraph notwithstanding. Moreover, the Foreign Corrupt Practices Act (1977) itself contains a number of loopholes. For instance, facilitation payments by companies (to ensure the granting of permits, visas, etc.) are not prohibited by the act, and can thus be interpreted as legitimized. On this, and how the Watergate scandal was a major impetus for adoption of the act, see Hoeffner 2001, esp. 58–59. On the influence of the Lockheed affair see Rosenthal 1989, esp. 704.

63   For this claim, and an analysis of early measures being taken by the European Union, see *TI Newsletter*, September 1996, 10.

64   The number of ratifications had increased to twenty-nine by early 2001 (*TI Newsletter*, March 2001, 5).

65   Like so much anticorruption legislation, the OECD convention is proving less effective than many had hoped. As Peter Eigen, chairman of TI, has pointed out (*TI Q*, December 2002, 1), five years after the convention was agreed to not a single company had been convicted of breaching it. Moreover, a substantial proportion of companies in major western states were still unaware of the convention by late 2002 — almost 50 percent in the United Kingdom and 62 percent in Germany, according to one survey (*TI Q*, December 2002, 4). For a history of the OECD Convention see Pieth 2003, while Heimann 2004 provides details of how and why the OECD convention is proving less effective than it should be, and proposes possible solutions.

66   Of the FATF's thirty-one member states as of mid-2002, none was a post-communist state. At the end of 2004 Russia remained the only post-communist member state.

67   Of potential significance is the United Nations Convention against Corruption, launched in Mexico in December 2003. This has been described by Peter Eigen as "the first comprehensive international framework for dealing with domestic and foreign bribery in the public and private sectors" (*TI Q*, December 2003, 1) and by Naím (2005, 96) as being, "for those in the trenches, the crowning event of the war on corruption." However, as of early 2003 many countries were still demonstrating a serious lack of commitment to some of the convention's basic principles, suggesting that it could make a very limited impact — see *TI Q*, March 2003, 4. Moreover, the convention does not become effective anyway until at least thirty states have ratified it, and Rooke (2004, 111) does not envisage it entering into force before "the end of 2005 at the earliest."

68   The World Bank names on its web site companies that it has blacklisted because of corrupt practices.

69   Another example of an anticorruption policy tailored by a western agency to the CEE and former Soviet Union countries is that adopted by the U.S. Agency for International Development in December 1997 — see Henderson 1998.

70   For a pithy analysis of some of the flaws, contradictions, and hypocrisy in the European Union's anticorruption policies for CEE see Cirtautas 2001.

71   On how the World Bank has become ever more overtly political because of its work on corruption see Marquette 2004.

72   Given the focus here on four CEE and CIS states, it is worth noting the suggestion by Feiler (2002) that similar problems may arise in connection with a forestry project in Bulgaria.

73   For examples of facilitation being used by major TNCs, see the "Cor-

porate News" section occasionally included in the *TI Newsletter* (for example in March 2001). The reader is reminded that facilitation payments for expediting slow government processes are — disappointingly — permitted under the Foreign Corrupt Practices Act (1977) referred to earlier.

74 For recent analyses of reputational risk see Larkin 2003, Rayner 2003.

75 In China particularly, there is evidence of private companies threatening legal action, ultimately because of official corruption. Perhaps the most familiar example is that of McDonald's, which lost a prime restaurant location in Beijing largely as a result of official corruption. McDonald's eventually agreed in late 1996 to move its flagship outlet in central Beijing, after receiving compensation from the municipal authorities. This story has been captured allegorically in the best-known Chinese novel about corruption in the 1990s, *Tian Nu* (Heaven's Wrath), by the pseudonymous Fang Wen (the book is officially banned). For an anthropological analysis of McDonald's in Beijing, and a brief reference to the legal case (215–16 n. 27), see Yan Yunxiang 1997.

76 Several Elf executives went on trial in January 2001 in connection with this case, and were eventually sentenced to both fines and prison terms (up to five years). But these were meted out to individuals; the proposal here is for extremely high fines or other punishments to companies themselves. For a brief introduction to the Elf affair and the role of the Treuhandanstalt (German privatization agency) see Doublet 2001; Yates 2001 provides a fuller analysis of the Elf scandal. Details of some of the penalties are in *TI Q*, December 2003, 3. And for a recent analysis that locates the Elf affair in the larger issue of unethical (including corrupt) behavior in the oil industry generally see Shaxson 2004.

77 An interesting variant on this theme concerns allegations about the Boeing and Airbus corporations, although the case does not involve postcommunist states. In 1994, allegedly, Saudi Arabia canceled a contract that it had signed with Airbus for the supply of airliners, after the CIA claimed that Airbus had bribed Saudi officials to secure the contract. Along somewhat similar lines, and again involving the CIA, a Brazilian contract with the French arms supplier Thomson-CSF was eventually lost to its American competitor Raytheon. This is a highly questionable example of economic espionage and collaboration between the state and the private sector, and in many ways it places the American intelligence service and state in an even worse light than the European aircraft or arms manufacturers. All information from *TI Newsletter*, June 1995; *Washington Post*, 24 July 2000 http://www.fas.org/irp/news/2000/07/irp-000724-echelon.htm, visited March 2003.

78 There were at least two cases during the 1980s of attempts by American corporations to sue other corporations for lost revenue in the wake of

overseas contracts allegedly secured through bribery; one concerned Indonesia, another Nigeria. But the courts dismissed the cases for want of jurisdic-
tion. It is precisely this kind of scenario that prompts the proposal here for an
international court to hear such cases.

79   It is interesting to compare our findings on Russia with some other
survey results cited in Owens 2002, 107. According to these, the proportion
of Russians who believe the reports in their national media has declined
markedly, from 70 percent in 1990 to 40 percent in 1996 and a mere 13 percent
in 2000.

80   For an early warning on media censorship under Putin see Panfilov
2000. In May 2000, in a case involving allegations made by *Życie* against
President Kwaśniewski, a Warsaw court rejected the defense's argument that
before publishing allegations journalists should only be expected to have
made investigations as thorough as was feasible, not to have incontrovertible
proof. Admittedly the court did not require the newspaper to pay compensation, only to apologize to the president. But the president won the moral high
ground, and a message had been sent to the media. The case was not related
to reporting on corruption as such, but the general principle pertained (all
from *EECR* 9, no. 3:31).

81   For an early collection of papers on this, albeit with specific reference
to the United States, see Nader, Petkas, and Blackwell eds. 1972.

82   For an early analysis of TI's techniques see Eigen 1996. Details on the
visits to Hungary, Poland, and the Czech Republic can be found in Transparency International 1996a; the information about the imminent establishment of national chapters is from *TI Newsletter*, September 1996: 8–9.

83   TI also sent missions to Slovakia and Romania during 1996, in May. As
in Czechia, only to an even greater extent, TI received a lukewarm welcome
from both the Slovak and Romanian governments (Transparency International 1996b). The visit to Slovakia occurred while Mečiar was still prime
minister—and that to Romania during Iliescu's first presidency, before the
parliamentary elections of November 1996 that resulted in a change of government. Shafir and Ionescu (1997, 52) argue that the main reasons for the
electorate's rejection of Iliescu and the Party of Social Democracy in Romania
(PDSR) in late 1996 were "the country's deteriorating economic performance
combined with recurrent corruption scandals in which PDSR officials or their
protégés were involved." It can be noted that TI planned to send missions to
several other post-communist states in 1997—Albania, Bulgaria, Estonia,
Latvia, Lithuania, and Slovenia—to discuss corruption and how to reduce it.
For the record, all states mentioned except Albania and Slovenia had established national chapters of TI by December 2002; the latter two still had no

chapter by the end of 2004. China appeared about to establish a TI chapter in early 2005 (*TI Q*, September 2004, 6), but still had not done so by March.

84 Skuratov was formally charged with abuse of office on 31 January 2000, but the case was closed in May 2001. On Boldyrev see Whitmore 1998 and Schmemann 1999.

85 Another unfortunate message was sent by the United States during the negotiations for the United Nations Convention against Corruption. The United States refused to agree to a proposal from others (including Russia!) for a mandatory provision on transparency in the financing of political parties, so that the final document was vague and weak on this issue — see Rooke 2004, 112.

86 The tragedy of the commons arises when individuals, unless checked by some authority, can pursue short-term, interest-maximizing activities even though they are aware that doing so is against not only the collective interest but their own longer-term interests — see Hardin 1968.

87 Singapore's score did decline marginally, from 9.26 in 1995 to 8.80 in 1996, and further still to 8.66 in the CPI for 1997. The significance of this trend should not be overstated. Singapore then improved again in the late 1990s, consistently scoring 9.1 in 1998, 1999, and 2000, before improving further in the early 2000s — to 9.2 in 2001, 9.3 in 2002, and 9.4 (its best score ever) in both 2003 and 2004.

88 Hong Kong reverted to Chinese rule in 1997.

89 Constantinescu's decision not to contest the presidential election of 2000 appears to have been based partly on opinion polls that indicated a very low level of support for him. In a public address Constantinescu attributed his presidential ineffectiveness to his failure to combat corruption, and his inability to curb the powers of the security police (*EECR* 9, no. 4:30).

90 Though it must be acknowledged that many post-communist politicians are damned if they do, and damned if they don't — see for example Handelman 2000 on Putin's dilemmas in fighting crime and corruption.

8: CONCLUSIONS

1 Krastev's argument is particularly germane to our critique of neoliberalism. He explains what he sees as the exaggerated focus of so many states and international organizations on post-communist corruption largely in terms of scapegoating — blaming corruption for the often disappointing results of reforms inspired by neoliberalism.

2 Interestingly, only one Catholic or Protestant CEE state, (Catholic)

Croatia, was in group D in 1999. But Croatia has improved its ranking in recent years, and by 2004 it was equal with Poland.

3   In dealing with the latter issue, he has begun to undo some of the good work relating to ownership; by 2004 this was having a destabilizing and hence negative effect on existing and potential foreign investors.

4   The only other still-communist state to be included in the CPI for 2000, Vietnam, fared relatively poorly, ranking 76th out of 90 countries assessed, with a score of 2.5 (and 100th out of 133 countries assessed in 2003, with a score of 2.4—compared with 3.4 for China, which ranked 66th).

5   However, see the argument below about the relationship between authoritarianism and corruption.

6   As mentioned briefly in note 23 to chapter 6, there has been a heated debate on the applicability of the term "transitional." Some analysts prefer the term "transformational." While many writers essentially blur the distinction between these two terms, Bryant and Mokrzycki (1994) make a generally persuasive argument for using "transformation" to refer to processes emerging from the past, and "transition" for processes that focus on destinations. While it can be questioned whether the actual words themselves connote such a distinction, it does make sense to use different terms to describe at least two related but conceptually distinct phenomena. For the record, my own preference is to describe the whole period between the collapse of one type of system and the crystallization of another as transitional, but to distinguish the earlier stages of transition from the later. In the former, which can usefully be called the transformational stage, people are still largely concerned with the legacy of the past and the establishment of new institutions and practices. One useful, though not infallible, yardstick for determining whether a country is still in this transformational stage is to consider the amount of emphasis on lustration or decommunization: the greater the emphasis, the more the society is still dealing with the past, and in this sense the more clearly it is still in the transformational stage. The later stage of transition can be called the consolidational phase. This is far more focused on the future than the past, and on crystallizing and normalizing institutions and practices. The emergence of what can legitimately be called a party system, as distinct from the mere existence of a multiplicity of political parties, is typically one of the indicators of having reached this stage. For a recent overview and critique of the transition literature and debate see Wiarda 2001; Bielasiak (2002, 208) argues that "the structuring of party systems remains to be fully accomplished in many states emerging from the communist experience." If an emphasis on lustration and the still highly volatile nature of party arrangements is taken as a key indicator, a surprisingly large number of post-communist states in CEE were still transformational in the early years of the twenty-first century.

7   For evidence of Kránitz's long-standing interest in corruption see Kránitz 1981. Her last point here accords well with our notion of legislative lag.

8   Typical of this attitude was that of a senior Hungarian official whom I
interviewed in September 1996. In conversation, I mentioned that I had been
in Singapore earlier in the year, and that the authorities there had apparently
been highly successful in bringing corruption down to manageable levels.
Before I could elaborate the kinds of policies adopted in Singapore, the
official smiled and declared that Hungary could also bring corruption under
control if it were prepared to use authoritarian methods. "But we are now a
democratic country," he said. Another example of this attitude is from Bulgaria: in December 1997 members of the opposition opposed a government
proposal to establish a financial police unit that was intended, *inter alia*, to
combat corruption, on the grounds that doing so would appear like an attempt to "revive the police state" (RFE/RL, 9 December 1997).

9   Neoliberalism can undermine the rule of law in western liberal democracies too, for example through secrecy based on so-called commercial-in-
confidence principles, and lenient treatment of corrupt officials by the legal
system. This tendency in turn undermines what has here been called the
bedrock of legal-rational legitimacy. But this is not a necessary scenario, even
under neoliberalism: the comparatively high levels of transparency in New
Zealand constitute one counterfactual, and there is no inherent reason why
corrupt officials cannot be subject to far harsher punishments than is currently the norm.

10   I am indebted to my colleague Mark Considine for pointing this out
to me.

11   Unfortunately it can also result in stagnation; this type of stability is
*dys*functional in the long term.

12   However, the reader is reminded of the survey data cited in chapter 3
suggesting that the Liberal Democrats are actually less prone to this activity
than many other parties.

13   A foreign visitor's first experience of this is often the attempt to obtain
a visa.

14   The best-known allegations were made by Gorbachev. However,
Luzhkov successfully sued the former Soviet leader for libel in connection
with these allegations.

15   Surveys of attitudes toward political party financing were conducted
by the author in late 2003 and early 2004 in six countries, including three of
those studied in this book (Bulgaria, Poland, and Russia). The basic methodology and survey companies were the same as for the surveys conducted in
2000. One question invited respondents to imagine an election in which there
were only two candidates—one somewhat corrupt but highly effective, the

other "squeaky clean" but far less dynamic and effective. The results favoring the somewhat corrupt candidate were uncannily similar in all three post-communist states (though different from two of the West European states that were also surveyed). Thus 23.7 percent of Bulgarians, 23.6 percent of Poles, and 24.5 percent of Russians opted for the first candidate. The differences between the Bulgarians on the one hand and the Poles and Russians on the other showed up in the levels of support for the second candidate and "don't know" responses. These were almost identical in Poland and Russia — with the cleaner candidate receiving 53.1 percent in both countries and "don't know" responses totaling 23.3 percent in Poland and 22.4 percent in Russia. But only 34.3 percent of Bulgarians chose the "clean" candidate, while a staggering 42.0 percent answered "don't know." Vitosha Research, which conducted the survey, was so surprised by the results that it asked respondents why they could not choose; apparently many respondents answered "don't know" because there was no "don't care" category (see note 41 to chapter 4). This response suggests a high level of political alienation — and almost certainly reflects the profound disappointment of many Bulgarians in the performance of the government created under former King Simeon II.

16   This is a highly truncated analysis of the potential functionalities of corruption and its reporting; for a much fuller version, plus overt consideration of its *dys*functions and further sources, see L. Holmes 2000 or L. Holmes 2002. A pithy recent overview of the functionality arguments, which cites a number of sources, can be found in Tanzi 2000, 123–26.

17   According to the World Bank, the average annual GDP growth rate from 1991 to 2001 in Bulgaria was –0.7, while the annual rates in 2000 and 2001 were 5.4 and 4.0. The Russian figures were more extreme, at –2.9, 9.0, and 5.0. Hungary fared better, at 2.8, 5.2, and 3.6; while Poland scored an average of 5.1 for the period 1991–2001, but a somewhat lower 4.0 in 2000, and only 1.0 in 2001. Of the five countries singled out in this book, China performed best, at 9.7, 8.0, and 7.3. All data from http://www.worldbank.org/data/countrydata/countrydata.html, visited October 2002.

18   The European Union is playing an important role in developing a culture of compromise *between* states too. Good examples are the agreements in 1996 between Hungary and Slovakia (May) and Hungary and Romania (September); all three countries sought membership in the EU, and knew that they had to reach compromises with their neighbors if their applications were to advance.

19   However, developing incrementalism prematurely (before the post-communist states have passed legislation in most major policy areas, including property rights) would probably delay democratic consolidation.

20   This said, Russia was still collecting income tax from only about 3

million of its more than 120 million adult citizens as of 2002 (*http://www*
.newsru.com/finance/20feb2003/declare.html — visited August 2003; I am grateful to Donald Bowser for alerting me to this source). In June 2004 Deputy
Prime Minister Aleksandr Zhukov announced that the average annual increase in income tax collection since 2001 was approximately 40 percent
(*Johnson's Russia List* 8240, 6 June 2004). While this might sound impressive,
the very low starting figure needs to be borne in mind: even allowing for the
large number of Russians on paltry incomes who would not be expected to
pay any income tax at all, improvements in tax collection still have a long way
to go.

21 Even though Putin was relatively unknown to many Russians before
mid-1999, that he was Yeltsin's chosen successor supports the point being
made here about familiarity.

22 It appears that some of the new, anticommunist politicians and officials have engaged in similar activities vis-à-vis privatization (stacking boards
with mates; various forms of insider trading; selling off enterprises cheaply to
family and friends), in part to ensure that they would not be beaten to the
post by the former communists. This is one case where the old adage "if you
can't beat 'em, join 'em" is particularly inappropriate. For a debate on the
connection between privatization and corruption, see Intriligator 1994 and
Zagórski 1995. It is argued here, more in line with Zagórski, that while the
privatization process creates new opportunities for corruption in any kind of
system, the possibilities and likelihood are greater in post-communist states,
given the legacies of communism — including the tradition of corruption and
the weak state.

23 For arguments that there have been some encouraging signs even in
countries such as Russia and Georgia see Rose 2000; Marsh 2000; Jones 2000.

24 It is acknowledged, however, that many other citizens either already
were, or increasingly became, skeptical about the advantages of joining the
European Union by the time of the referenda on membership held by many
CEE applicant states in 2002–3.

25 This is not to overlook or excuse the European Union's own corruption
and "democratic deficit"; there are times in the anticorruption struggle when it
looks as if the pot is calling the kettle black. Nor is it to deny a certain hypocrisy
of another kind on the EU's part. As has been demonstrated, Poland appears by
all criteria to have become more corrupt in recent years, while Bulgaria has
improved; yet Poland was admitted in 2004, Bulgaria was not. Obviously the
corruption factor is only one among many that interests the EU.

26 In an article published in 1997, James Arnold explicitly linked the recent
increase in press censorship in Kyrgyzstan to President Akayev's desire to clamp
down on the reporting of "his government's shabby anti-corruption record."

27   For evidence that the Russian gini coefficient has increased since 2001 see *RIA Novosti*, 30 April 2004, cited in *Johnson's Russia List* 8191, 1 May 2004.

28   This argument also applies to China. The reader is reminded of the point made in chapter 1 that there is considerable evidence from the PRC of what Gordon White (1993, esp. 147–69) calls "ideological decay" as a result of economic reforms since the late 1970s.

29   For a comparative and interpretive analysis of what is sometimes called the pink revolution see L. Holmes 1997b, 331–35, while Leftwich Curry and Barth Urban eds. 2003 provide an analysis of communist successor parties.

30   For recent analyses of various dimensions of trust in post-communist societies see Kornai and Rose-Ackerman eds. 2004; Kornai, Rothstein, and Rose-Ackerman eds. 2004. A more general analysis of trust, albeit with some focus on CEE, is Misztal 1996.

31   This assumption appears to be borne out by a Chinese analysis of high-level corruption in the PRC from 1978 to 2002, which concluded that perceived connections between senior officials and organized-crime gangs were affecting the communist party's legitimacy (*TI Q*, September 2003, 6).

32   Interestingly, the other countries in which corruption appeared to cause most concern were Brazil, France, and Turkey; for the source, see the following note. For evidence that corruption had again become the main concern of Chinese citizens, see the survey results in *CD*, 28 August 1999.

33   In Hungary 65 percent opted for criminality, 34 percent for unemployment, and 33 percent for inflation. In Russia 58 percent chose criminality as one of their top three concerns, compared with 42 percent for unemployment and 33 percent for a shortage of money. In Poland criminality scored the highest figure for inclusion among the top three, 74 percent, with 60 percent opting for inflation and 44 percent for shortage of money. It is worth noting that criminality was also top of the list in the United States (53 percent, compared with 34 percent for AIDS and 31 percent for narcotics) and the United Kingdom (63 percent, compared with 45 percent for unemployment and, perhaps surprisingly, 34 percent for environmental pollution). All data are from *EiSP* 1, no. 5:22–23.

34   Unlike the leaders of developing countries, communists could not even blame globalization. However, the communist states *were* affected by globalization; Lockwood (2000) goes so far as to argue that the collapse of the USSR was caused primarily by this.

35   For overviews see for example Clarke ed. 1991; Dunn ed. 1995. Since many of the writers whose views on the crisis of the state did not produce major follow-up arguments, it cannot be assumed that they continued to identify such crises. On the other hand, the logic of most of these arguments can be interpreted as suggesting that the crises constitute long-term developments.

36   For evidence that many Russians are aware of the possibility that the Georgian, Ukrainian, and Kyrgyz revolutions could spread to their own country see the article by Ivan Rodin in *Nezavisimaya Gazeta*, 8 April 2005.

37   For comparative survey data on this see for example Rose, Mishler, and Haerpfer 1998, esp. 141–59, although the findings reported there are by now somewhat dated.

38   At its most extreme, what could emerge is brutal anarchy. Two interviewees in Moscow in April–May 1997 (separately) cited this as a real possibility for Russia within two years. The rise of Putin has made this outcome less likely for now; but it is too early to be confident that it could not emerge in the next few years.

39   On this issue see Varese 1994; Hedlund and Sundström 1996.

40   The most readily accessible version of what some members of the British Labour Party mean by the third way was written by the man alleged to be Blair's favorite intellectual—see Giddens 1998 and 2000. For a collection of responses to Giddens and further elaboration of the concept of the third way see Giddens ed. 2001.

41   Justin Rosenberg (2005) has even argued that the age of globalization is already over.

Bibliography

Addis, D., K. Henderson, L. Lief, P. O'Rourke, and J. Denton. 1999. *Media Responses to Corruption in the Emerging Democracies: Bulgaria, Hungary, Romania, and Ukraine*. New York: Freedom House.

Alberti, A. 1997. "Political Corruption and the Role of Public Prosecutors in Italy." Williams and Doig 2000, 177–96.

Allnutt, L, J. Druker, and J. Tracy. 2001. "Central Europe, Southeast Europe and the Baltic States." Hodess with Banfield and Wolfe eds. 2001, 124–37.

Altukhov, S. 2001. *Prestupleniya Sotrudnikov Militsii*. St. Petersburg: Yuridicheskii Tsentr.

Alvazzi del Frate, A., and J. van Kesteren. 2004. *Criminal Victimisation in Urban Europe: Key Findings of the 2000 International Crime Victim Surveys*. Turin: UNICRI.

Anderson, J. 1998. *Report: Corruption in Latvia: Survey Evidence*. Washington: World Bank.

———. 2000. *Corruption in Slovakia: Results of Diagnostic Surveys*. Washington: World Bank and U.S. Agency for International Development.

———. 2002. *Governance and Service Delivery in the Kyrgyz Republic: Results of Diagnostic Surveys*. Washington: World Bank.

Anderson, J., O. Azfar, I. Imnadze, D. Kaufmann, Y. Lee, A. Mukherjee, and R. Ryterman. 2000. *Corruption in Georgia: Survey Evidence*. Washington: World Bank and U.S. Agency for International Development.

Anderson, J., B. Cosmaciuc, P. Dininio, B. Spector, and P. Zoido-Lobaton. 2001. *Diagnostic Surveys of Corruption in Romania*. Washington: World Bank.

Anderson, J., and A. Mukherjee. 2002. *Kazakhstan: Governance and Service Delivery: A Diagnostic Report*. Washington: World Bank.

Anechiarico, F., and J. Jacobs. 1996. *The Pursuit of Absolute Integrity: How Corruption Control Makes Government Ineffective*. Chicago: University of Chicago Press.

Anjaparidze, Z. 2001. "Fight a Losing Battle." *Prism* 7, no. 1. On line at http://

russia.jamestown.org/pubs/view/pri_007_005_006.htm, visited 30 January 2003.

Antonyan, Yu. 2003. "Tipologiya korruptsii i korruptsionnogo povedeniya." Gerasimov and Shchegortsov eds. 2003, 37–41.

Anusiewicz, T., T. Verheijen, and A. Dimitrova. 2001. "Tackling Corruption in Central and Eastern Europe." Caiden, Dwivedi, and Jabbra eds. 2001, 79–90.

Appel, H. 2001. "Corruption and the Collapse of the Czech Transition Miracle." *East European Politics and Societies* 15, no. 3:528–53.

Armenian Democratic Forum. 2001. *The Report of the Sociological Survey on Public Sector Reforms (for Households)*. Yerevan: Armenian Democratic Forum.

Arnold, J. 1997. "Kyrgyzstan." *Business Central Europe* 5, no. 38:66.

Bagehot, W. 1928. *The English Constitution*. London: Oxford University Press.

Bąk, M., P. Kulawczuk, and A. Szcześniak. n.d. [?2001]. *Polski biznes wobec korupcji*. Warsaw: Instytut Badań nad Demokracją i Przedsiębiorstwem Prywatnym.

Bakker, H., and N. Schulte Nordholt, eds. 1996. *Corruption and Legitimacy*. Amsterdam: SISWO.

Banciu, D., and S. Radulescu. 1994. *Coruptia si Crima Organizata in Romania*. Bucharest: Continent XXI.

Banfield, E. 1958. *The Moral Basis of a Backward Society*. Chicago: Free Press.

Barbacetto, G., P. Gomez, and M. Travaglio. 2002. *Mani Pulite: La vera storia*. Rome: Riuniti.

Bardhan, P. 1997. "Corruption and Development: A Review of Issues." *Journal of Economic Literature* 35, no. 3:1320–46.

Batory Foundation. 2000. "Postawy Polaków wobec korupcji, lipiec 2000 r. Dane szczgółowe z badania." On line at http://www.batory.org.pl/korupcja/pub.htm, visited July 2003.

Bayley, D., and C. Shearing. 1996. "The Future of Policing." *Law and Society Review* 30, no. 3:585–606.

Beck, A., and R. Lee. 2002. "Attitudes to Corruption amongst Russian Police Officers and Trainees." *Crime, Law and Social Change* 38, no. 4:357–72.

Beyer, J., and J. Wielgohs. 2001. "On the Limits of Path Dependency Approaches for Explaining Postsocialist Institution Building: In Critical Response to David Stark." *East European Politics and Societies* 15, no. 2:356–88.

Bielasiak, J. 2002. "The Institutionalization of Electoral and Party Systems in Postcommunist States." *Comparative Politics* 34, no. 2:189–210.

Blankenburg, E. 2002. "From Political Clientelism to Outright Corruption: The Rise of the Scandal Industry." Kotkin and Sajó eds. 2002, 149–85.

Bouissou, J-M. 1997. "Gifts, Networks and Clienteles: Corruption in Japan as a Redistributive System." Della Porta and Mény eds. 1997, 132–47.

Bowser, D. 2002. "Corruption, Trust, and the Danger to Democratization in the Former Soviet Union." *The Transition: Evaluating the Postcommunist Experience*, ed. D. Lovell, 80–95. Aldershot: Ashgate.

Bray, J. 2004. "International Business Attitudes toward Corruption." Hodess, Inowlocki, Rodriguez, and Wolfe eds. 2004, 316–18.

Brown, J. 1997. "Goodbye (and Good Riddance?) to De-communization." *Transitions* 4, no. 2:28–34.

Brusis, M., I. Kempe, and W. van Meurs. 2003. "Central and Eastern Europe and the Baltic States." Hodess with Inowlocki and Wolfe eds. 2003, 177–89.

Bryant, C., and E. Mokrzycki. 1994. "Introduction: Theorizing the Changes in East-Central Europe." *The New Great Transformation?*, ed. C. Bryant and E. Mokrzycki, 1–13. London: Routledge.

Buchanan, J., R. Tollison, and G. Tullock, eds. 1980. *Toward a Theory of the Rent-Seeking Society*. College Station: Texas A&M University Press.

Buiter, W., R. Lago, S. Fries, and P. Sanfey, eds. 2001. *Transition Report Update: April 2001*. London: European Bank for Reconstruction and Development.

Bull, M., and J. Newell, eds. 2003. *Corruption in Contemporary Politics*. Basingstoke: Palgrave.

Bunce, V. 1995a. "Should Transitologists Be Grounded?" *Slavic Review* 54, no. 1:111–27.

———. 1995b. "Paper Curtains and Paper Tigers." *Slavic Review* 54, no. 4:979–87.

Burnell, P., and A. Ware, eds. 1998. *Funding Democratization*. Manchester: Manchester University Press.

Burns, J. 1987. "China's Nomenklatura System." *Problems of Communism* 36, no. 5:35–51.

Button, M. 2002. *Private Policing*. Cullompton: Willan.

Caiden, G., O. Dwivedi, and J. Jabbra, eds. 2001. *Where Corruption Lives*. Bloomfield, Conn.: Kumarian.

Cangiano, M. 1996. "Accountability and Transparency in the Public Sector: The New Zealand Experience." Working Paper of the International Monetary Fund WP/96/122, November. Washington: International Monetary Fund.

Cardoso, F., and E. Faletto. 1979. *Dependency and Development in Latin America*. Berkeley: University of California Press.

Carothers, T. 2002. "The End of the Transition Paradigm." *Journal of Democracy* 13, no. 1:5–21.

Carter, F., and D. Turnock, eds. 1996. *Environmental Problems in Eastern Europe*. London: Routledge.

Castles, F. 2002. "Developing New Measures of Welfare State Change and Reform." *European Journal of Political Research* 41, no. 5:613–41.

Center for the Study of Democracy. 1998a. *Mnenieto na bulgarite za korupsiyata: mart 1997–yanuari 1998*. Sofia: Vitosha Research.

——. 1998b. *Attitudes of Citizens towards Public Administration*. Sofia: Vitosha Research.

——. 2001. *Annual Report 2000*. Sofia: Center for the Study of Democracy.

——. 2002a. *Annual Report 2001*. Sofia: Center for the Study of Democracy.

——. 2002b. *Corruption, Trafficking and Institutional Reform: Prevention of Trans-Border Crime in Bulgaria (2001–2002)*. Sofia: Center for the Study of Democracy.

——. 2003a. *Economy of Crime and Anticorruption Reforms*. Sofia: Center for the Study of Democracy.

——. 2003b. *Annual Report 2002*. Sofia: Center for the Study of Democracy.

Centre for Liberal Strategies. 2003. Untitled report on judicial handling of four alleged corruption cases. Sofia: Centre for Liberal Strategies.

Centrum Badania Opinii Społecznej. 1994a. *Sponsorowanie Instytucji Państwowych a Korupcja i Łapownictwo*. Warsaw: CBOS.

——. 1994b. *Nieuczciwość i Przekupstwo w Instytucjach Wymiaru Sprawiedliwosci*. Warsaw: CBOS.

——. 1995. *Czy Politycy Są Uczciwi?* Warsaw: CBOS.

——. 2000. *Korupcja i Łapownictwo w Życiu Publicznym*. Warsaw: CBOS.

——. 2004a. *Korupcja, Nepotyzm, Nieuczciwy Lobbing*. Warsaw: CBOS.

——. 2004b. *Postrzeganie Korupcji w Polsce*. Warsaw: CBOS.

Chuklinov, A. 2003. "Kratkii analiz dinamiki antikorruptsionnoi politiki v Rossii za poslednie 10 let (1992–2002 g. g.) i ee perspektivy." Gerasimov and Shchegortsov eds. 2003, 46–54.

Ciconte, E. 2004. "Research on the Flows and on the Routes of the Trafficking Aimed at the Sexual Exploitation in Italy of Women Coming from Eastern Europe." Paper presented at the W.E.S.T. [Women East Smuggling Trafficking] In-depth Conference, Bologna, November.

Cirtautas, A. 2001. "Corruption and the New Ethical Infrastructure of Capitalism." *EECR* 10, nos. 2–3:79–84.

Clapham, C. 1982. "Clientelism and the State." Clapham ed. 1982, 1–35.

———, ed. 1982. *Private Patronage and Public Power: Political Clientelism in the Modern State*. London: Frances Pinter.

Clark, W. 1993. *Crime and Punishment in Soviet Officialdom*. New York: M. E. Sharpe.

Clarke, S., ed. 1991. *The State Debate*. London: Macmillan.

Claussen, H. 1995. *Korruption im öffentlichen Dienst*. Cologne: Carl Heymanns.

Clinard, M. 1990. *Corporate Corruption*. New York: Praeger.

Coalition 2000. 2000. *Corruption Assessment Report 1999*. Sofia: Coalition 2000.

———. 2002. *Corruption Assessment Report 2001*. Sofia: Coalition 2000.

———. 2003. *Corruption Assessment Report 2002*. Sofia: Coalition 2000.

———. 2004. *Corruption Assessment Report 2003*. Sofia: Coalition 2000.

Cohen, A. 1995. "Crime without Punishment." *Journal of Democracy* 6, no. 2:34–45.

Collins, N. 2004. "Parliamentary Democracy in Ireland." *Parliamentary Affairs* 57, no. 3:601–12.

Collins, N., and M. O'Shea. 2001. *Understanding Political Corruption in the Republic of Ireland*. Cork: Cork University Press.

"Combating Corruption in Poland: Current Situation, Legal Institutions in Criminal Law." 1999. Paper presented at the Vice President's Conference on Fighting Corruption and Safeguarding Integrity among Justice and Security Officials, Washington, 24–26 February. On line at http://64.49 .225.236/Documents/GlobalForum99/Poland_CombatingCor_GF99 .pdf, visited July 2003.

Coulloudon, V. 1992. *Le Russisme: Enquête sur une démocratie*. Paris: Lattáes.

———. 1997. "The Criminalization of Russia's Political Elite." EECR 6, no. 4:73–78.

———. 1999. "Corruption and Patronage in Russia (1979–1999)." Paper presented at the Princeton–Central European University Joint Conference on Corruption, Budapest, October–November.

———. 2002. "Russia's Distorted Anticorruption Campaigns." Kotkin and Sajó eds. 2002, 187–205.

Cybulska, A., A. Sęk, M. Wenzel, and M. Wójcik. 2000. "Demokracja w Praktyce." Zagórski and Strzeszewski eds. 2000, 63–87.

Dallin, A., and G. Breslauer. 1970. *Political Terror in Communist Systems*. Stanford: Stanford University Press.

Dávid, I. 2000. "Fighting Corruption in Hungary." UNODCCP and UNICRI 2000, 15–19.

Deacon, B., et al. 1992. *The New Eastern Europe: Social Policy Past, Present and Future*. London: Sage.

DeBardeleben, J. 1991. *To Breathe Free*. Washington: Woodrow Wilson Center Press.

———. 1999. "Attitudes towards Privatisation in Russia." *Europe-Asia Studies* 51, no. 3:447–65.

Della Porta, D., and Y. Mény, eds. 1995a. *Démocratie et corruption en Europe*. Paris: La Découverte. Eng. trans. as Della Porta and Mény eds 1997.

———. 1995b. "Introduction: Démocratie et corruption." Della Porta and Mény eds. 1995a, 9–13.

———. 1995c. "Démocratie et corruption: Vers une analyse comparée." Della Porta and Mény eds. 1995a, 165–72.

———. 1997. *Democracy and Corruption in Europe*. London: Pinter.

Dikun, E. 2000. "The Kremlin Changes the Oligarchs' Diapers . . . for Which They Thank the President." *Prism* 6, no. 8 (on line), 31 August.

Ding, X-L. 2000. "Informal Privatization through Internationalization: The Rise of *Nomenklatura* Capitalism in China's Offshore Businesses." *British Journal of Political Science* 30, no. 1:121–46.

di Tella, R., and E. Schargrodsky. 2003. "The Role of Wages and Auditing during a Crackdown on Corruption in the City of Buenos Aires." *Journal of Law and Economics* 46, no. 1:269–92.

Dobel, J. 1978. "The Corruption of a State." *American Political Science Review* 72, no. 3:958–73.

Doig, A. 1996. "From Lynskey to Nolan: The Corruption of British Politics and Public Service." *Journal of Law and Society* 23, no. 1:36–56.

———. 2003. "Political Corruption in the United Kingdom." Bull and Newell eds. 2003, 178–90.

Dollar, D., R. Fisman, and R. Gatti. 1999. "Are Women Really the 'Fairer' Sex? Corruption and Women in Government." *Policy Research Report on Gender and Development: Working Paper Series No. 4*. Washington: World Bank.

Doublet, Y-M. 2001. "Elf Aquitaine: Grand Corruption Goes to Court." Hodess with Banfield and Wolfe eds. 2001, 145.

Dryzek, J., and L. Holmes. 2002. *Post-communist Democratization: Political Discourses across Thirteen Countries*. Cambridge: Cambridge University Press.

Dunlop, J. 1997. "Russia: In Search of an Identity?" *New States, New Politics: Building the Post-Soviet Nations*, ed. I. Bremmer and R. Taras, 29–95. Cambridge: Cambridge University Press.

Dunn, J., ed. 1995. *Contemporary Crisis of the Nation State?* Oxford: Blackwell.

Duyne, P. van, L. Huberts, and H. van den Heuvel. 2003. "Political Corruption in the Netherlands." Bull and Newell eds. 2003, 149–77.

Economic Crime Division. 2002. "The Prevention of Corruption in Central and Eastern Europe." Activity report based on regional seminar held in Bratislava, 19–21 November 2001. Strasbourg: Council of Europe, Directorate General 1, Legal Affairs.

Eigen, P. 1994. "Corruption: A Catastrophe to Developing Countries." Trang ed. 1994, 65–70.

——. 1996. "Combatting Corruption around the World." *Journal of Democracy* 7, no. 1:158–68.

——. 2003. "WTO Must Address Corruption in Procurement." *TI Q*, September, 1.

Eisenstadt, S., and R. Lemarchand, eds. 1981. *Political Clientelism, Patronage and Development*. Beverly Hills: Sage.

Eisenstadt, S., and L. Roniger. 1981. "Clientelism in Communist Systems: A Comparative Perspective." *Studies in Comparative Communism* 14, nos. 2–3:233–45.

——. 1984. *Patrons, Clients and Friends: Interpersonal Relations and the Structure of Trust in Society*. Cambridge: Cambridge University Press.

Esping-Anderson, G. 1990. *The Three Worlds of Welfare Capitalism*. Cambridge: Polity.

European Commission. 1997a. "Commission Opinion on Bulgaria's Application for Membership of the European Union." *Bulletin of the European Union*, suppl. 13/97. Luxembourg: Office for Official Publications of the European Communities.

——. 1997b. "Commission Opinion on Hungary's Application for Membership of the European Union." *Bulletin of the European Union*, suppl. 6/97. Luxembourg: Office for Official Publications of the European Communities.

Evans, J. 2003. "Political Corruption in France." Bull and Newell eds. 2003, 79–92.

Eyal, G., I. Szelényi, and E. Townsley. 1998. *Making Capitalism without Capitalists: Class Formation and Elite Struggles in Post-communist Central Europe*. London: Verso.

Feiler, J. 2002. "Fate of the Forest: Will the World Bank Replicate Amazonian Failures in Central and Eastern Europe?" *Multinational Monitor*, 23, no. 5. On line at http://multinationalmonitor.org/mm2002/02may/may02corp5.html, visited December 2003.

Fel'gengauer, P. 1996. "V voennom vedomstve gotovitsya bol'shaya chistka." *Segodnya*, 6 July, 1.

Fiorentini, G., and S. Peltzman, eds. 1995. *The Economics of Organised Crime*. Cambridge: Cambridge University Press.

Fish, S., and R. Brooks. 2000. "Bulgarian Democracy's Organizational Weapon." *EECR* 9, no. 3:63–71.

Ford, J. 1996. "Nuclear Smuggling: How Serious a Threat?" *National Defense University Strategic Forum*, no.59.

Frank, A. G. 1969. *Capitalism and Underdevelopment in Latin America: Historical Studies of Chile and Brazil*. New York: Monthly Review Press.

Freeland, C. 2000. *Sale of the Century: Russia's Wild Ride from Communism to Capitalism*. New York: Crown Business.

Freemantle, B. 1995. *The Octopus*. London: Orion.

Frentzel-Zagórska, J., and K. Zagórski. 1993. "Polish Public Opinion on Privatisation and State Interventionism." *Europe-Asia Studies* 45, no. 4:703–28.

Fric, P. 1999. "Corruption in the Czech Police." Paper presented at the Princeton–Central European University Joint Conference on Corruption, Budapest, October–November.

Friedman, E., S. Johnson, D. Kaufmann, and P. Zoido-Lobaton. 2000. "Dodging the Grabbing Hand: The Determinants of Unofficial Activity in 69 Countries." *Journal of Public Economics* 76, no. 3:459–93.

Fries, S., and P. Sanfey, eds. 2001. *Transition Report Update*. London: European Bank for Reconstruction and Development.

Frisby, T. 1998. "The Rise of Organised Crime in Russia: Its Roots and Social Significance." *Europe-Asia Studies* 50, no. 1:27–49.

Frydman, R., K. Murphy, and A. Rapaczynski. 1996. "Capitalism with a Comrade's Face." *Transition* 2, no. 2:5–11.

Frydman, R., and A. Rapaczynski. 1994. *Privatization in Eastern Europe: Is the State Withering Away?* Budapest: Central European University Press.

Frye, T. 1998. "Corruption: The Polish and Russian Experiences." *Economic Perspectives* 3, no. 5. On line at http://usinfo.state.gov/journals/ites/1198/ijee/frye.htm, visited September 2003.

Fukuyama, F. 1992. *The End of History and the Last Man*. New York: Free Press.

Fuszara, M. 1999. "Corruption as Shown in Polish, Czech, Slovakian and Bulgarian Press." Paper presented at the Princeton–Central European University Joint Conference on Corruption, Budapest, October–November.

———. 2000. "Obraz korupcji w prasie." Kurczewski and Łaciak eds. 2000, 39–62.

Gallup Organization and the Hungarian Gallup Institute. 2000. "Corruption Pilot Study: Focus Group among Public Officials." UNODCCP and UNICRI 2000, 43–48.

Galtung, F. 2003. "Are Anti-corruption Efforts Making a Difference? Introducing the TI Global Corruption Barometer." *TI Q*, June, 5.

———, ed. 1994. *Accountability and Transparency in International Economic Development*. Berlin: German Foundation for International Development with the Economic and Social Development Centre.

Galtung, F., F. Smith, and R. Homel. 2003. *The Transparency International Global Corruption Barometer: A 2002 Pilot Study of International Attitudes, Expectations and Priorities on Corruption*. Berlin: Transparency International.

Gambetta, D. 2002. "Corruption: An Analytical Map." Kotkin and Sajó eds. 2002, 33–56.

Gel'man, V. 1998. "The Iceberg of Russian Political Finance." Burnell and Ware eds. 1998, 158–79.

Gerasimov, V., and A. Shchegortsov, eds. 2003. *Nauchno-prakticheskaya konferentsiya "sotsiologiya korruptsii" (29 Marta 2003 goda) — Vypusk V*. Moscow: Russko-Nemetskoe Obshchestvo Prava i Ekonomiki.

GfK. 2001. *Corruption Climate: Central and Eastern Europe: Results of an International Research Project on Corruption in 11 Central and Eastern European Countries*. Prague: GfK Praha.

Giddens, A. 1998. *The Third Way: The Renewal of Social Democracy*. Cambridge: Polity.

———. 2000. *The Third Way and Its Critics*. Cambridge: Polity.

———, ed. 2001. *The Global Third Way Debate*. Malden, Mass.: Polity.

Gill, G. 2000. "Russia's Weak State: What Is to Be Done?" *Australian Slavonic and East European Studies* 14, nos. 1–2:99–132.

Gillespie, K., and G. Okruhlik. 1991. "The Political Dimensions of Corruption Cleanups: A Framework for Analysis." *Comparative Politics* 24, no. 1:77–95.

Girnius, S. 1995. "World Bank Survey on Bribery in Lithuania." *Open Media Research Institute*, 3 October.

Glavnyi Informatsionnyi Tsentr. 1997. *Sostoyanie Prestupnosti v Rossii za 1996 god*. Moscow: Ministerstvo Vnutrennikh Del Rossii.

Gleason, G. 1995. "Corruption, Decolonization and Development in Central Asia." *European Journal on Criminal Policy and Research* 3, no. 2:38–47.

Glinkina, S. 1998. "The Ominous Landscape of Russian Corruption." *Transitions* 5, no. 3:16–23.

Główny Urząd Statystyczny. 1990–2003. *Rocznik Statystyczny Rzeczypospolitej Polskiej*. Warsaw: Główny Urząd Statystyczny.

Glukhovsky, M. 1992. "The Criminal Economy." *Delovye Lyudi*, September, 14–16.

Gole, J. 1999. "Public Opinion Polls as an Anticorruption Technique." *LGI Newsletter* 2, no. 1:1–2.

Golik, P. 1999. "Cutting Gray Corners." *Warsaw Voice*, 18 April.

———. 2000. "Politicians Reveal All." *Warsaw Voice*, 30 January.

Gorbachev, M. 1987. *Perestroika: New Thinking for Our Country and the World*. London: Collins.

Goskomstat [Gosudarstvennyi Komitet Rossiiskoi Federatsii po Statistike]. 1990–2003. *Rossiiskii Statisticheskii Yezhegodnik*. Moscow: Goskomstat.

Gray, C., J. Hellman, and R. Ryterman. 2004. *Anticorruption in Transition 2: Corruption in Enterprise-State Interactions in Europe and Central Asia, 1999–2002*. Washington: World Bank.

Gray, C., and D. Kaufmann. 1998. "Corruption and Development." Transparency International and International Bank for Reconstruction and Development 1998, 21–31.

Graziano, L. 1980. *Clientelismo e sistema politico: Il caso dell'Italia*. Milan: Angeli.

Gregory, R. 1995. "Accountability, Responsibility, and Corruption: Managing the 'Public Production Process.'" *The State under Contract*, ed. J. Boston, 56–77. Wellington: Bridget Williams.

———. 2002. "Governmental Corruption in New Zealand: A View through Nelson's Telescope?" *Asian Journal of Political Science* 10, no. 1:17–38.

Grobelna, A. 1995. *Opinia Społeczna o Zamówieniach Publicznych*. Warsaw: Profile.

Grødeland, Å., T. Koshechkina, and W. Miller. 1998a. "'Foolish to Give and Yet More Foolish Not to Take': In-depth Interviews with Postcommunist Citizens on Their Everyday Use of Bribes and Contacts." *Europe-Asia Studies* 50, no. 4:651–77.

———. 1998b. "In-depth Interviews on the Everyday Use of Bribes in Postcommunist Europe." *ecpr News* 9, no. 2:7–9.

Grossman, G. 1977. "The 'Second Economy' of the USSR." *Problems of Communism* 26, no. 5:25–40.

———. 1996. "The Second Economy in the USSR and Eastern Europe: A Bibliography." Unpublished manuscript.

Gurov, A. 1990. *Professional'naya Prestupnost': Proshloe i Sovremennost'*. Moscow: Yuridicheskaya Literatura.

———. 1995. *Krasnaya Mafiya*. Moscow: Samotsvet.

Habermas, J. 1973a. *Legitimationsprobleme im Spätkapitalismus*. Frankfurt am Main: Suhrkamp.

———. 1973b. "What Does a Legitimation Crisis Mean Today? Legitimation Problems in Late Capitalism." *Legitimacy and the State*, ed. W. Connolly, 134–79. Oxford: Blackwell, 1984.

Hagelmeyer, I. 1994. Opening Statement. Trang ed. 1994, 11–13.

Hajdinjak, M. 2002. *Smuggling in Southeast Europe: The Yugoslav Wars and the Development of Regional Crime Networks in the Balkans*. Sofia: Centre for the Study of Democracy.

Hall, D. 1999. "Privatisation, Multinationals, and Corruption." *Development in Practice* 9, no. 5:539–56.

Handelman, S. 1994. *Comrade Criminal*. London: Michael Joseph.

———. 2000. "Shadows on the Wall: Putin's Law-and-Order Dilemma." *EECR* 9, nos. 1–2:88–91.

Hankiss, E. 2002. "Games of Corruption: East Central Europe, 1945–1999." Kotkin and Sajó eds. 2002, 243–59.

Hanley, E. 2000. "Cadre Capitalism in Hungary and Poland: Property Accumulation among Communist-Era Elites." *East European Politics and Societies* 14, no. 1:143–78.

Hann, C., ed. 2002. *Postsocialism: Ideals, Ideologies and Practices in Eurasia*. London: Routledge.

Haque, M. S. 1996. "The Intellectual Crisis in Public Administration in the Current Epoch of Privatization." *Administration and Society* 27, no. 4:510–36.

Harasymiw, B. 1969. "Nomenklatura: The Soviet Communist Party's Leadership Recruitment System." *Canadian Journal of Political Science* 2, no. 3:493–512.

Hardin, G. 1968. "The Tragedy of the Commons." *Science* 162:1243–48.

Hauk, E., and M. Sáez. 1999. "On the Cultural Transmission of Corruption." Working Paper no.392. Barcelona: University Pompeu Fabra, Department of Economics and Business.

Hawley, S. 2000. "Exporting Corruption: Privatisation, Multinationals and Bribery." *Corner House*, briefing no. 19. On line at http://www.thecornerhouse.org.uk/briefing/19bribes.html, visited January 2003.

He Bingsong. 1992. "Crime and Control in China." *Crime and Control in Comparative Perspectives*, ed. H-G. Heiland, L. Shelley, and H. Katoh, 241–57. Berlin: Walter de Gruyter.

He Zengke. 2000. "Corruption and Anti-corruption in Reform China." *Communist and Post-Communist Studies* 33, no. 2:243–70.

Hedlund, S., and N. Sundström. 1996. "Does Palermo Represent the Future for Moscow?" *Journal of Public Policy* 16, no. 2:113–55.

Heidenheimer, A., ed. 1970a. *Political Corruption*. New York: Holt, Rinehart and Winston.

———. 1970b. Introduction. Heidenheimer ed. 1970a, 3–28.

———. 1994. Introduction. Trang ed. 1994, 15–18.

Heidenheimer, A., M. Johnstone, and V. LeVine, eds. 1989. *Political Corruption*. New Brunswick, N.J.: Transaction.

Heimann, F. 2004. "Will the OECD Convention Stop Foreign Bribery?" Hodess, Inowlocki, Rodriguez, and Wolfe eds. 2004, 128–35.

Hellman, J. 1998. "Winner Takes All: The Politics of Partial Reform in Post-communist Transitions." *World Politics* 50, no. 2:203–34.

Hellman, J., G. Jones, and D. Kaufmann. 2000. "Seize the State, Seize the Day: State Capture, Corruption and Influence in Transition." World Bank Policy Research Working Papers, no. 2444.

Hellman, J., G. Jones, D. Kaufmann, and M. Schankerman. 2000. "Measuring Governance, Corruption and State Capture: How Firms and Bureaucrats Shape the Business Environment." World Bank Policy Research Working Papers, no. 2312.

Henderson, K. 1998. "Corruption: What Can Be Done about It?" *Demokratizatsiya* 6, no. 4:681–91.

———. 2000. "Halfway Home and a Long Way to Go: Russian and Kazakh Roads to Sectoral and Political Corruption." *Demokratizatsiya* 8, no. 4:481–514.

Henderson, K., and N. Robinson. 1997. *Post-communist Politics: An Introduction*. London: Prentice Hall.

Hess, H. 1998. *Mafia and Mafiosi: Origin, Power and Myth*. London: Hurst.

Hessel, M., and K. Murphy. 1998. "Stealing the State, and Everything Else: A Survey of Corruption in the Postcommunist World." Transparency International Working Paper. On line at http://www.transparency.org/working_papers/hessel/index.html, visited August 2002.

Heywood, P. 1995. "Sleaze in Spain." *Parliamentary Affairs* 48, no. 4:726–37.

Higley, J., J. Pakulski, and W. Wesolowski, eds. 1998. *Postcommunist Elites and Democracy in Eastern Europe*. New York: St. Martin's.

Hodess, R., with J. Banfield and T. Wolfe, eds. 2001. *Global Corruption Report 2001*. Berlin: Transparency International.

Hodess, R., T. Inowlocki, D. Rodriguez, and T. Wolfe, eds. 2004. *Global Corruption Report 2004*. London: Pluto.

Hodess, R., with T. Inowlocki and T. Wolfe, eds. 2003. *Global Corruption Report 2003*. London: Profile.

Hoeffner, T. 2001. "U.S. Law on Foreign Corrupt Practices and OECD Convention on Combating Bribery among Foreign Investors." World Bank 2001, 57–62.

Hoff, K., and J. Stiglitz. 2002. "After the Big Bang? Obstacles to the Emergence of the Rule of Law in Post-communist Societies." World Bank Policy Research Working Papers, no. 2934.

Hoffman, D. 2002. *The Oligarchs: Wealth and Power in the New Russia*. Washington: Public Affairs.

Holmes, L. 1993. *The End of Communist Power: Anti-corruption Campaigns and Legitimation Crisis*. New York: Oxford University Press.

———. 1996. "Poland and Hungary: Two Approaches to Post-communist Transition?" *Russia and Euro-Asian Bulletin* 5, no. 12:1–8.

———. 1997a. "Corruption and the Crisis of the Post-Communist State." *Crime, Law and Social Change* 27, nos. 3–4:275–97.

———. 1997b. *Post-communism: An Introduction*. Cambridge and Durham: Polity Press and Duke University Press.

———. 1997c. "Corruption in Post-communist Countries, with Particular Reference to Poland." Holmes and Roszkowski eds. 1997, 121–76.

———. 1998a. "Europe's Changing Boundaries and the 'Clash of Civilisations' Thesis." *Europe: Rethinking the Boundaries*, ed. P. Murray and L. Holmes, 19–42. Aldershot: Ashgate.

———. 1998b. "Corruption, Economic Rationalism, and the Crisis of the State." *La Trobe Forum* 12:14–15.

———. 1998c. "The Democratic State or State Democracy? Problems of Post-communist Transition." Jean Monnet Chair Papers, no. 48. Florence: European University Institute.

———. 1999. "Corruption, Weak States and Economic Rationalism in Central and Eastern Europe." Paper presented at the Princeton–Central European University Joint Conference on Corruption, Budapest, October–November.

———. 2000. "Funktionen und Dysfunktionen der Korruption und ihrer Bekämpfung in Mittel- und Osteuropa." *Jahrbuch für Europa- und Nordamerika-Studien*, vol. 3: *Politische Korruption*, ed. J. Borchert, S. Leitner, and K. Stolz, 117–44. Opladen: Leske and Budrich, 2000. Eng. trans. as Holmes 2002.

———. 2001. "Crime, Corruption and Politics: International and Transnational Factors." *Democratic Consolidation in Eastern Europe: International and Transnational Factors*, vol. 2, ed. J. Zielonka and A. Pravda, 192–230. Oxford: Oxford University Press.

———. 2002. "Functions and Dysfunctions of Corruption and Its Reporting in Central and Eastern Europe." *Corruption in Asia: Rethinking the Governance Paradigm*, ed. T. Lindsey and H. Dick, 50–70. Sydney: Federation.

Holmes, L., and W. Roszkowski, eds. 1997. *Changing Rules*. Warsaw: ISP PAN.

Holmes, S. 1994. "The End of Decommunization." *EECR* 3, nos. 3–4:33–36.

———. 1996. "Cultural Legacies or State Collapse? Probing the Post-communist Dilemma." *Post-Communism: Four Perspectives*, ed. M. Mandelbaum, 22–76. New York: Council on Foreign Relations.

Horne, C., and M. Levi. 2004. "Does Lustration Promote Trustworthy

Governance? An Exploration of the Experience of Central and Eastern Europe." Kornai and Rose-Ackerman eds. 2004, 52–74.

Hoser, R. 1999. *Victoria Police Corruption*. Doncaster, Victoria: Kotabi.

Howard, M. 2002. "The Weakness of Post-communist Civil Society." *Journal of Democracy* 13, no. 1:157–69.

———. 2003. *The Weakness of Civil Society in Post-communist Europe*. Cambridge: Cambridge University Press.

Hristova, K., and D. Kovatcheva. 2004. "Bulgaria." Hodess, Inowlocki, Rodriguez, and Wolfe eds. 2004, 166–70.

Hu Angang. 2002. "Corruption: An Enormous Black Hole: Public Exposure of Economic Loss Resulting from Corruption." *World Economy and China* 10:44–49.

Humphrey, C. 2002. *The Unmaking of Soviet Life: Everyday Economies after Socialism*. Ithaca: Cornell University Press.

Hungarian Gallup Institute. 2000. "Basic Methodological Aspects of Corruption Measurement: Lessons Learned from the Literature and the Pilot Study (1999 December)." UNODCCP and UNICRI 2000, 49–58.

Huntington, S. 1993. "The Clash of Civilizations?" *Foreign Affairs* 72, no. 3:22–49.

———. 1996. *The Clash of Civilizations and the Remaking of World Order*. New York: Simon and Schuster.

Hutchcroft, P. 2002. "The Impact of Corruption on Economic Development: Applying 'Third' World Insights to the Former Second World." Kotkin and Sajó eds. 2002, 115–38.

INDEM Foundation. 1998. *Russia vs. Corruption: Who Wins?* Moscow: INDEM Foundation.

International Monetary Fund. 2001. *World Economic Outlook 2001: Fiscal Policy and Macroeconomic Stability*. Washington: International Monetary Fund.

Intriligator, M. 1994. "Privatisation in Russia Has Led to Criminalisation." *Australian Economic Review* 2:4–14.

Jancar-Webster, B., ed. 1993. *Environmental Action in Eastern Europe*. Armonk, N.Y.: M. E. Sharpe.

Janos, A. 2000. *East Central Europe in the Modern World: The Politics of the Borderlands from Pre- to Postcommunism*. Stanford: Stanford University Press.

Jaskiernia, J. 1994. "Political Corruption in Poland." Trang ed. 1994, 61–64.

———. 1995. *Wizja parlamentu w nowej konstytucji Rzeczypospolitej Polskiej*. Warsaw: Wydawnictwo Sejmowe.

Jensen, D. 2000. "Russia: Analysis of Putin's Meeting with Tycoons." *RFE/RL*, 28 July.

Jiménez, F., and M. Caínzos. 2003. "Political Corruption in Spain." Bull and Newell eds. 2003, 9–23.

Johnston, L. 1992. *The Rebirth of Private Policing*. London: Routledge.

Johnston, M. 1989. "Corruption, Inequality and Change." Ward ed. 1989, 13–37.

Johnston, M., and Hao Yufan. 1995. "China's Surge of Corruption." *Journal of Democracy* 6, no. 4:80–94.

Jones, S. 2000. "Democracy from Below: Interest Groups in Georgian Society." *Slavic Review* 59, no. 1:42–73.

Jovic, D. 2003. "Southeast Europe." Hodess with Inowlocki and Wolfe eds. 2003, 190–202.

Kamiński, A. 1996. "The New Polish Regime and the Specter of Economic Corruption." Unpublished paper presented at the Woodrow Wilson International Center for Scholars, Washington, 3 April.

Kamiński, A., and B. Kamiński. 2004. *Korupcja Rządów: Państwa Pokomunistyczne w Dobie Globalizacji*. Warsaw: ISP PAN/TRIO.

Kanin, D. 2003. "Big Men, Corruption and Crime." *International Politics* 40, no. 4:491–526.

Karatnycky, A. 1998. "Introduction: Nations in Transit: From Change to Permanence." Karatnycky, Motyl, and Graybow 1998, 3–20.

Karatnycky, A., A. Motyl, and C. Graybow. 1998. *Nations in Transit 1998: Civil Society, Democracy and Markets in East Central Europe and the Newly Independent States*. New York: Freedom House.

Karklins, R. 2002. "Typology of Post-Communist Corruption." *Problems of Post-communism* 49, no. 4:22–32.

Karl, T., and P. Schmitter. 1995. "From an Iron Curtain to a Paper Curtain: Grounding Transitologists or Students of Postcommunism?" *Slavic Review* 54, no. 4:965–78.

Kaufman, M. 1998. "Corruption: What Can People of Good Will Do?" *Transitions* 5, no. 3:3.

Kaufmann, D., A. Kraay, and M. Mastruzzi. 2003. *Governance Matters III: Governance Indicators for 1996–2002 (Draft)*. World Bank web site, visited August 2004.

Kaufmann, D., A. Kraay, and P. Zoido-Lobaton. 1999a. "Aggregating Governance Indicators." World Bank Policy Research Working Papers, no. 2195.

———. 1999b. "Governance Matters." World Bank Policy Research Working Papers, no. 2196.

Kaufmann, D., S. Pradhan, and R. Ryterman. 1998. "New Frontiers in Diagnosing and Combating Corruption." World Bank Prem Note no. 7.

———. 1999. "World Bank Finds New Ways to Diagnose Corruption Symptoms." *Transition Newsletter*, January–February, 10–11.

Kaufmann, D., and F. Recanatini. 2001. "New Empirical Frontiers in Measuring and Evaluating Governance: Illustrations and Issues for Discussion." Paper delivered at the Carter Center, 30 October. On line at World Bank web site, visited July 2003.

Kaufmann, D., and D. Siegelbaum. 1997. "Privatization and Corruption in Transition Economies." *Journal of International Affairs* 50, no. 2:419–58.

Keane, M., and E. Prasad. 2001. "Poland: Inequality, Transfers, and Growth in Transition." *Finance and Development* 38, no. 1. On line at http://www.imf.org/external/pubs/ft/fandd/2001/03/keane.htm, visited September 2003.

Kelly, C. 2000. "Self-Interested Giving: Bribery and Etiquette in Late Imperial Russia." Lovell, Ledeneva, and Rogachevskii eds. 2000, 65–94.

Kettle, S. 1995. "Of Money and Morality." *Transition* 1, no. 3:36–39.

Kim, J. 2002. "Clientelism and Corruption in South Korea." Kotkin and Sajó eds. 2002, 167–85.

Kirichenko, N., A. Privalov, V. Chetokin, and G. Shvyrkov. 1995. "Pobeditelei ne sudyat." *Kommersant'* 22:16–24.

Kislinskaya, L. 2000. "Tsentral'naya Pressa Rossii ob Organizovannoi Prestupnosti i Korruptsii (Oktyabr'–Dekabr' 2000 g.)." Kodan and Brovkin eds. 2000, 87–97.

Klebnikov, P. 2000. *Godfather of the Kremlin: Boris Berezovsky and the Looting of Russia.* New York: Harcourt.

Kleshko, A. 2001. "Corruption at the Local Level." Senokosov and Skidelsky eds. 2001, 45–48.

Klitgaard, R. 1988. *Controlling Corruption.* Berkeley: University of California Press.

———. 1998. "International Cooperation against Corruption." Transparency International and International Bank for Reconstruction and Development 1998, 43–54.

Knapp, W., et al. 1973. *The Knapp Commission Report on Police Corruption.* New York: George Braziller.

Kneen, P. 2000. "Political Corruption in Russia and the Soviet Legacy." *Crime, Law and Social Change* 34, no. 4:349–67.

Koalitsiya 2000. 2003. *Doklad za Otsenka na Koruptsiyata 2002.* Sofia: Koalitsiya 2000.

Kodan, S., and V. Brovkin, eds. 2000. *Organizovannaya Prestupnost' i Korruptsiya: Issledovaniya, Obzory, Informatsiya.* Washington and Moscow:

Tsentr po Izucheniyu Transnatsional'noi Prestupnosti i Korruptsii pri Amerikanskom Universitete.

Kolarska-Bobińska, L. 2002. "The Impact of Corruption on Legitimacy of Authority in New Democracies." Kotkin and Sajó eds. 2002, 313–25.

Konstantinova, N. 1996. "Doklad L'va Rokhlina solidarno oprovergaetsya voennymi." *Nezavisimaya Gazeta*, 9 July, 1.

Kornai, J., and S. Rose-Ackerman, eds. 2004. *Building a Trustworthy State in Post-socialist Transition*. New York: Palgrave Macmillan.

Kornai, J., B. Rothstein, and S. Rose-Ackerman, eds. 2004. *Creating Social Trust in Post-socialist Transition*. New York: Palgrave Macmillan.

Korzhakov, A. 1997. *Boris Yel'tsin: Ot Rassveta do Zakata*. Moscow: Interbuk.

Koshechkina, T., Å. Grødeland, and W. Miller. 1997. "Different Perspectives on Coping with Officialdom in Four Post-communist Countries: A Focus Group Approach." Paper presented at the annual conference of the British Association for Slavonic and East European Studies, Cambridge, April.

Kosztolanyi, G. 1999. "Blind Justice: Crime and Police Corruption in Hungary." *Central Europe Online*, 29 July, visited September 1999.

Kotalik, J., and J. Garcia. 2004. *Transparency International Annual Report 2003*. Berlin: Transparency International.

Kotkin, S., and A. Sajó, eds. 2002. *Political Corruption in Transition: A Skeptic's Handbook*. Budapest: Central European Press.

Kovács, A. 1999. "Corruption and the Possibilities of Repressing Corruption — From the Viewpoint of the Hungarian State Audit Office." Paper presented at the Princeton–Central European University Joint Conference on Corruption, Budapest, October–November.

———. 2000. "Corruption and the Possibilities of Repressing Corruption." UNODCCP and UNICRI 2000, 21–25.

Kovács, J. 2002. "Approaching the EU and Reaching the US? Rival Narratives on Transforming Welfare Regimes in East-Central Europe." *West European Politics* 25, no. 2:175–204.

Központi Statisztikai Hivatal. 1990–2001. *Magyar Statisztikai Évkönyv*. Budapest: Központi Statisztikai Hivatal.

Kramer, J. 1994. "Political Corruption in Post-communist Russia: The Case for Democratization." Paper presented at the annual convention of the American Association for the Advancement of Slavic Studies, Philadelphia, November.

Kránitz, M. 1981. "A korrupció történetéből." *Kriminológiai és Kriminalisztikai Tanulmányok XVIII*, ed. J. Gödöny, 255–98. Budapest: Közgazdasági és Jogi Könyvkiadó.

———. 1994. "Corruption in Hungary." Trang ed. 1994, 105–9.

Krastev, I. 1998. "Dancing with Anticorruption." *EECR* 7, no. 3:56–58.

———. 2004. *Shifting Obsessions: Three Essays on the Politics of Anticorruption*. Budapest: Central European University Press.

Krastev, I., and G. Ganev. 2003. "Do Uncorrupt Governments in Corrupt Countries Have Incentives to Launch Anticorruption Campaigns?" *EECR* 12, nos. 2–3:87–93.

Kroes, L., and C. de Boer. 1996. "Police and Corruption in the Netherlands: Towards a Micro-perspective." Bakker and Schulte Nordholt eds. 1996, 119–35.

Kryshtanovskaya, O., and S. White. 1996. "From Soviet *Nomenklatura* to Russian Élite." *Europe-Asia Studies* 48, no. 5:711–33.

Kubiak, A. 2002. "Public and Official Opinion on Corruption in Government: Study and Report." On line at http://www.batory.org.pl/korupcja/pub.htm, visited July 2003.

Kupchinsky, R. 2002. "'Our Common Home,' Viktor Chernomyrdin, and Corruption." *RFE/RL Crime and Corruption Watch* 2, no. 14.

Kurczewski, J. 1999a. *Posłowie a Opinia Publiczna*. Warsaw: Instytut Stosowanych Nauk Społecznych, Uniwersytet Warszawski.

———. 1999b. "Corruption as Seen by Polish Parliamentarians (Summary)." Paper presented at the Princeton–Central European University Joint Conference on Corruption, Budapest, October–November.

———. 2004. "Is a Sociology of Corruption Possible?" *Polish Sociological Review* 2:161–81.

Kurczewski, J., and B. Łaciak, eds. 2000. *Korupcja w życiu społecznym*. Warsaw: Instytut Spraw Publicznych.

Kuz'minov, Ya. 1999. "Tezisy o korruptsii." On line at http://www.hse.ru/science/reports/kuzm9910/1.htm, visited July 2003.

Kwong, J. 1997. *The Political Economy of Corruption in China*. Armonk, N.Y.: M. E. Sharpe.

Łajtar, M. 2000. "Korupcja w policji." Kurczewski and Łaciak eds. 2000, 81–110.

Lambroschini, S. 2000. "Russia: Oligarch Meeting Offers Few Results." *RFE/RL*, 28 July.

Lampland, M. 2002. "The Advantages of Being Collectivized: Cooperative Farm Managers in the Postsocialist Economy." Hann ed. 2002, 31–56.

Lan Cao. 2000. "Chinese Privatization: Between Plan and Market." *Law and Contemporary Problems* 63, no. 4:13–62.

Lane, D., and C. Ross. 1999. *The Transition from Communism to Capitalism: Ruling Elites from Gorbachev to Yeltsin*. New York: St. Martin's.

LaPalombara, J. 1994. "Structural and Institutional Aspects of Corruption." *Social Research* 61, no. 2:325–50.

Larkin, J. 2003. *Strategic Reputation Risk Management*. Basingstoke: Palgrave Macmillan.

Lavigne, M. 1995. *The Economics of Transition*. Basingstoke: Macmillan.

Ledeneva, A. 1998. *Russia's Economy of Favours: Blat, Networking and Informal Exchange*. Cambridge: Cambridge University Press.

Lee, R. 1997. "Recent Trends in Nuclear Smuggling." Williams ed. 1997, 109–21.

———. 1998. *Smuggling Armageddon: The Nuclear Black Market in the Former Soviet Union and Europe*. New York: St. Martin's.

Leftwich Curry, J., and J. Barth Urban, eds. 2003. *The Left Transformed in Post-communist Societies: The Cases of East-Central Europe, Russia, and Ukraine*. Lanham: Rowman and Littlefield.

Leigh, D., and E. Vulliamy. 1997. *Sleaze: The Corruption of Parliament*. London: Fourth Estate.

Lemarchand, R., and K. Legg. 1972. "Political Clientelism and Development: A Preliminary Analysis." *Comparative Politics* 4, no. 2:149–78.

Letki, N. 2002. "Lustration and Democratisation in East-Central Europe." *Europe-Asia Studies* 54, no. 4:529–52.

Levada, Yu. 2000a. *Ot Mnenii k Ponimaniyu: Sotsiologicheskie Ocherki*. Moscow: Moskovskaya Shkola Politicheskikh Issledovanii.

———. 2000b. "Chelovek v korruptivnom prostranstve: Razmyshleniya na materialy i na polyakh issledovaniya." *EiSP* 5, no. 49:7–14.

———. 2001. "Corruption in Public Opinion." Senokosov and Skidelsky eds. 2001, 49–58.

Levin, M. 2001. "Is It Really So?" Senokosov and Skidelsky eds. 2001, 1–4.

Lewis, P. 1998. "Party Funding in Post-communist East-Central Europe." Burnell and Ware eds. 1998, 137–57.

Lewis, T. 1998. *Coverups and Copouts*. Auckland: Hodder Moa Beckett.

Lindelow, M. 2003. "Public Expenditure Tracking and Service Delivery Surveys." Paper delivered at the 11th International Corruption Conference, Seoul, 26 May. On line at www.worldbank.org/wbi/governance/pdf/11iacc_lindelow.pdf, visited July 2003.

Linz, J., and A. Stepan. 1996. *Problems of Democratic Transition and Consolidation*. Baltimore: Johns Hopkins University Press.

Lipset, S. M., and G. Lenz. 2000. "Corruption, Culture and Markets." *Culture Matters: How Values Shape Human Progress*, ed. L. Harrison and S. Huntington, 112–24. New York: Basic Books.

Lockwood, D. 2000. *The Destruction of the Soviet Union: A Study in Globalization*. Basingstoke: Macmillan.

Lopatin, V. 2003. "Sovremennoe sostoyanie i perspektivy antikorruptsion-nogo zakonotvorchestva v Rossii." Gerasimov and Shchegortsov eds. 2003, 84–94.

Łoś, M., and A. Zybertowicz. 2000. *Privatizing the Police State: The Case of Poland.* Basingstoke: Macmillan.

Lotspeich, R. 1995. "Crime in the Transition Economies." *Europe-Asia Studies* 47, no. 4:555–89.

Loungani, P., and P. Mauro. 2001. "Capital Flight from Russia." *World Economy* 24, no. 5:689–706.

Lovell, S., A. Ledeneva, and A. Rogachevskii, eds. 2000. *Bribery and Blat in Russia: Negotiating Reciprocity from the Middle Ages to the 1990s.* Basingstoke: Macmillan.

Lubin, N. 1995. *Central Asians Take Stock: Reform, Corruption and Identity.* Washington: United States Institute of Peace.

Lucky, C. 1997. "Public Theft in Early America and Contemporary Russia." *EECR* 6, no. 4:91–98.

Luneev, V. 1996. "Korruptsiya, uchtennaya i fakticheskaya." *Gosudarstvo i Pravo* 8:78–91.

———. 1997. *Prestupnost' XX Veka: Mirovie, regional'nye i rossiiskie tendentsii.* Moscow: Norma.

———. 1999. "Uglublenie sotsial'nogo kontrolya prestupnosti—odna iz predposylok resheniya sotsial'no-ekonomicheskikh problem (Materialy 'kruglogo stola')." *Gosudarstvo i Pravo* 9:60–86.

———. 2000. *Yuridicheskaya Statistika.* Moscow: Yurist'.

Maas, P. 1973. *Serpico.* New York: Viking.

Magatti, M. 1996. *Corruzione politica e società italiana.* Bologna: Il Mulino.

Makarov, D., et al., eds. 2000. *Materialy konferentsii "Rossiya i mirovoi opyt protivodeistviya korruptsii."* Moscow: Spark.

Manchin, R. 2000. "Assessment of the Status of Corruption: Discovering a Hidden Society Phenomenon." Paper presented at the 5th European Conference of Specialized Services in the Fight against Corruption, Istanbul, 15–17 November. On line at the web site of the Gallup Organization, visited August 2004.

Manolova, E. 1997. "No More Illusions." *Warsaw Voice,* 23 February.

Markwick, R. 1996. "A Discipline in Transition?" *Journal of Communist Studies and Transition Politics* 12, no. 3:255–76.

Marquette, H. 2004. "The Creeping Politicisation of the World Bank: The Case of Corruption." *Political Studies* 52, no. 3:411–30.

Marsh, C. 2000. "Social Capital and Democracy in Russia." *Communist and Post-communist Studies* 33, no. 2:183–99.

Marsh, C., and N. Gvosdev, eds. 2002. *Civil Society and the Search for Justice in Russia.* Lanham, Md.: Lexington.

Marsov, V., and A. Poleshchuk. 1993. "Skhvatka dvukh klanov v rukovo-dstve Rossii mozhet privesti stranu k polnoi anarkhii." *Nezavisimaya Gazeta*, 28 August, 1.

Mauro, P. 1995. "Corruption and Growth." *Quarterly Journal of Economics* 110, no. 3:681–712.

Mauss, M. 1970. *The Gift*. London: Cohen and West.

McAuley, M. 1997. *Russia's Politics of Uncertainty*. Cambridge: Cambridge University Press.

McCoy, J., and H. Heckel. 2001. "The Emergence of a Global Anti-corruption Norm." *International Politics* 38, no. 1:65–90.

McKay, J. 2003. "Political Corruption in Germany." Bull and Newell eds. 2003, 53–65.

Mény, Y. 1996. "'Fin de Siècle' Corruption: Change, Crisis and Shifting Values." *International Social Science Journal* 48, no. 149:309–20.

——. 1997. "France: The End of the Republican Ethic?" Della Porta and Mény eds. 1997, 7–21.

Michael, B. 2004. "The Rapid Rise of the Anti-corruption Industry: To-ward Second Generation Anticorruption Reforms in Central and Eastern Europe." *Local Governance Brief* (Budapest), spring, 17–25.

Milanovic, B. 1998. *Income, Inequality and Poverty during the Transition from Planned to Market Economy*. Washington: World Bank.

Miller, W., Å. Grødeland, and T. Koshechkina. 1998. "Are the People Victims or Accomplices?" Discussion Papers of the Local Government and Public Service Reform Initiative, no. 6. Budapest: Open Society Institute.

——. 1999. "What Is to Be Done about Corrupt Officials? Public Opinion and Reform Strategies in Post-communist Europe." *International Review of Administrative Sciences* 65, no. 2:235–49.

——. 2001a. "Confessions: A Model of Officials' Perspectives on Accepting Gifts from Clients in Post-communist Europe." *Political Studies* 49, no. 1:1–29.

——. 2001b. *A Culture of Corruption? Coping with Government in Post-communist Europe*. Budapest: Central European University Press.

Miller, W., T. Koshechkina, and Å. Grødeland. 1997. "How Citizens Cope with Post-communist Officials: Evidence from Focus Group Discussions in Ukraine and the Czech Republic." *Political Studies* 45, no. 3:597–625.

Minchev, V., et al. 2000. *Corruption and Trafficking: Monitoring and Prevention*. Sofia: Center for the Study of Democracy.

Ministry of the Interior [Hungary]. 2000. "Assessment of Corruption and Elaboration of a National Strategy in Hungary." UNODCCP and UNICRI 2000, 27–41.

Mishler, W., and R. Rose. 1995. "Trust, Distrust and Skepticism about Institutions of Civil Society." Glasgow: CSPP at the University of Strathclyde.

Misztal, B. 1996. *Trust in Modern Societies*. Cambridge: Polity.

Montinola, G., and R. Jackman. 2002. "Sources of Corruption: A Cross-
Country Study." *British Journal of Political Science* 32, no. 1:147–70.

Moore, B. 1967. *Social Origins of Dictatorship and Democracy*. Harmonds-
worth: Penguin.

Moran, J. 2001. "Democratic Transitions and Forms of Corruption." *Crime,
Law and Social Change* 36, no. 4:379–93.

Mukherjee, R., and O. Gokcekus. 2004. "Gender and Corruption in the
Public Sector." Hodess, Inowlocki, Rodriguez, and Wolfe eds. 2004,
337–39.

Mukhin, A. 2000. "Korruptsiya: mify i real'nost'." Makarov et al. eds. 2000,
123–39.

Mulvenon, J. 2001. *Soldiers of Fortune: The Rise and Fall of the Chinese
Military-Business Complex*. Armonk, N.Y.: M. E. Sharpe.

———. 2003. "To Get Rich Is Unprofessional: Chinese Military Corruption
in the Jiang Era." *China Leadership Monitor* 6:21–35.

Mungiu-Pippidi, A. 1997. "Breaking Free at Last: Tales of Corruption from
the Post-communist Balkans." *EECR* 6, no. 4:85–90.

Murphy, K., A. Shleifer, and R. Vishny. 1993. "Why Is Rent-Seeking So
Costly to Growth?" *American Economic Review* 83, no. 2:409–14.

Murrell, P. 1993. "What Is Shock Therapy? What Did It Do in Poland and
Russia?" *Post-Soviet Affairs* 9, no. 2:111–40.

Nader, R., P. Petkas, and K. Blackwell, eds. 1972. *Whistle Blowing*. New
York: Benton.

Naim, M. 1995. "The Corruption Eruption." *Brown Journal of World Affairs*
2, no. 2:245–61. Reprinted in Williams ed. 2000b, 263–79.

———. 2005. "Bad Medicine." *Foreign Policy* 147:96–95 [*sic*].

Nalla, M., and G. Newman. 1991. "Public versus Private Control: A Reas-
sessment." *Journal of Criminal Justice* 19, no. 6:537–47.

Natsionalen Statisticheski Institut. 1990–2003. *Statisticheski Godishnik*.
Sofia: Natsionalen Statisticheski Institut.

Nelken, D. 1996. "The Judges and Political Corruption in Italy." *Journal of
Law and Society* 23, no. 1:95–112.

Nelken, D., and M. Levi. 1996. "The Corruption of Politics and the Politics
of Corruption: An Overview." *Journal of Law and Society* 23, no. 1:1–17.

Nelson, T. 2000. "Russian Realities: Nuclear Weapons, Bureaucratic Ma-
neuvers, and Organized Crime." *Demokratizatsiya* 8, no. 1:145–59.

Newell, J., and M. Bull. 2003. "Political Corruption in Italy." Bull and
Newell eds. 2003, 37–49.

New South Wales Royal Commission into the New South Wales P(
Service. 1997. *Final Report*. Sydney: New South Wales Royal Comr
sion into the New South Wales Police Service.

Nomokonov, V. 2000. "On Strategies for Combating Corruption in Ru
sia." *Demokratizatsiya* 8, no. 1:123–28.

Noonan, J. 1984. *Bribes*. New York: Macmillan.

Nye, J. 1967. "Corruption and Political Development: A Cost-Benefit Analysis." *American Political Science Review* 61, no. 2:417–27.

O'Brien, J. 2003. *Wall Street on Trial: A Corrupted State?* Chichester: John
Wiley and Sons.

Offe, C. 2004. "Political Corruption: Conceptual and Practical Issues." Kornai and Rose-Ackerman eds. 2004, 77–99.

Oi, J. 1989. "Market Reforms and Corruption in Rural China." *Studies in
Comparative Communism* 22, nos. 2–3:221–33.

Okolicsanyi, K. 1992. "Hungarian Bank Closures: Regulators Miss the
Mark." RFE/RL *Daily Report*, 8 September.

Open Society Institute. 2002. *Monitoring the EU Accession Process: Corruption and Anti-corruption Policy*. Budapest: Open Society Institute.

Ortmann, A. 2004. "Transparency International Study Shows the More
Things Change, the More They Stay the Same." *Prague Post Online*, 5
August, visited August 2004.

Osiak, M. 2000. *Postawy Polaków wobec Korupcji*. Warsaw: Demoskop dla
Fundacji Batorego.

Owens, B. 2002. "The Independent Press in Russia: Integrity and the Economics of Survival." Marsh and Gvosdev eds. 2002, 105–24.

Palmier, L. 1983. "Bureaucratic Corruption and Its Remedies." *Corruption:
Causes, Consequences and Control*, ed. M. Clarke, 207–19. London: Pinter.

Panfilov, O. 2000. "Putin and the Media: No Love Lost." EECR 9, nos. 1–
2:60–64.

Pasuk Phonpaichit and Sungsidh Piriyarangsan. 1996. *Corruption and Democracy in Thailand*. Chiang Mai: Silkworm.

Pearse, H. 2001. "New Public Management Reform and Public Sector
Corruption: A Comparative Study of the United Kingdom, Australia
and New Zealand." M.A. thesis, University of Melbourne.

Pehe, J. 1998. "The Disappointments of Democracy." *Transitions* 5, no.
5:38–42.

Perlez, J. 1997. "Market Place: A U.S. Fund Manager in Prague Has Found
Privatization Corrupt." *New York Times*, 3 December, § D, 8.

Philp, M. 1997. "Defining Political Corruption." *Political Studies* 45, no.
3:436–62.

Pickvance, C. 1999. "Democratisation and the Decline of Social Movements: The Effects of Regime Change on Collective Action in Eastern Europe, Southern Europe and Latin America." *Sociology* 33, no. 2:353–72.

Pieth, M. 2003. "Banning Bribery: The Birth and Evolution of the OECD Convention." *TI Q*, June, 13.

Pine, F. 2002. "Retreat to the Household? Gendered Domains in Postsocialist Poland." Hann ed. 2002, 95–113.

Pirie, M. 1988. *Privatization*. Aldershot: Wildwood House.

Pitera, J., with M. Brennek, J. Kochanowski, A. Kojder, and J. Lęski. 2004. "Poland." Hodess, Inowlocki, Rodriguez, and Wolfe eds. 2004, 242–46.

Pollack, D., J. Jacobs, O. Müller, and G. Pickel, eds. 2003. *Political Culture in Post-communist Europe: Attitudes in New Democracies*. Aldershot: Ashgate.

Pope, J. 2000. *Transparency International Sourcebook 2000: Confronting Corruption: The Elements of a National Integrity System*. Berlin: Transparency International.

———, ed. 2000. *Rzetelność życia publicznego: podręcznik procedur antykorupcyjnych*. Warsaw: Transparency International Polska.

Potter, C. 2000. "Payment, Gift or Bribe? Exploring the Boundaries in Pre-Petrine Russia." Lovell, Ledeneva, and Rogachevskii eds. 2000, 20–34.

Pradhan, S., J. Anderson, J. Hellman, G. Jones, B. Moore, H. Muller, R. Ryterman, and H. Sutch. 2000. *Anticorruption in Transition: A Contribution to the Policy Debate*. Washington: World Bank.

Pribán, J. 2002. *Dissidents of Law: On the 1989 Velvet Revolutions, Legitimations, Fictions of Legality and Contemporary Version of the Social Contract*. Aldershot: Ashgate-Dartmouth.

Pryde, P. 1991. *Environmental Management in the Soviet Union*. Cambridge: Cambridge University Press.

Przeworski, A., M. Alvarez, J. Cheibub, and F. Limongi. 2000. *Democracy and Development: Political Institutions and Material Well-Being in the World, 1950–1990*. Cambridge: Cambridge University Press.

Przeworski, A., and F. Limongi. 1997. "Modernization: Theories and Facts." *World Politics* 49, no. 2:155–83.

Public Opinion Foundation. 2002. "Corruption in Russia." On line at http://english.fom.ru/virtual/frames/, released 31 January, visited January 2003.

Pujas, V., and M. Rhodes. 1999. "Party Finance and Political Scandal in Italy, Spain and France." *West European Politics* 22, no. 3:41–63.

Putnam, R. 1993. *Making Democracy Work: Civic Traditions in Modern Italy*. Princeton: Princeton University Press.

Quah, J. 1995. "Controlling Corruption in City-States: A Comparative

Study of Hong Kong and Singapore." *Crime, Law and Social Change* 22, no. 4:391–414.

Queensland Criminal Justice Commission. 1997. *Integrity in the Queensland Police Service: Implementation and Impact of the Fitzgerald Inquiry Reforms*. Brisbane: Criminal Justice Commission.

Radaev, V. 2002. "Corruption and Administrative Barriers for Russian Business." Kotkin and Sajó eds. 2002, 287–311.

Ramge, T. 2003. *Die grossen Polit-Skandale*. Frankfurt am Main: Campus.

Raun, T. 1997. "Democratization and Political Development in Estonia, 1987–96." *The Consolidation of Democracy in East-Central Europe*, ed. K. Dawisha and B. Parrott, 334–74. Cambridge: Cambridge University Press.

Rayner, J. 2003. *Managing Reputational Risk: Curbing Threats, Leveraging Opportunities*. Chichester: John Wiley and Sons.

Razinkin, V. 1995. *"Vory v Zakone" i Prestupnye Klany*. Moscow: Kriminologicheskaya Assotsiyatsiya.

Reddaway, P., and D. Glinski. 2001. *The Tragedy of Russia's Reforms: Market Bolshevism against Democracy*. Washington: United States Institute of Peace Press.

Reed, Q. 1995. "Transition, Dysfunctionality and Change in the Czech and Slovak Republics." *Crime, Law and Social Change* 22, no. 4:323–37.

———. 2002. "Corruption in Czech Privatization: The Dangers of 'Neo-Liberal' Privatization." Kotkin and Sajó eds. 2002, 261–85.

Rees, S. 1995. "The Fraud and the Fiction." *The Human Costs of Mangerialism: Advocating the Recovery of Humanity*, ed. S. Rees and G. Rodley, 15–27. Leichhardt: Pluto Press Australia.

Reinikka, R., and J. Svensson. 2003. "Survey Techniques to Measure and Explain Corruption." World Bank Policy Research Working Papers, no. 3071. On line at http://ideas.repec.org/p/wop/wobael/3071.html (econ.worldbank.org/files/27279_wps3071.pdf), visited July 2003.

Reinikka, R., J. Svensson, and B. Kurey. 2002. "Public Expenditure Tracking Surveys." On line at http://www.worldbank.org/poverty/empowerment/toolsprac/tool18.htm, visited July 2003.

Reisch, A. 1993. "Corruption Scandal Hits Hungarian Banking." *RFE/RL*, 10 September.

Remington, T. 1994. "Introduction: Parliamentary Elections and the Transition from Communism." *Parliaments in Transition*, ed. T. Remington, 1–27. Boulder: Westview.

Repetskaya, A. 2000. "Korruptsiya v Pravookhranitel'nykh Organakh (po rezul'tatam sravnitel'nogo kriminologicheskogo issledovaniya)." Kodan and Brovkin eds. 2000, 78–84.

Rigby, T. H. 1982. "Introduction: Political Legitimacy, Weber and Communist Mono-organisational Systems." *Political Legitimation in Communist States*, ed. T. H. Rigby and F. Fehér, 1–26. Basingstoke: Macmillan.

———. 1988. "Staffing USSR Incorporated: The Origins of the Nomenklatura System." *Soviet Studies* 40, no. 4:523–37.

———. 1999. "New Top Elites for Old in Russian Politics." *British Journal of Political Science* 29:323–43.

Rigby, T. H., and B. Harasymiw, eds. 1983. *Leadership Selection and Patron-Client Relations in the USSR and Yugoslavia*. London: Allen and Unwin.

Roldan, A. 1989. "A Brief Psychology of Corruption." *Psychology* 26, no. 4:53–55.

Roniger, L. 2004. "Political Clientelism, Democracy and Market Economy." *Comparative Politics* 36, no. 3:353–75.

Rooke, P. 2004. "The UN Convention against Corruption." Hodess, Inowlocki, Rodriguez, and Wolfe eds. 2004, 111–15.

Rose, R. 2000. "Uses of Social Capital in Russia: Modern, Pre-modern, and Anti-modern." *Post-Soviet Affairs* 16, no. 1:33–57.

Rose, R., W. Mishler, and C. Haerpfer. 1998. *Democracy and Its Alternatives*. Cambridge: Polity.

Rose-Ackerman, S. 1978. *Corruption: A Study in Political Economy*. New York: Academic Press.

———. 1999. *Corruption and Government: Causes, Consequences and Reform*. New York: Cambridge University Press.

Rosenberg, J. 2005. "Globalization Theory: A Post Mortem." *International Politics* 42, no. 1:2–74.

Rosenberg, T. 1995. *The Haunted Land*. New York: Random House.

Rosenthal, M. 1989. "An American Attempt to Control International Corruption." Heidenheimer, Johnstone, and LeVine eds. 1989, 701–15.

Ross, C. 2003. "Putin's Federal Reforms and the Consolidation of Federalism in Russia: One Step Forward, Two Steps Back!" *Communist and Post-Communist Studies* 36, no. 1:29–47.

Roszkowski, W. 1997. "The Afterlife of Communism in Poland." Holmes and Roszkowski eds. 1997, 83–111.

Roth, J. 1997. *Der Sumpf*. Munich: Piper.

Roth, U. 2003. "How Switzerland Fights Money-Laundering." Paper presented at the journalists' seminar of the Swiss Bankers Association, 5–6 June. On line at www.swissbanking.org/en/roth-e-03-06-05.pdf, visited October 2003.

Rothacher, A. 2003. "Political Corruption in Japan." Bull and Newell eds. 2003, 106–19.

Rowley, C., R. Tollison, and G. Tullock, eds. 1988. *The Political Economy of Rent-Seeking*. Boston: Kluwer.

Rubnikovich, O., and I. Rodin. 1993. "Rutskoi oproverg obvineniya." *Nezavisimaya Gazeta*, 20 August, 1.

Rupnik, J. 1999. "The Postcommunist Divide." *Journal of Democracy* 10, no. 1:57–62.

Sabbat-Swidlicka, A. 1993. "The Legacy of Poland's 'Solidarity' Governments." RFE/RL *Research Report*, 5 November, 19–22.

Saich, T. 2004. *Governance and Politics of China*. 2d edn. Basingstoke: Palgrave Macmillan.

Sajó, A. 1994a. "Traditions of Corruption." Trang ed. 1994, 43–45.

——. 1994b. "Legal Socialization in Hungary under Communism and some Implications for the Future." *Comparative Social Research* 14:97–109.

——. 1998. "Corruption, Clientelism and the Future of the Constitutional State in Eastern Europe." EECR 7, no. 2:37–46.

——. 2002. "Introduction: Clientelism and Extortion: Corruption in Transition." Kotkin and Sajó eds. 2002, 1–21.

——. 2003. "From Corruption to Extortion: Conceptualization of Postcommunist Corruption." *Crime, Law and Social Change* 40, nos. 2–3: 171–94.

Sakwa, R. 1999. *Postcommunism*. Buckingham: Open University Press.

——. 2000. "Russia: From a Corrupt System to a System with Corruption?" Williams ed. 2000a, 123–61.

Samuelson, P. 2004. "Where Ricardo and Mill Rebut and Confirm Arguments of Mainstream Economists Supporting Globalization." *Journal of Economic Perspectives* 18, no. 3:135–46.

Sartori, G. 1970. "Concept Misformation in Comparative Politics." *American Political Science Review* 64, no. 4:1033–53.

Satarov, G. 2001. "Corruption, Western and Russian." Senokosov and Skidelsky eds. 2001, 5–11.

——, ed. 2002. *Diagnostika Rossiiskoi Korruptsii: Sotsiologicheskii Analiz*. Moscow: INDEM Foundation. On line at http://64.49.225.236/rc_survey.htm#Russia, visited January 2003.

Savitskii, V. 1996. "Judicial Power in Russia Today." *Review of Central and East European Law* 22, no. 4:417–23.

Scamuzzi, S., ed. 1996. *Italia illegale*. Turin: Rosenberg and Sellier.

Schilizzi, S. 2002. "Triple Bottom Line Accounting: How Serious Is It?" SEA Working Paper 2/10.

Schloss, M. 1998. "Combating Corruption for Development: The Role of Government, Business and Civil Society." Transparency International and International Bank for Reconstruction and Development 1998, 1–20.

Schmemann, S. 1999. "What Makes Nations Turn Corrupt? Reformers Worry That Payoffs and Theft May Be Accepted as Normal." *New York Times*, 28 August, § B, 11.

Schmidt, F. 1998. "Sleaze Spreads in Pauperized Albania." *Transitions* 5, no. 3:50–53.

Schmitt, C. 2004. *Legality and Legitimacy*. Durham: Duke University Press.

Schmitter, P., and T. L. Karl. 1994. "The Conceptual Travels of Transitologists and Consolidologists: How Far to the East Should They Attempt to Go?" *Slavic Review* 53, no. 1:173–85.

Schneider, F., and D. Enste. 2000. "Shadow Economies: Size, Causes and Consequences." *Journal of Economic Literature* 38, no. 1:77–114.

Schöpflin, G. 1984. "Corruption, Information, Irregularity in Eastern Europe: A Political Analysis." *Sudosteuropa* 33, nos. 7–8:389–401.

Scott, J. C. 1972. *Comparative Political Corruption*. Englewood Cliffs: Prentice-Hall.

Senokosov, Yu, and E. Skidelsky, eds. 2001. "Corruption in Russia." *Russia on Russia*, issue 4. Moscow: Moscow School of Political Studies and Social Market Foundation.

Seton-Watson, H. 1965. *Nationalism Old and New*. Sydney: Sydney University Press.

Shafir, M., and D. Ionescu. 1997. "Radical Political Change in Romania." *Transition* 3, no. 2:52–54, 101.

Shaxson, N. 2004. "The Elf Trial: Political Corruption and the Oil Industry." Hodess, Inowlocki, Rodriguez, and Wolfe eds. 2004, 67–71.

Shearing, C., and P. Stenning, eds. 1987. *Private Policing*. Beverly Hills: Sage.

Shelley, L. 1995. "Organized Crime in the Former Soviet Union." *Problems of Post-communism* 42, no. 1:56–60.

——. 1998. "Organized Crime and Corruption in Ukraine: Impediments to the Development of a Free Market." *Demokratizatisya* 6, no. 4:648–63.

——. 2000. "Corruption in the Post-Yeltsin Era." EECR 9, nos. 1–2:70–74.

——. 2002. "Transnational Crime: The Case of Russian Organized Crime and the Role of International Cooperation in Law Enforcement." *Demokratizatsiya* 10, no. 1:49–67.

——. 2003. "Crime and Corruption: Enduring Problems of Post-Soviet Development." *Demokratizatsiya* 11, no. 1:110–14.

Sheng Xue and Gao Zhan. 2002. "The Zhu Xiaohua Case: A Window into Chinese Hardball Politics." *China Brief* 2, no. 21. On line at http://china.jamestown.org/pubs/view/cwe_002_021_004.htm, visited January 2003.

Shevtsova, L. 2001. "From Yeltsin to Putin: The Evolution of Presidential Power." *Gorbachev, Yeltsin and Putin: Political Leadership in Russia's Transition*, ed. A. Brown and L. Shevtsova, 67–111. Washington: Carnegie Endowment for International Peace.

———. 2003. *Putin's Russia*. Washington: Carnegie Endowment for International Peace.

Shkaratan, M. 2001. *Bosnia and Herzegovina: Diagnostic Surveys of Corruption*. Washington: World Bank.

Shlapentokh, V. 2003. "Russia's Acquiescence to Corruption Makes the State Machine Inept." *Communist and Post-Communist Studies* 36, no. 2:151–61.

Shleifer, A., and R. Vishny. 1993. "Corruption." *Quarterly Journal of Economics* 108, no. 3:599–617.

Sík, E. 1999. "Some (but Mostly Methodological) Thoughts about the Sociology of Corruption—From an East European (but Mostly Hungarian) Perspective." Paper presented at the Princeton–Central European University Joint Conference on Corruption, Budapest, October–November.

———. 2002. "The Bad, the Worse and the Worst: Guesstimating the Level of Corruption." Kotkin and Sajó eds. 2002, 91–113.

Šiklová, J. 1996. "Lustration or the Czech Way of Screening." *EECR* 5, no. 1:57–62.

Singh, G. 1997. "Understanding Political Corruption in Contemporary Indian Politics." *Political Studies* 45, no. 3:626–38.

Skaperdas, S., and C. Syropoulos. 1995. "Gangs as Primitive States." Fiorentini and Peltzman eds. 1995, 61–82.

Slay, B. 1996. "Banking Scandals Send Political Reverberations." *Transition* 2, no. 22:41–45.

Smilov, D. 2002. "Structural Corruption of Party-Funding Models: Governmental Favouritism in Bulgaria and Russia." Kotkin and Sajó eds. 2002, 327–51.

Sparkes, R. 2002. *Socially Responsible Investment: A Global Revolution*. Chichester: John Wiley and Sons.

Steen, A. 1997. *Between Past and Future: Elites, Democracy and the State in Postcommunist Countries: A Comparison of Estonia, Latvia and Lithuania*. Aldershot: Ashgate.

———. 2004. "How Elites View Corruption and Trust in Post-Soviet States." Hodess, Inowlocki, Rodriguez, and Wolfe eds. 2004, 323–25.

Sterling, C. 1995. *Crime without Frontiers*. London: Warner.

Sutch, H. 1999. "What Transition Countries Can Learn from New Zealand's Experience of State Reform." *Rappel* 5, no. 3:3–5.

Sutch, H., with M. Dybula and J. Wojciechowicz. 2000. *Corruption in Poland: Review of Priority Areas and Proposals for Action*. Warsaw: World Bank.

Svensson, J. 2003. "Who Must Pay Bribes and How Much? Evidence from a Cross Section of Firms." *Quarterly Journal of Economics* 118, no. 1:207–30.

Sweeney, J., et al. 1996. "Russian 'Mafia' Invades Britain." *Observer*, 15 December, 16–17.

Szilágyi, A. 2002. "Kompromat and Corruption in Russia." Kotkin and Sajó eds. 2002, 207–31.

Szilágyi, Z. 1996a. "Slowing the Pace of Economic Reform." *Transition* 2, no. 20:40–43.

——. 1996b. "Privatization Scandal Threatens Coalition's Future and Public Confidence." *Transition* 2, no. 25:46–47, 64.

Taagepera, R. 2002. "Baltic Values and Corruption in Comparative Context." *Journal of Baltic Studies* 33, no. 3:243–58.

Tanzi, V. 2000. *Policies, Institutions and the Dark Side of Economics*. Cheltenham: Edward Elgar.

Tanzi, V., and H. Davoodi. 1998. "Roads to Nowhere: How Corruption in Public Investment Hurts Growth." Transparency International and International Bank for Reconstruction and Development 1998, 33–42.

Tarchalski, K. 2000. *Korupcja i Przywilej*. Warsaw: Semper.

Tarkowski, J. 1995. "Political Patronage." *Politicus*, August, 32–38 [special issue].

Tarschys, D. 2003. "Taxes and Bribes: Assessing the Extraction Burden in Orderly and Disorderly Societies." *European Review* 11, no. 3:365–83.

Thomas, T. 2001. *World Bank Corruption Surveys*. Washington: World Bank. On line at http://www.worldbank.org/poverty/empowerment/toolsprac/tool17.htm, visited May 2004.

Tiffen, R. 1999. *Scandals, Media and Corruption in Contemporary Australia*. Sydney: University of New South Wales Press.

Tikhomirov, V. 1997. "Capital Flight from Post-Soviet Russia." *Europe-Asia Studies* 49, no. 4:591–615.

——, ed. 1999. *Anatomy of the 1998 Russian Crisis*. Melbourne: Contemporary Europe Research Centre.

Tillier, A. 1996. "Interpol Tries to Curb Spread of Russian Mafia." *European*, 21–27 March, 4.

Timofeyev, L. 1994. "Tenevaya Privatizatsiya." *Izvestiya*, 14 May, 5.

Ting Gong. 1994. *The Politics of Corruption in Contemporary China: An Analysis of Policy Outcomes*. Westport, Conn.: Praeger.

——. 1997. "Forms and Characteristics of China's Corruption in the

1990s: Change with Continuity." *Communist and Post-Communist Studies* 30, no. 3:277–88.

Todorov, B., O. Shentov, and A. Stoyanov, eds. 2000. *Corruption and Trafficking: Monitoring and Prevention*. Sofia: Center for the Study of Democracy.

Tolz, V. 1998. "Forging the Nation: National Identity and Nation Building in Post-communist Russia." *Europe-Asia Studies* 50, no. 6:993–1022.

Torański, B. 1994. "From Yellow Curtains to Golden Parachutes." *Warsaw Voice*, 25 September, 8–9.

Trang, D. 1994. Foreword. Trang ed. 1994, 7–10.

——, ed. 1994. *Corruption and Democracy*. Budapest: Institute for Constitutional and Legislative Policy.

Transparency International. 1996a. *Report of the Mission of Transparency International to Hungary, the Czech Republic and Poland*. Berlin: Transparency International.

——. 1996b. *Report of the Mission of Transparency International to the Slovak Republic and Romania*. Berlin: Transparency International.

——. 1996c. *Sharpening the Responses against Global Corruption*. Berlin: Transparency International.

——. 2000a. "Transparency International Releases the Year 2000 Corruption Perceptions Index" [press release]. Berlin: Transparency International. On line at http://www.transparency.org/cpi/2000/cpi2000.html.

——. 2000b. "Gender and Corruption: Are Women Less Corrupt?" [press release]. Berlin: Transparency International. On line at http://www.transparency.org/pressreleases_archive/2000/2000.03.08.womensday.html.

Transparency International and the International Bank for Reconstruction and Development. 1998. *New Perspectives on Combatting Corruption*. Washington: Transparency International and the Economic Development Institute of the World Bank.

Transparency International Polska. Forthcoming. *Mapa Korupcji w Polsce*. Warsaw: Transparency International Polska.

Treisman, D. 1998. "Russia's Taxing Problem." *Foreign Policy* 112:55–66.

Trepp, G. 1996. *Swiss Connection*. Zurich: Unionsverlag.

Tsipko, A. 2000. "Will Putin Confiscate the Oligarchs' Property?" *Prism* 6, no. 8 (on line), 31 August.

Tsyganov, Yu. 1996. "Corruption in the PRC: Payment for Economic Education." English-language version of a paper published in the *Sisa Journal*, Seoul, 8 August, presented to the author in Moscow, April 1997.

——. 2001. "Farewell to Oligarchs? Presidency and Business Tycoons in

Contemporary Russia." *Russia after Yeltsin*, ed. V. Tikhomirov, 79–102. Aldershot: Ashgate.

Ukhmanov, V. 1999. "Sovremennoe Zakonodatel'stvo Belarusi i Rossii o Konflikte Interesov." Paper presented at the Princeton–Central European University Joint Conference on Corruption, Budapest, October–November.

UNODCCP and UNICRI. 2000. "Joint Project against Corruption in the Republic of Hungary: Preliminary Assessment and Feedback on the Corruption Pilot Study." *Global Programme against Corruption Working Paper*. Vienna: United Nations.

Vaksberg, A. 1991. *The Soviet Mafia*. New York: St. Martin's.

Vannucci, A. 1993. "Scambi e collusioni: analisi di un caso." *Il Progetto* 74:75–86.

Varese, F. 1994. "Is Sicily the Future of Russia?" *Archives européennes de sociologie* 35:224–58.

———. 1997. "The Transition to the Market and Corruption in Post-socialist Russia." *Political Studies* 45, no. 3:579–96.

Vásárhelyi, M. 1999. "Public Opinion Regarding Corruption." *Review of Sociology*, special issue, 82–94.

Verheijen, T., and A. Dimitrova. 1996. "Private Interests and Public Administration: The Central and East European Experience." *International Review of Administrative Sciences* 62, no. 2:197–218.

Veslo, A. 1996. "Generalov portit dachnyi vopros." *Nezavisimaya Gazeta*, 20 July, 2.

Wagener, H-J. 2002. "The Welfare State in Transition Economies and Accession to the EU." *West European Politics* 25, no. 2:152–74.

Walecki, M. 2000a. "Geneza finansowania partii politycznych w Polsce." Walecki ed. 2000, 48–62.

———. 2000b. "Dochody polskich partii politycznych — regulacje prawne i praktyka." Walecki ed. 2000, 86–115.

———. 2000c. "Wydatki polskich partii politycznych." Walecki ed. 2000, 116–38.

———. 2003. "Money and Politics in Central and Eastern Europe." *Funding of Political Parties and Electoral Campaigns*, ed. R. Austin and M. Tjernström, 71–93. Stockholm: International Institute for Democracy and Electoral Assistance.

———, ed. 2000. *Finansowanie polityki: Wybory, pieniądze, partie polityczne*. Warsaw: Wydawnictwo Sejmowe.

Wallerstein, I. 1974. *The Modern World System*. New York: Academic Press.

Wang Shaoguang. 2003. "The Problem of State Weakness." *Journal of Democracy* 14, no. 1:36–42.

Ward, P. 1989. Introduction. Ward ed. 1989, 1–12.

——, ed. 1989. *Corruption, Development and Inequality*. London: Routledge.

Webster, W., ed. 1997. *Russian Organized Crime: Global Organized Crime Project*. Washington: Center for Strategic and International Studies.

Weingrod, A. 1968. "Patrons, Patronage and Political Parties." *Comparative Studies in Society and History* 10, no. 4:377–400.

Werlin, H. 1972. "The Roots of Corruption: The Ghanaian Enquiry." *Journal of Modern African Studies* 10, no. 2:247–66.

——. 1994. "Revisiting Corruption: With a New Definition." *International Review of Administrative Sciences* 60, no. 4:547–58.

Werner, S. 1983. "New Directions in the Study of Administrative Corruption." *Public Administration Review* 43, no. 2:146–54.

White, G. 1993. *Riding the Tiger: The Politics of Economic Reform in Post-Mao China*. Basingstoke: Macmillan.

——. 1996. "Corruption and the Transition from Socialism in China." *Journal of Law and Society* 23, no. 1:149–69.

White, S., R. Rose, and I. McAllister. 1997. *How Russia Votes*. Chatham, N.J.: Chatham House.

Whitford, R. 1997. "Whistle-blower." *Business Central Europe* 5, no. 38:52.

Whitmore, B. 1998. "Russia's Top Crime Fighter." *Transitions* 5, no. 3:35–39.

——. 1999. "Something to Fight for." *Transitions* 6, no. 1:18–20.

Wiarda, H. 2001. "Southern Europe, Eastern Europe and Comparative Politics." *East European Politics and Societies* 15, no. 3:485–501.

Willerton, J. 1992. *Patronage and Politics in the USSR*. Cambridge: Cambridge University Press.

Williams, P., ed. 1997. *Russian Organized Crime*. London: Cass.

Williams, R., ed. 2000a. *Party Finance and Political Corruption*. Basingstoke: Macmillan.

——. 2000b. *Explaining Corruption*. Cheltenham: Edward Elgar.

Williams, R., and A. Doig, eds. 2000. *Controlling Corruption*. Cheltenham: Edward Elgar.

Williams, R., J. Moran, and R. Flanary, eds. 2000. *Corruption in the Developed World*. Cheltenham: Edward Elgar.

Williams, R., and R. Theobald, eds. 2000. *Corruption in the Developing World*. Cheltenham: Edward Elgar.

Woodall, B. 1996. *Japan under Construction: Corruption, Politics and Public Works*. Berkeley: University of California Press.

World Bank. 2001. *Combating Corruption: Poland's Anticorruption Strategies and International Lessons of Experience*. Warsaw: World Bank.

Wu Naitao. 1997. "Amended Criminal Law Contains 260 More Articles." *BR* 40, no. 17:17–19.

Yan Sun. 2001. "The Politics of Conceptualising Corruption in Reform China." *Crime, Law and Social Change* 35, no. 3:245–70.

Yan Yunxiang. 1997. "McDonald's in Beijing: The Localization of Americana." *Golden Arches East: McDonald's in East Asia*, ed. J. Watson, 39–76. Stanford: Stanford University Press.

Yang, M. 1989. "The Gift Economy and State Power in China." *Comparative Studies in Society and History* 31, no. 1:25–54.

Yates, D. 2001. "France's Elf Scandals." Caiden, Dwivedi, and Jabbra eds. 2001, 69–78.

Yong Guo and Angang Hu. 2002. "Administrative Monopoly in Economy Transition in China." Research paper of the China Institute for Reform and Development, China Reform Forum. On line at http://www.chinareform.org/cgi-bin/ResearchPaper/ResearchPaper_main.asp?Ggwk_ID = 37&Ggwk_Type = 1, visited July 2003.

———. 2004. "The Administrative Monopoly in China's Economic Transition." *Communist and Post-communist Studies* 37, no. 2:265–80.

Zagórski, K. 1995. "Privatisation and Crime: Danger of Oversimplification." *Australian Economic Review* 2:5–13.

Zagórski, K., and M. Strzeszewski, eds. 2000. *Nowa Rzeczywistość: Oceny i opinie, 1989–1999*. Warsaw: Dialog.

Zanga, L. 1995. "Corruption Takes Its Toll on the Berisha Government." *Transition* 1, no. 7:12–14.

Zhilin, A. 1995. "Quotation of the Month: 'Criminal Financial Dealings Dramatically Increased in Russia.'" *Transition* [World Bank/PRDTE] 6, nos. 11–12:9–10.

Zhongguo Falu Nianjian. 1993–2002. Beijing: Falu Chubanshe.

Zon, H. van. 1999. "Captured by the Past: The Political Economy of Ukraine." Paper presented at the conference Transition from Planned to Market Economies Ten Years On, Berlin, November.

Zwart, F. de. 1996. "Personnel Transfer in Indian State Bureaucracy: Corruption and Anti-corruption." Bakker and Schulte Nordholt eds. 1996, 53–64.

Index

corruption: acceptability of, 293–94;
administrative, 42, 308–9 n. 41;
advantages of, 278–80; Asiatic, 18;
authoritarianism and, 12, 274–75,
284–85; among bank officials, 82–
83, 313 nn. 36–37, 326 n. 78, 331
n. 18, 350 n. 52; black, 23, 40, 304
n. 18; among border control
officers, 72–74, 125–41; business-
to-business, 17–18, 22, 303 n. 15,
322 n. 54; causes of, 97, 176–210,
276, 335 n. 2, 335 n. 6, 340 n. 39,
341 n. 46; civil society and, 186–
87, 286; class structures and, 191–
94; communist legacy and, 11,
183–87, 191, 203–6, 208–9, 216,
235, 238, 244, 273–74, 277–78,
283; in communist systems, 26,
46–48, 84–85, 86; convictions for,
95, 97, 98, 99, 100–103, 212, 213–
14, 345 nn. 5–6; cultural aspects
of, 17–20, 22–23, 179–82, 185,
271–72, 335 n. 7; among customs
officers, 72–74, 124–41, 157, 182,
217, 228, 231–33, 236, 324 n. 62,
326 n. 75; dangers of investigating
or reporting, 146–48, 260, 329 n.
3; definitions of, 13, 17–31, 91,
102, 143, 297 n. 1 (Introduction),
301 n. 3, 302–4 nn. 11–19, 306 n.
31, 322 n. 54; delimiting, 26–29,
306–7 n. 33; democratization and,
161, 174, 200, 275; among diplomats, 78, 125, 131–35, 138–39;
disadvantages of, 144, 149, 174,
262, 344 n. 1; discretionary decision making and, 189, 229–30, 338
n. 26, 340 n. 39; dynamism of,
280–88; economic, 18; economy
and, 3–4, 151–58, 186, 189–91,
196–97, 200, 203–7, 272–75, 279,
281, 286, 338 n. 27; electoral, 52–
53, 85–86; environment and, 151,
158, 253, 330 nn. 7–8, 352 n. 72;
eruption of, 287, 299 n. 16; examples of, 44–89; experience of, 116–

22, 142, 315 n. 5; foreign entities'
role in combating, 241–43, 247–
48, 284; as form of protectionism,
343 n. 51; future of, 268–69; gender and, 237–38; grand, 163, 167,
184; grass-eating, 22, 39, 121, 325
n. 69; gray, 23, 40, 304 n. 18;
group targeting and, 252; hotlines
and, 328 n. 91; hypotheses on, 9–
12, 270–75; impact of, 40, 78,
146–75; inequality and, 143, 193,
286; international climate and,
194–202; international organizations' role in combating, 248–53,
262–63, 284; international ramifications of, 159–60; among judicial
officials, 8, 33, 74–75, 124–41,
236, 324 n. 62, 326 n. 75, 326 n. 80,
334 n. 38; legalist approach to, 23–
24; legal safeguards against, 212–
17; legislation and, 189, 190, 191,
203–5, 207–8, 212, 222–27, 281;
legitimacy and, 11–12, 137, 160–
75, 186, 240, 276–77, 279–80,
288–92, 325 n. 69, 328 n. 91, 334
n. 38; among local officials, 66–68,
124–41, 326 n. 76; measurement
of, 9, 45, 90–91, 142–45, 315 n. 1,
329 n. 95; measures against, 109,
166, 238–40, 332 n. 30, 349 n. 47;
meat-eating, 22, 39, 121, 323 n. 58,
325 n. 69; media coverage of, 8–
11, 14, 44, 60–61, 77, 84–89, 115–
16, 144, 146, 170, 217, 258–60,
285, 320 n. 39, 320–21 n. 43, 326
n. 82, 329 n. 1, 349 n. 46, 354 n.
79, 359 n. 26; methods of combating, 211–69; among military
officers, 75–78, 85, 124–41, 147–
48, 159, 217, 220, 227, 244–45,
313 n. 32, 326 n. 78, 336 n. 15;
minimalist approaches to, 23–25,
31; among ministerial staffs, 68–
69, 124–41, 150, 217, 219–20, 312
n. 22; among ministers, 58–59, 61,
62–64, 76, 79–80, 125–41, 193,

LESLIE HOLMES

is a professor of political science at

the University of Melbourne.

Library of Congress
Cataloging-in-Publication Data

Holmes, Leslie.
Rotten states? : corruption, post-communism, and
neoliberalism / Leslie Holmes.
p. cm.
Includes bibliographical references and index.
ISBN 0-8223-3779-7 (cloth : alk. paper)
ISBN 0-8223-3792-4 (pbk. : alk. paper)
1. Political corruption — Europe, Eastern. 2. Political
corruption — China. 3. Post-communism — Europe,
Eastern. 4. Post-communism — China. 5. Europe,
Eastern — Politics and government — 1989-   .
6. China — Politics and government — 2002-   .
I. Title.
JN96.A56C644 2006
364.1'323 — dc22   2005031587